The Lost Generation

Other books by this author include

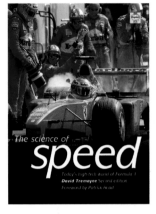

**The Science of
Formula 1 Design**
*Expert analysis of the
anatomy of the modern
Grand Prix car*
ISBN 1 84425 340 6
£19.99

The Science of Speed
*Today's high-tech world
of Formula 1*
ISBN 1 85960 650 4
£19.99

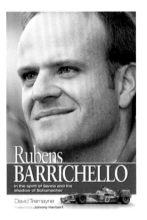

The Science of Safety
*The battle against
unacceptable risk in
motor racing*
ISBN 1 85960 664 4
£19.99

Rubens Barrichello
*In the spirit of Senna and
the shadow of Schumacher*
ISBN 1 84425 200 0
£18.99

The Lost Generation

THE BRILLIANT BUT TRAGIC LIVES OF RISING BRITISH F1 STARS
ROGER WILLIAMSON, TONY BRISE AND TOM PRYCE

By **David Tremayne** Foreword by **Tom Wheatcroft**

DEDICATION

For Roger, Tony and Tom and those who loved them and those who supported them, for young lives lost and promise unfulfilled, and inspiration left behind.

    Also to Tom Wheatcroft and David Purley. Those people who matter know just what they did.

© David Tremayne 2006

David Tremayne has asserted his right to be identified as the author of this work

All rights reserved. No part of this publication may be reproduced, stored in a retrieval system or transmitted, in any form or by any means, electronic, mechanical, photocopying, recording or otherwise, without prior permission in writing from the publisher.

First published in August 2006

A catalogue record for this book is available from the British Library

ISBN 1 84425 205 1

Library of Congress catalog card no 2005935265

Published by Haynes Publishing, Sparkford, Yeovil, Somerset BA22 7JJ, UK.
Tel: 01963 442030 Fax: 01963 440001
Int. tel: +44 1963 442030 Int. fax: +44 1963 440001
E-mail: sales@haynes.co.uk
Website: www.haynes.co.uk

Haynes North America Inc.,
861 Lawrence Drive, Newbury Park,
California 91320, USA.

Page layout by James Robertson

Printed and bound in Great Britain by J. H. Haynes & Co. Ltd, Sparkford

PHOTOGRAPHIC CREDITS

Brise family collection: p38, p39, p40, p41, p42, p122, p123.

Janet Hunt collection: p114/115, p124, p125, p147, p171 bottom, p200 top.

Pryce family collection: p28, p29, p30, p31, p32, p33 left, p34, p35, p59 top, p72 top, p118 top, p119, p120 right, p121, p134 top, p216 bottom.

Williamson family collection: p14/15, p16, p17, p18, p19, p20, p21, p22, p23, p24, p25, p46, p48, p59 bottom, p109, p116 top and bottom, p117 top, p254, p259 bottom.

Jacqui Hamilton collection: p92 top, p92 bottom.

LAT Photographic: p43, p47, p54, p55 right, p58 bottom, p60, p64 top, p69 bottom, p70 bottom, p80 top, p93, p107, p111, p112, p134 bottom, p151, p186, p187 top and bottom, p188, p191, p192, p193, p200 bottom, p201 top and bottom, p233 top and bottom, p234, p235, p236, p237, p258 bottom, p259 top.

Sutton Motorsport Images: p7, p8/9, p44/45, p49, p50, p63, p66/67, p68, p74, p76/77, p78, p82/83, p89, p90/91, p95, p98, p101, p102/103, p120 left, p126/127, p130, p132, p133, p135, p136, p141, p142/143, p153 bottom, p154/155, p156, p157, p160/161, p162, p163, p164, p165, p166/167, p168/169, p170, p171 top, p172 top, p173 top and bottom, p174/175, p176 top and bottom, p177, p181, p182, p183, p184, p185 top, p190, p194/195, p196, p197 top, p198, p205, p217, p220, p226, p227 top, p228/229, p231, p232, p238, p240, p241, p242/243, p244, p247, p249, p255, p258 top.

Grand Prix Photo (Peter Nygaard): p13, p53, p58 top, p61 bottom, p70 right, p79 left, p85, p86, p87, p104/105, p129, p139, p148/149, p150, p158, p178, p179 top and bottom, p180, p185 bottom, p197 bottom, p202/203, p214/215, p218 top and bottom, p219 top and bottom, p221, p223, p224, p225.

Anon: p62, p70 top, p80 bottom. p81, p113 top, p128, p153 top, p167 bottom, p172 bottom, p189 top and bottom, p199, p222, p230.

Cledwyn Ashford collection: p61 top, p64 bottom, p71, p169 top.

Chris Meek: p72 bottom left and right.

Attualfoto: p227 bottom.

Author's collection: p10, p12, p69 top, p253 left and right, p257.

Brunswick News: p106.

Mike Dixon: p56/57, p65.

DPPI: p73.

Jutta Fausel: p117 bottom, p118 bottom.

Ferret Photographic: p26/27, p33 right, p36/37, p113 bottom.

John Fitzpatrick: p146.

Haymarket: p75.

Leicester Mercury: p19.

Leonard: p96 left and right, p97 left and right.

Simon Lewis: p55 left, p79 right, p131, p145.

Gerry Stream: p250/251.

Contents

Acknowledgements

One name on the cover of a book always hides a multitude that helped its progression from mind to page. These are the people to whom my gratitude goes: Jenny Anderson, the Brise family's friend; Mario Andretti, for his memories of Tony at Long Beach; Cledwyn Ashford, Tom's retiring childhood friend for his trust in lending his treasured memorabilia to a complete stranger; Nando Boers, for sharing his superb and hard-hitting VPRO Television interviews with Ben Huisman and Hermann Brammer; Pete Briggs, who had to endure Zandvoort; Janet Hunt (née Brise) and her husband John, for their hospitality, frankness and illuminative memories and anecdotes; Pam Brise, for talking about her beloved son and husband; Nick Brittan, Tony's manager and family friend; Peter Collins, 'Mr Taciturn,' a true friend and a great talent-spotter even three decades ago; Stuart Dent for his support and for getting the message about the impending book out there in the first place; Mike Doodson, for his memories and excellent contemporary journalism with *Motoring News* and *The Motor*; Mike Earle, for his stories of David Purley; Bernie Ecclestone for memories of Tony; Alexander Fasel, for his unending enthusiasm and support; Ian Flux, for all his recollections; Trevor Foster, for his friendship over many years, and for sharing his memories of Roger and Tom; Bill Harding for memories of Tom; Howden Ganley, for sharing his Zandvoort memories; Bob King for memories of Tom and Royale; Jacqui Hamilton (née Martin), for selflessly sharing memories of the man she loved; Alan Henry, who every time I think I have pulled back a book on him turns out to have done two more. 'AH' had a deep friendship with Tom, and shared his memories no matter how painful they sometimes were; Bette Hill, for a morning of memories; Steve Holter; Alan Howell for his memories of November 1975; Jeff Hutchinson; Brian Jones for friendship and anecdotes; Glyn Jones for memories of Roger; Nick Jordan, for his brilliant recollections of life working with Roger and Tony, for his willingness to share his enduring passion for motorsport and to trust me with some of his treasured memorabilia of a great time in his long career; Jorge Koechlin for his memories of days at Red Webb's; Niki Lauda, for being as candid and informative as ever; Jacques Laffite, for his story of Kyalami; John Love for connections; Andrew Marriott, *Motoring News*'s famed 'ARM', who was such a part of the sport's fabric as a writer and team manager in those days and who now covers it for television; Chris Meek, for memories and a raft of photographs and clippings; Max Mosley, under whom safety has now become paramount; Richard Noble for advice on altimeters; Jackie Oliver, for memories of a fun lunch; Fred Opert; Tim Parnell, a genuine Roger fan; Freddy Petersen for memories of Kyalami 1977; Ian Phillips, to whom Roger meant so much; Annie Proffit, for her memories of Long Beach 1975; Jack and Gwyneth Pryce, for their friendship and hospitality, and their courage in talking about the racing son they so loved and the elder son they also lost; Nella Pryce for sharing her memories with unflinching courage; Alan Rees, who perhaps rated Tom more than anyone else; Dieter Rencken for his enthusiastic support and help with all matters South African; Alex Ribeiro, for his candid memories of Tony and their infamous collision in Monte Carlo; David Richards, who survived that brush with a wall on the Tour of Epynt with Tom in 1975; James W Roberts, a young upcoming writer with tremendous enthusiasm and affection for Tom, for his help in providing contact details, with fond memories of a happy day spent in Ruthin with Jack and Gwyneth Pryce, and respect for his moving BBC Radio documentary on Tom aired late in 2005; Nigel Roebuck, the first man to puncture the myth of 'arrogant' Tony Brise; Tim Schenken for memories of Tom; Beulah Schoeman for her help with the South African side of the story; Marcus Simmons, who carried on the spirit of *Motor Sport* magazine with the appreciation that the past is as important as the present; the late Louis Stanley who, for all his pomposity, had a heart that was very much in the right place whenever young lives were shattered by a sometimes cruel sport; Quentin Spurring for his unselfish help with Formula Three research; Sir Jackie Stewart, whose courageous safety crusade helped to stop the sort of senseless tragedies that stole Roger and Tom; Hans Stuck, for his candour and memories; Barbara and John Upton, for bringing Roger back by sharing their fond recollections of her brother; Leigh Trevail for connections; Neil Trundle for memories of Tom; Tony Vlassopulos, for his enthusiasm and generous assistance; Jeremy Walton, for his *Motoring News* memories; John Watson, for recollections of Tom; Tony Watson for memories of Tom; Sir Frank Williams, for recollections of Montjuich Park; and George Witt, for insights into the Kyalami story. And to the respective editors of *Motoring News* (now *Motorsport News*) and *Autosport* for permission to quote from the many interviews from those days when both publications were virtually the sole source of inside information for motorsport-hungry enthusiasts.

Much as the late Ken Norris stood out in the list of acknowledgements for *Donald Campbell – The Man Behind the Mask*, so Tom Wheatcroft must be singled out here. I first met him at Donington during an Aurora Formula One meeting in 1979. I was standing in the pit lane, just another face in the crowd, next to a broad man in a shabby old raincoat who contemplated the pouring rain before turning to me with a broad smile to say, 'Bloody marvellous, in't it!' And it was! That captured the essence of racing, and the essence of the man himself. He cared: about the circuit, about the sport, and about the fans.

The ebullient Leicester builder and developer also selflessly believed in one of the most talented British drivers of the 20th century, and bared his soul as we toured his beautiful Donington Collection one day in 1990 when *Motoring News* (which I was editing at the time) was sponsoring a racing car show at Donington. I figured a tour by 'Wheaty' himself would make a great double-page centrespread preview feature, with him explaining the stories behind the acquisition of some of the star exhibits. And I admit that I did have the ulterior motive of hoping to walk him round to Roger's cars. I wasn't sure back in

those days whether he would open up on the subject and it seemed a subtle way of getting him to talk for the book *Racers Apart*, in which there would be a chapter on Roger. I needn't have worried; we didn't need to get as far as Roger's Marches and GRD. When we stopped by the BRM P180 that Roger had driven so quickly in a test at Silverstone early in 1973, Tom opened a vein. I'll always be grateful to him for his candour that morning, and have a lump in my throat when I think of it.

It was my wife's inspired idea to ask him to write the foreword to this book, and I was so pleased when he agreed. Wheaty, the hard man with a laugh like an old tractor starting up, is one of the most important people in the history of British motorsport. Over the years he has given so much to the sport while taking so little, and so ill deserved to lose what was stolen from him that shameful day at Zandvoort in 1973.

Friends reunited. In July 2003, Ian Phillips, Tom Wheatcroft, Barbara Upton and Trevor Foster gathered for the unveiling of David Annand's striking sculpture of Roger Williamson, in Donington Park's Garden of Remembrance.

Foreword

by Tom Wheatcroft
Owner, Donington Park Circuit

I have known David Tremayne for many years now, and have enjoyed his books. Having received the manuscript to *The Lost Generation*, I just couldn't put it down. One cold March morning I set about reading it all, only turning the last page just before bedtime. I felt exhausted, as if somehow I had gone back 30 years and relived those times; still a heady mixture of triumph, and tragedy. Like David, I can remember where I was and exactly what I was doing on the days each tragedy took their toll. The feelings of anger and despair still haunt me.

I knew Tom and Tony well, we had competed against them, joked with them and shared that motorsport camaraderie. And Roger: as each year passes and 29 July stares at me from the calendar, I still get that overwhelming feeling one gets deep inside as emotions build. They don't get any less.

Thirty years to the day since his death, my son, Kevin, created a memorial to Roger in Donington's Garden of Remembrance. He knew that day was for me. He was as emotional as I was, and went away for the weekend so that I could be alone with my memories. A very special act, as he too loved Roger like a brother.

It was a sad day, but a fitting opportunity to be reunited with the likes of Ian, Nicky, Trevor, Jacqui and many of the old gang. It brought back some of the happier memories.

Motor racing is an indelible part of my soul, and I have remained involved at many levels, but the day we lost Roger, part of my motor racing spirit died.

The Lost Generation is a wonderful tribute to these three extraordinary young men, three of the many whom I've witnessed in my 60 years in motorsport.

For Roger, still nothing can take his place in my heart.

Oadby, 2006

Roger and Tom ready to go racing. Nothing more need be said.

Introduction

The seeds of this book were sown a long time ago: back in a very different era of motorsport when safety standards fell woefully short of what we have come to take so much for granted today; back in dark days when it was common for two or three drivers to die in action each season – to be 'left behind'.

Back when, as a young wannabe racer and writer who had little idea how to go about starting either career, I devoured *Motoring News* and *Autosport* each week, and enjoyed identifying the young hotshoes who were beginning to make a name for themselves.

Roger Williamson came into focus first, thrusting his way insistently into the limelight in Formula Three in 1971, initially with a privately-run March, and then walking off with two of the three titles in 1972. I saw his first race in a GRD 372 at the *Daily Express* International Trophy at Silverstone that year, when he left his opposition floundering like hoboes chasing a speeding train.

The most impressive thing about Roger was his sheer determination. No matter what happened, he simply would not give up. His head would cock forward as he adopted a unique crouch in the cockpit, but it never dropped in defeat. When Vittorio Brambilla, the aptly titled 'Monza Gorilla', edged him off the track and down an escape road at Monza in 1973 during the Formula Two race, Roger just gathered everything up and set off after leader Patrick Depailler. He outran Brambilla and caught Depailler, those Grand Prix winners of the future, and beat them fair and square that day to score his first outright victory in the category.

Never give up. It became my personal mantra. It still is.

Then came Tom Pryce and Tony Brise, both of whom had mixed it with Roger in Formula Three. Tom was the first of the pair to get to Formula One, two years after I had put off approaching him at that same International Trophy meeting when he was driving a Formula Three Royale. The Welsh star was quiet and introspective, reserved with people he did not know. That suited me just fine, because I was that way myself. I walked down the paddock on the Club Straight and there Tom stood, apparently deep in thought, by the tatty green D. J.

Tom Tremayne's Project 1 TKM kart bears the subtle five orange vertical stripes on its Nassau panel and the sides of the nose as Restless Spirit Racing's tribute to Tom Pryce, after whom the author's son was named; Lydd 2000.

Bond Racing transporter and the black Royale RP11 wearing the number 42. I took a photo but left it too late that day to approach. Just as I summoned the courage to go and speak with him, somebody else beat me to it. It was the closest I ever got to meeting one of the 'Lost Generation'.

Tony, to begin with, struck me as being a different character altogether, a little too arrogant for my taste (my only source of information being the weekly racing magazines) but clearly blindingly quick. I suppose it also bothered me subconsciously that we were of similar age, and there he was and there I was: one a burgeoning star, the other on the sidelines. It took an interview with him by Nigel Roebuck in *Autosport* in 1975 to correct my various misconceptions, by which time Tony's performances in Teddy Savory's Formula Atlantic Modus, and then Graham Hill's eponymous Formula One car, had marked him out in the clearest terms as a World Champion of the future.

I felt such an affinity with Tom that, seven years after his death, my wife and I celebrated the birth of our first son by christening him Tom. When I wrote the book *Racers Apart* in 1990 I concluded the chapter on the Welsh star, 'Tom Pryce was one of the people after whom I named my elder son. I hope one day he might grow up proud to share the name of someone who set such an example in his behaviour and his attitude to life and people.' I'm proud to say that 'my' Tom has grown to do just that, and in some ways to emulate the 'other' Tom. Any parent knows the weight of emotional responsibility that naming a child entails, and Tom was not named lightly. Later, in our karting days, few people understood the meaning behind the five vertical stripes that our blue and orange Project One carried on either side of the nose and the Nassau panel, but all that mattered was that *we* knew that they represented our homage to the black stripes Tom Pryce wore on his helmet. And though I have been to many places and seen many remarkable, moving and sometimes emotionally uplifting things in a 30-year career as a motorsport writer, my proudest moment came at the Anglesey circuit, not far from Ruthin in North Wales. The announcer for the Formula Honda race informed the crowd, meagre as it was, that 18-year-old Tom Tremayne was named after the local hero. If Thomas Maldwyn Pryce was up there somewhere, listening in, I hope that he understood and approved.

I remember exactly what I was doing and where I was when I learned of each of the tragedies. Roger's I saw, along with millions of other viewers, on the late

Silverstone's International Trophy meeting, 1972. By the DJ Bond transporter Tom is deep in conversation alongside his Royale after the author's reserve got in the way.

afternoon television news. Black and white, as I recall, in our household back then. It was 29 July 1973. The upturned March, flame and smoke, David Purley's valiant rescue attempt. The sombre timbre of tragedy in the newscaster's modulated voice. Two years later my business partner and I were busy decorating some flats in Ealing. It was 29 November 1975. Rather than waste time studying too hard for our economics degrees we had set up a company to generate some income and three of us did a block of nine flats in 63 days, working flat out. It was a Saturday evening towards the end of that job, foggy and cold, when the news about Tony Brise and Graham Hill came on our paint-spattered radio. On my way home I was shocked to find myself weeping for people who had, after all, been strangers; but there in that grief came an understanding of why fans' affinities with the characters in their sports never deserve to be treated lightly or derided.

A close friend, Pete Finch, and I were erecting a Dexion warehouse structure in Maidenhead, working

for another mate while waiting for the breaks that would open up our 'real' careers. It was 5 March, another Saturday, in 1977. Pete had a radio in his battered old Hillman Super Minx and I kept dashing in and out to tune in and see who was doing what at Kyalami in the South African Grand Prix. In those days you didn't get a full report, just updates at regular intervals. The news about Tom was simply too devastating to take in.

Each tragedy was somehow harder to take. The cruelty of individual fate – that these gifted racers should each so suddenly be left behind, their huge potential now forever unfulfilled – evoked overwhelming feelings of anger and despair in equal measure. More than 30 years later they still do. The injustice was so desperate. Not for the first time in my life, I felt deeply moved during the writing of their stories for this book. A strong affinity on an emotional and, for me, cathartic journey. Not even that great record breaker, Donald Campbell, the greatest influence on my life, evoked in me quite the same depth of feeling when I wrote his biography as one of those passionate things that you know you have to do before your time is over. Rationalising it, I think that was because Campbell at least had his

Tony as he will forever be remembered: charging hard at Zandvoort in 1975.

moments of great triumph, a devoted band of followers, public recognition of his talent, his unquestioned place in the pantheon.

When these things happen, a little part of you dies, too. Call it transferred hope. My friend Alan Henry, who had great affection for Tom Pryce and knew him well, refers to such events as the days the circus leaves town, when you learn the hard way that motor racing can indeed be a cruel sport. Somewhere inside you a light dims, something is torn loose. Some try to distance themselves thereafter. Writer Eoin Young, whose 'Straight From The Grid' column in *Autocar* so influenced me from 1967, tried to do so after his very close friend Bruce McLaren was killed in 1970, but later admitted on the death of Denny Hulme 22 years later that he had not, after all, succeeded.

For me, each tragedy became another step in an evolving mission. This book is part of that mission, a long overdue celebration of their lives. A means of keeping their memories – of keeping *them* – alive. Of ensuring that successive generations of motorsport fans know who Roger Williamson, Tony Brise and Tom Pryce were and what they did. Not forgetting that great man's man David Purley. Don't ask me to explain it better than that, but there it is. To me it is terribly

important that they be remembered, and that they might yet inspire future generations of racers.

When, in 2003, I finally finished *Donald Campbell – The Man Behind the Mask*, friends who knew of my admiration for the speedking and the 30-year emotional investment I had made in the project kept asking what I could follow it up with. For once even I was satisfied with that one. But there was never any question in my mind. I always knew exactly what my next 'passion' book was going to be because it, too, had been in my head for the best part of three decades. We all need heroes, people who inspire and motivate us with their deeds, their successes and their defeats, and how they deal with all three. These were three of mine. They always will be. If not a week, then certainly not a month goes by without something reminding me of one or all of them, just as if it was yesterday and the fire of their futures still burned bright. In my mind – and, I hope, in this book – they live still.

David Tremayne
Darlington, 2006

CHAPTER 1

Beginnings

Roger

'The effort he puts into his driving always looks to be double that of anyone else in the race.'
Ian Titchmarsh

Everyone is familiar with the *accrochage* – the spraying of Champagne on the victory rostrum. Since Jo Siffert and Dan Gurney made it part of the post-race ceremonies at Le Mans in the sixties it has become the enduring image of motorsport victory. To the victors, the spoils. It might be wasteful, but it generates great photographic opportunities.

It often puts me in mind of the words from a song by Andrew Wintersgill, 'Elegy to Campbell', in which he pays tribute to the great speedking. The last verse runs:

> *The boathouse is empty, the jetty lies rotten.*
> *New heroes are basking in the spray of Champagne.*
> *Speed is the king in the realm of ambition,*
> *Great are the glories but short is the reign.*

The reign can indeed be short. In an era in which we have become used to the fact that Michael Schumacher was top dog from 1994 pretty much through to 2004, it is easy to forget that greats such as Jimmy Clark and Jackie Stewart had only six short years as the yardsticks (1962 to 1967 and 1968 to 1973, respectively). Some, such as Denny Hulme in 1967, Mario Andretti in 1978 or Jody Scheckter in 1979, were kings for less than 12 months. But at least they were all kings, and had their days in the sun when the world feted their success and the Champagne stung their eyes on rostrums across the globe.

Only one of the three subjects of this book ever stood on a grand prix podium (thanks to two third places), and though each had the talent to go all the way to the very top none was to be blessed by Fate. Each would die before they had the chance they deserved to

By the time Roger was five, his father, Dodge, had built him a small car that he would drive at the Leicester speedway while Williamson Snr. was racing there.

realise their true potential, before race wins and championship titles crowned their sublime ability.

Roger Williamson was born on 2 February 1948 in Leicester, to Herbert Lawrence Williamson and his wife Hilda. Herbert, a tough and feisty little man who was quick with his fists, was universally known as 'Dodge' and dealt in cars when he wasn't racing speedway bikes.

On 11 June 1949, Thomas Maldwyn Pryce was born in Ruthin, North Wales, where his father Jack was at that time a farm hand and his mother Gwyneth a nurse.

And on 28 March 1952, pig farmer and stock car ace Johnny Brise and his wife Pam celebrated the birth of their first son, Anthony, in Dartford, Kent.

Nola Williamson was nearing 16, and her sister Barbara 14, when their little brother Roger came along. 'I used to change his nappies!' remembered Barbara,

BELOW: *Roger Williamson, aged two, atop one of father Dodge's Buick limousines.*

OPPOSITE PAGE: *Dodge Williamson switched from speedway riding to karts as the new sport gained popularity in the Fifties. Before long, Roger joined him. The famed crouch and the 'Sideways Williamson' moniker evolved as Roger won trophy after trophy, and the British Championship in 1966.*

whose love of children would later lead her into nursery nursing. But husband John Upton, whom she met in 1958 and married in 1961, remembered that her sibling fondness did not prevent her once from inadvertently dropping her brother on his head. In later life, Barbara recalled, 'We didn't talk an awful lot, to be honest,' meaning heart-to-heart. 'He was more a sort of man's man, you know. I think he'd talk more to John than to me.'

Roger began competing early in his life, perhaps inevitably, given the close bond with his father. Dodge raced in speedway events whenever he wasn't running Northend Motors & Coaches, in Leicester's Northgate Street.

'Dodge very much influenced Roger into going racing,' Barbara said, but he was no karting dad pushing on an unwilling child in the hope of living out his own aspirations. Racing was in the genes.

When Roger was five Dodge built him a little car to drive at Leicester's speedway stadium whenever Dodge was racing there. But when Roger finally made his competition début, aged 11, he relied on his own legs in cycle speedway. While Roger was busy pedalling away – 'I was never very good at it because my legs were too small!' – Dodge had taken up karting and soon became one of Leicester's fastest competitors.

'Karting was just coming in, so Dodge had to have a go,' John said. 'Bill Price and Ken Norton were also there. They were the top three around here. They formed the Leicester Kart Racing Club, used Mallory Park, and the old hairpin, the Melbourne Loop, at Donington.'

It was only a matter of time before Roger joined him, as he turned 12 in 1960. 'There was a minimum age and you had to be 13, so they said he was 13,' John revealed. 'Roger won the British title, and several others, racing mainly at places such as Shenington, Lakenheath, Fulbeck. And Donington, of course.'

These days young racers can start in 50cc Cadet karts before graduating either to 100cc Junior TKMs or Rotax machines. But Roger went straight in the deep end in a Special Class Four with a 200cc engine and four-speed gearbox.

'They had a 100-mile race at Donington, which Dodge and Roger did together,' John said. 'They came third. I always remember, there was an old local farmer and his son; they were ridiculed a bit because they were just plodding along, but they won the race! They just kept going, while all the others were spinning or scrapping with each other. And once, I think it was at Shenington, Dodge won a race going backwards after spinning over the finish line.'

In 1964, the year in which John Surtees narrowly won the World Championship from an unlucky Jim Clark, Roger immediately showed speed. That year he was runner-up in the British Championship to Roger

Keele, and to Steve Thompson in 1965. He finally won the Special Class Four kart title in 1966.

It was in karting that he developed the Williamson crouch, so redolent of determination and commitment. 'Oh yes, he always had that!' John remembered. 'And sometimes they called him "Sideways Williamson."'

Writer/commentator Ian Titchmarsh once wrote, 'The effort he puts into his driving always looks to be double of that of anyone else in the race.'

It wasn't always a positive story. John remembers a day when Dodge asked Roger to drive the family car round the back to the garages. 'Roger braked a bit late, and ended up crashing into the big fence at the bottom! But he didn't do much damage.'

Roger Williamson, the racer, was an unassuming, happy-go-lucky young man who was nevertheless deadly serious about his racing. 'He wasn't studious,' Barbara

A move to cars was inevitable, and by 1967 Roger was terrorising much bigger cars with this self-prepared ex-Ian Mitchell 850cc Mini.

laughed. 'He was more of an action man! He liked football, too.'

On the track he was a charger, who quickly became notable for his determination. 'He got the never-give-up thing off his dad,' John said. 'He would push and push and just keep going. Roger couldn't wait to go karting.'

The hunger in Roger's driving was also a legacy from Dodge, 'and from Roger himself,' John stressed. 'His dad drove him on, but that was because Dodge was always interested in Roger's racing, and seeing him do well.'

Barbara Williamson confirmed a story told by Trevor Foster, who would later work with Wheatcroft Racing in Formula Three and Formula Two. 'Roger's mother was unbelievable,' Foster said. 'Roger had all these trophies from karting. And Hilda used to be up at five o'clock every morning and she systematically polished these trophies. They might as well have been cleaned once a fortnight, but there was always this thing where she did them religiously, every day, before Roger'd get up for his breakfast.'

But Hilda Williamson did not like to go to the races, according to Barbara. 'She was very nervous about it. If

we did go, mum and I were usually in the bus rather than in the pits or near the car. A lot of the drivers used to come and have a sandwich and a cup of tea.'

In 1967, Roger and Dodge purchased an 850cc Mini from fellow racer Ian Mitchell. It was a successful season by any standard, with 15 class wins – some of them outright victories – a second and a third. In Snetterton's Two-Hour race Roger finished fifth with the smallest car in the field, and easily won his class. To sweeten things further, he claimed class records at Mallory Park, Llandow, Rufforth and Cadwell Park. His performances at Snetterton won him the John Aley Saloon Car Championship.

Bolstered by the success, Roger and Dodge were determined to move into single seaters for 1968, even though the best car they could afford was an ex-Bev Bond Cooper T72 at a time when Brabham, Chevron and Lotus were dominant. 'It was ancient, but all that money would allow,' Roger told writer Dave Middleton in his first published interview in *Autosport* in May 1970.

After two unspectacular outings, which confirmed that the engine lacked grunt, Roger was pushing hard at Cadwell, the most demanding circuit in England, when he got caught up in another driver's moment. 'I tried to avoid him but just couldn't,' he reported. 'I shot up a bank, turned over three times in the air, came down the bank and slid along the track upside down.'

Roger refused the offer of a ride in the ambulance and a medical checkover. Instead, he sat on the bank glumly surveying the wreckage. 'All I could do was ask Dad if it would be okay for the race – and there was the car on the side of the track with its wheels and suspension hanging off...'

They took the mess back to Leicester and started to rebuild it, but Roger's Formula Three career was destined to go on hold for another three years. John Upton explained, 'Ken Norton used to work with Dodge as a part-time mechanic and Dodge used to get him to do jobs on the Cooper. Ken was in the garage welding, and he was working quite near the Cooper's petrol tank. And he caught one of the fuel pipes with the flame and the thing just went up. He pushed it out of the garage pretty quick and eventually the fire brigade came out, but that was the end of the Cooper.' There was no insurance.

Bruised but unbowed, the Williamsons scraped together what money they could and went back to saloon car racing with a 1650cc Ford Anglia 105E. It had wide wheels but was only marginally tuned. Roger raced it five times in 1968, without notable success.

In his acclaimed book *How To Go Saloon Car Racing*, racer Nick Brittan, who had himself dominated with his famous Super Speed-entered Green Bean Anglia, suggested that the ideal weapon for ultimate class victory might be an Anglia fitted with a Formula Three engine. The Williamsons heeded the advice and for 1969

The plan was always to go single-seater racing as soon as possible. An elderly Cooper T72 was Roger's pride and joy until it was consumed by fire after a welder let the flame get too near a fuel line.

installed the 997cc Holbay Formula Three engine that was all they'd salvaged from the Cooper.

They worked their way patiently through broken gearboxes and differentials until steady development improved reliability. But a spate of broken camshafts still kept Roger from the winner's circle. At Mallory he was even overtaken by a wheel and driveshaft. 'I wondered whose it was,' he told Middleton. 'Inevitably it was mine, and with only four minutes left to repair it after the car was recovered we had a real rush job. We tried to get the race held up, but without luck, and failed to reach the line by a few seconds.'

There was consolation to follow, however. The remaining 10 races yielded eight wins and two second places before the Williamsons put the car on a serious diet over the winter. They ran their amateur team in professional style, assisted by mechanics Eric Hassell and Peter Williams, the former an employee of Northend Garage, the latter a professional draftsman. Eric worked out the suspension set-up, Peter had expert knowledge of metallurgy. John Upton witnessed the transformation. 'They built the car up in the row of garages at the back of the old house in Barkby Road that they'd had converted into a big workshop. They just completely stripped it down and put on aluminium and fibreglass panels to lighten it. They did really well with that.'

With the refreshed engine producing 123bhp, the revised red and yellow machine was blisteringly quick, and its feisty little driver stunned his rivals with victory after victory on his way to an extraordinary outright triumph in the prestigious Hepolite-Glacier Saloon Car Championship. He scored maximum points with his remarkable 14 class victories.

Back in saloons, the Williamsons built up this heavily modified Anglia for 1968. With the Cooper's Holbay F3 engine installed, Roger subsequently won the Hepolite Glacier Saloon Car Championship in 1970.

In March, *Motoring News* reporter Andrew Marriott watched him at Oulton Park in the first round of the series. 'The giant-killer was Leicester's Roger Williamson who, since last season, has further lightened his 1-litre Anglia and had the engine freshly built by Holbay. All to good effect, for he immediately took the lead and screamed round to win by 10 seconds...'

The televised race at Thruxton typified his style; starting from the sixth row in the wet, he was leading after three laps. 'And by then there would have been some big twin-cam racers of double his Anglia's capacity, driven by the likes of Dave Brodie,' *Motoring News* penman Jeremy Walton remembered, 'plus Gerry Marshall in a proper Dealer Team Vauxhall jobbie.'

Ian Phillips was then a struggling journalist who hitched to many races. Subsequently, although he was seen as a 'sponger' by Dodge who tried to discourage it, he would form a strong friendship with Roger. His first memory of them leaves an interesting insight into the way the Williamsons viewed their racing. 'When I first met them at a race it was a long, long way away from home,' he recalled. 'Castle Combe, I think. They were simply amazed that somebody actually wanted to talk to *them*. I think that must have been 1969 or 1970 with the Anglia, and it just sort of struck a vein somewhere. Then, when they went into Formula Three, Roger and I became good mates.'

Glyn Jones, now in charge of heritage at Lola Cars, provided another. 'I used to mechanic for Martin Birrane in 1969 when he was racing his Ford Falcon. I was at college at Shrewsbury and really that was too far from London to go home there. So instead after a race I used to go to Leicester and Roger would put me up overnight. I'd go to the races with him in the coach, we'd take it in turns sleeping and driving, and then at the track I'd go off to help Martin! But despite being in an opposing camp I was always treated as one of the family. I was only 19 at the time, and I have many happy memories of those days. The Williamsons were a lovely family and they looked after me as a teenager.'

Marriott arranged for Walton to test Roger's Anglia at Mallory Park for *Motoring News*. Walton, who would forge a strong friendship with Roger as he covered the Hepolite-Glacier races that year and later bumped into him regularly in Formula Three, recalled, 'My diary for track test day Friday 3 December 1970 simply says, "Williamson great and his car okay, though Anglia and Dodge were a bit scary and we had a helluva lot of trouble starting the car."'

At the end of the year Roger and Dodge faced a new crossroads. Roger expressed some interest to Middleton in racing in G5 sportscars in the long term, but still really hankered after a single-seater. More than anything, he was keen to see how well he could perform against the better-known drivers. As he said to Marriott, 'Would you look to saloon car racing for a driver? No, of course you wouldn't. And that's another good reason for going single-seater.'

John stopped going to so many races when Roger moved up to Formula Three, mainly because with the mechanics there wasn't enough room in the converted coach that Dodge had created as their transporter. 'They scraped together everything they could to buy the March,' John said, 'and they went into financial debt, with hire purchase, to do it. They were so keen to get the car, and Roger was really keen to get back into a single-seater.'

The regulations for Formula Three had changed for 1971, with the famed 1000cc 'screamer' engines being replaced by 1.6-litre production-based units. Roger opted for March's new 713M chassis and a Holbay engine, and set off once again down Formula Three's yellowbrick road.

The new season was expected to be close-fought, and there would be three major titles to shoot at: the Shell, Lombank and Forward Trust British F3 championships. The major contender was expected to be tough Australian Dave Walker in the works Gold Leaf Team Lotus car with which he had won races the previous season. Then there was veteran Bev Bond, another tough guy who would be piloting the slippery wedge-shaped Ensign built by Walker's former team-mate, Mo Nunn.

Roger with saloon ace Dave Brodie, with whom he enjoyed a close, knockabout friendship.

Or James Hunt, the upcoming public schoolboy who would soon earn himself the nickname 'Hunt the Shunt'. Colin Vandervell, the son of Anthony Guy Vandervell whose patriotic green Vanwalls had put Britain on the Formula One map back in the fifties, would be aboard a new Brabham BT35.

Little was expected from Roger; despite his karting pedigree he was still seen as a 'tin-top' racer. It did not take him long to change perspectives, however. He took his first victory in the opening Lombank round at Mallory Park in March, albeit only after Hunt had been disqualified for an airbox infringement and Formula Ford makeweight Andy Rouse had crashed his Dulon. Other good results followed, even though by April he had yet to adjust the damper settings. In the Lombank series there were other wins: at Brands Hatch in May and June, at Crystal Palace in August and September, and again at Brands the day after the second London success, and in October.

Walker was top dog in both the Forward Trust and Shell series, winning seven and eight of the races, respectively, in each. But Roger beat him in the Forward Trust race that was also a Lombank round in September, and again fair and square in a great Shell fight at Oulton Park, one of the most challenging circuits, on 21 August. Roger led to begin with, was overtaken by Walker, repassed him and was in turn passed again, but always kept the Australian under so much pressure that Walker tried to protect his line at Lodge on the last lap, knowing Roger's reputation as a late braker. Roger cannily hung back, got on the power sooner as Walker's chosen line carried him to a wider exit, and outdragged the Gold Leaf Lotus into and out of Deer Leap and over the finish line. It was a great piece of strategic thinking that outfumbled the acknowledged master of the art. Hunt, who started from pole, finished 12s adrift.

Roger won again at Brands on 24 October, in the event that supported the non-championship Formula One Victory Race organised by circuit manager John Webb to celebrate Jackie Stewart's second World

In 1971 Roger proved the surprise of the season after he and Dodge scraped together enough to buy a Formula Three March 713M on hire purchase.

Championship title. Sadly Roger's performance that day would be overshadowed by the tragic death of the popular Swiss racer Jo Siffert after his Yardley BRM crashed on the descent to Hawthorn's Bend, and the fact that Scheckter had lost the Formula Three race through a puncture and victor-on-the-road Patrick Depailler, together with Hunt, had been disqualified. But with 10 victories in championship events and another in a non-championship race at Thruxton, Roger emerged as the undisputed find of the season.

What impressed onlookers as much as the victories and his confidence at the wheel, was his sheer determination. At Brands Hatch in April he finished second to Bond after a scrap with Hunt in which he passed his fellow Englishman round the *outside* of Paddock Bend, three years before Jacky Ickx was fêted for pulling a similar manoeuvre on Niki Lauda to win the Race of Champions. The next day, Roger fought all the way to another second place, at Silverstone, after a furious and successful scrap with Andy Sutcliffe.

To put things into perspective, Walker won three Lombard rounds, Hunt and an upcoming Australian

called Alan Jones two apiece, and Vandervell, Sonny Eade, Steve Thompson, Scheckter and David Purley took one each. Roger won seven. In the Shell series Bond got closest to Walker's eight victories with his three, and behind Roger on two came Scheckter, Vandervell, Depailler and Jochen Mass with one apiece. In the Forward Trust championship, Walker had his seven wins while Roger, David Morgan, Mike Walker and Sandy Shephard each took one.

By the end of his first full season in Formula Three, Roger had won the Lombard North Central Championship, come second in both Shell Super Oil and the Forward Trust and been voted BP Superman of Year. He had also won the top Grovewood Award, a prestigious accolade made by John Webb and a panel of journalists on behalf of Grovewood Securities which owned Brands Hatch and a number of other British race circuits.

None of this, however, could have happened without the intervention of a Leicester builder and developer called Tom Wheatcroft. He had initially sought to introduce himself to Roger the previous year as he celebrated victory in the Anglia at Mallory Park, 'but he was busy signing autographs. It wouldn't have been right to interrupt his moment.' Instead, they met after Roger had finished a smoking seventh overall in the most prestigious event of the year, at Monaco. The Holbay's piston rings were worn and it needed a rebuild, but since they hadn't even made the first payment on the hire purchase agreement that was out of the question. Roger and Dodge were contemplating the harsh facts of motor racing finance in the Formula Three paddock, when they were approached by a heavy-set individual with a ready smile, a broad Leicester accent and a laugh that could drown out a cement mixer. Tom remembers that he simply asked why Roger didn't put in his spare engine for the next race. Relating the incident to *Autosport*, Roger said: 'This nutcase comes up and asks, "Have you got a spare engine?" When I told him we hadn't he just said, "Go and buy another one and charge it to me!"'

Frederick Bernard 'Tom' Wheatcroft was a larger than life character, an ex-soldier who brooked no argument and had a lifelong detestation of petty authority and red tape, but his occasionally abrasive mien hid a heart of gold. After World War Two he had developed a successful building business, and amassed an impressive collection of classic racing cars. Now, having formerly helped racer Derek Bell in Formula Two, he was motivated purely by the wish to help a local lad who had impressed him.

In the end Wheatcroft had to persuade Roger Dunnell of Holbay of his own bona fides, and promise to pay to have Roger's original engine rebuilt too, before a deal could be struck. He went home happy.

Roger, seen outside Greater St James's Church in Leicester, was never afraid to work for a living. In between races, he often acted as chauffeur with his father's wedding hire sideline.

'I thought I'd never see the boy again,' he admitted, 'but I admired how he drove there. He finished up seventh, and I think he started about 18th.' But later that week, back home in Leicester, Wheatcroft's wife Lenchen answered the front door close to midnight, and informed her puzzled husband that a 'black boy' was calling on them. 'I thought that were odd, because I didn't know any black boys,' Tom said. It was, however, Roger, covered in oil after changing a rear axle on Dodge's bus. He was heading for a race at Silverstone once he'd cleaned up. But before that he was determined to take the first opportunity to repay the debt from Monaco as best he could. In his grimy hands was a ticket for Tom to Silverstone.

'I thought twice about it because I had a lot on that weekend,' Tom confessed, 'but I were touched. And eventually I decided to go, after the first thing I found myself thinking when I woke up that morning was, "I wonder how the boy's getting on?"'

Wheatcroft put more pressing things to one side and went to Silverstone. He arrived in time to see the wrecked March being hauled back to the paddock after Roger had shunted it in practice. He had pushed a little too hard on worn tyres, having attempted to make do with the set from Monaco. He was white-faced from lack of sleep when Wheatcroft arrived, and was telling his crew: 'That's my career finished.'

Wheatcroft thought otherwise. Besides being instrumental in soliciting financial support of £5,000 apiece from Dunlop and BP, he persuaded Max Mosley, then the head of March Engineering, to let Roger's crew use the March factory in Bicester as their base to rebuild the car overnight. He gave Mosley an undertaking to reimburse him if anything went missing while 'his' boys were working there, even though that would never have been the case with Hassell and Williams.

The relationship between driver and builder gelled as Tom became more closely involved, sponsoring Roger for the rest of the season. But despite Tom's growing largesse, Roger remained cost-conscious. Often he refused new tyres even when Wheatcroft beseeched him to get a new set. 'We don't need them, Tom,' he would say. 'I can make up the time.' And very often he did.

Roger, with mechanics Peter Williams (left) and Eric Hassell (right).

Tom loved the lad for the way he never took his support for granted. Before long, he came to regard Roger as another son. He would leave the grid shortly before the formation lap, giving Roger five minutes or so to collect his thoughts. 'But there were never a time when I didn't get a gentle elbow in the ribs at some stage, and a "Thanks, Tom," from him,' Wheatcroft revealed. 'Wi' some people, that means nothing, but that were 100 per cent his heart. You'd know be 'is eyes. He were such a nice lad, and a racer. Oh, absolutely a racer. A Villeneuve type.' Wheaty was referring to Gilles.

Roger gained another major supporter that year, a mechanic from Berwick-upon-Tweed called Nick Jordan who had proved himself with Dave Brodie's famous Run Baby Run Ford Escort and Lotus Elan team after years working in Jock McBain's Ford dealership in his native Scotland.

'I met Roger halfway through 1971,' he said. 'The Formula Threes were running with the saloon cars. I got chatting to him, with mechanics Eric Hassell and Roger Chalk, and Rosalyn Bates (Roger's then girlfriend), and Roger asked me if I wanted to join him. I'd always had an inkling to work on single-seaters, and I felt very proud to be actually asked. I was virtually inexperienced as a race mechanic at the time. In fact, Wheaty had me down on the books as a plasterer and brickie!'

Jordan recalled Roger's complete honesty. 'He got tyres free from Dunlop and he would sell them on when they

Financial help from Tom Wheatcroft transformed Roger into the one man who could challenge – and beat – champion-elect Dave Walker. At Oulton Park he vanquished the Gold Leaf Team Lotus driver, earning that week's Autosport front cover.

were used. And he'd hand Tom the £400 or whatever he got back. And they weren't the best tyres back then, the Dunlops, I'm sorry to say. I think we had a disadvantage with them, but Alec Maskell was very good and dear old Harry Downing at BP was fantastic. We'd go to a 10-lap Forward Trust bash somewhere and we'd go to the pumps and load up with about 200 gallons of BP five star. And Harry would say, "You don't need as much as that for the car, do you?" And I remember Tom turning round, "Ah, it's a bit thirsty sometimes!"'

At the end of the season Roger threw a party to say thanks to all the friends who had helped him during the season. As a special gift, he donated his March 713M to the Donington Collection. 'It was the best Christmas present I could think of giving Tom,' he said. The car remains there to this day.

Had Fate been benign, Roger and Tom might have gone all the way together, like Jackie Stewart and Ken Tyrrell. What they achieved together in 1972 would be proof of that.

CHAPTER 2

Beginnings

Tom

'He was a lovely guy, and underlying that was this latent skill that he had. He came alive in the cockpit of a racing car.'
Bob King

While Roger Williamson was making such a name for himself, Thomas Maldwyn Pryce had been developing his own taste for the sport. He had first driven a baker's van at the age of 10 (being permitted to turn it round in a field during deliveries and usually paying for his excessive zeal by having to pick up all the cakes in the back afterwards) and informed his parents he wanted to be a racing driver when he was only 12. His boyhood hero was Jimmy Clark, and he decorated his bedroom with pictures of racing cars. Gwyneth Pryce recalls that her son wept when the great Scottish champion was killed at Hockenheim on 7 April 1968. 'He was very upset when Jochen Rindt was killed, too,' his father Jack recalled.

When he had informed his parents of his ambition to go racing, Gwyneth had reacted the way most mothers would: 'Oh, Mald,' – he was always Mald or Maldwyn at home – 'people like us can't afford to go motor racing.' Jack was a policeman in Ruthin, where Tom was born, and she was a district nurse. And a feisty one at that. 'At that time they didn't let policemen's wives work,' she said. 'But I was not going to let that stop me. We couldn't have afforded to live properly on just a policeman's wage. The chief constable telephoned me one day, and obviously knew that I was working. He hummed and hahhed about it, and said something about not being too worried if it was governmental work. I carried on anyway, and pretty soon everyone else's wives were working too!'

The Pryces were close friends of the Ashfords, Norman and Marion. Norman Ashford was a

In 1971, wearing five vertical stripes on his helmet to help his father identify him, Tom supplemented his Formula Ford and SuperVee outings with a series of winning drives in the new Formula 100, driving T.A.S. Racing's Royale sports car.

policeman, too. They lived in neighbouring villages, the Ashfords in Llansallan in Denbighshire, the Pryces in Nantglyn.

Why Jack joined the force is a sad tale. The Pryces' elder son David John died in hospital at the age of three, and Norman Ashford was delegated to inform them and prepare a report. Jack was working on a farm at the time and was sufficiently inspired by Norman's sensitivity to join up himself. But Gwyneth also recalled that, once they had paid the £78 it cost to have David buried, they were broke.

They were from rural communities and, with four other friends who were also policemen, Jack would meet regularly to practice for the sergeants' exam. 'I think Jack passed before my father did. They used to call one another by their number,' recalled Norman's son Cledwyn. 'My father was 86, Jack was 416.'

For Jack, it would be reminiscent of his wartime days when he had shown his innate courage as a tailgunner in a Lancaster bomber, one of the most godless jobs in the conflict.

Jack was an open, friendly man, with the same economy of movement that his son would display. 'Gwyn was very reserved,' Cledwyn said. 'She was so proud of Maldwyn, and he was his mum's boy. There was a very close relationship between them.' Gwyneth was extremely determined and hard-working, other traits that her second son inherited. After defying the chief constable and starting her own business as a midwife-cum-nurse, she went on to found her own nursing home in Old Colwyn.

'Jack and he were not so much just father and son as best mates,' Cledwyn continued. 'They were very close, too, and had the same interests.' They had gone to see the motorcycle races one year on the Isle of Man, and had been down to circuits in England such as Aintree and Oulton Park when Tom was eight. Jack took his son with him when he collected his first new car, a black Austin A35. 'I didn't want them to deliver it because I knew what delivery drivers can be like. But Austin was worried what the unions might make of that if I collected it direct from the factory. So we went down to Coventry, Mald and I. I think he must have been about 10. We met up with some Austin people just outside the factory. Mald and I then motored all the way back to Ruthin.'

Tom and Cledwyn grew up together. 'We used to go

Below: Thomas Maldwyn Pryce, aged six, with Sandra, the young girl who Jack and Gwyneth Pryce fostered successfully until her mother could have her home again. Below right: Tom (right) and a friend on the farm. His father said he loved being able to get dirty.

to each other's houses. Whenever he came to mine I used to hide all my toys so he wouldn't play with them, then when I went to Nantglyn, Maldwyn would do exactly the same thing! In the police houses you had a footpath that went all round. We used to go like hell around there. Maldwyn was mad-keen on cars.'

In keeping with their character, the Pryces agreed to help their son all they could even though the world of motorsport was alien to them. Tom got his love of cars from Jack but Gwyneth didn't like racing, and even when her son would win the Race of Champions, she would sit in their caravan in the paddock and listen to it on the radio, rather than watch.

'Maldwyn was a bright lad, but I don't think he liked school,' said Cledwyn, who went on to become a head teacher. Education had been unsettling for Tom as Jack's job frequently took them to different Welsh towns, and it was a relief to him when he left it at 16. But Gwyneth shrewdly insisted that he take up an agricultural apprenticeship as a tractor mechanic at Llandrillo Technical College in St Asaph. 'He said to me, "Oh, Mam, what do I want to mess about with flaming tractors for?" And I said, "So that if things don't work out for you, you'll have something to fall back on. We could maybe set you up with a small garage or something..."'

'I wanted to be a pilot, but I don't really think I was bright enough,' Tom told Alan Henry in an interview with *Motoring News* published in July 1975.

His first steps in motor racing came in 1969 with a preliminary test at Mallory Park in Leicestershire at the famous Motor Racing Stables. He was 20 years old. Former Team Lotus star Trevor Taylor, once team-mate to Tom's hero Jim Clark and then a star of Formula 5000, put him through his paces there.

From Mallory Park he graduated to a series of school races run at Brands Hatch in Kent and Silverstone in Northamptonshire by MRS, the first coming at the former venue in September. 'I could only afford to race once a month,' he told Henry. 'The races were about £35 a time. But I sold my Mini and my parents offered all the help and encouragement I could have wished for.'

Tom's future wife Nella remembered, 'It was really through Jack and Gwyn that Thomas got going. They were very, very unselfish. And Thomas told me, "I always said to them, if I'm not any good, I'll stop. I won't carry on wasting your money."'

Though it was immediately clear that he *was* quick, that did not stop MRS instructors from criticising him. 'I was always being hauled up in front of them and told that I wasn't putting enough effort into my driving. Other pupils seemed to rush about the place, fiddling with their cars and making a great effort; I simply seemed to drive the cars as I found them.'

MRS ran a series called the *Daily Express* Crusader

Tom, aged six, at Nantglyn School, towards the end of the third row looking at camera.

Championship in conjunction with the newspaper, a contest exclusively for school pupils in private races. The tantalising prize was a Formula Ford Lola T200 worth £1,500.

Brian Jones, the voice of Brands Hatch (and countless other circuits in more than three decades of commentating), took up the story. 'Tom was not the most vocal of chaps! He was a country lad.

'The *Daily Express* Crusader thing had some lengthy title that include the words "cradle of champions," I seem to remember. Geoff Clarke of MRS set up the whole competition and had very good support from the *Daily Express*. We used to sit all Saturday night hashing it over in the Green Man by Silverstone, damaging their gin and whisky supplies, after the races on a Saturday morning. Then David Benson would write it all up in the paper.

'Geoff had an agreement in principle to buy a Royale from Bob King as the overall prize, but that coincided with the Brazilian Torneio for Formula Fords and the early results from Brazil suggested that the Lola T200 might be the car to have. So Geoff sat in the UK looking at these results and reading the runes, and decided to plump for the Lola. When Bob said recently that the first prize was a Lola T200, second prize two Lola T200s, he was right! At the time he was very disappointed and irritated when Geoff changed his mind. And, of course, that Lola coincided with Eric Broadley's short wheelbase period. I think Thomas Maldwyn Pryce learned more from that car than he did from most others!'

Everything would be decided in the final round, one race held in public at Silverstone the day before the 1970 International Trophy. 'I made it to this final,' Tom continued, 'and I was on the third row of the grid. But I walked the race to win easily.'

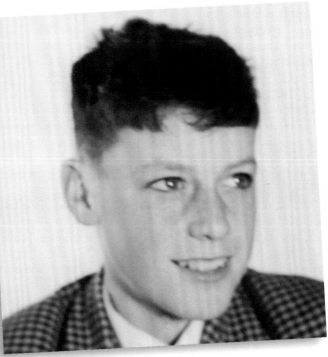

ABOVE: *Sergeant Jack Pryce, from whom Tom inherited his love of cars and with whom he enjoyed a particularly close relationship.* RIGHT: *Tom in a school photograph, aged ten.*

Jack Pryce proudly added a footnote. 'It started to rain in the race, and while everyone else was moaning about that Mald was rubbing his hands with delight. He always loved racing in the rain! He was second to begin with but then just left all the other drivers behind.'

Jones provided some further background to the fairytale story. 'Coincidentally, that race marked my first involvement with the British Racing Drivers' Club, and Tony Salmon was the secretary of the meeting. We pitched up with these six very tired Lotus 51s, some of which I seem to remember had been fitted with the later 61 wedge-shaped bodies. We were tolerated at best by the BRDC, but they looked down their noses at us. The cars were absolutely clapped out, but we were contracted to run six of them in our private races, and we repaired them as meetings went on. That inevitably led to delays. Friday's scheduled practice session came and went; we missed our slot because we were still fixing these cars. I had to plead with Tony to let us go out at the end of the day. Fortunately, and perhaps because the meeting was also sponsored by the *Daily Express*, he agreed to let us run then.

'Now, it was very important that all six cars were identical, so we hired a man from Securicor to watch them overnight. We had determined that all the cars had to run with a 6,000rpm limit. Special rotor arms were fitted and sealed. The morning of the race, Saturday, I arrived and immediately checked the cars. Five of them still had their 6,000rpm rotor arms, one did not. I probably shouldn't reveal the name of the driver whose car miraculously now had an unrestricted rotor arm, but

I can categorically tell you that it was *not* Tom Pryce's. Had that change not been noticed, it is possible that one competitor might have run away with the race. However, the plot was uncovered and everyone ran with 'legal' cars. But then one of them failed to start, because of a flat battery. The driver in question was being financially supported by his mother who, from memory, ran a fish and chip shop in the Midlands. After the race she pursued me with her umbrella and I spent a long hour trying to persuade her that it was a pure mechanical fault and not some dastardly plot to stop her child becoming a Formula One driver. It was a disaster.

'Anyhow, the race started. A man called Chris Smith, who I believe later went on to become a senior executive for Oyez, the legal publisher, built up a substantial lead and should have won. But the weather was pretty awful that weekend and now it began to pour with rain. And suddenly Tom Pryce was *flying*. He closed the gap to Chris Smith, overtook him, and went on to win comfortably. Later he received his prize, the Lola, from Sir Max Aitken, the *Express* proprietor.

'Tom took the car back to Brands Hatch and was allowed to garage it in the old stables at the bottom of the paddock, and in return for working as a mechanic on the MRS school cars, to test it pretty much whenever he wanted to.'

Suddenly, Tom's immediate racing future seemed rosy. From being the tractor mechanic with nothing but hope and the money for the odd race, he now owned a brand new car, and the deal with MRS and the *Daily Express* included the provision of oil, fuel and tyres.

After talking things over with his parents he abandoned his agricultural engineering apprenticeship and moved south to settle in a guesthouse in West Kingsdown, just along the road from Brands Hatch. He would see if he really could make it as a racing driver while being able to make some money for living expenses from his job as a mechanic. He was ready to take on the world.

'I really hated moving from Wales,' he admitted, but 'Red' Webb, his new landlady, was a grand character well used to welcoming lonely racing drivers who were wondering quite what they had let themselves in for while following their destiny. It was not uncommon for her to help them out when they stayed at High Elms.

'Red Webb was a most extraordinary woman,' Jones recalled with warm humour. 'Nobody seemed to know her real first name, but she was always just Red because of her hair colour.

'Going into West Kingsdown, there was this large blue house on the right where she lived with her inoffensive husband who tended to keep himself in the background. Red kept an open house for impecunious young drivers. People like Tony Trimmer, Ray Allen – and Tom. She was beloved by all, but it was a sort of love-hate thing. She was an unbelievable woman. Diminutive, but huge in character, and incredibly dominant. She would eff and blind – her language would have made a sailor blush. She'd shout upstairs to a driver still lazing in bed of a morning, "Get out of that effing bed, your breakfast is ruining down here!" She nagged them rotten, but she also loved them to bits. And if they couldn't afford to pay her, then they just owed her. For me she was one of the huge unsung figures in British club racing history.'

Jorge Koechlin was an aspiring Peruvian racer who arrived in Britain with little money and Red's address. 'I went there with Danny Sullivan. Tony Trimmer and Ted Wentz were already there, then this white Ford Cortina arrived and this lanky fellow got out. I think he was still wearing Wellington boots. He could hardly speak English! His name was Maldwyn but we all called him Thomas. He called me "Pancho". We became quite good friends.'

Koechlin, whose great-granduncle Paul had won the first-ever motor race, the 1895 Paris-Bordeaux-Paris and later produced his own grand prix car, worked at the Elden company on Formula Ford cars while racing his old Merlyn Mk20A.

'Thomas and I changed its engine once,' he said. 'You had to compress the doughnut driveshaft constant velocity joints with a Jubilee clip, but we were both poor mechanics at that time and struggled like mad with that.

'In those days *Motoring News* and *Autosport* came out on Thursday, but we wanted to be ahead of the game. Thomas used to drive me to Swanley and I'd get the train up to Victoria. Invariably I'd find *MN*, and 60 per cent of the time *Autosport*. I'd read *MN* on the train back, while Thomas was waiting. I'd give him the *MN* and we'd sit under a lamp post, him reading that and me *Autosport*.'

Koechlin also talked of illicit lappery of Brands Hatch at night, sometimes with girls to impress, after they discovered a gate at Dingle Dell that was always unlocked or unlockable.

'When Thomas ran in Formula Two at Rouen, I remember Danny asking him how he'd gone so fast there, and Thomas just replied, "They put the rear wing down so the Esses were flat." That was how easy it was for him.'

They tested whenever they could, leaving Red's at six in the morning. Wednesdays and Saturdays it would usually be Brands; Tuesdays, Snetterton, Thursdays, Silverstone. 'Lola and Lotus would bring cars along,' said Jorge. 'Thomas was always running cars for Bob King. We'd have our own cars or would sit around with

Tom with the Austin A35. He went down to Longbridge with his father to collect it.

our helmets, ready to drive anything. We were both hopeless at testing, didn't know anything about camber and castor, but we were good at telling them where the limit of their cars was.' When they weren't testing they would spend their afternoons talking racing in Red's sticker-covered lounge. 'We'd mull over how much Scheckter's dad was spending on his racing; what Emerson was being paid; how we went round tracks. We sat in the bay window looking out into the garden, and it used to drive Red's Labrador Susie mad…

'We used to reckon Red's full breakfast was worth a second a lap, because if you got wind in the cockpit you drove faster to make it go away!'

Jorge also thought that Red was jealous of Nella and some of the other girls. Certainly she preferred to help her boys. 'She even once lent me £135 to go and buy a new engine,' Tom told Henry, adding quickly, 'But I paid back every penny, of course.' His upbringing would not have allowed him to do anything else.

Nella remembered one occasion, however, when Tom was late picking her up. 'He arrived eventually and I asked him what had happened. He said that he had done something to upset Red and she'd ended up tipping his evening meal over his head! He'd had to go back upstairs and wash his hair and change his clothes.'

In his early days at High Elms, Tom might call home and say he was feeling fed up; Jack would whizz down in five hours in his Lotus Cortina, and Tom would drive them both back up to Wales. He loved the peacefulness of his birthplace; Jack remembers that he would stop and get out of the car at Braeburn, Clocaenog, just to listen to the silence. In later years, after Kyalami, Jack would be particularly grateful for the time they spent together on those trips.

Cledwyn once made a similar journey with Jack. 'He was himself a superb driver! A safe driver, but fast. A friend of mine, Elwyn Hamilton, had a big Peugeot and we went down to the British Grand Prix once, with his little boy Ken. We stayed locally and met up with Jack and Maldwyn at the track. Jack's car broke down, so Jack and Gwyneth decided to come back with us. Elwyn was a garage manager, quite a careful driver. And he said, "Do you want to drive, Jack?" Jack didn't hesitate. "Oh, yes, I know my way quite well."

'Well, I've never seen anything like it in my life! We sailed home in the most incredible amount of time. He went through London like that!' He snapped his fingers. 'Jack drove like a bat out of hell! Elwyn didn't say a word for about two hours. He was glued to his seat. We got back in half the time.'

Tom eventually ran an MGB GT, BCA 565L, in which he was once banned for three months for doing 106 mph (even though he swore he was doing only 86). He maintained it himself, and was a good mechanic. 'One time I had an MG 1100 and Mald told me I was over-revving it and that I'd blow it up one day,' Jack recalled. 'And that's exactly what happened!'

Besides his growing reputation on track, Tom was also making one for economy of words. Upon his arrival at MRS he had been told Maldwyn was too complicated for English tongues and that they would call him Tom Pryce. Jack recalled the time that photographer Max le Grand, who then lived locally, called in to see Red. 'She urged him to go upstairs and talk to this quiet Welsh bloke who was trying to go racing. It was not a very enlightening conversation. Max: "So how are you enjoying being down here, then?" Mald: "All right." Max: "And how is the racing going?" Mald: "All right."

'It wasn't that Mald was rude or anything. He was just shy and reserved with people he didn't know,' Jack explained.

'He never liked the glamour, didn't like being pointed out,' Red said.

Jones recalled with a guffaw: 'If he said "Good morning" to you, that was a conversation!'

'I considered that we were childhood friends,' Cledwyn Ashford said in 2006, 'but I would never presume. With Maldwyn being such a private person, you gave him space when he was racing.' They drifted apart a little as teenagers, as life took them in different directions, but Tom always made Cledwyn feel more than welcome on the days when he would go and see him race. 'I would not make a fuss,' Cledwyn said, 'because Maldwyn was not a fuss-maker. He wouldn't give you the big hug, "Hello, mate, how have you been?" No. That was not his scene. On race day, he would be in that caravan and you did not go in there.

'He said what he meant. He was a very straight talker, like his mother. I remember the time she might make a bit of a fuss; she would only get "the look" from him, and she'd know that was it. Don't go there.'

Tom's first race with the Lola was naturally at Brands Hatch, but very soon he began to learn the hard way that a short wheelbase single-seater can be unforgiving. Exiting Clearways in practice he missed a gear and in a flash the Lola was parked in pieces on top of the grass bank, where it was viewed with dismay by its bewildered driver.

'I just hadn't a clue what to do with a smashed up racing car,' he told Henry. 'I didn't know a thing about the business, where to get it fixed or who to approach. It just sat in one of the Brands lock-ups for days with me just looking at it, wondering what on earth to do with it.'

Somebody from MRS finally put him out of his misery and pointed him in the direction of Arch Motors, which at that time was the place to go for such things. They straightened the damaged chassis and fixed everything else for £50.

The little Lola would play a crucial part in Tom's racing career, not just because it got him going in the

TOP LEFT: *Jack had to cajole Tom into letting him take this photograph of him in his first racesuit.*

TOP RIGHT: *Down at the shabby garages in the Brands Hatch paddock, Tom and a friend pose with the Lola T200 that he won in the Crusader series.*

CENTRE: *Commentator Anthony Marsh interviews Tom, under the watchful eye of Daily Express proprietor Max Aitken (left), on the day he won the Crusader series at Silverstone in April 1970.*

LEFT: *Tom in the Lola at Crystal Palace in 1970, before Jack suggested he add the five black vertical stripes to his helmet so that he could identify his son more easily in the Formula Ford pack.*

Tom didn't have a passport until he started racing, aged 20. This is its photo.

first place, but because it helped him to develop the car control that would later be compared with the sideways kings of the game, Jochen Rindt and Ronnie Peterson.

'The T200 taught me a lot,' he said. 'It had such a short wheelbase that it tended to break away suddenly. I was always spinning the thing all over the place. But it gave me a good idea about car control and I won quite a few races in it.'

Former soldier Ray Allen was one of the resident hotshoes of Formula Ford at Brands and was a senior trainer at MRS. On one occasion he ventured the opinion to Tom that he really should be getting more out of the Lola than he was. 'So Mald told him to take it out himself and have a go if he wanted,' Jack recalled. 'Ray did just that, and he couldn't get it going as quickly as Mald did! It was a difficult car to drive, that one.'

The famous vertical stripes on Tom's white helmet came around this time. 'We were at Castle Combe,' Jack said. 'I was having a lot of trouble recognising Mald in the pack of cars whizzing past, so I said he had to do something to make his helmet stand out more.' This was of course in the days long before racing parents felt the need for their offspring to have £500 paint jobs on their helmets even before they had started to race, and the Pryces' practical solution was to add five vertical black stripes.

At the end of the year Henry reviewed the Formula Ford season in *Motoring News*. Colin Vandervell, Peter

Hull, Peter Lamplough, Bob Evans and Andy Rouse had been the pacesetters, together with Derek Lawrence, Ian Taylor, Tony Roberts and Bernard Vermilio, but Henry also mentioned two rookies. 'Right at the end of the season,' he wrote, somewhat presciently as it would turn out in both instances, 'two novices emerged from the close-fought series of Brands FF races, both of whom could develop real flair next season. They were Tom Pryce and Richard Croucher, and to win in the hot company they kept was certainly a step in the right direction.'

In 1971 Tom continued to make a name for himself. A new sportscar category had been introduced the previous year by John Webb, the enterprising manager of Brands Hatch whose abrasive manner often disguised the heart and soul of a true motorsport enthusiast. Webb was a far-sighted visionary who frequently imported successful US series to the Britain, such as Formula 5000 and Formula Atlantic, or else invented his own. Formula F100 fell into the latter category and was for two-seater sportscars using production engines and Firestone's F100 road tyre. Towards the end of the previous year Tom was somehow inveigled into calling Bob King, to see if he would lend him one of Royale's new RP4 sportscars.

'Tom was such a shy boy and he would never push himself,' King recalled. 'He just phoned one day and asked if he could come and quickly see me. There was a race the next weekend at Brands Hatch for sportscars, "Do you think I could borrow the F100?" After a lot of argy-bargy I said, "Okay, take it away, but look after it. If you break it you are going to have to buy it."'

Recognising the unlikelihood that Tom would have been so forward without intense provocation, King racked his memory. 'I think what actually happened was that Geoff Clarke just said, "Why don't you give Bob King a ring and see if he'll lend you a car?" I really hadn't heard of Tom beyond whispers from Brands Hatch, but I liked him immediately he came in the door.'

Jones recalled that situation. 'I do know that Geoff lobbied Bob hard about helping Tom. I am sure that he would have been inspirational in making that happen, though I suspect it would have happened before he fell out with Tom over a contract. I don't think Geoff would have made that sort of effort after that. But it was him, I think, who persuaded Bob that Tom was a guy who should be helped, and I know that Tony Lanfranchi, who was also involved driving for Royale, also rated Tom very highly.'

King continued, 'It sounds very old-fashioned, but he was very polite, very nice, he was genuine. And it wasn't a thing I would normally do, just saying, "Take the car." I couldn't afford to. But with him it just seemed right. When I think about it, his approach was self-effacing: "I know you're not going to give me a car, but I may as well ask since I'm here..."

'It was that, I suppose, that made me feel, "Yeah, let's give him a go." So Tom took the car away and won the race by a country mile, beating much quicker cars.' But what impressed King even more was what happened after that. 'When he brought the car back on Monday morning, it was pristine, absolutely like new. I was really so impressed with that. He'd done a nut-check all round and cleaned it all up. And that's when it started with him. We gave him a test drive in a Formula Ford, and that just started him on the road.

'Tom was just a lovely personality, and I'm not saying that just because he is no longer with us and you can get too sentimental about these things. He was a lovely guy, and underlying that was this latent skill that he had. He came alive in the cockpit of a racing car.'

Subsequently, having taken over Les Leston's car for a few races in 1970, in 1971 he drove one of the new Royales for TAS Racing. He dominated the series and won the crown with embarrassing ease. But he was well aware of what he had and had not achieved, and did not let the success go to his head. 'The trouble about F100 was that there wasn't really anybody in it, even though it was fine for getting experience,' he admitted. Certainly he was establishing a reputation for spectacular sideways motoring, but who was he actually beating?

He continued to race the Lola at times (sponsorship negotiations for something better having stalled), winning with fastest lap at Brands at the end of February ahead of Croucher and the rising Tony Brise (who'd spun and had to fight his way back up). And having become a regular performer at Brands, he attracted patronage from Toby St George-Matthews which later that season enabled him also to move up to the newly emergent Formula SuperVee category, promoted by Volkswagen. He drove one of St George-Matthews' new Royale RP9s, which at that time was the car to have. As his natural ability blossomed he won races with it, and took podiums in European events. In July, he and St George-Matthews vied for the lead at Silverstone prior to retiring, Tom having flown in specially after winning the Formula 100 race at Brands Hatch earlier in the day.

'The next stage in all of this came when a chap called Tom Smith, a quiet businessman from Essex who kept himself in the background, helped to fund some of Tom's racing,' Jones said. 'He played a significant role in his development around that time, and without that I'm not sure what Tom would have done.'

Royale Racing Cars had been born out of Bob King's Racing Preparations business, which King had set up while pursuing his own ambitions behind the wheel. He had purchased the assets of the famous Coventry Climax Formula One engine company from Jaguar, to whom it was an embarrassment; and after he'd moved his own racing operation out of the garage by his home in Edgware to a factory in nearby Park Royal in north London, he moved again to set up a manufacturing base

at Huntingdon in late 1971 in order to be closer to suppliers such as Arch Motors, Titan and Specialised Mouldings. There was space in its new factory to run a Formula Three team, and Bob liked the idea of being able to sell cars in that category. After testing the new Royale RP11 for King at Snetterton near the end of the season, Tom débuted it at the Victory Race meeting at Brands on 24 October. He qualified 13th for the first heat, setting his time of 1m 36.4s in the damp Saturday morning session when it was bettered only by Vandervell and Williamson, and after teething problems with gear ratios, brake balance and tightening steering hampered the car the previous day. He ran in the top 10 in the race before dropping back with vicious oversteer to finish 13th as Roger won from Hunt and Vandervell. He started the final 27th, after Mike Walker, Jody Scheckter and Claude Bourgiognie had filled the top three places in heat two. He made up places hand over fist, until he came across Gerold Pankl's wayward Lotus at Druids and was helped into retirement.

A week later veteran racer and proven Formula Three winner Bev Bond took over the car for a Lombank round, but Tom had another outing at Lydden in November. As Roger won the first heat, the crowd was entertained by Tom's spectacular progress as he chased Peter Hull home in third place. More oversteering motoring brought him sixth place in the final, which David Purley won for Ensign.

King was sufficiently impressed with Tom's performances to nominate him as the official Royale Formula Three driver for 1972.

The Pryces, seen here as Tom, Nella, Gwyn and Jack attended a friend's wedding, were a very close-knit family. Nella is still in regular contact with Jack and Gwyn, who celebrated their 80th birthdays and their 60th wedding anniversary in 2006.

CHAPTER 3
Beginnings

Tony

'He was very thoughtful, a deep thinker like his father, and he had that deep knowledge of cars which came from growing up with his father. He was a clever chap, actually.'
Pam Brise

It was so inevitable that Anthony Brise would become a racing driver, that it might have been preordained. His parents, John and Pam, met through a mutual friend in the forties and soon realised they did not want to live without each other. John was the son of a builder in Dartford and then became a pig farmer, moving into the business when it was at its zenith. His success financed a pleasant lifestyle that enabled him to indulge his passion for motor racing.

At 19 he acquired a pre-War SS100, then moved into the newly emergent Formula 500 category that would subsequently spawn great talents such as Stirling Moss, Peter Collins, Stuart Lewis-Evans and Don Parker. The cars were relatively simple single-seaters generally powered by the 500cc JAP engine. John bought one of the dominant Coopers, and soon proved himself to be quick. His performances attracted Daphne Arnott, for whom George Thornton had designed an unusual little car. The Arnott had first appeared in 1952, and for 1953 John was offered the works drive. This was a mixed blessing. Thornton had plumped for a relatively conventional concept as far as the rear-engined chassis was concerned, but specified double wishbone, torsion bar suspension, pannier fuel tanks and a short wheelbase. This was advanced thinking, but it was all a little too much ahead of its time and it was not an easy or rewarding car to drive. Ivor Bueb, who would go on to win Le Mans in 1955, soon reverted to a Cooper. John had to persevere with the works car, but his best

The Elden Formula Ford, like Tom's Lola, was a tricky short wheelbase car, but soon Tony was winning races. He was always the man to beat at his local track, Brands Hatch.

result was fourth place in a 100-mile race at Silverstone. A streamlined version with enclosed bodywork was constructed, and proved more successful; he set some 500cc class records with it (which would stand for decades) at the banked Montlhéry circuit outside Paris.

In the mid-fifties stock car racing was emerging in Britain, and John made the switch enthusiastically. This was not the NASCAR-type of stock car that was then becoming popular in America, but more akin to the sprintcar genre that ran on dirt tracks over there. John built himself a car comprising a Mercedes chassis, Jeep rear axle, Massey Ferguson tractor gearbox and an Oldsmobile Rocket 88 V8 engine bored out to 7.5 litres.

In an interview in August 1975 with Nigel Roebuck in *Autosport*, Tony still enthused about the monster. 'Dad's last engine was incredible! It had roller cams and all kinds of tweaks. None of the opposition bothered to do more than buy a bog-standard engine, and they had to rebuild them all the time, whereas his engine just stayed in all season! There were great bumps in the rocker covers and no-one could understand why. Dad used to say that these allowed more oil around the rockers; in fact, the real reason was that the engine had such a high-lift cam that the rocker covers got in the way!'

Tony had been the perfect age to be seduced by racing as his father's successes reached their peak. John

Initially John went circuit racing, with this Cooper in the highly popular Formula 500.

won the World Stock Car Championship in 1956 when Tony was four, and the British Trophy in 1957. He then emulated Jack Brabham by scoring back-to-back World Championships in 1959 and 1960.

It is not surprising that he built seven-year-old Tony a downhill racer, but this was no ordinary wooden crate type of soapbox favoured by young children in the fifties; it had a tubular chassis and suspension. Before long it had a moped engine, too, so Tony could tear round the family farm. 'It was great,' he told Roebuck. 'The thing had a clutch and accelerator, and no brakes!'

The next craze to sweep Britain was karting, which originated in America early in the decade. John was barely covering his rising costs in stock cars, and the new category had instant appeal. He started off as works driver for Getkart, and Tony had opportunities to sample the 4.5hp machine. By 1960 John was making the Brisekart, and it was inevitable that Tony would join him in racing one.

These were the days before the RAC began to regulate karting and to insist on a minimum age, so eight-year-old Tony frequently found himself racing adults when he and John ventured to nearby Tilbury. Over the years that track would resonate with karting dads throughout the UK as a tough place to cut your teeth. 'The other drivers used to get very annoyed by being beaten all the time due to such a favourable power-to-weight ratio and they made me start from the back of the grid,' Tony told *Motoring News* in November 1973.

ABOVE: *Rising costs obliged John to move into stock car racing, where he built his own monsters and quickly made a major name for himself.* RIGHT: *He won three stock car World Championships – in 1956, '59 and '60 – but gave up his own sporting activities to guide his eldest son's burgeoning career.*

For four years Tony raced with increasing success at Tilbury, before the RAC stepped in to separate young drivers from the adults. The new age limit was 13 and he was only 11, but like Roger he lied about his age, adding the requisite two years to qualify for the new Junior class. The winning continued, at tracks all over the UK, but potential aggravation loomed as he moved up to the Senior category in his '16th' year, when of course he was still only 14. Incredibly, nobody raised an eyebrow, either through ignorance or a benign inclination to indulge a fast young racer, and the success continued. Running in the Villiers Class, Tony finished runner-up in the British Championship in 1966, the year Roger won in Special Class Four.

By this time John had effectively retired from racing himself, preferring to focus his efforts on the burgeoning talents of both his eldest son, and his 18-month younger brother Tim. 'Being John he just stopped all interest in himself and concentrated on Anthony,' Pam Brise said. 'He really enjoyed it, but what really used to make me

ABOVE: *John, with Tony and his brother Tim, as they embarked on the karting trail.* ABOVE RIGHT: *John was there with Tony when he graduated to Formula Ford with the Elden in 1971, seen here at Oulton Park.*

cross was that he would never interfere with the running of the karts or cars. I used to say to him, "You know what's wrong, why don't you go and tell them." And he'd say, "No, it's nothing to do with me. It's up to them." He would give them their space. Very proud he was, in a lot of ways. It's a Brise trait, I think.'

This blend of support and insistence that Tony should work things out for himself certainly helped the younger Brise to stand on his own feet, and was perhaps where the first seeds were sown of the reputation he would gain for arrogance.

In 1967 Tony raced a 40bhp, 200cc Montessa-powered gearbox kart and won the RAC British Kart Championship for the class which was held at tricky Cadwell Park. He also won the Bouley Bay hillclimb in Jersey, but was disqualified. 'They said I was a Junior and therefore too light!' Ironically, John was competing with the same kart and was awarded the victory.

That season Jim Clark was the dominating force in Formula One with the new Cosworth-powered Lotus 49, and that's when Tony's thoughts first turned towards racing cars. 'It seems like Tony was always racing,' Pam said, 'and I think he always wanted to do something with cars.'

Tony followed Clark's exploits closely that year, and at the same time John was also beginning to entertain thoughts of a switch. The problem was one of finance. They stayed with karts, and Tony continued to win. He

also won the Bouley Bay hillclimb for the third time, and by 1969 was joint British Champion in the 250cc category. Still they could not escape the category, and 1970 saw only a limited season for a man who should have moved up long before.

'As kids we all grew up together,' said Jenny Anderson, whose brother Bob Simpson was a school friend of Tim who worked on Tony's machinery. Her husband Gary would later work in Formula One with Brabham, McLaren, Jordan, Arrows, Stewart and Jaguar. 'To begin with we went to St Paul's in Swanley Village, a tiny, beautiful church school. Bob, myself and sister Kate were the only kids in the village, where my parents ran a small butcher's shop. It was like a private school, there were only 12 in our class.

'Tony and Tim were 18 months apart, the same ages as me and Bob. Tony and I were close, and so were Tim and Bob. I remember that Tony and Tim would come to school with the kart on top of the car whenever they had won! John Brise adored cars and had a red Ferrari, but as they lived at the end of a bumpy lane he only ever used it on special occasions.

'John and Pam were so close. As a family they were such a tight unit. John was a very sensible man, well thought of as a local businessman but somebody who never looked for the limelight. Mrs Brise, as we called Pam then, was a beautiful, stunning woman. They adored their kids, and their kids adored them. They were a lovely family.

'I went to the Brise house regularly. When Pam and John went on holiday, Pam's mother Nana Hills could just about manage looking after the three boys, but I used to go over and help look after Simon, who was nine years younger than Tim.

'Eventually Tony went off to Eltham College, while the rest of us went to the comprehensive in Swanley. Tony told me he was taken to Eltham College by Mick Jagger once, but I never figured out if he was just pulling my leg. The thing that surprised me as far as racing went was that Tony had asthma, you could hear it in his chest sometimes. But it never stopped him.'

By the end of 1970, John and Tony were desperate to move to cars, and at last serendipity played its role. The Hampsheir brothers, Brian and Peter, lived not far from them in Dartford and had been building racing cars since 1961. At the end of 1970 they harboured ambitions to emulate March, the company that had been set up in 1969 by Max Mosley, Alan Rees, Graham Coaker and Robin Herd to manufacture proprietary racing cars. Such had been March's dramatic success that, having produced a prototype Formula Three car for Ronnie Peterson to drive in that first year, it had leapt into 1970 making Formula One, Formula Two, Formula Three, Formula Ford and CanAm cars! When the Hampsheirs approached their bank manager he may have been aware that March had been nicknamed 'Much Advertised Racing Car Hoax' in the specialist press, and declined their request for funding. But he did suggest that they speak to John and Tony, who also had an account at his branch.

'So up they came,' Tony related to Roebuck, 'asking for a certain amount of money, but we had to laugh at them as we certainly didn't have that sort of money. Eventually we did a deal: we funded a chassis on the understanding that if we liked it when we first drove it, we would keep it. If we didn't, they would refund our money. Anyway, I drove it and, not knowing any better, I thought it was reasonable.'

Thus was born the Elden Mk8, with which Tony would carve a name for himself in Formula Ford racing. It was an unusual-looking car, with a short wheelbase reminiscent of his father's 500 Arnott and a square, drooping nose; but, in his hands at least, it was an effective little tool. His first race in the red car came on 17 January 1971 at Brands Hatch, where he finished fourth behind Richard Croucher, Val Musetti and Russell Wood, and set fastest lap to everyone's surprise. *Motoring News* distinguished itself by publishing his photo captioned as Croucher, but before long there would be no mistaking the 19-year-old from Dartford. 'If ever there was an advertisement for karting it was this FF thrash,' wrote Alan Henry, 'with the youngsters Croucher and Brise proving that driving by the seat of one's pants certainly does qualify you for single-seater racing.' Mentioning Tony's fastest lap, he added, 'We'll have to forget the old Elden and adjust ourselves to this extremely quick newcomer.'

Next time out at Brands, in February, Tony took his first car victory and again set fastest lap, albeit in a four-

ABOVE: *Tousled Tony, aged 19.* BELOW: *His efforts in his first season of Formula Ford were sufficient to attract much attention, including an Autosport front cover. Here he hustles the Elden in pursuit of Colin Crang's Merlyn at Crystal Palace, where he broke the lap record.*

car field. But 1971 was a difficult season for him as his father had imposed one key condition: he had to pursue an education so that he had something to fall back on if racing proved unsuccessful. He had already achieved two A-levels at Eltham College, and in September 1969 had enrolled at Birmingham's Aston University on a four-year Business Studies degree course. University life precluded much midweek testing, and he missed races in May as exams intervened and the Elden underwent a complete rebuild.

'We started a development programme on it,' Tony told Roebuck, 'and it went on as long as we had the car. Fairly soon we reached a point where there was no more development we could do. However, fortunately, we'd got it going well at Brands because all our testing was done there, and we'd got some sponsorship from Scholar Engines. Doug Wardropper of Scholar used to race stock cars against my father, and one day he came up and offered us free engines! We said we weren't sure he was doing the right thing – it wasn't much of a car, after all, and I was new to racing – but he said he knew that if my father was involved, the project would be a success.'

It was. By the end of the season he had won 22 FF

Tony's performances were so impressive that team manager Peter Warr invited him to test Dave Walker's championship-winning Lotus 69 partway through 1971.

races with the Mk8, which had been rebodied and repainted yellow. Everywhere he went he proved to be a man to be reckoned with. At Snetterton in March, on his first visit to the Norfolk track, he beat local ace Martin Watson by four-tenths of a second. First time out at Oulton Park, in the rain, he beat fellow comingman Ian Taylor, even after briefly sliding off the road at Island Bend. He lapped all but six cars. At Brands Hatch in June came two decisive wins. *Motoring News*'s headline and report from its 29 July issue perhaps best summarised the year. 'Brise and Brodie brilliant', the former said, while reporter Hilary Weatherley added, 'First there was Schenken, then Fittipaldi, then Vandervell. Is it possible that Tony Brise will be the next one to make the big time? On Sunday's form the answer is obviously yes.'

There were less auspicious moments, too. He didn't always win, and at Crystal Palace in August he parked the Elden in the barriers at North Tower while battling to make up ground on eventual winner Colin Crang after a previous mistake had dropped him back.

In August, the Brises had the opportunity to swap the car for the Merlyn Mk20 which Richard Croucher had used to stunning effect all season, and suddenly Tony gained a second a lap. It put his performances in the Elden into further perspective. He won a further six races in that car and clinched the Brands Hatch-based Townsend Thoresen Formula Ford Championship. He

ABOVE LEFT: *His Formula Three race début came at Brands at the end of the year in the works ex-Colin Vandervell Brabham BT35, however, courtesy of team owner Bernie Ecclestone. Was Tony as good as everyone said? 'No,' Ecclestone replied in 2006, 'he was better. He would have gone all the way.'*
ABOVE: *Father and son: Tony and Johnny in 1971.*

was also runner-up to Bernard Vermilio in the BOC Oxygen series. There were two fillips at the end of the year. The first was the performance of brother Tim, who had moved up to Formula Ford in the Elden and showed good speed. At Brands Hatch in October Tony won in the Merlyn ahead of Vermilio, with Tim a close third.

Thus his impressive first season earned him one of the new Grovewood Awards nominations, together with Vermilio.

The final boost came when Ford paid for him to go to South Africa with the Merlyn to compete in the Sunshine Formula Ford series. But the regulations demanded locally made tyres, which ruled out the Firestone Torino that had served him so well in the UK. He opted for Firestone's Cavallino, but was blown off in the first race by Jody Scheckter's brother Ian in an indentical car shod with India radials. After that bruising wake-up Tony got a set of Indias. Scheckter beat him twice more and he beat Scheckter twice, but retirement in the final race sealed the title in the South African's favour and left Tony as runner-up.

'I found the experience invaluable,' he told *Motoring News*. 'I always do well on new tracks because I don't take long to learn them.'

The Brises now faced the question of what to do in 1972. With so many wins there was little point in staying in Formula Ford. Formula Three was the logical option. There had been rumours in August that Ensign builder Mo Nunn might hire him to replace Bev Bond in his little team, but in the end an invitation came from an even more auspicious source. John Brise knew Bernie Ecclestone, the former manager of Stuart Lewis-Evans and Jochen Rindt who had just purchased Motor Racing Developments and the Brabham operation from Sir Jack Brabham's partner Ron Tauranac. 'Bernie phoned and offered me a drive in the ex-Vandervell Brabham BT35 Formula Three car,' Tony informed Roebuck. 'Naturally, I accepted!'

The blue car bore the legend alongside the cockpit, 'Tony Brise driving for Brabham'. He won a Formule Libre race with it first time out at Brands Hatch in November, beating more powerful cars, Clive Santo's Formula Atlantic Palliser and Patrick Sumner's Kitchiner. His next two outings came at Brands on Boxing Day; in the first, a combined Formula Three-Formula Atlantic thrash, he started from the back after practice problems and finished third in the Formula Three section before being dropped a place by a penalty for a jump start. In the second, for Formula Threes and Formula Fords, he again started near the back but closed right up on Roger's troubled new March 723 and the winning Ensign driven by a former paratrooper called David Purley – who would later play a key role in the 'Lost Generation's' developing story.

'He was a good person,' Pam Brise said, looking back on her lost son. 'When he was young and was still at Eltham College and had his sights on being a racing driver, local people used to call him arrogant. But college can knock that out of you. He enjoyed his time at Aston University, even though he was racing and studying at the same time. He really was a lovely guy. He was very thoughtful, a deep-thinker like his father, and he had that deep knowledge of cars which came from growing up with his father. He was a clever chap, actually. And he liked flying. He said that he thought he might take it up even when he was in his early racing days. He told us, "It's much nicer. Motor racing is so cut-throat!" And that was back then!'

CHAPTER 4

A dominant force

Roger, 1972

'His determination, ambition and will to win were the same as the world-class rally Finns I came into contact with, total commitment. Roger saw nothing else but victory as a worthwhile result.'
Jeremy Walton

At the start of 1972, Roger Williamson was the best known of the 'Lost Generation', following his surprise successes in 1971. And his star was set to continue its rise.

The British Formula Three scene was complicated at that time by the presence of three championships. The most prestigious was the Shell Super Oil series, followed by the Forward Trust and the Lombard North Central. Having won the Lombard in 1971 Roger focused on the Shell and Forward Trust series, but his campaign did not get off to a promising start. After their success with the March 713M the previous year, Tom Wheatcroft stuck with the Bicester marque but its side-radiatored 723 soon proved a disappointment. Whatever set-up changes or modifications they tried made little difference to its performance. The car was no match for the new GRD 372 driven by works driver Andy Sutcliffe, who won three of the first six races.

'I remember at Mallory Park,' Nick Jordan said, 'Roger came in and said, "Christ, at Gerard's I'm not sure of this." Gerard's was flat even then, a ballsy corner, and he just didn't feel right about the car there.'

Roger hit back with a Shell win at Oulton Park on 31 March despite the March's shortcomings, but his

As so often in 1972, Roger was out in front immediately in the Formula Three race supporting the GP at Clermont-Ferrand.

The 1972 March 723 was a handful, but that didn't stop Roger winning with it at Oulton Park early in the season.

next victory came in a brand new GRD at Silverstone's International Trophy meeting on 23 April. There he left the opposition for dead after breaking the slipstream tow early on, putting in a perfect performance which increased the hold he would have on the Shell series all year.

Thirty years later I recounted the story to Jochen Mass of watching from the side of the track as Roger dominated that race. When I said that he was so far ahead of the next man that I couldn't even remember who had finished second, Jochen smiled quietly and said, 'Actually, I did.' He fought all the way to bring his March home four-tenths of a second ahead of Peter Hull's Brabham. Roger's margin of victory was a hair under 14 seconds, a vast amount by Formula Three standards.

'We built the car in four days,' Jordan said, 'but we had all sorts of problems. We ran it up the Silverstone Club Circuit straight and we had a fuel pump problem. Jo Marquart's fuel system didn't work so well, so we were putting all sorts of extra pumps in. And the wheels were letting air out. They were cast magnesium and full

of pinholes. So I nipped down to the local hardware store, got a tin of clear varnish, and there I was with the tyres off, shellacking these wheels. But after that they were fine.'

Three weeks later Roger won again at Silverstone, in a Forward Trust round, this time in the works GRD after the Wheatcroft car had been damaged the previous day at Monaco, and there was no stopping him. Shell victories followed at Anderstorp in June, Brands Hatch in July, Oulton Park in September and Snetterton in October; Forward Trust triumphs at Cadwell Park and Thruxton in July and Thruxton again in September; and Lombard wins at Mallory Park in July and Cadwell in September. On top of that he won European races at La Chartre in June and Clermont-Ferrand in July, and walked the race at Paul Ricard in front of the Formula One team managers until his car's intake manifold failed to hold a vacuum at post-race scrutineering.

Jordan has particularly fond memories of those French outings. 'Roger won La Chartre from Tony. There was a real tussle between them during the heat as the organisers made sure that they were both in the same heat so that at least one Frenchman was on the front row for the final!

'The final result was Roger first, Tony second, and

Jacques Coulon third. This was a first-class result for the British pair; they collected four cups between them: three for Tony for the heat win, fastest lap, and second place in the final. Tony was very quick and had Roger on the grass twice, blocking him big time during the heat in which they finished first and second. Roger was absolutely livid; it was the only time that I recollect they had a real go verbally during their racing. But there was good convivial banter between us all at the presentation in the local town hall.

'Clermont was one of Roger's best races. He was running tiny little wings on the front and we'd made up our own rear wing, with no centre. We were up against the Alpine-Renaults of Jean-Pierre Jabouille, Christian Ethuin, Patrick Depailler, Michel Leclère and Alain Serpaggi; there was a whole bunch of them and it was a good grid. Roger came in and there were 10 minutes to go, and he was third or fourth quickest. And he said, "There's a long climb up that hill... Take the wings off." Now I don't think the Dunlops were the best tyres there either, not as good as the Michelins that the French guys had. But he went out and stuck the thing on pole by about three-tenths, just like that.

'He touched a wall, but said that right away he'd had an extra 100 revs all the way up the hill, and knew that was time he was gaining.

'He had massive commitment, without a shadow of a doubt. They didn't call him 'Sideways Williamson' for nothing. He'd sussed that one and he'd made his mind up, and the night before when he knew he was on pole, he said, "I will win this."'

There was fun afterwards. 'Myself and Eric got a prize from Ecurie Antar, the fuel company, although we were sponsored by BP. We collected something like 500 francs, or 50 quid, the two of us, which was like a fortune. I was on 20 quid a week then. And we got this jeroboam of champagne. Harry Marks was there, this grey-haired guy who was at that time in every photo. And there were about eight people around this table and Tom was in the middle, and he goes, "Aaargh," you know how he goes, and he's winking at me. He gets the cork out and I'm thinking, "He's gonna blast Harry." And he swung round, but Harry knocked it on the floor and it smashed. There were about two gallons of Champagne all over this floor. It was good fun!'

Ricard may or may not have been payback for Depailler's disqualification at Brands Hatch the previous October. 'Roger qualified well, right up the front.' Jordan recalled, 'but he was going backwards in his heat because he had a slow puncture in the right-hand front. When he was coming into the right-hander, the last corner on the last lap, the thing was smoking and he was *still* outbraking people. He finished 13th so started 26th on a grid of 32, on the

left-hand side. I remember the white line was a metre away from the barrier. He said, "I know exactly where I'm going at the start, and I'm that far back that they won't be watching me. I know that the car's good."

'He took off at the start and came round in seventh or eighth place at the end of the opening lap. Unbelievable. It was three laps from the end that he passed Leclère on the pit straight to take the lead. What was really nice about it was that the French crowd appreciated the fact, because they were fed up with the Alpine-Renaults beating everybody. When Roger overtook them they were very, very happy that he had won.

'Then we went to scrutineering. The vacuum diaphragm unit on the rear of the engine was an aluminium casting riveted together. That casting was porous. When they checked the engine for vacuum afterwards, it should have pulled 14 inches of mercury. I know for a fact, because I rebuild historic Formula Three engines now, that a little bit doesn't make any difference; you need to have a fairly reasonable sized hole to make any difference. It was pulling something like 13.7, 13.8, the needle was hovering. The ruling then was that if it

The switch to a GRD 372 saw him walk away from the opposition first time out at Silverstone's International Trophy race meeting, where he won by 14 seconds.

ABOVE: *After the decisive victory, (left to right) BP's Harry Downing, Eric Hassell, Nick Jordan, Dodge Williamson and Eric Chalk anxiously await their turn in the scrutineering bay.*
BELOW: *Competition Car's Number 4 cover of 1972 perfectly captured the Williamson crouch as Roger set about making amends for a poor start at Monaco.*

didn't pull the necessary vacuum you could take the cylinder head off, regrind all the valves and then retest it. But when it got to that point, the organisers had made their minds up they were going to disqualify Roger. That was wrong. It was right technically, but I think, for the show that was put on, it was wrong. In the UK they would have said there was no gain.'

In July Roger won five races in a row, in September three. He finished second on three occasions, to Sutcliffe while driving the March at Snetterton's Lombard round in March; at Zandvoort's Shell round in April when he battled wheel-to-wheel with eventual winner Mike Walker; and at Brands Hatch's Shell round in October when he was beaten by promising Frenchman Jacques Coulon in a Martini. The Brands performance was little short of sensational, however, as Roger was the only topliner to gamble on slick tyres in a race which remained soaking wet. Showing his ability to bring a car home, he backed all this with a third at Silverstone in June, fourths at Mallory Park in March and April, Thruxton in August and Brands Hatch in October, and fifths at Brands in March and Crystal Palace in September. More often than not he also set fastest lap.

The GRD was a great car and he certainly benefited from the strength of his Holbay engines and the depth of Wheatcroft's team organisation. But the slippery Iberia-sponsored Ensigns of Rikki von Opel and Mike Walker were serious competition, too, as were Tony and Alan Jones in their GRDs and Tom in the Royale. In the cockpit Roger demonstrated fearsome determination – epitomised by his famous crouch – tremendous speed and a willingness to fight all the way regardless of the odds. He never seemed to know when he was beaten. Nowhere was that more evident than at Monaco in May. He won his heat comfortably but made an uncharacteristically poor start from pole position in the final when ranged against French rising star Patrick Depailler; he was fighting back in superb style when he made a rare mistake on the wet track and crashed out. The following day he bounced back with that victory in Sutcliffe's 372 at Silverstone.

Jordan particularly remembered two British races: Thruxton, where he beat Mike Walker, and Snetterton, where he just pipped Tony. 'Walker was leading at Thruxton and there was only the last lap to go. Roger's mental approach before a race would be: "If they can stick with me over the first two laps on cold tyres, if I haven't got the break of 100 yards or so, I know I've got a real fight on my hands." He was

OPPOSITE PAGE: *Surrounded by the Elf-funded hopefuls of France, Roger sets off from pole position at Clermont-Ferrand.*

fantastic on cold tyres. Anybody who can drive that first or second lap on cold tyres will have that margin. It's not rocket science. It's like, can you do it or can't you? You either have that car control, or you don't.

'Roger sold Mike a dummy coming up into the chicane and kept pushing to the outside. He knew he couldn't get past Mike's slippery Ensign otherwise, and there was something on Roger's engine anyway that sounded like a cracked exhaust but was actually a chipped valve. But he just swung down the inside, big old lock-up, and managed to squeeze through into the chicane. He got the win on the line. I remember Mo Nunn was pretty hacked off about that. He thought Roger had better engines. There was always a big needle between us and Ensign.'

The Snetterton race saw Roger and Tony share the same race time after a fabulous duel. 'Tony just gave him too much room in the Bombhole. He said to me afterwards, "I cannot believe where he put his car, I just gave him a foot too much. I gave him 12 inches of road I didn't need to give him."

'That was when Roger won the championship. And we went into the Snetterton bar and sunk a few scoops, and there was Jo Marquart crying, he couldn't believe it. He was quite emotional. A good race car designer, a hard-working guy.'

By season-end Roger had achieved his aims of winning the Shell and Forward Trust championships. Yet despite the effect all this success had on his standing on the international motorsport stage he remained the same man he had always been – willing to stop and talk with old friends in the paddock and possessed of an infectious sense of humour and vigorous enthusiasm for life. He was an uncomplicated young lad who adored motor racing, and loved it even more when he had a car capable of winning.

He had also made his Formula Two début that year courtesy of Wheatcroft, who hired a March 722. In the rain at Oulton Park at Easter he ran third until spinning at Esso with 10 laps to go. At Rouen in June he non-started after his engine ingested a nut. 'Our fault,' Jordan said tersely.

In between, he finished fifth in his heat at Pau, and impressed in the final.

'This is gonna blaspheme someone!' Jordan chuckled. 'John Coombs Racing was running François Cevert and Patrick Depailler in Marches and Jean-Pierre Jabouille in an Elf. We needed an engine and Bruce Stevens from Race Engine Services said he'd got one, "but it's from Cevert's car and it's got a misfire. You can have that. I can cure the misfire."'

Alan Henry knew the engine of old and described it in his *Motoring News* report as 'the unloved Coombs 1930 "misfirer", which showed no less an inclination to run roughly when installed in the Wheatcroft March.'

'Roger called Tom,' Jordan continued. 'A deal was struck with Mr Coombs, around £2,500 for that engine. Roger offered to give him a cheque for it, but Mr Coombs said that if Tom Wheatcroft gave his word on it that was fine. So Mr Coombs said they were going off for dinner, but to come up to the hotel about nine o'clock. I could tell they were stringing it out, messing us about. So Roger and I went up there, they'd finished dinner, it was about nine in the evening, and Roger asked if was it possible somebody could come down, open the truck up and get the engine because we wanted to get it all together. At this particular point Peter Warr, Richard Divila and a whole range of rival guys knew we were in a pickle and said that anything we needed, they'd help with. They knew we were on the back foot, they liked Roger and thought it was good to have him in the show. The others are all sitting on sofas in this hotel, and this guy Brian Lewis, who was with Mr Coombs, I'll always remember, just said to Roger, "Why don't you go and play just in the Formula Threes, Roger? This is too big for you, this Formula Two."'

An interesting comment, given Roger's début performance at Oulton, or that in Pau Depailler had qualified his Coombs March in 1m 16.5s for the front row of the first heat, while Roger (still misfiring) was fourth fastest for the second, with 1m 16.3s behind Cevert (15.4s), Peter Gethin (15.6s) and Jean-Pierre Jaussaud (15.6s).

'My hackles went up. Okay, I'm only a mechanic, but we had passion. And all of a sudden Mr "Noddy" Coombs said, "Well unfortunately Roger, the price of the engine just went up." And he bumped the price up – I was there, I saw and I heard all of this – to around £3,200. And Roger just said, "Well, you've got me by the balls. I'll need to ring Tom, but would you take my word for it? We need the engine." And they were like, "Yeah, we can see that." It was like they were really putting the knife in and twisting it.

'As we were leaving the hotel, Roger said, "Nick, tomorrow I can guarantee you I will not do anything silly for the first half of the race. For the first 20 laps I will stay out of trouble. But then watch."

'As a driver he was *extremely* determined. He'd made his mind up before he'd even got in the car. He was difficult to talk to the last minute in the cockpit. I remember one time at Mallory him telling a journalist who was asking him questions, more or less on the line, to "Go away."

'It was hard work, that whole 1972 season. I don't know how many races we won, but some of them were absolutely terrific.'

There was plenty to smile about in France; the success made up for the disappointment in Monte Carlo.

Pau was one of them. Roger got Cevert's engine, and took it gently to begin with. Gethin ultimately won for Chevron from Depailler. 'Roger'd made it up to about 10th or 11th, and all of a sudden he just lit up and was driving about two seconds a lap quicker. He just kept going forward. He was catching Gethin by about a second a lap. But as he went up the hill after 37 laps a rubber oil pipe split and just nipped the engine. That was that. But when we went to pick the car up and bring it back down the hill, the crowd were still up on the bridge and on the track, and the cheering that went on... They'd seen a motor race, and the French really appreciated it whenever they saw somebody having a go. They were pretty nationalistic, but they could see this guy was pretty good. I had a lump in my throat about that.'

At Oulton Park in September he qualified only 14th but came through to finish seventh as Ronnie Peterson headed home Niki Lauda and an impressive James Hunt.

Roger also competed in three Formula 5000 races. Tony Kitchiner ran a McLaren M10B in the British series which catered for single-seaters powered by 450bhp five-litre American stockblock engines. Kitchiner had modified the car heavily, and called it the Kitchmac. Accessories king Gordon Spice had driven it, and now Tom Wheatcroft hired it for the two final races so that Roger could increase his experience and gain more points in the national Tarmac Championship for British drivers. It was an ageing car that was generally outclassed by the latest models from McRae, Surtees, Chevron and Lola, but that didn't bother Roger. He was more concerned about reaching the pedals.

'The car was a bit of a nail, and Roger didn't fit it,' Jordan said. 'You could only adjust the pedals minimally, and Roger being short couldn't reach them. Bodger Jordan made some blocks for the pedals! There was no seat and we were stuffing jerseys down his back. "How are you feeling now, Roger?" "Yeah, I'm all right. Can you bring the steering wheel a bit closer?" So we packed that with some washers to bring it out.

'When we tested it at Oulton Park he drove the wheels off it! He was *so* fast. And Tony Kitchiner said, "The car's never been that quick before!" He was something like two seconds quicker round there than it had ever been.'

Roger made an immediate impression with fourth fastest qualifying time for the 13th round of the series at Oulton on 14 October, behind pole-sitter Brian Redman in the Chevron B24, Graham McRae's eponymous GM1 and Alan Rollinson's Duckhams Lola T300. Behind him

Another decisive victory came on home ground at Brands Hatch, in front of the Formula One team managers in the Grand Prix-supporting Shell series round.

were fancied runners such as Steve Thompson in a Surtees TS8, John Cannon in the lightweight March 72A, Teddy Pilette in a new McLaren M22, Ian Ashley in a Lola T190 and champion-elect Gijs van Lennep who was obliged to race team-mate Ray Allen's McLaren M18 after damaging his Surtees TS11 in a crash in Friday's practice.

Redman and McRae opened up an immediate lead over Rollinson, while after a poor start Roger soon passed both Thompson and Cannon to run fourth. Redman lost the race after tripping over backmarker Jock Russell on the 13th lap, leaving McRae to head Rollinson home. Roger was headed for the final podium slot when Cannon misjudged an overtaking attempt at Lodge corner on the penultimate lap. Cannon was an ex-patriate Briton who had moved to Seattle. His principal claims to fame were winning a wet CanAm race at Laguna Seca in an elderly McLaren against the might of the works team in 1968, and subsequent success in the American Formula A (5000) series. He was a good driver and the mistake he made attempting to overtake Roger was uncharacteristic, but when he took an impossibly tight line into Lodge he punted the Kitchmac into the sleepers. Roger was lucky to escape unharmed as the chassis was almost cut in two, and was classified seventh. Cannon was fined £50 for a 'gross misjudgement'.

Jordan assisted Kitchiner to rebuild the chassis, working day and night to ready the car for the John Player Challenge Race meeting at Brands Hatch the following week. There, Redman again took pole position, from Australian veteran Frank Gardner in the new Lola T330. McRae was third fastest from Rollinson, van Lennep, Cannon, Thompson and Roger, whose elderly machine was a handful over the Kentish track's famed bumps.

Redman and McRae lapped the field as the Englishman won narrowly from the New Zealander, leaving Gardner to head home van Lennep and Rollinson. Roger was only a few seconds behind Rollinson's Lola, having successfully challenged a fading Cannon for sixth place after the latter's March developed understeer. The Kitchmac really had no business running anywhere near the hares, and in his two outings in the unfancied machine Roger had done more than enough to confirm his class.

The car was also entered for the non-championship Formula One/Formula 5000 race the following day, allowing Roger to make his début in a Formula One race even though he was actually driving a Formula 5000 car. He just made the grid for this one, having to start at the back as he had still been sorting the car when the Formula 5000s had to qualify in damp and cold conditions on Friday. And he nearly didn't make it.

'We'd got a brand new Alan Smith engine in the car,' Jordan related, 'and just before the race we went to fire it up but they hadn't put the distributor cap on properly;

the rotor arm did some damage. This is 10 minutes before the pit lane closes. We're in the shit. Kitchiner has this guy John Carpenter working for him, and Carpenter says, "It's okay, I know how to fix it." And he jumps straight into the back of Count Rudi van der Straten's VDS truck, and there were three brand new engines sitting there. He undid the distributor from one, pulled it out. I'm saying, "John, you can't do that!" and he's saying, "No, it's okay, I know them. We'll give it them back afterwards." So we put it in Roger's engine, lined up all the timing marks, pushed the car and got it started.'

The track was damp, and after starting on wets Roger quickly began to move up the field, but as the track dried out the tyres began to shred. Jordan urged Wheatcroft to bring Roger in before tyre failure caused an accident. 'The tyres were absolutely canvas when we finally called him in. That was sad, because he was going all right before the tyres became "shredded wheat". That was another good effort.'

In the quest for Tarmac points Roger also drove a GRD in the previous day's Formula Atlantic race. He qualified seventh after an oil pipe split, and finished sixth. The race was won by Tom, who proved unstoppable in the works Royale.

In 2006, writer Jeremy Walton recounted his contemporary impressions of Roger. 'He was a hero I could relate to versus the "club-plus" standard drivers of the day – Gerry Marshall, Dave Brodie – in superior vehicles. It was obvious even at this level that he belonged in a single-seater.

'He always had time for you, and had absolutely no side. If he said "Hello" to you once, he'd always acknowledge your presence thereafter, however tense the race environment.

'His determination, ambition and will to win were the same as the world-class rally Finns I came into contact with, total commitment. Roger saw nothing else but victory as a worthwhile result. He didn't throw tantrums if he'd lost or mechanical failure intervened (which it frequently did in the Anglia era), but he was only really sunny and satisfied if he had won.

'He took no account of reputation or superior machinery – they were all there just to be beaten.

'His humour was cheerfully rude. After that Ricard win, from which he was subsequently disqualified, I said to him at a function, "Roger, just how did you beat all those top frogs on home ground, that must've taken some doing. What's the secret?"

'He looked thoughtful for a moment or two, and I saw his eyes start to twinkle as urine was going to be extracted from a journo. There was a bit of Leicestershire Wheaty in his voice as he said, "Well they're all just drivers aren't they? Have good days and bad days... So long as I have a good crap before a race, I'm okay and I'll have a good day. Don't get frightened after that..."'

ABOVE: Nick Jordan stuffs pullovers behind Roger as he prepares for his Formula 5000 début in the Kitchmac at Oulton Park. ABOVE RIGHT: The Kitchmac was a modified McLaren M10B that was past its best, but Roger was headed for third place before an ill-starred overtaking move from John Cannon almost destroyed the car. RIGHT: After a mammoth rebuild the Kitchmac was back in action at Brands Hatch. Here Roger forces it to challenge champion-elect Gijs van Lennep's Surtees and Alan Rollinson's Lola T300 for fourth place. BELOW: Roger pushed hard despite front wing damage, and finished an impressive sixth.

CHAPTER 5

Fast moves

Tom and Tony, 1972

'I just couldn't believe it – I froze on the spot. The next thing I remember is being picked out of a shop front, where my car had been hurled by the impact.'
Tom Pryce

When Tom Pryce took his unfancied Royale RP11 to a dominant win in the opening Shell round at Brands Hatch in March 1972, at the prestigious non-championship Formula One Race of Champions meeting, there was widespread astonishment.

The Royale was a works car run by Dave Bond, who owned a bodyshop and repair company that traded as D.J. Bond. Royale had to borrow an old nail engine from builder Vegantune, but Tom put the red car on pole position and then simply ran away and hid from opposition that included drivers of the calibre of Roger, Jochen Mass and James Hunt, who was sacked from his works March ride soon afterwards. Such was the manner of the victory that many teams voiced the opinion that the Royale had to be running underweight.

'He won that by a country mile. And that was with us really slowing him down,' team boss Bob King recalled. 'I remember thinking, "For God's sake, hang on to it, Tom!" I gave him the slow signals, but he said as soon as he slowed he lost concentration, so he didn't really slow down that much. But he won it at a walk.'

Tom's victory was observed by aspiring racer Rick Morris, later to become something of a legend in Formula Ford. He told Paul Lawrence, author of the Royale history *Nowhere To Hide*, 'I did three or four school days at Motor Racing Stables and made friends with Tom Pryce, who was coming through like a rocket at the time with his Royale RP11. I saw that famous

After battling at La Chartre earlier in the season, Tom and Tony had nothing but praise for one another following their gripping duel in the Archie Scott Brown Trophy race at Snetterton in October 1972.

Tom produced a major surprise by winning the Formula Three race supporting the 1972 Race of Champions in his unfancied Royale RP11. There were arguments about its weight afterwards, but elsewhere he proved that his speed had been no fluke.

Formula Three race where he went faster and faster and faster every lap, and won the race. I was in the grandstands at Paddock watching this and it was one of the most amazing performances I've ever seen in my life. Once again that fired me up about racing.'

King continued, 'After the race there was talk of a big engine, and then Colin Vandervell protested us. I had happened to see Colin walking round with a great big sheet of lead all rolled up under his arm, so I knew what he was thinking. We came from nowhere and suddenly won this big Formula Three race with an unknown car and an engine on loan from Vegantune, what they called a "cooking" engine.'

The signs had been there the previous week at Brands, however, which was when King had learned how to make his car quick. 'We took it down there for a general practice day on a Thursday and we were two or three seconds off the pace. I knew the car should have been better than that, and after working out everything I thought the only thing we could do was change tyres. We had a contract with Dunlop, and I went and saw them and said that I'd got to try Firestones, so they agreed to release us. We put the Firestones on, then sent

OPPOSITE PAGE: *At Mallory Park Tom chased after Roger's March 723, in turn pursued by James Hunt and Barrie Maskell.*

Tom out and on his third lap he set a fantastic time. We were a second quicker than anybody else – which I found hard to believe! We brought him in and sat on the pit wall, and watched everyone else. Tom was just so quick, absolutely natural. And there were some big names there.'

Andrew Marriott, then a journalist for *Motoring News*, recalled that race with a smile 34 years later. 'I'm sure the Royale was running underweight there. I was the one who protested. I was running Colin Vandervell and he finished seventh, so I protested the top six. Vandervell liked that! And they were all underweight! It was just too embarrassing so the organisers decided that the weighbridge certificate was out of date... But I don't think that detracted from Tom's performance that day.'

Brian Jones also laughed at the memory. 'My own observation is that I'm not sure any circuit's weighbridge would have had a valid certificate back then – they were notoriously neglected. I would detect the hand of John Webb in that situation!'

King is adamant his car was fully legal, but admits the result took him by surprise. He had intended only to do half a dozen races in the category as a means of boosting sales for 1973. Now he suddenly had demand and no real means of satisfying it. 'The protest obviously took the shine off the win, and somehow the momentum of that was a bit lost, which was a shame,' he said ruefully.

ABOVE: *Tony's choice of a Brabham BT38 was not ideal for Formula Three. Here he chases eventual winner Tony Trimmer's JPS Lotus 73 at Mallory Park, where he could only finish fifth.* BELOW: *At Zandvoort Tom and the Royale challenged established stars Roger and Mike Walker for the lead, until a wandering backmarker caused him to have a massive accident.*

There was almost a repeat of the Brands performance at Oulton Park on Good Friday, when Tom was leading comfortably. 'Then I blew it. I spun away the lead for no reason.'

He was also blisteringly quick at Zandvoort, fighting for the lead with Roger and Ensign's Mike Walker before dropping back to be classified ninth after crashing when a backmarker put him off the road. As a consolation he set fastest lap.

'That was an horrendous crash,' King recalled. 'He came off at just the wrong place. The barrier was there but they hadn't tapered the edge of it. He came off when he was going very, very quickly, and hit the barrier sideways and it sliced the car in half. Tom was unharmed, but that really was a nasty accident.'

The bubble really burst at Monaco, during practice for the Formula Three race that supported the famous grand prix. Climbing up the hill through Massenet on the way to Casino Square, the Royale cut out and coasted to a halt. A wire had come loose in the ignition and Tom climbed out to try and fix the problem. While he was doing this Peter Lamplough lost control of his car, and struck the Royale. Tom was still standing beside it, and suffered a broken leg. The RP11 was destroyed.

'I was fiddling about with the car when I suddenly saw Lamplough coming straight towards me,' Tom told Alan Henry in *Motoring News*. 'I just couldn't believe it – I froze on the spot. The next thing I remember is being picked out of a shop front, where my car had been hurled by the impact.'

King remembered, 'Louis Stanley stepped in there, introduced himself, and said, "Whatever I can do for Tom..." which was very good of him.'

Tom was clearly very quick, but he was also expensive. 'I've got to say that he nearly closed us down with all the accidents!' King admitted. 'He didn't know enough, and perhaps it was partly my fault for promoting him a little quickly. His learning curve was fairly sharp. And one of the reasons that he kept coming off, even though I kept telling him, was that he didn't realise he shouldn't get too close. Even back then he was being affected by the downwash, the turbulence behind another car. He really couldn't seem to get that through his head. Gear ratios: he had no idea. He didn't care – he just drove! We used to sit down in the transporter and try to work out the ratios from his memory of what the rpm was at any given point, and it was almost impossible. But we made an educated guess what we thought they should be. It took him a little while to pick up those finer points – but, ooh, was he quick!

Tony (56) found the BT38 a poor match for the GRDs and the French Alpine Renaults at Monaco.

Despite the Brabham's shortcomings, Tony gave Roger a hard time at La Chartre, though some of the tactics he used to keep the GRD driver behind him in their heat did not endear him to the Wheatcroft camp. Roger won overall, with Tony a brash second.

'He did try really hard to understand. And really he had no right to be as quick as he was because there was quite a bit left in the development of the car, more we could do to make it faster. Not much left to come from him, because he just drove it to the limit already. If we'd got the car as good as Tom was, then we'd have had a winning combination that was very hard to beat. He was just naturally quick, and he just came alive when he was sitting in the car.'

Tom was back in action again shortly and again featured strongly. 'I was back at Brands on pole position in five weeks…' He showed well elsewhere, too, but garnered only fourth behind Andy Sutcliffe, Liechtenstein's Rikki von Opel and Tony in that Lombard round at Brands Hatch in June, and sixth in the wet Shell round there in October.

At the same time, he ran for Toby St George-Matthews' Team Rumsey Investments UK Formula SuperVee team in an RP14, winning the title with ease. 'I won just about every race I went in for,' he admitted almost sheepishly.

King subsequently put him into Royale's Formula Atlantic RP12 for the remainder of the season. This was an RP11 with Formula Atlantic engine, and bigger wheels, tyres and brakes. In the bright yellow and blue machine Tom was dynamite. He put the car on pole position for each of the final three races of the season, winning the finale at Brands Hatch's John Player Challenge Race and beating champion-elect Bill

Gubelmann in the more popular March chassis.

These were happy days for the Welsh star. 'I think Tom was homesick, actually, to begin with,' Marriott suggested. 'But when he got into grand prix racing he had Nella with him and he was much more confident then. But back in those early days it was a weird deal when you tried to contact him. If you ever phoned the house up, if you were trying to find him in Ruthin, they answered it in Welsh. I particularly remember that.'

With the hindsight of more than 30 years, King remembered: 'We were always a bit short of dough in our racing and had to limit really how much we could do. Although we ran teams in Formula Three, Formula SuperVee, Formula Ford, Formula Atlantic and Formula 100, it took money to do that because we never charged any of the drivers a penny.

'One time we blew an engine in practice and I didn't have a spare, and Tom Wheatcroft got to hear about it and said, "Go and help yourself, lad." I said, "What do you mean?" He said, "Well, there's another engine in the back of our truck, go and take it." And that just blew me away; you don't get that kind of thing today.'

Wheatcroft was not the only benefactor, though. But for Bob King, Tom's career might well have slipped away after its early promise. 'I don't know if it made me a bad businessman or too soft or what, but I never had a contract with my drivers,' he revealed. 'I just had a principle that if they were that quick, then we wanted them anyway. That's what would sell us cars: win on Sunday, sell on Monday. It was literally that; you were existing week by week. That's what put the strain on me, and after so many years I just popped. I couldn't take the continual strain of making production cars – a lot of them – and running three or four teams, all of them very different.'

But King had no doubts that it had been worth it. 'Looking back, I just think what a great privilege it was to have known Tom, and to have known what he was like, his family and his girlfriend Nella. As a personality, there was no-one that I could say I liked better.'

Tom did, however, have an initial contract with MRS. And the way in which he dealt with it showed that, while he might be a country lad from, as Brian Jones liked to put it, 'Welsh Wales,' he was not one to put up with what he perceived to be an unfair situation.

'Conditional upon winning the Crusader series was that the winner had to sign a management contract with MRS,' Jones revealed. 'And though he signed it, Tom objected to it. I remember sitting in the old clubhouse at Brands Hatch after that Silverstone International Trophy race weekend in 1970, with Geoff Clarke, Tom and his father, battling over this contract. Tom and Jack said it was too onerous and that they weren't going to be bound by it. Now we could take them to court to enforce it, or we could accept that and effectively tear it up.

'Geoff was by nature quite a litigious fellow. He had sued several people in the past. But this time, for whatever reason, he agreed to accept that Tom would not be bound by the contract. I think he realised that you could lead a horse to water, but you couldn't force it to drink. Trying to be objective three decades later, I would say that resisting that contract was the best thing that Tom did. Of course we were disappointed to 'lose' him, but I honestly don't think he would have progressed the way he did if he had been shackled to us. And we did want him to succeed. It was quite clear that he was very talented, and at MRS we were all very excited about him. If he'd had to stay with us, I'm not sure we would have generated the right opportunities for him.'

While Roger Williamson and Tom Pryce grabbed the early headlines in 1972, Tony Brise's fuse was burning at a slower rate and it was not really until the end of a difficult year that people began to take serious notice of him. Having cleaned up in Formula Ford in 1971 and graduated to Formula Three at the end of that season as John Brise did the deal with Bernie

Ecclestone, the Brises decided to opt for one of the first new Brabhams – the BT38 – to come from the drawing board of Geoff Ferris for 1972 and went racing with backing from Montessa Motorcycles, which John imported from Spain.

Just as Roger had quickly found that March's 723 was no match for GRD's 372, so Tony realised that the BT38 was also lacking something. As Roger ruled the roost in his new Wheatcroft GRD, challenged only by Rikki von Opel and Briton Mike Walker in the Iberia Ensigns, Tony struggled and was unable to show his true potential. On 29 April he took his first victory, but it was in a relatively poorly supported Lombard round, and though he headed home strong contenders Damien Magee in a Palliser, Andy Sutcliffe and eventual Lombard champion von Opel, observers began to forget that this was the man who had made a winner out of

After switching to a GRD, Tony was a match for Roger. Here, each a heat winner, they leave the grid for the Shell series finale at Brands Hatch in October, with Tony on pole. Jacques Coulon, on the outside of the front row, won from Roger.

Switching from Formula Three to the works Formula Atlantic Royale proved another step forward for Tom; by the end of the season he was the man to beat.

the difficult short wheelbase Formula Ford Elden. Later he beat Magee, Bob Evans and Mike Walker in a Lombard round at his local Brands Hatch circuit on 13 August, repeating the feat over Russell Wood and Jac Nelleman in a non-championship event at the Jyllandsring in Denmark the following weekend.

Jenny Anderson remembered that Brands race, because it was the scene of one of two major shunts that befell Tim (the other being at Mallory). 'I ran up to Druids and there he was upside down in the car. Tony won that race, and I often think now of the Schumacher brothers when I think of that. Tony had to go by each lap knowing that it was his brother in that car, and not knowing if he was all right. I think you have to be a special kind of person to be able to carry on and to shut that out, to have that faith that they were okay.' Eventually, Tim's motorsport success would come in rallying.

Elsewhere, Tony became resigned to lower placings. He was second to von Opel at Thruxton's Lombard round in April, to Roger at La Chartre and to Mass at Thruxton, where younger brother Tim brought his GRD 372 home fourth to make John's day. There were thirds at Snetterton in March and Brands Hatch in June, both Lombard rounds, and fourths at Chimay (where David Purley completed his hat-trick of victories), in the Forward Trust race at Thruxton in June, and in Oulton Park's Lombard race in August. But Tony was satisfied only with victories, and father and son knew that they had to reorganise their campaign if the season was not to become a disaster.

Of the BT38, he told Nigel Roebuck in the interview in *Autosport,* 'It was just a bad car, I'm afraid. Very unpredictable round corners, and very slow in a straight line. We tried everything to make that car work, but nothing made any significant difference to it.' In the end

they managed to massage the handling into something sanitary, but the aerodynamic problem went unresolved. It was not, according to Tony, the sole reason for the lack of straightline speed.

Younger brother Tim really liked his GRD 372, so John ordered one for Tony without further preamble. They had to rescue his fading reputation. It arrived by September and the improvement was immediate. At Cadwell Park that month Tony shadowed Roger all the way home, ahead of Mass, and was third behind Roger and Walker at Thruxton.

'Our biggest problem was engines,' he told Roebuck. 'Ecclestone had given us an introduction to Holbays. I knew that something was wrong. Okay, the GRD was a hell of an improvement over the Brabham, but we still weren't going that much quicker. We'd be pushing Rikki von Opel, that sort of thing, but we were way behind Mike Walker and Roger. It was obvious to me that we were getting poor engines – or, at least, very ordinary "cooking" engines. So my father told Holbays we'd had enough and we were getting out. Anyway, a few weeks later, an engine arrived; it didn't look any different, but it certainly went differently, and suddenly I was pushing Roger Williamson rather than Rikki…'

Having been pushing himself and his car to the limit all season, he suddenly found the key that unlocked the mysterious door. 'That needed quite a bit of mental adjustment, believe me! You couldn't feel much difference, but it certainly showed on the stopwatch. I don't want anyone to think I'm all bitter and twisted about this engine business, because I'm not. But I mention it because it had a tremendous effect on my two years in Formula Three.'

Interestingly, he told *Motoring News,* 'My best engine was an ex-Sutcliffe and ex-Rousselot unit which was as good as the best but certainly not better – it's just a matter of who goes through the corners quickest, after all.'

The first win in the GRD came at Mallory Park on 1 October when he dominated the Shell round by winning both his heat and the final, outpacing von Opel and Colin Vandervell by nine seconds. He also won the Forward Trust round at Thruxton at the end of the month, leading home circuit aces von Opel and Walker. But perhaps his most impressive performance came when he raced wheel-to-wheel with Roger in the Archie Scott Brown Memorial race at Snetterton in October. Both won their heats and started from the front row for the final. After 30 nail-biting laps they crossed the line millimetres apart and were so close that they shared the same race time: 45m 24.4s.

Roger got the victory by a whisker, but Tony had the consolation of a new lap record of 1m 29.4s at 109.13mph. It was a tremendous performance against the formula's established yardstick, and finally marked Tony out as a future star. He loved their duel.

'A wonderful race,' he recalled to Roebuck. 'Everybody had said the transformation from Formula Ford to Formula Three had been too much for me. There was a great deal at stake. It was a great race all the way, against an intelligent, safe driver, and I was very happy to finish second, virtually level with him. At that stage of my career, there was no way I was going to risk falling off at the last corner.'

There was further satisfaction to come at Brands Hatch two weeks later; he was beaten by von Opel in the Lombard race, but finished ahead of both Jones and Roger in their similar cars. He might have finished only sixth overall in the Shell series, 60 points adrift of Roger, and second to von Opel who most assuredly was not in his league in the Lombard series, but changing chassis had finally allowed him to unlock his latent potential.

'I should have won the Lombard series,' he lamented to *Motoring News*, 'but Rikki von Opel had been testing at the circuit during the week with his Ensign, and breezed past me when I was in the lead to win the race and the title.'

Writing his seasonal review of the Formula Three season for the respected annual *Autocourse*, journalist

Ian Phillips, now the commercial director of Midland F1 Racing in Formula One, said of Roger, 'There have been a large number of drivers who have shone in Formula Three this year, but all must take a back seat to Williamson.' But there were encouraging words also for Tony and Tom. 'Brise possibly showed more natural talent than anyone in Formula Three,' Phillips wrote of the former, adding, 'He will be a formidable competitor next year.' And of Tom he said, 'Unfortunately the team was underfinanced and Pryce got involved in more than his fair share of incidents which meant that the equipment was not always the best. With the right sort of backing he could be one of the very best.'

So 1972 was Roger Williamson's time, the year in which he delivered as the motorsport world's most promising comingman. For Tom Pryce and Tony Brise, it had provided further opportunity to show their true talent. But their time had yet to come.

After their clean and gripping duel in the Archie Scott Brown Trophy race at Snetterton, Roger just clinched the victory by a whisker from Tony's identical GRD.

CHAPTER 6

Stardom beckons

1973

'I have to admit that up until that point I had never been a fan. But I certainly was after watching him. Roger was absolutely blinding through there.'
Peter Collins

Roger moved up full-time to Formula Two in Tom Wheatcroft's Ford-powered GRD 273 for 1973, but though he won his heat from pole at Thruxton at Easter, it was already clear that it was an unwieldy car. The talented Frenchman Jean-Pierre Jarier was dominant in the works March-BMW, and after Roger had crashed the GRD at Nivelles in Belgium following a brake problem, Tom Wheatcroft decided that enough was enough. Roger was quite happy to continue with the GRD and never once suggested a change – and Tom might have stayed with it – but GRD boss Mike Warner liked to play mind games, and at Nivelles boasted to Wheatcroft that he could read his and thought Tom had just ordered two new Marches.

'Up until then it had never dawned on me,' Wheatcroft admitted, 'but after he said that I thought, "Bugger it! We've had enough of struggling!" I told Roger that on our way back to the pits we had to pass Max Mosley, so we might as well do a deal with him.' They did.

First time out at Rouen, in the wake of his friend Gerry Birrell's death in practice, Roger was walking his heat until the engine lost oil pressure after 10 laps. After watching him there, a once sceptical Peter Collins was sold on his ability. The Australian would later manage the Lotus, Williams and Benetton Formula One teams and be instrumental in nurturing the latent talent of

By winning the final race at Brands Hatch as Alan Jones slumped, Tony gained the points he needed to take the prestigeous John Player Formula Three title by two points.

drivers of the calibre of Nigel Mansell, Johnny Herbert, Mika Häkkinen, Alex Zanardi, Kimi Räikkönen, Vitantonio Liuzzi and Neel Jani.

'I was still living in Australia then and was working for Air New Zealand, so I was able to get free flights. I stayed with my sister, who was living in Ladbroke Grove in west London. We travelled to Rouen in Peter Windsor's Ford Escort. My sister slept in the car, and Peter and I slept underneath it!

'When we got there on the Saturday morning Birrell had just been killed on the run down the hill to Nouveau Monde. Later on I watched Roger going through there in the Wheatcroft March.'

The downhill sweep was one of the greatest tests of a driver's mettle, a frighteningly fast descent that required courage and complete commitment. David Purley, who would later play such a poignant role in the Roger Williamson story, lacked nothing in either department. But even Purley, the man they would later call 'Brave Dave', admitted using an old tactic from his paratrooper days to generate a sufficient surge of adrenaline to keep his foot flat on the throttle there: he screamed into his helmet.

'I'd heard of Williamson, after all his success in Formula Three,' Collins said, 'but have to admit that up

until that point I had never been a fan. But I certainly was after watching him. He was absolutely blinding through there. His engine note was still solid, the motor was still screaming as he came through, whereas others were feathering the throttle. He had real commitment and class. I became a big fan of his that day. I came away thinking that he had a major future.'

If any race confirmed that class and commitment, it was the Monza Lotteria. But they arrived late after the transporter broke down, then discovered that it was too high to get beneath one of the two bridges leading into the paddock. Practice had already begun, so they had to unload the car and equipment, and hump it through to the pits. Roger changed into his race suit as they sped to the paddock in the back-up estate car.

He had never seen Monza before, and qualifying was partway through when the March was finally ready to go. Yet within half an hour he was second fastest. 'He literally just warmed the car up and then, boom! He was straight into it,' mechanic Trevor Foster recalled. 'He would come in and say, "I just can't believe these chicanes. I'm going to drive straight across one soon because I keep coming up to them thinking, "I'm not going to brake yet, not yet, not yet, NOW!" And the next lap he'd do the same thing but go a little bit deeper.'

Roger took pole, a tenth of a second ahead of local ace Vittorio Brambilla who was driving a similar car but knew his home track intimately. Roger won the first 20-lap heat easily, by 11s from Frenchman Patrick Depailler

GRD's 273 Formula Two car was a handful, yet Roger still managed to win his heat with it at Thruxton against the superior BMW-engined Marches.

ABOVE: *He proved unstoppable at Monza in his second outing in Tom Wheatcroft's new March 732 BMW, despite the best efforts of 'Monza Gorilla' Vittorio Brambilla. This was Roger's finest hour.* RIGHT: *At Misano Adriatico he was headed for his second Formula Two triumph, until electrical failure intervened.*

in an Elf-Ford, and Brambilla. But it all went wrong at the start of the second. He and Depailler were eyeball to eyeball going into the first chicane when Brambilla, the 'Monza Gorilla', collided with him and sent them both down the escape road. As Roger went to rejoin, Brambilla did his utmost to delay him in his own haste to do likewise. Depailler, meanwhile, had the race on a plate. Roger saw his chance and blasted by Brambilla, and then began the drive of his career. There were 19 laps left in which to catch and pass Depailler. He was seventh at the end of that dramatic lap. Four laps later he was within 10s of Frenchman Jacques Coulon, running second in his similar March-BMW. Within three more laps Roger had taken the place, and before half-distance was within 11s of Depailler and could thus win on aggregate. But that wasn't Roger's way. On lap 15 he took the outside line into the first chicane and actually overtook the Frenchman, only to spin. Nothing daunted, he spun the March back in the right direction and started over. With three laps to go he tried again, and this time his move succeeded and he sped home to a superb victory. In years to come, even Gilles Villeneuve couldn't have done it better.

The appreciative Italian fans hadn't seen fighting spirit like it since Jim Clark's recovery drive in the 1967 Italian Grand Prix. 'I got that drunk after the track management took us out for a lovely meal that night,' Wheatcroft recalled happily.

At Misano Roger led again, but this time electrical problems stopped him.

Ian Phillips was by then covering Formula Two for *Autosport*, 'I think the most distinctive thing about Roger's driving style was how he sat in the cockpit. That crouch. Some people have natural style and grace, and I don't think you could ever say that about the way Roger drove. He just wanted to get stuck in, and he did it the way he knew best, which compromised in a way. It

was just a case of, "I'm going to get in there and show those bastards..."'

Wheatcroft remembered, 'One day he came into the pits and sat on the counter, very quiet, and I said, "Are you all right?" And he replied, "Well, Tom, I can't understand it. I really pushed them last four laps, and I'm only on the second row." I sez, "Well, you've got violent understeer." He were feathering the inside edge of the front tyres, so they fiddled with the car and he went out again, and when he came in that time he said, "It felt like I never tried." And he were on pole!

'He never came in and said it was the car, *never* blamed the car. If anything weren't right, he thought it were him that were off. He were like Jimmy Clark; he didn't bother about an anti-rollbar's thickness or whatever. If he'd got a handling problem he'd let the back go more, go in a bit quicker and let the back go and cut the understeer. He were so natural it were beyond believing. He were just like Jimmy in that respect. But I always used to think of Roger and Fangio: they were the same height and both had the same sort of determination just to get that time.'

Trevor Foster loved working with him. 'He was very likeable as a driver, very down-to-earth, matter-of-fact, straightforward. Never any bullshit. If he thought the car wasn't right then you knew it was down to the car. But if he wasn't driving right, he'd be the first to stand up and say, "Don't worry about it, it's down to me." I've even known him in qualifying actually to stop, get out of the car, and walk around, sort himself out. He'd tell you to leave the car, then he'd get back in it and go out and do the business. He was a real thinker in that sense.

'Looking back I would have to say that he wasn't one of the most technical guys, but he knew the basic things he wanted and if you gave him them, then he was what you'd call just naturally quick. As far as engineering was concerned, he wasn't actually that strong. But he would drive round a problem. When he went out, he'd often come back in and say, "That's as quick as it'll go. That's it." You knew then that if you said, "No, that isn't quick enough," he could go out and do another 10 laps but he wasn't going to go any quicker. Whatever he got to, he was always straight on to it.

'We just loved him. We thought he was brilliant. He was that sort of driver. He just used to raise his standards all the time. And he never used to give up. Just look at that Monza Lottery...'

Meanwhile, Tom was furthering his reputation, too. In 1973, he continued driving in Formula Atlantic in Britain for Bob King, the unique Royale RP12A now repainted light blue and silver. He won three races, and should have added the season opener at Mallory Park to that tally. He took his fourth consecutive pole position there and looked an easy winner until a plug lead worked loose, created a misfire, and allowed David Purley to pass with a lap to go. Later at Brands Hatch his RES engine blew up, and elsewhere similar misfortune dogged him.

BMW's Jochen Neerpasch was one of many impressed by Roger's quiet ability, and the speed he showed in the new March.

'He was always very quick in that, and the car itself was quick from the onset,' King remembered happily. He recalled one race in particular, at Brands Hatch. 'It was really pouring down. Tom said that the car was awful in the wet,' – and if Tom Pryce said that the car must have been *truly* awful – 'so we put four road tyres and wheels on it, sent him out in the race, and he won.'

An example of why King thought Tom was inexperienced came at Oulton Park. The rebuilt RES engine was blowing the O-rings out of its carburettors in qualifying, but as Purley opened a lead in the wet Tom came flying up past Colin Vandervell and Cyd Williams, and closed on Purley in traffic: he was poised to challenge for the lead when he got too close to the Briton's March, lost front-end downforce, and slithered to a stop on the infield at Cascades. At least on that occasion he didn't hit anything solid...

There had even been talk of resurrecting the Royale RP7 Formula 5000 car, which had been on the drawing board since 1970, for Tom to drive. 'We penned it and had a full set of drawings prepared for it,' King revealed. 'We just needed to press the button. We considered building it for Tom, but it just wasn't viable. I'm glad I didn't in retrospect. It would have been a very costly machine.'

Such was King's regard for Tom, however, that as early as April 1972 his name had been connected with Bob's most ambitious plan yet: to graduate to Formula Two later that season. The deal came about via Liechtenstein driver Manfred Schurti, who was able to source significant funding from his homeland and planned a two-car team for himself and Tom. Though one RP20 was eventually built, the plans never came to genuine fruition and the project ultimately led to King quitting the business. By the time he would leave Royale, the loyal Tom had already found himself racing in that formula in a Motul M1 for Ron Dennis and his partner Neil Trundle at Rondel Racing.

The invitation had come from Dennis to test one of his cars. Property developer and amateur racer Chris Meek and his business partner Malcolm Wayne were keen to sponsor a driver in Formula Two, via their company Titan Properties. 'Chris drew up a list of names and I seemed to be the first one who was home when Ron rang,' was Tom's version of events related modestly to Alan Henry. 'I went down to test the car, and drove eight races for the team that season.' He also did the odd Atlantic race in a Motul, at Oulton Park and Silverstone.

'I was first attracted to Tom's talent when I drove in the same Formula Atlantic events. He reminded me of myself at his age,' Meek recalled. 'He had the same will to win, without the finances. As a person he was unassuming, delightful and completely dedicated.'

Tom immediately acclimatised to the greater power and was soon hustling the ex-Jody Scheckter Motul with

his distinctive oversteer style. He made his Formula Two début in June at Nivelles, one of the blandest circuits in modern history, and finished 14th after qualifying 16th. He'd finished eighth just behind Roger's GRD in the first heat, but lost time with a pit stop in the second as the throttle pedal had bent sideways under his heavy right foot and was catching the inside of the monocoque. He showed strongly in the second heat at Hockenheim, after overheating stopped him in the first, and then he showed all his gusto at Rouen where the curves and downhill plunges clearly did not daunt him before overheating again claimed his car. Much of the time he was plagued by the Motul's tendency towards excessive oversteer (even by Tom's elevated standards), poor engines or by niggling problems such as sticking throttles.

But his most impressive outing came in a race at the Norisring – an old Nazi stadium in Germany which became infamous as the place where the great Mexican Pedro Rodriguez had been killed in a sportscar race in 1971. Tom qualified fifth, ahead of more experienced Motul team-mates Bob Wollek, Tim Schenken and Henri Pescarolo, and ran third initially in the first heat behind March runners Jacques Coulon and Hans Stuck and ahead of Bill Gubelmann, his old Atlantic sparring partner. Coulon was cruising for a win when a screw vibrated out of his BMW engine's rotor arm, so now Tom was leading, 'until the brakes failed and I dropped

Tom was delighted when he was asked to test the Formula Two Motul M1 at Goodwood on behalf of Rondel Racing. 'It's the first time I've ever had anyone more interested in me than they are in the car,' he enthused about proprietor Ron Dennis's minute attention to driver comfort detail.

back to second place behind Schenken.' The rears were locking, and with 10 laps left he ran wide in the hairpin and momentarily stalled, allowing the Australian to take the lead; he recovered to finish second. In the second heat he overtook Schenken to run second to flying champion-elect Jean-Pierre Jarier in the works March, but Schenken stayed close and slipped ahead when Tom ran out of brakes again. On aggregate Schenken won with Tom second, which was to be his best-ever result in Formula Two. Reporting the race for *Motoring News*, Murray Taylor wrote, 'The Welshman must be the find of the European Championship as, apart from J-PJ, he is one of the few bright lights in a rather uninspiring year for new driver talent.'

As a result of the deal that put him into Rondel Racing, Meek took over running Tom's career for the remainder of 1973, but it was an uneasy alliance, particularly once the Formula Two season was over. Tom told Alan Henry, 'I just found myself sitting around for six months waiting for Meek to come up with

something, so the start of 1974 didn't really look any brighter than the previous two seasons.'

Interestingly, Bob King had never felt the need to put Tom under contract, and his comment on the subject explained all you need to know about his racing philosophy. 'We could have done, but we actually never had anybody under contract. The commercial side of our business was selling racing cars. I never expected to earn money out of contracts with drivers. And had anything come along that would have taken Tom further forward, I would never have considered standing in his way.'

At the end of 1973 Tom won the premier Grovewood Award in recognition of his efforts. But he was not particularly happy about it. 'He didn't really want it,' Jack remembered. 'I mean, he did, but in some ways he regarded it as a jinx on a driver's career. And he was terrified when he had to get up and make an acceptance

LEFT: *Tom with Chris Meek. The property developer was of crucial assistance in helping him to move up the ladder, but according to Jack Pryce they fell out over Meek's contract.*

OPPOSITE PAGE: *Tom was very quick but unlucky at Rouen. In 2006 team-mate Tim Schenken said of him: 'I was the star of the Rondel team, and then suddenly Tom arrived and he was bloody quick! He sure gave me a fright!'*

BELOW: *According to Jack Pryce, Tom was a little embarrassed by Meek's Titan dollybirds at Snetterton's Atlantic race (left), but flew in the second Formula Two heat at Hockenheim.*

speech. He was as pale as a wall, and I really thought he was going to faint. He hated having to speak in public.'

Tony, meanwhile, was content to stay for another season of Formula Three to gather experience, and on the strength of his end-of-season performances in 1972 with the GRD marque boss Mike Warner offered him the works seat with a brand new 373 and his own 372 as back-up. Tony was also negotiating for a drive with the Baty Group but that eventually went to talented rival Ian Taylor, so he accepted Warner's offer on the condition that promised development of the car would be forthcoming.

Over the winter he had been pondering ways of raising his publicity profile, and approached the local BBC Radio Medway, and the *Kent Messenger* newspaper group with a proposal to broadcast and write about his racing programme. Medway accepted immediately, while *Kent Messenger* went one better and offered unexpected sponsorship. He enjoyed his writing so long as he had done well in a race.

Initially, the GRD was competitive with the heavily revised new March 733, a stubby little car which featured a full-width rounded nose and was a smaller clone of the successful Formula Two car. But the promised development of the GRD did not materialise even though works DART driver Alan Jones was just keeping his head above water. For the second season running Tony's racing

career was headed for trouble. Drivers such as Taylor, Russell Wood, Mike Wilds and Mo Harness were grabbing the headlines and once again he was falling behind and at risk of losing his hard-won reputation.

'The problem was that our disadvantage was not noticed at the beginning of the year,' he told *Motoring News*, 'because so many of the races were in the wet and the GRD, being a flexible car, was terrific in those conditions.' By May it was obvious that the March was better, and John Brise simply told his son that thereafter he would be driving one. Soon he was winning again, and went on to clinch the prestigious John Player Formula Three Championship and then the Lombard North Central only weeks later. But it was a more patchy season than he would have liked and the story behind the successes was one of a constant struggle with engines. At one time with the March he suffered an unaccountable four failures in six weeks.

OPPOSITE PAGE: *Once again Tony found himself in the wrong car at the wrong time in 1973. GRD's 373, seen at Monaco, was not competitive with March's 733.*

BELOW: *After Johnny Brise insisted on buying a March, Tony (here passing Pedro Passadore at Oulton Park) was back up with the front runners.*

'Once more it was a question of third or fourth again,' he said to Roebuck. 'Occasionally, we got a good engine, but we could never count on it. It was a bit of a farce, really. We weren't even consistently mediocre. Sometimes we had a good motor, sometimes not, and it threw me completely. On top of that, of course, I was acquiring a reputation for being inconsistent. Eventually we got a March 733. I didn't agree at the time, I must say, but my father just went and bought it, and it turned out to be the right thing to do. As soon as we got it, we went quicker. The March was effective. I'd liked the GRD; in fact, it was a nice car to drive, very forgiving and very quick in a straightline, but it wasn't effective. I've driven several cars like that. Anyway, the March was a big improvement and, believe it or not, we found in the end that there was something like half a second a lap gained simply by the exhaust system that came with it! It was much better than Holbay's own system!

'Throughout the season, I never had a really good motor… at least, not until the last race of the year. That was at Brands Hatch, and there were double points for that race. It seemed to be a foregone conclusion, actually. I think Alan Jones had only to finish in the top six to win the championship, irrespective of what happened to anyone else. Practice didn't go well for us. I blew up one engine and we were just preparing to change it when Holbays gave us another one. It wasn't one of ours, it didn't have our marks on it – we all had our own, and we'd wander round the paddock every race, checking to see who had the quick heads that particular week! Anyway, we put this engine in, and after 10 laps, I had a lead of 10 seconds, which later grew to 20 seconds at one point. We had a fuel pump problem later in the race, but still managed to win. Alan, if you remember, finished seventh [sic], so we won the championship.'

The story of that race epitomised Tony's fighting spirit. It actually transpired that the engine he was given by Holbay was one of Mike Wilds's, which irked his Dempster Developments backers since Holbay had not sought permission to lend the Brises the unit. But of greater concern as the televised start neared was the question of tyres. The track was wet, but drying, and because of the presence of BBC's *Grandstand* cameras, nobody was allowed to change rubber on the grid. Ian Taylor had taken pole from Tony, Frenchman Michel Leclère, Japanese Masami Kuwashima and title contender Jones. Only Leclère opted for wets, and it was the wrong choice. Tony blasted into the lead and was never headed; but – by the flag nearly 48.5 minutes later – it had been a

At Brands Hatch in October 1973, Tony came from behind to challenge Alan Jones for the prestigious John Player Formula Three Championship.

On the podium at Brands Hatch, Tony celebrates his dramatic success, applauded by John Player PR and journalist Mike Doodson (right).

close-run thing as his new engine's fuel pressure dipped alarmingly and he had been coasting through some of the corners during the final laps. His lead had been reduced to 1.8s over championship-contender Russell Wood and Taylor, and it was not until he received his trophy from Ronnie Peterson that Tony finally realised he had won the title; Jones had actually needed to finish no higher than seventh but managed only eighth with a weakening engine, so Tony scored 123 points to the Australian's 121 and Wood's 119. Had Tony not been disqualified from second place at Mallory Park the previous week, however, the gap over Jones would have been larger.

His win in the Lombard North Central series was initially called into question. He had clinched the title after finishing fourth behind Richard Robarts, Wilds and Taylor at Brands Hatch on 4 November; he and Robarts actually scored the same number of points, but Tony was awarded the title because of his greater number of wins. However, Robarts's sponsor Myson had video evidence showing that Tony had overtaken Ted Wentz's slow Elden under yellow flags at Druids bend, after Val Musetti had spun. Tony argued that he

had only done so because Wentz was going so slowly, and the American admitted that he had waved Tony through because he had no wish to spoil other drivers' races. In the end the matter was resolved, with Tony keeping his title.

During the year there had been an unbecoming incident in one race. He had already had a run-in with Bobby Brown at Oulton, hanging around to block him after the American driver had earlier spoiled his own race. Then, at Mallory Park in October, he lost second place behind Wilds after allegedly swerving at Brian Henton down Stebbe Straight and putting him on to the grass. An irate Henton had protested, and the stewards upheld it and disqualified Tony for a dangerous manoeuvre.

Nevertheless, Ian Phillips wrote of him in *Autosport*'s seasonal review, after rating him second to Leclère, 'With the exception of Jody Scheckter he has more natural talent than anyone I have seen racing in the 1600 formula, though he lacks the determination of a Roger Williamson or a Dave Walker to see him through when the odds are against him.'

Of the new generation of British talent, John Watson had been the first to race a Formula One car, taking the former Eifelland March 721 to a solid sixth place in the non-championship John Player Challenge Race at Brands Hatch in October 1972. The following year, both he and James Hunt were entered for the Race of Champions there in March. Watson was the unfortunate victim of a sticking throttle which put designer Gordon Murray's dramatic new Brabham BT42 into the bank at Druids, breaking one of the popular Ulsterman's legs. Hunt, however, distinguished himself with an excellent drive to third place in an ageing Surtees TS9B entered privately by Lord Hesketh, right on the tail of runner-up Denny Hulme whose McLaren was the leading Formula One car. In an upset of form, former BRM pilot Peter Gethin beat the Formula One cars for the first time in his Formula 5000 Chevron.

As remarkable as Hunt's drive that day was the fact that he was there at all. Having been sacked by March the previous year, he had stumbled into the arms of the portly peer who had aspirations to run his own racing team. When their efforts with the unloved Formula Three Dastle nosedived, Hesketh took the unusual step of moving up to Formula Two instead with a March 712M. Suddenly Hunt came into his own and immediately showed such form in the race at Oulton Park in September, where he challenged the works March 722s of Ronnie Peterson and Niki Lauda, that he turned his reputation around overnight.

As inspired by the Race of Champions result as he had been disappointed by poor results in Formula Two

early in 1973 with a rented Surtees TS14, Hesketh then doubled up again and decided to move into Formula One full-time. He bought a March 731G from Max Mosley (the man who had sacked Hunt in the first place) and hired March designer Dr Harvey Postlethwaite to engineer it for his little team, which was still managed by former Dastle racer 'Bubbles' Horsley. Hunt made his grand prix début at Monaco and was classified ninth, after dropping back from sixth place in the dying moments when the engine broke. By mid-season he was really making a name for himself, finishing sixth in France and then fourth in the chaotic British Grand Prix at Silverstone.

Because of Hunt's sudden emergence and his excellent performance on home soil, Roger's début in a Wheatcroft-sponsored works March made few headlines at Silverstone. In truth, the works 731G was no match for the Hesketh car, which had been completely rebuilt to a very high standard and had benefited from the development work invested by Postlethwaite.

Mosley had begun the season with lofty ambitions

Roger was all smiles as he prepared to make his long awaited grand prix début at Silverstone, where he sported the trademark cap that girlfriend Jacqui Martin said was his only vanity.

March's 731G was a pale shadow of the Bicester marque's successful Formula Three and Formula Two models, but was all that Tom Wheatcroft could hire at short notice. Roger was beset by brake troubles in practice.

for a single-car team to be driven by the brilliant but perennially unlucky New Zealander Chris Amon, who had been team leader in 1970 and was scheduled to return after a two-year spell with the French Matra team. But then Amon was suddenly and unceremoniously sacked by Mosley, allegedly because money he had promised had not come through. The reality was that March was the party that failed to deliver on financial commitments, and firing Amon was the only way to avoid an embarrassing catastrophe.

'Max wanted to win the championship that year with a single car for Chris, but then lost interest,' March mechanic Pete Briggs recalled. 'The car was never developed like the Hesketh car was; there were only the three of us running it.'

March's team comprised Briggs, Pete Kerr and Dave White. The primary driver was the promising Jean-Pierre Jarier, who had been a contemporary of Hunt's in Formula Three and then Formula Two. French veteran Henri Pescarolo had also driven the car in Spain. Briggs didn't rate Jarier: 'He was so hard on the lightweight Hewland gearbox that was originally fitted that we had to fit a heavier FG400 to cater for that,' he revealed. That was another reason why the works car did not handle as well as the Hesketh 731G.

Tom Wheatcroft hired this car as a toe-in-the-water exercise for Roger to gain more experience in Formula One after he had briefly tested for BRM in February. The plan was to run it in England, Holland and Italy. Despite the March's shortcomings, and a complete lack of testing mileage in it, Roger attacked his new challenge with his customary determination. 'We all reckoned Roger was pretty good,' Briggs said, and the Leicester driver qualified for his first Formula One race in 22nd place with a best lap of 1m 19.5s. This compared to Hunt's 1m 17.6s in the better-developed Hesketh 731G which also had the benefit of Firestone tyres compared to Roger's Goodyears. The former were said to be slightly quicker, though on some cars were less durable than the latter. David Purley had lapped his similar March in 1m 18.4s but didn't start after crashing at Becketts, and Mike Beuttler did 1m 20.1s in his yellow Clarke-Mordaunt-Guthrie-Durlacher version. The Wheatcroft car was something of a dog, for Jarier had similarly struggled to get a decent time out of it in his races, and Roger's case was hampered further by a persistent brake problem. He twice damaged the nose in practice after going wide and running over the grass.

Unfortunately, his grand prix début lasted only a lap. Like six other unlucky racers he became an unwitting victim of a first-lap accident triggered when Jody Scheckter, another of his Formula Three sparring partners, spun the third works McLaren M23 exiting the daunting Woodcote corner at 150mph. The South African had already made his Formula One début the previous year in a McLaren M19C in America and had driven two races in 1973. His last, in Paul Ricard, had seen him leading the field in the M23 until a collision with reigning champion Emerson Fittipaldi, which was adjudged to have been the Brazilian's fault. Now, having qualified sixth, Scheckter had passed team-mate Denny Hulme for fourth place going into Woodcote on the opening lap – but his M23 lost the battle he was forcing it to wage against the laws of physics. As its speed exceeded the level of grip available, the white car ran wider and wider until it got on to the grass on the exit to the last corner and then looped back across the track, spinning through 360 degrees before crunching nose-first into the pit wall. The impact bounced it back into the path of 22 oncoming vehicles, and carnage ensued.

Stewart, Peterson and Carlos Reutemann made it through ahead of the accident. Those immediately behind Scheckter – Hulme, team-mate Peter Revson, Hunt and Clay Regazzoni – all got through virtually unscathed. So did others even further back: Howden Ganley, Jacky Ickx and Emerson Fittipaldi. The rest did not. The track became littered with damaged cars: George Follmer's Shadow, Andrea de Adamich's Brabham, Jean-Pierre Beltoise's BRM, and all three Surtees of Carlos Pace, Mike Hailwood and Jochen Mass.

Roger had been running well after a good start, but like many others was unsighted by flying debris and dust. He spotted what appeared to be a gap and tried to run close to the pit wall, but was tagged and launched as one of the Surtees cars veered across the road after being hit by somebody else and closed the gap at precisely the wrong moment. Roger's car was pitched precariously on to its right-hand wheels as it walloped Scheckter's wreckage, but stayed the right way up and slithered to a halt. Roger was able to jump out, but the 731G was seriously damaged and in no state to take the restart.

'It all happened so fast,' Roger told his local paper, the *Leicester Mercury*. 'I turned into Woodcote, saw all the dust flying about and got on brakes, but everything was cold because it was only the first lap. I started to slide towards the dust and I was aiming for the pit wall, thinking there wouldn't be any cars about there. But I had to swerve to miss the back of one car, then there was another one and nowhere for me to go. I took off, hit Jody Scheckter's car, then the pit wall and ended up under the bridge. All the drivers were just glad there was no fire, because we all had full tanks, of course.'

By contrast, Hunt fared much better, but he had been mighty lucky. He had lost his 731G's tall airbox after Scheckter's rear wing had fluttered through the air and sliced it off – narrowly missing his head – but was able to borrow a smaller spare from Beuttler's team. Thus re-equipped, the tall Englishman went on to drive the best race of his career to that point. The stubby white March held on to the John Player Lotuses of Peterson and Fittipaldi, and to the Yardley McLarens of eventual winner Revson and Hulme, to grab a fighting fourth place by the end.

Not surprisingly England hailed a new hero, for Hunt had driven with a maturity that had been lacking in many of his Formula Three forays. The fact that Roger was in an inferior car that took no further part after the great shunt explains in some measure how a man who was so clearly superior to Hunt in terms of results the previous year would come to be so overlooked by history.

But Roger quickly bounced back from the disappointment and immediately set his sights on the next race, the Dutch Grand Prix at Zandvoort. It would put his name on television screens and the front page of every daily newspaper.

His race ended in the aftermath of Jody Scheckter's 360-degree spin exiting Woodcote corner at the end of the first lap. Roger was left to climb from the wreckage of his car after finding himself trapped by the pit wall with nowhere to go.

CHAPTER 7

Renaissance in the dunes

29 July 1973

'The back part of the track was interesting, very demanding with all these hills and sand dunes, but a lot more needed to be done to the track.'
Jackie Stewart

One day in July 1973, Roger Williamson paid a visit to his friend and mentor Tom Wheatcroft. Theirs was an easy relationship, the ebullient developer and the outgoing but respectful young lad. On the surface Roger had everything to be upbeat about. That astute talent-spotter and team owner Ken Tyrrell had very quietly expressed interest to Ford's Walter Hayes in signing him as the replacement driver for the great champion Jackie Stewart who, unbeknown to all in the racing world at that time bar Tyrrell and Hayes, intended to retire at the end of that season. It should have been the ultimate dream for any young racer. Since 1968 Tyrrell's team had been one of the leading contenders. With Matra chassis, Stewart narrowly missed the world title that year and won it convincingly in 1969. In Tyrrell's own cars he was dominant again in 1971, and after illness in 1972, was a strong contender for the 1973 crown. But Roger was a loyal man, and was loathe to do anything to upset Tom.

'Roger come up the office one morning,' Wheatcroft recalled. 'He were there all day and then he come home and had a meal with me. It were just after the nine o'clock news, and after being with me all day from about nine o'clock in the morning, he finally said to me, "Oh, Tom, I'm worried."'

This was not what Wheaty expected from a driver who had a contract with Tyrrell on the table, awaiting only his signature. 'Roger looked terrible, and said, "I'd like to stay with you, Tom, and drive for you."'

Despite some clutch trouble...

Wheatcroft was astounded, but deeply touched by his protégé's loyalty. 'I said, "Well, Roger, we'd only hold you up. Ken's forgot more than we'll ever know."'

They talked long into the night about their future together, and laid plans accordingly that centred around Wheatcroft running his own Formula One operation in 1974. But in the meantime the works March was there for Roger to drive in the Dutch Grand Prix at the end of the month.

On the morning of the 29th, race day at Zandvoort, Ben Huisman climbed into his yellow Porsche 911 and drove to the track from his rented summerhouse in a southern boulevard in the town. It was a trip of just over a mile. As his wife and two young sons took their grandstand seats, Huisman headed for the paddock to resume his duties as clerk of the course, the man in effective charge of the Dutch Grand Prix. There he met up with his partner, track director Johan Beerepoot. This was to be their big day: the culmination of months of unrelenting effort that had enabled them to bring the race back to their track.

Zandvoort had always been popular with drivers and teams alike. Located by the coast near Haarlem, it had a pleasant ambience and a reputation as a circuit on which you could race. Two fast corners led on to the pit straight, which was followed by the Tarzan hairpin, where the braking area was a popular passing zone. But a shadow had been cast over the venue following the death of Piers Courage in the 1970 race, the immensely popular old Etonian crashing the de Tomaso he was driving for Frank Williams's fledgling team. Courage had lost control in one of the fast sections of the course, and hit a bridge support. Trapped in his car, he was burned to death in the ensuing fire that raged for much of the race. Unable to quell the flames because of the Italian car's magnesium construction, marshals had ultimately resorted to burying the machine with sand until the event was over. Compounding the tragedy, initial reports claimed that the driver had escaped the inferno. The Swiss driver Jo Siffert had stopped there only moments earlier when his works March had expired with engine failure, and he had been mistaken for Courage. Lady Sarah Curzon, Courage's wife, was initially told that her husband was okay.

There was a race in 1971, which was run in the wet and saw rainmasters Jacky Ickx and Pedro Rodriguez slugging it out for Ferrari and BRM, but there was no event in 1972 as the drivers boycotted Zandvoort on safety grounds. The Commission Sportif Internationale (the CSI, at that time the sporting branch of the FIA) had inspected the circuit just before Christmas 1971 and declared it sub-standard. Track director (and designer) John Hugenholtz estimated the cost of upgrading it at £70,000. Later there was an argument between the Nederlandse Autorensport Vereniging (NAV, Holland's national automobile club) and the drivers over safety standards, and the CSI came down on the side of the drivers. There was also the problem that, in Holland, taxation took 50 per cent of the gate receipts, making it very difficult to make a profit. It did not take long for the venue to deteriorate, with weeds pushing through the asphalt in places. Even in late 1971 there was talk of the city of Zandvoort closing it down and turning it into a pleasure park, the local Labour Party and 13 citizens trying to sign its death knell in the forerunner of social protests that would lead to the closure of many tracks in the nineties.

For Huisman and Beerepoot, closure was completely unthinkable. Huisman handled the finances for the track, while Beerepoot was the secretary of the NAV. In 1972 they began planning how to resuscitate their circuit.

Huisman explained, 'The council wanted to close the circuit and that is why we joined forces and said, "No way! We have to race. Motor racing at Zandvoort has to remain possible." Johan and me took the lead and said, "We have to raise sufficient funds. Subsequently I moved to Zandvoort. The track was run-down. The pit boxes and pit lane were a complete shambles.

'I met heavy opposition from the municipal council and all odds were stacked against us. And our adversaries had strong backing from third parties.'

Huisman and Beerepoot formed an organisation, Circuit Exploitatie Nederland Autorensport Vereniging (CENAV) with Beerepoot as the president and an investment of 2.5 million guilders (1.1 million euros). According to Huisman, the money came 'from everywhere. Sponsors bought the pits and an investment bank lent us money. We had a lot of participants. The financing was pretty well organised, nothing wrong there.'

The track was resurfaced, run-off areas were widened and they erected steel barriers all round. New pit garages and a new control tower completed the revamp. Huisman invested so much of his time in pursuit of his passion that he took a leave of absence from his paper business in Elburg; it almost went bankrupt as a result but he would not be deterred from what he now saw as his life's mission.

Months earlier he had picked up double World Champion Jackie Stewart from Schipol Airport near Amsterdam and driven him to inspect the new Zandvoort. Stewart did this sort of thing regularly in his role as representative of the Grand Prix Drivers' Association (GPDA). Huisman had an orange BMW 2002, a quick car in its day, but knowing that Stewart did not care for people who drove quickly on the road he deliberately refused to exceed 50kmh just to tease the Scot. Doubtless Stewart's patience was exercised by the juvenile tactic, and today Huisman admits, 'We weren't really talkative. Our personalities did not really fit. He wanted to go slow and, just like I did with my father earlier, I lowered my speed even more.'

One of the reasons why there was no love lost between Stewart and Huisman was that the Scot called a spade a spade, and as the leading safety crusader of his generation he had been incensed two years earlier by the Dutch organisers' lack of concern for changes the GPDA had sought. At the 1971 race the long-haired Scot had shot from the hip. Even before Courage's death there, the GPDA had asked for improvements. In the edition of that week's *Motoring News* which, ironically, had a story about the 1971 grand prix and a photo of Roger winning at Brands Hatch on its front cover, Stewart was quoted as branding Zandvoort 'malignant', while criticising the organisers' failure to honour promises they had previously made.

'They've done a token amount that's not nearly enough,' he said. 'I'm extremely annoyed; their behaviour has been extremely bad. Maybe the track only has a few years to go – I can understand that – but we've been hijacked into coming here. We were committed to the race, and the work hasn't been done.'

CSI officials had inspected the place and imposed their own requirements, but even though they were not met either, the race was allowed to go ahead.

'The drivers in this case relied on their own governing body, the CSI,' Stewart continued. 'The report (on the circuit's lack of up-to-date safety facilities) was not made solely by the GPDA but in conjunction with the CSI.

'I'm not sorry to see anything go that's unhealthy, and as far as I'm concerned this is malignant. If one set of organisers can get away with it, then so can the others.'

Stewart's remarks caused a furore at a time when he – and others – were trying to enlighten attitudes in racing, and to save lives. Future events would prove him to be absolutely correct in his assessment of Zandvoort. Thirty years later, even Huisman had to admit that.

'We walked across the circuit,' he said of the day of Stewart's inspection. 'I wasn't a member of the Stewart fan club. I found him a pain in the arse.'

But then he added, 'In hindsight he was right. He had to race and had to ensure that he would survive to tell the tale.'

…Roger was able to acclimatise himself better…

...to the March 731G...

Thanks to shortcomings that went unnoticed by Huisman, Roger would not survive.

The Dutchman preferred the black and white Niki Lauda, or the outgoing Graham Hill, with whom he got on so well that they visited one another at home on more than one occasion. Huisman also liked playboy James Hunt and had enjoyed a dinner with the Englishman and Roger the previous year in Hilversum. 'That serious Stewart, that is a different piece of cake,' he observed.

Together with Beerepoot and a man called Smallegange, who had been responsible for some of the construction work, Stewart and Huisman walked round the renovated track. For the men who dreamed of reviving Zandvoort this was a crucial day, for Stewart had the authority to turn down their venue. The Scot asked a lot of questions, as was his way, and remembered, 'The back part of the track was interesting, very demanding with all these hills and sand dunes, but a lot more needed to be done to the track.' However, Huisman thought they were on the home straight. Their race, and their track, would survive. That was what was uppermost in his mind.

That morning of 29 July, Zandvoort's two saviours rode round it on a motorcycle. Each was gratified by what they saw. Flags waved all around the circuit, the sun was shining and the place was alive with spectators who came in their droves to occupy grandstand seats or to perch on top of the sand dunes. There were 80,000 of them, creating traffic jams everywhere.

The icing on the cake, and still something of a rarity in those days, was that they had arranged for live television coverage which would be provided by the Dutch NOS network. This was an historic first for Zandvoort. Previous coverage in 1971 had embraced only pre-race activity and recorded highlights. The presenters were Henk Terlingen and Frans Henrichs, and to give them an extra something to talk about, Dutchman (and reigning European Formula 5000 Champion) Gijs van Lennep was driving one of Frank Williams's Iso Marlboro cars.

That happy morning gave no hint whatsoever of the tragic events that were to unfold, and few – if any – drivers realised that not all of the safety work had been carried out properly.

While Huisman and Beerepoot were taking their ride, volunteer marshal Herman Brammer was collecting his lunchbox, which contained an apple and a bottle of soft drink. It was his stipend for volunteering to be a

...as he ran in company with the likes of Carlos Reutemann.

marshal at Post 10, near Tunnel Oost on the sweeping curves at the back of the circuit that Stewart had described. This was Brammer's second day in the role; he had wanted to be there for practice on the Friday, too, but had been unable to secure time off from his grammar school teaching job. He had been marshalling since 1967 and was a member of the Officials Club Automobielsport (OCA). In 1970 he had been an unfortunate witness of Courage's fatal accident, at Post 10.

'I remember I was waving two yellow flags because there was hardly any sight for drivers who were approaching,' he recalled of that incident. 'The black smoke was blowing right over the track.' Back then, as race director, it was Huisman who had the thankless task of informing Frank Williams that Courage had perished. 'It was exceptionally tragic, poor Frankie-boy,' he remembered 30 years later.

In light of what had gone before, and what was to follow, it is important to put that era of motor racing into its correct perspective – especially when reviewing it all these years later in an age when the 'nanny state' is so vocal and some no longer regard it as one of the great freedoms for a man to choose the manner in which he cares to risk his life. Back then, people had different views on what constituted unacceptable risk, though this

was the time when Stewart's safety crusade was at its zenith. Since his crash at Spa in 1966, the great Scottish champion had campaigned tirelessly for safety standards to be enhanced.

Deaths were always mourned within the brotherhood of racing drivers, but they were also an accepted part of the game in those days. The seventies alone had already seen the violent passing of topline drivers such as Bruce McLaren, Courage, Jochen Rindt (who had become the sport's only posthumous World Champion in 1970), Ignazio Giunti, Hans Laine, Pedro Rodriguez, Jo Siffert and Jo Bonnier.

Only weeks before Zandvoort, the highly promising Scottish racer Gerry Birrell had been killed at Rouen.

The famed Indianapolis 500 race had also been cursed that terrible season. In practice, popular veteran Art Pollard had died. Then, after poor weather which necessitated a delay from the scheduled Saturday date to Wednesday, the race had barely started when Salt Walther was injured in an explosive accident on the startline that involved 11 cars, and resulted in photographs being sent around the world of his fiery, upturned McLaren, his feet visible as they protruded from the shattered footbox. Worse still, upcoming American David 'Swede' Savage suffered a horrible accident as the race progressed. After fighting for the lead, he crashed his STP Eagle very heavily in Turn Four. This time the images showed his body strapped to the remains of his car which resembled nothing more than a flaming haversack. A fire truck rushing to the scene the wrong way down the pit lane then hit and killed Armando Teran, one of the STP crew members. Savage lingered in hospital until succumbing to liver failure after 33 days; he was 26.

'It's important to put Roger Williamson's accident into the perspective of the era,' Stewart said three decades later. 'Back then racing drivers did die. It was a terrible thing, but it happened time and again. You never really got used to it, but it was always there. When my son Paul was at school in Switzerland one day he came home in tears and asked my wife Helen when I was going to die – they had been talking about it at school and another kid had said that I was a racing driver, and racing drivers got killed.

'One time Helen and I sat in bed counting all the friends we had lost to racing. We stopped when we got to 50...'

So these were bloody times, when death was a regular habitué of the paddocks of the world. Brammer knew this as well as the next man, but even witnessing the horror of Courage's accident had not deterred him from his passion for the sport. That was how it was back then. You were horrified and saddened, you mourned, but you had to move on. But few of the people truly affected by the tragedies ever forgot. Stewart, in particular, was pilloried by the misguided as he fought for the change that helped turn the sport into the much safer – but, of course, never entirely safe – form of entertainment that it is today, when any death would have a deleterious effect on the multi-million dollar investments by multi-national companies.

Brammer could not afford to race so, like many young men and women, his role as a track worker enabled him to get as close as he could to the sport he loved. That is why he was at Zandvoort that Sunday morning. Yet, despite the ever-present risk of fire, all he wore were his regular street clothes. The only concession to his marshalling role was a black and white chequered OCA tabard that he slipped over them. He was given no helmet, nor fireproof clothes or fire-fighting aids. Huisman and Beerepoot had spent their budget on the track, not on such equipment for others who were, after all, only volunteers.

Poppe de Boer had left his home in Haarlem that morning. His father, Cees, ran a photographic agency and had been a regular visitor to Zandvoort since 1960. Poppe planned to start his day as an accredited photographer at the Hunzerug corner behind the pits before walking round the track as the race progressed. He would shoot photographs of the leaders and, of course, local hero van Lennep.

The Dutch driver had competed in the 1971 race in a Surtees TS7 entered privately by Stichting Autoraces Nederland. He raced a new TS9 for Team Surtees in America later that season, before switching to race entrant Jackie Epstein's Surtees TS11 in the 1972 European Formula 5000 Championship in which he was victorious. A few weeks before this Dutch Grand Prix he received a call from representatives of Marlboro; they were sponsoring Frank Williams's team, and were offering him a ride. It was the perfect means of increasing the spectator attendance. Van Lennep had won the Targa Florio sportscar classic earlier that year, sharing a Porsche Carrera RSR with Swiss driver Herbert Muller, but his Formula 5000 season had so far been unhappy. He was the winner of the 1971 Le Mans 24 Hours classic endurance race (with Austrian driver Helmut Marko in a Porsche 917), but, even so, he had hitherto been unable to raise the 400,000 guilders (181,000 euros) that John Surtees wanted for a seat in his eponymous team. 'To be honest, until the offer came from Marlboro I had deleted Formula One from my mind,' van Lennep recalled. 'But when I hung up the call, I thought that just a few Formula One races a year would be nice. Long-distance racing demands 90 per cent from you. Formula One is much more; it claims 100. It was one of my problems. Since I had crashed heavily at Spa in 1967 I had always been on the edge of too little physical condition.'

Marlboro was determined to persuade van Lennep to race, and Williams was obliged to accept the deal. Van Lennep agreed, but the drive was not the passport to success that racing a Williams would subsequently become for so many future champions. 'Williams did not mean a thing in those days,' he laughed. 'Frank did not have money, he did not have anything.'

Around two o'clock, Huisman waved the drivers and cars out onto the track. Timing was much more lax than it is today, when everything runs to a clearly defined, television-driven schedule. But he told them to hurry up otherwise he would close the pit lane. 'Nobody was in a hurry,' he recalled. As one by one the cars went out of the pit lane on their grid formation lap, he and Beerepoot turned and congratulated each other once again. They had done it, and each man felt understandable pride. They had saved their nation's race.

As ever, Roger brought total commitment to extracting the maximum from a tricky little car that was no match for James Hunt's Hesketh version.

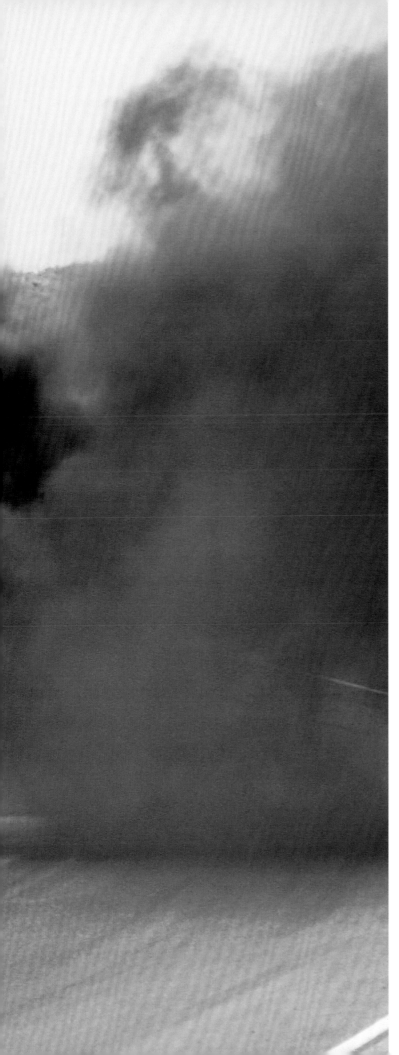

CHAPTER 8

Infamy at Zandvoort

29 July 1973

'I couldn't get the car over. I was trying to get people to help me, and if I could have turned the car over or even just lifted it a bit, he would have been all right, we could have got him out.'
David Purley

At the front of the starting grid, Ronnie Peterson in his black and gold John Player Lotus was ready for battle with the blue Tyrrells of Jackie Stewart and François Cevert. Peterson's team-mate Emerson Fittipaldi, however, had qualified only 16th after a nasty ankle-bruising crash in practice. With a lap of 1m 22.72s Roger should have shared the seventh row with both the reigning World Champion, and former Champion Graham Hill. This time – apart from Hunt in the modified Hesketh version – he was the fastest March driver. He had been 12th fastest in Saturday morning's first practice session, and that time subsequently left him 18th overall in a brand new chassis built up with Formula Two-style nose and narrow track after Silverstone. Roger's time was two seconds slower than Hunt's, but his car had suffered clutch slip in qualifying and the unit had eventually expired before he'd really had the chance to go for a quick lap on Saturday.

As the drivers got out of their cars and milled about on the grid, awaiting the start, Gijs van Lennep, who had qualified 20th, strolled back to pass the time with Roger. As he observed, 'He was a nice chap and I liked him.' Roger should have been on the seventh row, but when the March refused to start initially and was late

Flames surround the upturned Wheatcroft March and obscure David Purley's heroic rescue attempts. At this stage, Roger was still alive in the cockpit.

ABOVE: *Always relaxed before a start, Roger shares a joke on race morning with James Hunt, Tom Wheatcroft and Denny Hulme, giving the lie to clerk of the course Ben Huisman's later claim to have been the only man to know Roger.* BELOW: *More serious was Roger's conversation with team owner Max Mosley as they mulled over the 731G's shortcomings.*

getting out of the pits for the formation lap, he was moved to the back row.

On the second floor of the control tower Ben Huisman checked with the timekeepers. They were ready. The fire brigade was also ready, and on the first floor the OCA had made contact with all the marshals' posts around the track. Everything was set. A ladder stood against one wall of the tower. In case Huisman could not hear the timekeepers he would be able to scoot up the ladder to get closer. 'These guys were my eyes and my ears,' he admitted. It was a far from sophisticated method of communication, and it was highly inefficient as events would prove, but so much about Formula One was like that back then. Hindsight is always 20/20 vision.

Huisman climbed onto a small platform in the pit lane near the start-finish line as the drivers were strapped back into their cars and fired their engines. As spectators stood and craned their necks, Huisman waved the Dutch flag to start the race. Some of his fellow citizens had wanted the track to die, so it is not hard to imagine the elation he felt as, instead, it now came to raucous life at his command and obliterated the months of effort and heartache.

Twenty-three cars piled into the Tarzan turn, with Peterson grabbing the lead from Stewart and rising Brazilian star Carlos Pace shoving his Surtees into third place ahead of Cevert.

By the seventh lap, Peterson led Stewart and Cevert. Van Lennep was 12th, separated from the three leaders by Pace, James Hunt, Denny Hulme, Carlos Reutemann, Peter Revson, Clay Regazzoni, Jean-Pierre Beltoise and Wilson Fittipaldi. Roger was running 13th, chasing the Dutchman's Iso Marlboro. After his back-row start, he had completed the opening lap in 16th place but soon carved his way through in a style reminiscent of his Formula Three and Formula Two days. On the second lap he had passed Mike Beuttler's privately-backed March (which then stopped with electrical problems) and Hill, and a lap later he overtook David Purley, his old Formula Three sparring partner. Purley tucked in behind him as they chased after van Lennep. Much would later be made by national newspapers of the close friendship between the two British drivers, but in truth they knew each other the way many young racers know rivals: to chat to, and have a drink with, in the paddock, but not being much closer than that.

Van Lennep negotiated the curve by Post 10, near Tunnel Oost, for the eighth time. This was a very fast full-throttle, full-speed section of the track. From the Tarzan hairpin drivers looped back to the tight left-hand Gerlachbocht corner before climbing up Hunzerug. From there they hit fifth gear working through a sweeping left/right combination before dropping to fourth gear for the Scheivlak right-hander. Then it was back up to fifth gear and 165mph for another left-right flick, Hondenvlak, which led to a straight that crossed Tunnel Oost and on to an even tighter right-hander which was immediately followed by a tight left. It was a very challenging part of the track, one that van Lennep remembered well 30 years later.

'Tunnel Oost was a very nice turn, a real turn. It was difficult. You had grip, but when you came out of the turn there was no space. There was just a few metres of grass, then a guardrail and a steep dune and on top of that, the woods. It was a very tight turn. There you needed to do it exactly right. There was not a lot of space for error, not a lot of space for compensation if anything went wrong. When you were on the inside of the turn, if you got only a little bit too far from the inside edge of the track, you would miss a lot on the outside. Tunnel Oost was a matter of centimetres; a bit like Blanchimont at Spa or the 130R bend at Suzuka. The car's handling had to be neutral at that speed. To be honest, I always felt happy when I passed Tunnel Oost cleanly. I was always very aware of that turn. When coming through Scheivlak, I always thought to myself, "Two more curves to go..."

'Sometimes I thought "Is it me or is it the car?" if I saw someone like Cevert passing me, and I watched them slam and slide their car through there, and run six metres further away from me. I thought I should not

have too much oversteer there, and then looked at the black skid marks they left on the track. Amazing! When you make one little mistake, time stands still. You just do not have time and space to correct it, especially there.'

Only seconds after van Lennep had passed Post 10 by Tunnel Oost and headed for the right-hander, Roger sped through the previous left-right flick. Herman Brammer was looking to the right, tracking his fellow countryman, when he heard a loud bang and the unmistakable sound of metal hitting metal. A car scraping down the guardrail. He spun round to the left to see what was happening.

What he saw was Roger's March, now in full flight. Subsequently, photographic evidence would prove conclusively that he did not make a mistake, that his car suffered a tyre failure. As it negotiated the right-hander before Tunnel Oost, the March was captured on film at the very moment in which the outer left-hand edge of the full-width nose delaminated as a result of debris from a burst left front tyre. The one that provided the grip he needed. Without it, the car ran wide until it struck the guardrail on the outside of the track. It would

Roger leads David Purley past Jackie Oliver's crashed Shadow in the Gerlach corner behind the pits.

Early in the race Roger leads Purley; they are in the sequence of corners close to where the accident subsequently happened.

transpire that, despite all the exhortations of Jackie Stewart, the GPDA and the CSI, the barrier had not been mounted correctly. Its steel support posts had simply been sunk into sand without any of the concrete packing that should have anchored it properly. The March hit the barrier at an angle of 45 degrees, and then slid along it for the length of five of the posts. With nothing to prevent these posts from moving in the sand, the barrier bent back at a 40-degree angle and acted as a launching ramp.

The ensuing accident was captured by a film cameraman positioned behind the barrier, a little further down the track from the March's point of initial impact. Here is what happened in some of the most harrowing footage ever broadcast from a race track:

After hitting the barrier, the March is thrown upside down and comes into shot skidding and already trailing flame and shedding parts. Still upturned and heading backwards, it slides down the road before turning at 40 degrees and stopping after perhaps 200 metres, its rear end facing towards the barrier just before the apex of the second right-hander opposite Post 10. Orange flames lick around the cockpit and underside as it comes to rest.

David Purley stops his March before the second right-hander, on the grass on the left-hand side of the track. He erupts from the cockpit and runs across the track at 90 degrees to his own car, after waiting for two others to speed by. There is flaming wreckage to the right of the road that includes the March's front left wheel and oil catch-tank. Purley then sprints down the right-hand verge to the blazing car. He immediately tries to push the March back on to its remaining wheels, working on the right front. At this stage he is alone.

Two men run across the track, neither of them dressed to deal with fire. One is wearing a leather coat with a fur collar, the other is a marshal with his distinctive OCA checkered tabard.

Purley runs back across the track, opposite the flaming car, to grab a fire extinguisher located out of shot. The March is still blazing.

Purley runs back to the car, accompanied by a policeman and one other man. Now there are five people at the scene.

Initially Purley cannot make the extinguisher work, and the car is well ablaze. Eventually he gets the extinguisher going and begins to douse the cockpit area with extinguishant powder. For a moment the flames abate, and he moves round the front of the car and plays the extinguisher along the underside. The flames return.

Purley nearly gets the fire under control, and at this stage a concerted effort to right the car might have been successful. The problem is one of leverage. But the other men who might have helped are just standing around. 'Fur Collar' waves down passing drivers, while talking into a hand-held radio.

The fire erupts again, and the policeman feebly tries to kick dirt on to it. He does not even stoop down to use his hands, but just kicks it like a bully on a beach. Apart from Purley, nobody has a clue what to do.

Purley moves back round to the cockpit and plays the extinguisher over it again, trying to safeguard Roger. The car is well ablaze again. There is no point at which it has not been surrounded by orange flame.

The extinguisher runs out.

Purley makes desperate signals to the other men as the flames increase significantly. He tries again to lift the car via the right front wheel, waving all the time for assistance. Fur Collar tries to help briefly, placing one hand on the right front wheel, as does the policeman, but then the policeman pulls Fur Collar away. All three are very close to the car and therefore the flames. The heat must be unbearable to men in civilian clothing. Another man, with what appears to be another fire extinguisher, runs across the track.

Fur Collar pulls and pushes Purley clear, into the middle of the road, where Purley angrily chops away the man's arm with his own right hand. They stand helplessly in the middle of the track, so absorbed in what they are doing that they are almost oblivious to the approaching traffic. Another man runs across the road to the accident scene, but it is too late and he merely stands there, nonplussed, not knowing what to do. The fire is now completely out of control.

Purley stands on the left-hand verge, utterly disconsolate. A young girl guide tries to usher him away but he shakes her arm free. He begins to walk towards his car, shaking his head in anguish, but then turns and walks back towards the burning March. He takes a last look at the inferno, from the left-hand side of the track. Despair is written in every verb of his body language.

First there is white smoke billowing across the track. But as the fire takes real hold it turns black, rendering the orange flames ever more stark. Drivers have to go blindly through it. Some slow down more than others.

Purley actually stands on the track, frantically waving at them to slow down, perhaps even for somebody to stop. Nobody does.

Motoring News reader Leonard Coleman, who had been spectating with his brother on a sand dune 100 to 150 yards before Tunnel Oost, sent the paper his own eyewitness report, which was published in the 9 August edition. His account, which began at 3pm, made very hard reading, particularly at the end:

At first the fire was quite small, the flames being about six feet high and being carried away from the car by the wind. I was so upset that I am a bit vague about the next minute or so, but, as I remember, Purley was pushing on the right-hand rear wheel in an attempt to right the car, and he was obviously expecting the two marshals who joined him to help him. They just looked on, seemingly frozen with fear.

Approximately 30 seconds elapsed before a fire extinguisher was brought, and there was some difficulty making it work. After another five seconds the marshal started using it but standing about five yards from the car, and on the opposite side to the seat of the fire, which was in the engine bay. Purley grabbed the extinguisher, ran round the car and exhausted the contents into the seat of the fire, unfortunately without much effect.

Probably he expected help by this time, but the same two marshals were still standing there doing absolutely nothing. At this point the crowd started shouting, and my brother and I were calling out to get Williamson out, and bloody quick. I should think that by now some 90 seconds had elapsed, and the fire was getting bigger. Purley made another attempt to right the car, pushing on the right-front wheel, but by now the flames were getting bigger and he was being forced back. Purley then signalled with his arms for help (two police officers were now on the scene, not doing anything), and my brother and I moved forward. Then I realised that it was almost certainly too late, or would be by the time we had climbed over a five-foot barbed wire fence, and spectators could get mixed up with the race traffic, producing a disaster of even greater proportions.

One man did get over the fence, but he was immediately "arrested" by a policeman.

The fire raged without anyone doing a thing for several minutes, and at 3:08 a khaki-coloured fire engine with three men aboard drove up and stopped at the first fire, that involving the oil tank. The crowd shouted at them and they got back into the wagon and drove to the car. It took them another minute to get their hoses out and working, and they sprayed powder which didn't do much good as every 10 or 15 seconds the fire re-ignited.

This happened eight or 10 times, then at 3:18 a red fire engine drove up and attacked the wreckage with water, which cooled the car down and eventually finished the fire. The car was eventually righted at 3:25. A piece of cloth about a yard square was produced and it was left to Purley to cover the body, still in the car. By this time we were so sickened and distressed that we left the scene.

At no time did we see an ambulance, and for a good 15 or 20 minutes the smoke and powder completely obscured the track. The marshals' post at the scene of the accident was crewed by three men, none of whom had any protective clothing. One of them, the flag marshal, left his post and walked about 20 yards up the track.'

Brammer admitted that he was scared to death, and immediately thought of Piers Courage. 'Oh no, not another one.' He remembered that the Wheatcroft March's onboard fire extinguisher was activated, probably by Roger rather than automatically, and that he could see him trapped in the cockpit with insufficient space between the cockpit sides and the road to squeeze out to safety. Brammer's adrenaline kicked in, and he ran to the side of the track and immediately began to wave the yellow flag to warn the other drivers.

His colleague Hans Rens and another OCA track official were two of the men seen crossing the track and running to assist Purley. Both were unable to add their effort to overturning the car because it was burning so fiercely, and they lacked protective clothing.

Brammer described his fire-fighting colleagues to journalist Nando Boers in 2003 (for the interview with Ben Huisman see pages 109-110). Brammer recalls, 'There was an old fire-fighter and a young fire-fighter for whom it was only his first or second time around. So you can not really blame the young one. But the older fire-fighter was sitting on top of a sand dune watching the race – hardly ready to act instantly.

'After the accident he descended from that dune to the track with the fire extinguisher. When he climbed over the Armco, Purley grabbed the fire extinguisher from his hands.'

Elsewhere, policemen too scared to offer help but emboldened by their dogs, occupied themselves restraining the anxious crowd, cutting off any potential rescue attempt from that source. Appalled television

After the incorrectly installed metal barrier acted as a launching ramp, Roger's March was thrown upside-down along the road, shedding parts and bursting into flame as it went.

viewers watched the tragedy unfold, but back in the control tower, in a terrible irony, there was no television screen. From Post 10 a marshal should have called the tower to inform Huisman of the accident but, more than 30 years on, nobody knows who this man ought to have been. It was neither Brammer nor Rens. In any case, the unidentified man faced an impossible mission because, according to Brammer, the telephone cable had somehow been damaged. Huisman claimed that the vital message 'Post 10, crash, fire', never reached him. Due to this crucial lack of information, he was never in a position to consider stopping the race so that due assistance might have been despatched.

But that begs the question: to whom was 'Fur Collar' speaking on his hand-held radio? And what happened to the message he must have been transmitting?

Out on the track the other drivers were plunging through smoke and flame.

'I was ahead of the accident, so I only saw it on the next lap and then thereafter,' Stewart recalled in 2005. 'We often had to drive through fire, so there was no reason for the race to be stopped the way it would be today. It had not been stopped for Piers's accident when again we had to drive through fire. Or Jo Schlesser's at Rouen in 1968. We had to drive through fire quite a lot of the time back then.'

Was there ever a more chilling condemnation of safety levels of the era?

Alan Henry concurred with Stewart. Talking in 2005, he said, 'The thing you have to remember, and it sounds terrible saying it today, is that during that summer so many drivers were killed that you just got into the mindset as a young writer that it was what happened. The normality with which you confronted it wasn't in any way dismissive, but it was taken for

granted. There was sadness and an obituary, and the next week you went on to something else. There was never really any backtracking or analysis the way there would be today.'

Henry, who has been at many race tracks on such sad days, and lost several friends to the sport he loves, was far from being cynical or unfeeling. He was just putting into perspective how motor racing was back then.

Roger's tragedy would be the first time that the signs of much-needed change emerged so publicly.

'I didn't know it was Williamson's car,' Stewart continued. 'I didn't know whose it was. It was very clear that the fire wasn't being put out, but in those days that wasn't unusual. It was just another example of the inadequacies of the whole infrastructure. It wasn't until the end of the race that I knew who it was, whereas I had known it was Piers because I saw his distinctive fighter pilot's helmet lying on the track...

'It was a holocaust. In those days you slowed down while you were under the yellow flags getting to an accident, then you went through the fire, and then you went fast again until you came around the next time. Not many people caught you up, because everybody was doing the same thing. The biggest issue was that there were a lot of people there, by the time I arrived at the scene. I was looking for marshals; they could inform me. In a car you see the accident completely differently from what spectators see. And, don't forget, this was a fast part of the track. When you reduced speed you had to be careful that nobody got caught unawares and ran into the back of you. Naturally you had to look in your mirrors as well as ahead; your mind was in a different zone to that of any of the spectators.'

Those were valid points, well made, by the man

Black smoke obscures reference points as Wilson Fittipaldi and Gijs van Lennep thread their way through the accident scene, but in the pits Ben Huisman was still deluding himself that the smoke came from tyres set afire by errant children.

whose own safety crusade did more to save lives than any other.

'We drove by at crawling pace,' van Lennep remembered. 'Except Mr Peterson, who just screamed by. I noticed a driver standing next to the crashed car. After the race that appeared to have been Purley, but at the time I thought, "Okay, the guy rolled out from under his car. He's okay."'

Van Lennep's Williams team-mate, the New Zealander Howden Ganley, had yet another version. 'That race was probably the worst I have ever been involved in. It began badly and then turned, although I was not immediately aware of that fact, into a total tragedy.

'I got slightly delayed at the start, but when I arrived at the left-hander behind the pits at full speed I discovered that the cars in front seemed to have braked much too soon. There was no chance of getting slowed

way down to their pace, so I finished up punting Niki Lauda off into the dirt and breaking the nose and right front wing on my car. After the race I had an angry Niki demanding to know why I had run into him, but I was able to point out that he was going much too slowly and deserved to be run into, which seemed to calm things down somewhat.

'I continued in the race but very soon I was getting showered with shredded green glassfibre, so accepted that I would have to stop for a new nose and wings. This done I rejoined, and soon came across what had obviously been some sort of accident around the back of the circuit. Dave Purley's March was stopped on one side of the road, and another car was much further along, upside down. There were bits of bodywork scattered about, and some fairly long skid-marks on the road. No marshals appeared to be doing anything very much, so it seemed obvious to me that both drivers must be okay. Next lap around I could see flames licking around the overturned car, and there was a lot of fire extinguisher powder in the air. Then a couple of laps later I had Purley shaking his fist at me, which puzzled me. As he had been behind me there was no way I could have caused his accident, and if somehow he had been hit by Niki after our contretemps then it was only very slightly my fault.

'A lap or two more and the overturned car, which by now I had identified as Roger Williamson's March, was well ablaze and I did wonder why the big fire engine parked just up the road at the next corner was not being brought into action, or why there was not a lot of marshal activity. Had things been really serious there would have been a red flag, wouldn't there? But it seems that was not the policy at Zandvoort.'

It is worth noting that races were *sometimes* stopped in those days. The non-championship event staged at Brands Hatch in October 1971, to celebrate Stewart's second world title, had been stopped when Jo Siffert met his end. And only weeks prior to Zandvoort, the British Grand Prix had likewise been stopped after Scheckter's monumental misjudgement. Had Huisman understood in time the seriousness of the accident, he surely could have done likewise and stopped his race.

'When we came in after the race, and were told that Roger had been trapped in the car and died in the flames, it was absolutely devastating,' Ganley continued, going on to make the point that even without intervention by the fire engine or the marshals several drivers, in their Nomex overalls, could have righted the car and extracted Roger had a red flag been deployed to illustrate the gravity of the situation, so giving them the chance to help.

'I have festered on this ever since,' he admitted in 2005. 'It is something I will never forget. The message went out loud and clear – the drivers needed to look out for each other. Do not rely on officialdom to do the right thing. It was significant that at the last grand prix of the year at Watkins Glen when François Cevert had his (fatal) accident in practice, every driver stopped instantly and ran to the scene to see if they could help.'

It is interesting that some drivers were able to identify the cars and drivers involved even as they drove by, and that Ganley took the inactivity of the marshals to be a sign that everything was okay – though, like several others, he was puzzled as to why Purley was shaking his fist at him.

Zandvoort marked Alan Henry's first foreign grand prix for *Motoring News*. 'I went over with Mike Tee and Jenny on the ferry from Harwich to the Hook of Holland, on the Wednesday or Thursday,' he remembered, 'and Roger and his girlfriend Jacqui were on the next table. I knew less about him on a personal level than I did Tom Pryce and Tony Brise. I remember meeting him for the first time when I went to Mallory Park that time when Jeremy Walton tested Roger's one-litre Anglia.

'I thought Roger was a tough bastard. I was never quite convinced that he was as good as Tom and Brise, but I began to be convinced in the last few weeks of his

life when he won the Monza Lottery in that March-BMW. That was really good. As I recall that actually turned some people's opinion. I remember them thinking, "Blimey, perhaps this *is* quite a big deal."

'I remember sitting in the grandstand, watching the smoke, and realising that it either had to be Purley or Williamson. There were no cameras around or television screens in the press room; you just waited to see. Then Purley came back to the pits a long while later, driving with his belts undone, and that was when we realised it was Roger. But I don't think we realised for a long time what had really happened.'

From Hunzerug, photographer Poppe de Boer saw the smoke, grabbed his equipment bag and started running through the dunes. It took him around five minutes to reach the scene of the accident, where he remembered seeing only smoke, misery and disaster. His instincts kicked in and dispassionately he photographed the smouldering car, completely unaware whether or not the driver was still aboard. He simply registered and recorded the scene with his camera. It's what photographers do in such moments, when instinct overrides any other considerations.

Close by, Brammer was becoming increasingly frustrated. He could see every moment of the tragedy unfolding, but his duty was just to stand there and keep waving the yellow flag.

Eventually, from his position in the control tower, Huisman spotted the spiral of black smoke, but still there was no telephone message from Post 10. Yet again one must ask, who was Fur Collar contacting? What happened to his message? Huisman faced a terrible dilemma. His emotional investment in the resurrection of Zandvoort was persuading him that nothing on the track could have caused the smoke; this was perhaps because to consider such a thing was unthinkable for a man who had worked so hard to enable his beloved circuit to survive. But, given the fact that he had seen smoke such as this during Piers Courage's accident, it is incredible that he now rationalised it to himself thus, 'It could not have happened on the track because lap times remained the same...'

This was wishful thinking at best, and his desire to believe the best then overrode his other instincts. As he climbed the ladder to the timekeepers he clung to an even more desperate and ridiculous hope: that perhaps spectators had set fire to some old tyres; that, as the white and then black smoke billowed hundreds of feet into the sky at the accident scene. When he arrived on the first floor, he found that the timekeepers knew nothing. They were all so sure they had built the perfect, safe racetrack that they too clung to the belief that it had to be a false alarm. Looking at things from a distance of more than 30 years, it is tempting to believe that they deluded themselves purely because they believed what they wanted to believe. If that was the case then, quite simply, their blind faith cost Roger Williamson his life.

'Later we knew something had happened but the message we received was, "Accident, driver OK. He is standing next to his car,"' Huisman recalled. Unforgivably, it was Piers Courage all over again. Had nothing been learned since 1970?

It was at the 20-lap mark, 12 laps or more than 15 minutes after the accident, that Huisman finally realised that something was terribly wrong. 'Naive? Absolutely,' he admitted to Boers. 'But things were happening during races all the time and I am not a person who panics quickly. None of the drivers came into the pits to let us know something was going on.'

Given the culture of racing at the time, that was as unlikely as Frank Williams's cars were to win a grand prix. In such circumstances the drivers kept doing what they were there to do while assuming that the authorities would take the necessary steps to protect them. At Zandvoort they did not.

Had Huisman even thought to have checked, the lap charts would have pinpointed that, while one driver might be standing by a car, there were actually two cars missing. After driving through the smoke for a lap, GPDA president Denny Hulme, the 1967 World Champion, purposely drove his McLaren very close to the pit wall, shaking his first in anger that the race was not being stopped. After the race he had harsh words with Huisman on that very issue.

After the interminable and unforgivable delay, the elderly Bedford firetruck was despatched to the scene from the Gerlach corner, the left-hander that followed Tarzan. It was heavy, with 500 litres of water on board. It had trouble exceeding 40kmh and crawled pathetically up the climb out of Gerlachbocht known as Hunzerug. By the time that it finally arrived at the accident scene, Roger was beyond help. Further round the track another vehicle had been much closer to the accident scene, but driving it against the flow of traffic, or even reversing it, along the grass verge was not considered an option. That was one of the few decisions that afternoon that was perhaps understandable. Eventually, long, long after it mattered, the fire was extinguished. Again, it seems callous to us now that the firemen simply turned the March the right way up and left Roger aboard until the sacred race had run its terrible course. But that was the way things were done back then. The real height of callousness and cowardly behaviour, however, was to hand Purley the sheet and leave it to him to cover Roger's body. The Dutch officials themselves could not even afford him that small dignity.

'It gets serious when a fire truck enters the track,' Huisman admitted all those years later. 'But the message, "He is dead"... I really do not know when that came in. It even might have been my own conclusion. It took a long time before we knew for certain. The story just grew.'

After 72 laps Stewart was flagged off the victor, but his face on the rostrum betrayed no satisfaction or elation even though, with 26 wins, he had now moved ahead of his late fellow countryman Jimmy Clark as the Formula One record-holder. His face was the same mask that Jochen Rindt's had been three years earlier when he had learned in his moment of victory of his friend Piers Courage's death. Van Lennep's return netted him a World Championship point for sixth place, but that mattered little to Dutch television reporter Frans Henrichs who had the unenviable task of reporting the tragedy to his viewers. The Dutch driver cursed when he received the news of the man to whom he had spoken on the grid. 'Goddamn! But I have seen him getting out of his car!' Henrichs told him that it was, in fact, Purley he had seen.

Many other drivers made the same mistake, whizzing past the scene with that truncated clock time, as Stewart put it. Such was the level of their concentration and their focus on the right-hand side of the track where all the action was going on, that most of them did not take on board Purley's abandoned March on the left-hand side, let alone connect it with the upturned wreckage 200 metres further on.

'I remember very well the car lying upturned to the inside of that corner,' said Niki Lauda in 2003, long after he had won his three world crowns. 'You are concentrating, "Where can I go by?" Always you see David Purley, and you start to think, "Still there. Is that guy crazy? It's only a car. Leave it the hell alone and get out of the way." After a while you could drive flat out through there, no problem. No sticking throttle slides, nothing like that.

'There were a couple of unfair things. One was this Dutch arsehole who hassled me afterwards about why we didn't stop, and I explained to him that while we were driving by we couldn't see that Roger was in the car. We all just thought that Purley was trying to save his own car from burning. So nobody stopped. Nobody understood that somebody was still inside the burning car.

'I explained all this to this guy but he just never stopped, so in the end I told him to fuck off. Finally I said to him, "Look, I'm not here to be a fireman. I'm a racing driver, that's why I didn't stop." But of course when I said that I didn't know that Roger was dead. The bastard later made me seem very callous.

'Tom Wheatcroft was one hell of a guy and I knew him better than I knew Roger. But I thought Roger was a completely normal guy and absolutely a talented British driver.'

In the immediate aftermath recriminations flew, though, interestingly, Stewart, Huisman's declared enemy, says that he doesn't remember any of the arguments that followed even though they were highly acrimonious. It is likely that he simply switched off, compartmentalised his thinking.

'Keep in mind, in those days there was a lot of this going on. You just felt, "Not another one." I don't recall a shouting match. In my experience I don't think I ever saw that. Whether it was Jo Schlesser, or Piers, or any of the others. When you are driving the car there is no way you could make a judgement. You had such a short window of clock time when you were seeing any accident, and to make a song and dance about something you had such limited knowledge of wasn't my style. You didn't know what had caused the accident; you didn't know the circumstances. You had every right to ask, "Why did it not take a shorter time to get the fire put out?" but in those days these fires went on and on. Piers's car was still smouldering at the end of the race, and so was Roger's.'

Huisman knew he was in for a hard time, and first sought out the OCA track officials of Post 10. This was a sensible and understandable precaution, but what he did next speaks volumes about what was really going on in his head. When Brammer had given his account of what happened to him, Huisman made him sign a document promising not to speak of what he had seen. 'After 30 years we might have reached the term of limitation and therefore I speak about this for the first time,' Brammer told Nando Boers in 2003.

'Afterwards, colleagues wanted to talk,' he added. 'After the race I was pretty calm when I had left the circuit. Just like when you cut your fingers: first you do not feel any pain. But later... Eventually I could talk about it in a sensible manner, I had lost the panic I felt during the afternoon.'

A tent near the control tower became the platform for heated debate as drivers, team bosses and journalists gathered to confront the race directors. Huisman sat at a table and watched the angry scene unfold. 'It scared me,' he confessed to Boers, and who would not have felt fear in his position? 'Everybody ran in and out, there

Far too little, and far too late. The fire tender has finally arrived and the fire is doused. Purley's abandoned car can be seen to the right of the track.

In the immediate aftermath the March has at last been righted, and it is left to the gallant Purley to cover the smouldering wreckage with a sheet.

were heated discussions, people were calling each other names. I thought, "Where the hell am I?"' But then he added something that appears outrageously stupid. 'Everybody was shouting about Williamson, but the only one who knew him was me. Last year I had dinner with him in Hilversum. Denis Hulme, who called me nasty names, never met Williamson.'

Actually, Hulme had certainly met Roger at Silverstone earlier in the month, if not before. Hunt knew him, as did Purley and Mike Beuttler, and others. In the circumstances to have claimed some sort of

special friendship with Roger, to have effectively staked such a claim over Roger's fellow pilots, was simply crass.

Hulme was incensed by what had happened. As Huisman sought to absolve himself from failing to have the race stopped, or even knowing that anything untoward had happened, the gritty New Zealander roared, 'Bullshit! I let you know something was going on every time I drove by you.'

Hulme's team-mate, Peter Revson, who himself had less than a year to live, voiced the opinion that Roger would have had a chance had the race directors responded faster and more accurately and the race had been stopped so that his car could be turned back over. Some might see this as the drivers being wise after the event, and could argue that they could have stopped

themselves at any time, had they wished. But race-driving is like boxing: you have a job to do and you do it, either driving the car or punching the other guy, and you don't stop until a red flag or a chequered flag or a mechanical failure makes you, or until the referee intercedes.

Some time later, however, champion motorcyclist Mike Hailwood, who earlier that year had received the George Medal after saving Clay Regazzoni's life by dragging him from his blazing BRM in South Africa, made an emotional confession to Alan Henry. 'I've never forgiven myself for not stopping to help Roger that day,' said a man of rare class, honour and dignity. 'A lot of us thought of doing that, but the only one of us brave enough to actually do it was Purley.'

Hailwood was a most singular man.

After an hour the meeting finally broke up. Spleens had been vented and some very harsh things said, but none of it helped Roger Williamson or his shattered family, friends and team. 'It felt like a cold shower,' Huisman said. He left to go to Graham Hill's camper, where they drank beer together. Both of them were desperately tired and depressed. 'Not so good Ben,' said Hill quietly, the incident doubtless bringing back memories of all the horror and cruelty he had seen in his own lengthy career at the top. 'Not so good.'

Huisman left a few minutes later and headed out to Tunnel Oost, where he encountered a pensive Ronnie Peterson. Perhaps the Swede was trying to make his own sense of the tragedy. Huisman then headed back to his rented summerhouse on the boulevard in Tijn Akersloot, next to the beach.

CHAPTER 9

Aftermath

Zandvoort, 1973

'The only point I want to make is, and that was the whole issue back in 1973, we didn't give Roger Williamson a chance to survive. I was totally responsible.'

Ben Huisman

'We had taken the kids horse riding, just outside Leicester, when we got the phone call,' John Upton said. 'Normally, Roger would have been up there with us. There were a couple of horses up there, and one time he attempted to mount one when it didn't have a saddle. That was Roger... He was fearless. He'd have a go at anything.'

'We got the call from Tom Wheatcroft's secretary Anita,' Barbara Upton continued. 'She'd gone to mother's and phoned from there. Fortunately I don't think mum ever watched it on television. The first she knew about it was when Anita turned up at the house. Tom had called Anita from Holland, and they had a plan that if anything ever happened she was to go and tell mum. I suppose when you are in that sort of thing you have to be prepared for that... Dad, of course, was at Zandvoort.'

In another poignant touch, it was Charlie Purley who flew Dodge Williamson back from Holland. 'Dad was never the same after the accident,' Barbara said. 'Never the same...'

As Roger's girlfriend Jacqui Martin was being escorted from the track, Purley – left desolate by his sense of anger and frustration – departed for his hotel in Bloemendaal where Roger had also stayed. Later, Purley told Ian Phillips, 'I just couldn't turn the bloody car over. I could see Roger was alive and I could hear him shouting, "For God's sake get me out of here!" but I couldn't get the car over. I was trying to get people to help me, and if I could have turned the car over or even just lifted it a bit he would have been all right, we could have got him out.' Later, when the immediate grief

By irony, the cars of Roger and David Purley were lined up side by side in the paddock on race morning.

This Brunswick News photo is the only image that proved once and for all that Roger's accident was caused by tyre failure rather than driving error. The left-hand side of the March's nose is clearly damaged as the front left tyre begins to fail.

had receded, he admitted, 'I didn't even think about the heroism or any of that rubbish. I just did what comes naturally to a trained soldier who sees a fellow in trouble.'

Alan Henry remembered seeing Purley the following week, at the German Grand Prix at the Nürburgring. 'Purls just rolled his overalls down to his waist and undid the bandages on his arms. And it was just like that popper stuff that you wrap fragile things in nowadays. His arms were literally rippled all the way up to the inside of his elbows where he'd been pushing on the car, trying to lift it. All the blood vessels had popped in both of his arms.'

Briggs and the shattered March team set about clearing up, trying to do something to make sense out of something that had no sense.

Nick Jordan had left Wheatcroft to join Modus, after one clash too many with the volatile Dodge, and was watching Tony win the Formula Three race at Brands Hatch. 'Roger, James Hunt and Alan Jones were all pretty friendly; it was all good banter and we all travelled together. Somebody like Tom Pryce wasn't outside the loop, but he was quite introverted and kept himself to himself, while Tony was sort of a year behind. After the race Jonesy came up to me. "Come here," he says, and he put his arm round me. He took me along past the tower on to the grass banking as you go towards the tunnel. We walked down there, 40 yards or so, and then he said, "Sit down. I've got something to tell you. We knew before the race but we didn't want you to know." And I just burst into tears, I did – because I really loved the guy. I'll be totally frank and honest: Roger gave me a chance in motor racing that I'll always be grateful for.'

Ironically it seemed that Jackie Stewart, the man he

didn't like and the champion of safety, was the only one who understood Ben Huisman's predicament. The Scot did not believe the race should have been stopped. 'I don't think that was necessary,' he said 30 years later. 'Today the safety car would be sent on to the track. But today's drivers just don't understand how things were back then. We had to live with the knowledge that anything fatal could happen at any time, to anyone.'

Stewart was not being provocative, nor was he condoning in the slightest what had happened; he was simply refocusing the perspective.

Looking back from 30 years' distance, former March team principal Max Mosley, did not spare the organiser. 'You would have thought that with double-waved yellows, you would have made the original fire truck go back to the scene,' he said trenchantly. 'The whole thing was a cock-up that wouldn't happen today, because we have sensible people running the races, and sensible people in the medical and emergency cars. In the end it always comes down to the same thing: it's not the cause of an accident that matters, it's the consequence.

'Had the car not been upside down, Roger would have got out of it. The marshals were, I think, very cowardly. If that had happened opposite the pits, everybody would have turned it up the right way whether they were dressed properly or not. It was possible to do it.

'All the organisers did for Roger was to get the car back to the garage, then come to ask if a couple of us would go down and get his corpse out. That was their only real concern. It was all so unnecessary. It could and should have been avoided. Roger was a good driver, sensational. He would have been a big star.'

Mosley himself was not entirely blameless, however, according to Pete Briggs. 'Afterwards I was packing things up and there was a small television set; the accident suddenly came on that and I was there watching it, and Jacqui was standing right beside me...

'I had to tell Dodge and Tom what had happened. There I am in the middle of all this, and Max comes up and says, "Got to go. I'll leave it all to you..." We cleared everything up and had to go back a month later for the car after the police impounded it. I retired from racing for two years after that...'

Eventually, an official report confirmed what David Purley already knew. Roger had been alive and physically unharmed when the March came to rest.

A life, not to mention a brilliant career, was needlessly wasted through lack of vision, imagination, planning and preparation – and courage – on the part of men who saw only the fragment of what they wanted to see within the big picture.

Nigel Roebuck made an interesting observation. 'The height of irony was that when Lorenzo Bandini was killed at Monaco in 1967, the next race was held at

Zandvoort. And all the way round the circuit, if you look at the photos, there were marshals wearing these heavy silver suits as a reaction to what had happened to Bandini. Six years on, they had nothing...'

In the immediate aftermath, poor Tom Wheatcroft could not come to terms with his protégé's death. When he was asked to go to Haarlem to identify the body he understandably could not do so alone, and so sought Louis Stanley's help. As ever in such circumstances, the corpulent and florid BRM boss rose to the occasion. He was often seen as a pompous man and did little in his behaviour to temper such views, but in such situations he was peerless. BRM team manager Tim Parnell recalled. 'Big Lou had his chauffeur. At the end of the race Tom asked Big Lou, "Would you drive me to the hospital? Do you know where it is?"

'Whatever you say about Big Lou, he was absolutely brilliant at such times, getting injured drivers immediately to hospital or getting them back to England pretty rapidly, that sort of thing. You have to give great credit to him for that, and in this Zandvoort business he was remarkable.

'Big Lou said, "Yes, my car and chauffeur are at your disposal. Parnell, get in." We all climb in to this big Cadillac that took up half the BRM paddock space, and off we set. We get to the exit of the track, just before the main road, and there is a policeman directing all the traffic. Big Lou gets out: "Parnell, let us have a word to get the directions from this policeman." He speaks to this guy, who only speaks a little bit of English. It was almost impossible to follow his directions, so Big Lou puffed himself right up and said, "I am Lord Louis Stanley and we have had a serious incident here today with one of our drivers who is on the critical list, possibly beyond, and we want to get immediately to this hospital. Please get in the car and direct us to the hospital. I want you to come immediately." Blow me, this policeman climbs into this massive car, and off we went, leaving all the traffic snarled up. But there was nothing amusing about that day. Losing Roger was a great, great tragedy.'

Later that night, to compound Tom's awful burden – he kept asking himself over and over if the accident had in some way been his fault – the police came to arrest him. With car owner Max Mosley already on his way home, Wheatcroft was the focus of their attention. In Holland, as in Italy, the law requires a culprit whenever somebody dies in a racing car. Thanks to Purley's intervention, the British consul had Tom released and also helped with the sad details that lie beneath the surface of such accidents: the employment of an undertaker and the arrangements to get a body home.

Stewart had handled such thankless tasks after Piers Courage's death. His tale was another chilling reminder of the other side of the sport, of life. 'I was one of the few who knew what to do. Very few passenger airlines back then would accept coffins. We had to find out if they had to be zinc- or lead-lined. And there were only two or three undertakers in all of Europe who would do that. You had to have all of their numbers.'

Later, writing of that terrible day in his book *Grand Prix, The Legendary Years*, Stanley summarised the sheer horror of the tragedy with eye-stinging clarity. 'The mortuary was a simple building with a church-like atmosphere except that instead of an altar there was a coffin. The attendant gave me a key to unscrew one end and the lid was raised. If ever there was a condemnation of motor racing, it was there. Roger Williamson, in stained flame-resistant suit, had both hands raised before his face as if to fend off the approach of death. The instinctive urge was to take those outstretched hands and help him out. The formalities completed, the lid was screwed back. Roger Williamson was now only a name on the roll of motor racing victims.

'Back at the Bouwes Hotel everyone was excited over a championship victory, but that night, and ever since, I can see again the horror on the face of the young man who lay alone as others celebrated.'

Not since the death of Jim Clark at Hockenheim in April 1968, or the non-fatal but spectacular accidents to Graham Hill and Jochen Rindt at Montjuich Park a year later, had the sport been so forcibly confronted with its own inadequacies and the long overdue need for drastic change.

David Purley proudly raises the George Medal – the highest award for civilian bravery – after his heroic efforts to rescue Roger at Zandvoort.

Roger's needless death rightly provoked an outcry and an outpouring of emotion. Questions were even asked about the race in the Dutch Parliament.

This made absolutely no difference to the men who ran Zandvoort. A Formula 5000 race was run there in late September, only two months later. *Motoring News* ran a stinging editorial after complaints from drivers that there had been zero improvement in the organisation. When Teddy Pilette spun and came to rest in a potentially dangerous position, it was left to fellow driver Bob Evans, who had spun there earlier, to push him clear. There were no marshals, just a policeman and a small boy. The meeting was run by the same people who had run the grand prix. 'We had hoped to commend the organisation for raising its standards of marshalling in the ensuing weeks,' the paper said, 'but instead the marshals earned nothing but criticism throughout the meeting. They were, the drivers said, indecisive with their flag signals, unable to flag the correct car on every occasion, and didn't understand the proper use of flags anyway.'

The failure to learn any of the lessons from Roger's death was unforgivable.

By August, the GPDA, under the presidency of the vocal Denny Hulme who, like Jackie Stewart, had seen far too many friends die in racing, had acted. It appointed Stanley as director of circuit safety, with the power to withdraw drivers if tracks licensed to stage grands prix did not meet agreed safety standards.

The controversy this aroused was matched earlier in the month by Stanley's own well-intentioned proposal that all marshals at races should carry twin-pack fire extinguishers. The packs weighed 68 pounds, provoking a backlash from British marshals who pointed out how fit every man would have to be to wear them all day yet still be capable of fast intervention in the event of a similar tragedy to Zandvoort's. RAC researchers pointed out that they had already found such packs to be impractical. The GPDA, however, insisted that they should be mandatory from 1974 – even though, three months earlier, its own studies had suggested that Stanley's research, under the auspices of the Jo Siffert Advisory Council, was inferior to the RAC's.

Stanley told the media that his appointment had the blessing of Prince von Metternich, the president of the CSI, and intended to work closely with the governing body. 'We aim for very close co-operation with circuits and officials,' Stanley said. 'Most will be cooperative, I'm sure. But I fear that one or two circuit owners will suffer from, shall I say, a surfeit of national pride, and may resent our work. I hope this will not happen.'

Almost immediately RAC motorsport director Dean Delamont invited Hulme, Ken Tyrrell, McLaren's Teddy Mayer and Frank Dew from fire-fighting company Pyrene, to a high-powered meeting in Belgrave Square to review the situation.

The RAC had initiated research into fire-fighting procedures following Siffert's fatal crash at Brands Hatch in October 1971, and in conjunction with Pyrene had set out to find a system of fighting fires that would work and be practical for *all* circuits and *all* race meetings. After several months a detailed handbook was published by the RAC outlining the proposals, among them a 'two-by-two' system employing two lots of paired marshals, each with a suitable fire extinguisher.

At the same time Stanley had assembled a group of experts under the aegis of the Jo Siffert Advisory Council, with the same broad aim.

In March 1973, the Fire and Medical Safety Committee of the GPDA indicated that, having assessed proposals from all the groups concerned, it

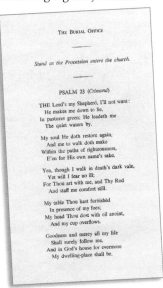

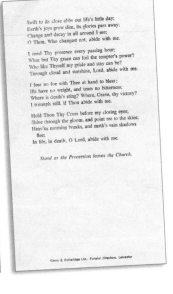

favoured the RAC's and recommended that its ideas be adopted by the CSI. They were practical, would not entail massive financial outlay for circuits, and could be used as effectively at a club race as at a grand prix.

Now, however, the GPDA was backing Stanley, to the disappointment of many others who had invested much time and effort into seeking a suitable fire-fighting solution.

The haggling was entirely well-meant, but perhaps missed the real crux of Roger's accident, which was not that fire-fighting methods per se needed improvement, but that Zandvoort's system had been so woefully inadequate and should never have been condoned by the CSI in the first place.

Meanwhile, at the Nürburgring during the German Grand Prix that followed a week after Zandvoort, David Purley was awarded the Prix Rouge et Blanc Joseph Siffert from Bernard Cahier, president of the International Racing Press Association, in honour of the fighting spirit that Siffert had shown prior to his untimely death.

In August, Tony Salmon, on behalf of the British Racing Drivers' Club and as a mark of respect from followers of motorsport worldwide, made a special award to Purley at the Radio Luxembourg meeting at Brands Hatch, and later the British Automobile Racing Club awarded him its Browning Medal in recognition of his valour.

Subsequently, he was also awarded the George Medal, the highest civilian recognition for bravery. Greg Field, who went on to work for the Onyx, Lotus and Benetton Formula One teams, met him in 1969 and worked for his Lec Racing operation from 1973 to the end of 1976. 'To be honest, he quite liked all the attention after that,' Field said, though Purley always maintained it was his paratrooper training that kicked in when he saw a fellow racer in trouble, and that he remembered little of his actions until the immediate, poignant aftermath. 'He used to scoff at the GM, and we used to kid him it meant Gaberdine Mac, and that he was a dirty old man! Once it had all settled down, though, he'd sign his name, David Purley, GM.'

Later in August, Delamont, with the express permission of the CSI, announced several recommendations arising from Zandvoort. 'A review of fire-fighting measures on international circuits will be carried out,' he said, 'and, as part of this, copies of the RAC's fire-fighting manual have been sent to other grand prix organisers.' Stanley's controversial twin-pack extinguishers had quietly been forgotten.

Delamont also announced that in the event of further serious accidents, a pace car would be deployed from the pits immediately, to pick up the race leader and slow the field during fire-fighting and rescue operations. It was an adoption of the system used for many years in American racing, and though the first use of it would prove to be disastrous in Canada later that year, it was a sensible step and one that could have saved Roger's life had it been in effect at Zandvoort.

It was also agreed that henceforth all Formula One grids would be lined up on the two-by-two system that is so familiar today (albeit side by side rather than staggered), and that only race organisers and team personnel would be allowed in the pits during practice, qualifying and races.

A year after the tragedy, Tom Wheatcroft was finally shown a copy of the official report by Mr Ryshouwer, the official Dutch delegate to the International Technical Commission of the CSI. It completely exonerated Roger of any driving error, and confirmed that tyre failure was the initial cause of the accident. It stated that the left front tyre deflated 'immediately', causing the March to veer 15 degrees off course and into contact, first with the concrete kerb on the outside of the corner, and thence with the steel barriers. It further found that the barriers had not been installed correctly and that as a result they bent backwards under the weight of the impact and acted as a launching ramp.

The investigators found that the car's throttle was jammed open, and confirmed that this was as a consequence of the 140mph impact rather than the cause of it.

By far the most damning evidence in the report, however, concerned the cause of death. In the immediate aftermath the Dutch authorities had circulated information that Roger had died virtually on impact. Purley was vehemently able to deny that deliberate misinformation, having been the only man to get close enough to the burning car to hear Roger shouting from the cockpit. But now the report confirmed that he had sustained no physical injuries whatsoever and had died from the inhalation of hot gases.

'That proved that he must have been alive for at least three minutes, which points the blame at the marshalling as they had ample time in which to put the fire out,' Wheatcroft said.

The Williamson tragedy struck a shattering blow against Jackie Stewart's safety crusade, but ultimately it led to better fire-fighting techniques, better equipment and greater safety measures. All of that came far too late for Roger, but his brutal passing was the catalyst for change.

In 2003, Dutch journalist Nando Boers interviewed Ben Huisman for a documentary programme commemorating the 30th anniversary of the tragedy.

Boers asked Huisman whether Stewart had ultimately been right about all the extra work that still needed doing to the circuit that he had saved. 'He felt that a lot had still to be done,' Huisman replied, before admitting, 'In hindsight... let's put it this way: remember the 2003 Grand Prix of Brazil, with that rain? You cannot say, "They had to stop the race." I say, just like Allard Kalff on Dutch television, "If you can't stop, you can always go slower."

'The only point I want to make is, and that was the whole issue back in 1973, we didn't give Roger Williamson a chance to survive. I was totally responsible. When someone died in grand prix racing in 1973 it was nothing out of the ordinary. But on that circuit, on that particular spot, the chances to survive a crash were virtually nil. That is the sole criterion. Nowadays you have to make sure that such a chance exists. You have to run into a patch of really bad luck when you kill yourself on the track. In those days you were lucky when you didn't.'

Boers then began to press his questioning, beginning with the eighth lap.

Huisman: 'We see smoke, but don't hear anything. Perhaps someone had set fire to some tyres or something like that. We said, "Can't be that important as the lap times are still the same."'

Boers: 'Who saw the smoke first?'

Huisman: 'Someone might have yelled, "Look, smoke!" Then we started to analyse: Any news from a marshal post? No. I climbed the ladder. "Have you heard anything?" "No." Well, it might be something back in the woods. Lap times? Anyone entering the pit lane? Must be a fluke.'

Boers: 'But, there are enormous clouds of smoke, and you think it is a small fire with tyres...?'

Huisman: 'Yes, something like that. We were not thinking of the race itself.'

Boers: 'Never one thought...?'

Huisman: 'No, nothing could happen on our circuit. We did build a safe circuit. What could happen on our circuit?'

Boers: 'Weren't you a little bit naive?'

Huisman: 'Yes, I think so. Without a doubt. Nothing could happen. But then it sinks in: something is wrong.'

Boers: 'Who reported that?'

Huisman: 'The marshals.'

Boers: 'It fits in your story that no-one is aware of anything at the timekeeping office...?'

Huisman: 'We were unaware, and then we found out...'

Boers: 'When was that?'

Huisman: 'During lap 20 we thought, "Something is wrong."'

Boers: 'Because there was still smoke?'

Huisman: 'Then we sent the fire truck.'

Boers: 'How is it possible that a race director decides, "It's early in the race, the race can go on." Was that normal in those days?'

Huisman: 'Listen, there are three reasons: we had no information that something serious had happened and, secondly, how do you get everything going again? That would not have been easy with 70,000 spectators. After consulting the sports commission I decided, "I will not stop the race." And, third and above all, lap times did not decline.'

Was Huisman solely looking at Ronnie Peterson's times? Remember how Gijs van Lennep accused the Swede of going through the accident zone at scarcely abated speed?

Boers: 'But you missed two cars?'

Huisman: 'If there would be crashed cars on the track, you must lower speed. But there was no reason for it. They all drove with the same speed. And what I never understood is that not a single driver entered the pit lane wondering why no action was taken.'

Boers: 'How do you look back at this period?'

Huisman: 'In hindsight we described it as a Titanic experience. It is a new ship which is unsinkable. Hadn't we built a new circuit, the safest of all? I think this is a black page in my book. Perhaps I have saved some lives another time as well.'

Boers: 'Do you still think of it?'

Huisman: 'Yes. Man can't determine his own destiny. It proves that it is impossible to have everything under control. It depends on so many elements but people expected me to control them all. You will not hear me say, "Not my fault." No. The others were not to blame.'

Boers: 'Did you have sleepless nights?'

Huisman: 'Might have. Roger Williamson was still young and we took away his chance to live a normal life. And he was a nice young man, too.'

Boers did not shy away from asking Herman Brammer the hardest question. Did he feel, at any time, any responsibility for Roger Williamson's death? 'No,' the marshal replied, 'I have always been thinking Roger was dead when his upside-down car hit the track. I do not feel responsible.' Sadly, however, Roger was very much alive as his car burned.

In July 2003, Huisman travelled with the Dutch television crew to Donington, where Tom Wheatcroft unveiled David Annand's statue of Roger. Jacqui Martin, now Jacqui Hamilton, was also there.

'I did talk to him, even if only very briefly,' she said. 'I thought the fact that he was there was actually quite nice. I suppose it was laying a ghost for him.'

Tom Wheatcroft was not told of Huisman's presence until after the elderly Dutchman had left. Writing in his autobiography *Thunder In The Park* in 2005, Wheatcroft said, 'It had been a highly emotional day and even after all those years I don't think I could have found forgiveness in my heart.'

DEFINITION OF A HERO

David Purley

'I floated down from 10,000 feet on top of his 'chute, looking through the hole in the centre at his tin hat. If I'd chosen to scramble off the edge and my tangled 'chute hadn't opened, I'd have been a goner.' – David Purley

No account of the career of Roger Williamson could ever be complete without the story of David Purley, a racer of the old school and a man of unimpeachable courage.

Purley was a maverick, a man's man and a husband's nightmare. He lived – and raced – on his own terms. He detested the drudgery of testing, and was attracted only to the adrenaline rush of wheel-to-wheel combat. He loved the inherent risk. That was small wonder, given his remarkable background.

He was expelled from his progressive co-educational school because, as he once told Alan Henry for *Motoring News*, 'An alarm clock failed to go off when it should have'.

Having arrived in the world shortly after the cessation of World War Two, Purley found himself working in the vehicle maintenance depot at Lec Refrigeration, the company his father had formed after moving out of fishmongering.

'We'd got one lorry and one shop on the seafront,' Purley said, 'but just to keep the right image dad painted number 17 on the front of the truck, then repainted it every other week to give the impression that we'd got a fleet of them!'

When he was 17 Purley was, for a time, the nation's youngest pilot but offended authority when he buzzed the seafront at Bognor. Subsequently he became the company pilot. 'I chose that for two reasons,' he admitted. 'I might mature a bit quicker, and I might avoid killing myself!'

Father and son had a turbulent relationship, and one day when he and Charlie had one of their clashes of temperaments he stormed off to London on his motorbike. There he worked for six months on a demolition site before, despite his £48 weekly stipend, he enlisted on a whim for the Coldstream Guards. 'The winter came and I reckoned that perhaps demolition work wasn't such a good idea after all. So there I was, driving along the Chiswick High Road when I saw this Army Information Centre. I went straight in and joined up.'

He went up to Sandhurst within a year and was clearly officer material. Before long, he found himself enjoying two years of adventure-packed service, six months of that in troubled Aden.

He liked to tell the story of a landmine there which

David Purley: former paratrooper, company director, racing driver and thrill seeker.

destroyed the armoured car he was in, killing six of his companions. He was unscathed. On another occasion, his parachute failed to open on one drop, and he floated down atop his NCO's inflated 'chute. Purley escaped with a broken ankle while the unfortunate recipient of his hitch-hiking was knocked unconscious.

'I was the first jump on the port side and my platoon sergeant was first on the starboard,' he relayed. 'Unfortunately, we hadn't mastered the technique of jumping from a Hercules and we collided under the belly of the aircraft. My parachute got tangled up and I floated down from 10,000 feet on top of his 'chute, looking through the hole in the centre at his tin hat. If I'd chosen to scramble off the edge and my tangled 'chute hadn't opened, I'd have been a goner.'

Even then some might have accused him of having a death wish, but Purley simply loved living his life to the full. After discovering the camaraderie and challenge of motor racing through his friend Derek Bell, he bought himself out of the Army in 1968, invested in a Datsun dealership in Middleton-on-Sea, and somewhat predictably chose a brute of a racing car: a big blue AC Cobra which he eventually reduced to component parts in a huge accident at Paddock Bend at Brands Hatch. He replaced the Cobra with one of Derek Bennett's new Chevron B8 sportscars before switching to single-seaters, first with a Formula Three Brabham BT28 and then an Ensign. He was widely regarded as a rich kid with

Purley began single-seater racing in 1970 with this Brabham BT28. He twice won the challenging Grand Prix des Frontieres in Chimay with it.

expensive toys, but he raced strongly against the Williamsons, Brises, Pryces and Hunts.

There was a circuit called Chimay which nestled on the border of France and south-west Belgium. It was not one of those that grabbed the imagination and the headlines in the manner of the old Nürburgring, the old Spa-Francorchamps, Rouen or Clermont-Ferrand. But it was David Purley's personal fiefdom.

Chimay ran clockwise over a 6.75-mile lap through the north edge of town and then out into the countryside via a series of fast sweeps and flat-out curves, culminating in a dangerous high-speed plunge downhill on the main Beaumont to Chimay road. The GP des Frontieres was held annually for Formula Three cars, and was a flat-out blind slipstreamer in which only the brave stood a chance. Between 1970 and 1972, Purley reigned supreme. In 1970 and '71 he beat James Hunt, in 1972, Tony. He was braver than Dick Tracy, but you didn't beat drivers of Tony's calibre, or James's, without having plenty of natural flair, too.

Chimay epitomised everything that Purley held dear about racing. There was none of the exotic veneer of Monaco, nor the sterility of nearby Nivelles. It was a place for unadulterated motor racing, like it had been in the fifties when Purley was growing up. He would probably have fitted best into that bygone era, as a swashbuckling privateer. It was a place where you pushed the risk as hard as you dared, knowing that mistakes exacted the highest price. Purley was quite happy with that deal.

He won the odd race besides Chimay, and set fastest lap in his heat (and overall because the final was wet) at Monaco in 1972. But it had not been until he made his

Formula Two début in his private March 722 at Oulton Park earlier that year, and put it on pole position ahead of the emergent Niki Lauda, or later lost the 1973 Formula Atlantic title only after mechanical failure in the final round, that the racing world began to see him in a different light.

'He was born 20 years too late,' suggested Mike Earle, his friend who ran his cars for him. 'He would have been the ideal fifties driver. He would sit in the bar all night, literally, drinking and drinking, and tip up the next morning, all bright. "Okay chaps? Right, let's go!" He used to love it. Absolutely *love* it!

'What was good about him was that he was frightened of no-one. He just had that about him. It didn't matter who it was. If someone told him it couldn't be done, he'd just go and do it.'

For his bravery at Zandvoort, Purley was awarded the George Medal, the highest civilian award for gallantry. As Tom Wheatcroft said, 'I liked him as a fella. You couldn't have got a nicer fella than David.'

In an interview with Nigel Roebuck in *Autosport* in 1976, Purley talked about that day at Zandvoort. 'What happened was purely a reflex action. In Aden, if one saw a burning tank or something, one tried to help the people inside. With Roger's accident, it was exactly the same. It was a case of a man needing help. I have no recollection of it at all; I don't remember stopping the car, getting out, running across the road, or anything. I can remember trying to get the marshals to help. Afterwards I said some pretty nasty things about them, but they simply weren't equipped to deal with the situation. I mean, one of them was wearing a plastic mac. Now, if he goes near that car, he's dead, isn't he?

Much was made by the national media of the close friendship between Roger and David, but as this drivers' briefing photo from Oulton Park suggests, they knew one another socially without being bosom buddies.

The people who *did* have the right equipment were 200 yards up the road. This is where I do hold strong views on safety. If a man does have an accident, then he should have the right to expect that everything possible will be done for him, and as soon as possible.'

One of the saddest aspects of Roger's tragedy was that not even a man of Purley's extraordinary calibre, the bravest of the brave, could rescue him.

See also 'Life as a Lion', page 260.

Purley was always super-fit. Here at Monza in 1973 he chases Frank Williams and James Hunt in a running race round the track.

CHAPTER 10

The women they loved

'I think the problem that I had, if I'm actually honest, is that I was very, very, very much in love with him.'
Jacqui Martin

'I always thought that was very attractive, and that people who were quite shy often had more to them, hidden away.'
Nella Pryce

'My cousin Richard wasn't quite sure whether Tony was right for me! It took him three weeks to get my telephone number!'
Janet Brise

It provides an interesting insight into the 'Lost Generation' that all three drivers had steady relationships in their lives.

Roger met Rosalyn Bates at a dance in 1967 when they were both 19. Affectionately, he used to call her 'Smells'. For a time they shared a rented house in Stoneygate in Leicester, and had an on-off engagement. Rosalyn was keen to get married, but each time she pushed, Roger demurred, saying, 'I wouldn't think of getting married while I'm a racing driver. It wouldn't be fair.'

The first time they broke up was in 1971, but they stayed in touch and Nick Jordan, Roger's mechanic who rented a room from them, remembers her still being on the scene in mid-1972. 'I got pretty friendly with Roger. I lived in Maidenhead at the time, in bedsitter-land, which was fairly rough for my wife Irene as we were newly married. Then we moved up to Leicester, and I

MGB and silly string: Jan and Tony prepare to escape in their going away clothes after their wedding on 29 June 1974.

ABOVE: *Baby Roger, aged six months, is fussed over by sisters Barbara (14, with bow) and Nola (15).*

BELOW: *Roger and his first love, Rosalyn Bates, photographed in 1969.*

OPPOSITE PAGE: *Roger found plenty to laugh about with his new girlfriend, Jacqui Martin, at Nivelles in 1973, even if his GRD's on-track performance left much to be desired.*

lived with Roger and Rosalyn, number 27 Stoneygate Road, I think it was. I seem to remember that she then went off with another driver, after she and Roger finally split up around May that year.' Thereafter, she decamped for a new life in Spain's Playa de Aro.

'Ros really wanted to get married,' Roger's sister Barbara confirmed, 'but Roger wouldn't because of the life he was leading. He didn't want to commit himself while he was racing, and I think Tom warned him off it as well! Dad didn't like him having a girlfriend either, because it was a distraction!'

It was during one of their periods of estrangement that Roger met a vivacious brunette called Jacqui Martin.

'It was all Ian Phillips's fault!' she recalled with a chuckle more than three decades later. 'In 1972, I had a promotions company employing girls to do exhibitions, working on stands, laying bodies across cars. One of my clients was Haymarket and I used to supply girls for the stands at their different exhibitions. *Autosport* had one at the Racing Car Show.

'The first day I was there making sure everything was all right, and this very scruffy guy in a velvet suit, looking as though he had just got out of bed, walked on to the stand. Mr Phillips. I said, "Who the hell are you?" And he said, "Well, who the hell are you?" That's what started our enduring friendship!

'It was at that show that he introduced me to Roger. It was January. After the second day Roger said to me, "Right, I'm off to Brazil, come with me."'

'I couldn't go because I was working. I just said, "Don't be ridiculous!" But he insisted, "I want you to come with me." But I didn't go. I kicked myself, because I'd never been to South America. Then, when he came back, he'd just bought a house in Markfield. He was terribly chuffed about it, "I can do what I like now," sort of thing.

'He sort of had a girlfriend, Ros, but it was an on-off thing. I was living at the time with my parents in Bedford, so it was only a hop, skip and a jump up the motorway to Leicester. Every time Roger went to a race he said, "Oh, come with me," so we had a laugh and a giggle, and stayed in all sorts of weird and wonderful hotels. I was always interested in motor racing because my father used to take me to Goodwood.'

Roger knew that Rosalyn had distrusted racing, and went to some lengths to alleviate any fears Jacqui harboured. 'Every time we used to go to a circuit, when he was doing Formula Three and Formula Two, Roger used to get a car and say, "Right, I'm taking you round the track so you know what's going on." And he'd start off at 40 miles an hour, and build up speed until you got to the point where you were hanging on. It terrified the life out of me in a way, but I always felt incredibly safe. There was something about the way he drove.

'Now this is pure sentimentality. Basically, I'm quite

tall; if I wear heels, I'm six foot. And Roger wasn't actually that tall, only five-eight. So really he wasn't the sort of person I'd be attracted to because I like to look up at somebody, or at least look them in the eye. But there was something charming about Roger that made me think, "Oh, he's lovely." And one of the things that made me fall for him – and I don't know how to put this without sounding rude – was that when he drove the one thing that fascinated me was his hands. It's not supposed to sound sexual, but it is. The way he used to caress the steering wheel… There was something about it that actually fascinated me, and was very sexy. It was quite a turn-on, really, especially when he was driving very fast.

'The other thing that was nice about Roger was that he didn't have any enemies. He would always talk to anyone, but especially people he'd met before, even just once. He remembered people from his past, from the Anglia days, even from karting. Nobody could not like him. You didn't have to be bosom pals or anything, but you know what I mean.'

Much media fuss was made in the aftermath of Zandvoort of the great Mike Hawthorn-Peter Collins 'Mon Ami Mate' type of friendship between Roger and David Purley. Nick Jordan and Jacqui Hamilton put that into better perspective.

Jacqui (sitting, left of the picture) listens as Roger and John Macdonald share a joke with a visitor at Rouen.

'David was doing a Formula Two race and so were we, with the March, and David needed an engine,' Jordan said. 'He drove up from Bognor Regis and we loaded our engine into the back of David's car. And it was, "Well, Roger, how are we going to work this deal?" And Roger just said, "Don't worry, David, just give me the engine back in one piece and we'll work something out." It was a kind of gentlemanly between the two of them. I don't think they were close friends, but they were mates and there was a respect there from each other.'

'They weren't great mates, but each was a friend,' Jacqui confirmed. 'They would have a drink together, that sort of thing. The trouble is, David always used to come on to me, and that used to get Roger really uptight! But then David would come on to anybody, so it wasn't exactly very flattering to me.'

It took a lot to annoy Roger, unlike his father. 'Any time he was taken out or couldn't finish, couldn't still be out there, he wasn't happy,' Jacqui continued. 'But he didn't sulk, he didn't go round kicking things, stamping his foot. He just went very quiet, and it would take a day, then he'd be back to being Roger. He had a very silly, but nice, sense of humour. Obviously Ian was around and he was such a good mate, of mine and Roger's. There were quite a few times when Roger had gone off to a race and I'd drive out there with Ian; we had some great laughs together. Tom Wheatcroft used to make me laugh, too.'

Soon Roger and Jacqui were an item, but in some ways they were an odd couple, the little racing driver from a mechanic's background and the daughter of a quite well-to-do family. 'He was in many respects quite shy,' Jacqui said. 'I don't think he could quite make out why I liked him. This is not trying to blow my own trumpet because I don't mean it that way, but I was more sophisticated than he was, and I had a completely different lifestyle and had been brought up in a completely different way. And he couldn't understand why I fell madly in love with him. There were silly things. I've always liked red wine, and when we used to go out for a meal he'd say, "I suppose you want some of that red stuff?" He rarely drank wine, but if he had some he'd say, "Hmm, it's not bad, is it?" He was never a great drinker, and he always used to tease me and say, "You'd better choose the wine, I haven't got a bloody clue what I'm doing!"'

Then there was the flat cap, which appeared sometime in 1972. It was better than the old trilby he used to wear in the Anglia days. Roger was completely and utterly unpretentious by nature, but Jacqui recalled, 'He used to wear that hat. He said, "You've got to have a gimmick, something that people recognise you by," and as soon as the helmet came off at a track, the hat went on. It suited him down to the ground. So he was image-conscious the more he mixed in the Formula Two and

Formula One milieu, conscious of other people having a certain style. I think it was also a bit of a lucky charm.'

Jacqui does not mind talking about that day at Zandvoort now, but admitted that it took her many years before she was ready. One of her memories was of the trip out, when Alan Henry saw her and Roger on the ferry. 'Oh yes!' she laughed. 'And we sneakily got a cabin and got up to no good! Why not?' Looking back, that little moment of stolen fun takes on greater poignancy.

'The morning of the race Roger was off somewhere and a certain gentleman (Mr Purley) came on to me. "When you get back to the UK, do you want to come out for a drink?" I said, "I don't think so!" I liked him, don't get me wrong, but...

'Another thing I remember: it was the most fantastic day, really sunny. It was beautiful. Everybody was happy. Okay, he was never going to win in that car, but things were all right.

'I watched the start at the first corner, then I said I'd have a better view watching it on the 'box' in the transporter. We saw the smoke, but there wasn't a television camera round that side so nobody knew what had happened. I just sat there, and we didn't think anything bad about it. But then somebody said, "It looks like Roger's car." Even then they didn't know exactly what had happened. Okay, we knew there had been an accident, and obviously it was a fairly major one, but it wasn't until later that we understood.

'I went to the pits, and they really didn't know properly. The communication system wasn't great. Then suddenly it all came out, and I don't remember very much after that, apart from the fact that they said it was Roger and it didn't look as though he was alive. Then they took me back to the transporter and said "Sorry", and all I can remember was being totally and utterly numb. Somebody said, "Right, we need to get you out of this as soon as possible." I was bundled into a taxi and taken to the airport. Somebody phoned my father, to make sure he was at Heathrow to pick me up. The airline put me in first class so they obviously knew, and they said, "There won't be anybody sitting next to you." I got to the other end and my ex-boyfriend was there with my father. I just went home to my parents – I couldn't go back to my flat in London.

'Then, of course, it was like a four-day wonder in the newspaper. Everywhere you looked, whenever you turned the television on or whatever, it was there. And I just remember seeing all these pictures and thinking, "That isn't real. That isn't Roger."

'Looking back, it was the stupidity of it. A fire tender wasn't allowed to go against the traffic. I mean, how daft was that? I couldn't understand why the guy in the fire vehicle didn't just say, "Excuse me, but sod it, there's somebody in that car! There's somebody's life at stake."'

Sometimes, she admitted, she torments herself watching

Nella Warwick-Smith was initially very camera shy! Behind her is Tom's prized blue MGB. Enjoying the success of her nursing home venture, his mother Gwyn took him to see the car in the showroom, and only when he said how much he liked it told him that it was already his...

old films such as *Grand Prix*. 'It was over the top, with lots of accidents; you watch them and you feel masochistic in a way. That was a bloody good film, but on the other hand it always used to make me cry. And I thought, "You're doing this and you're stupid". Which I am.'

She also admitted that even now she will walk down a street and suddenly catch a glimpse of somebody who resembles Roger. 'And it's stupid, because you just know they are not around. One side of your brain says, "Don't be stupid," while the other side says, "It's what you've been waiting for."'

Sometime in the months after Zandvoort, or perhaps Monza, which was scheduled to be his final Formula One outing that year, when the time was right Roger had planned to start looking for engagement rings. It seemed he had changed his mind about permanent attachment as a race driver. 'I didn't say no!' Jacqui smiled. 'And, of course, it never happened...'

She had not watched the harrowing footage from Zandvoort for many years, but did so via the tape of Nando Boers' Dutch documentary. 'It was unreal, it wasn't anything to do with Roger. I know that sounds bizarre, but I was three steps away from it. I don't think I will ever watch it again. I think the problem that I had, if I'm actually honest, is that I was very, very, very much in love with him. But I do not know, and I will never know, where we would have gone. Subsequent men in my life have said, "The trouble is that you had the most fantastic relationship, nothing bad in it at all, so it's always going to be top of your list as a relationship because it was killed off when it was absolutely brilliant." I mean, we never had a chance to have an argument, to disagree about things. If I say perfect that's a bit over the top because nothing is perfect, but it was fantastic. I think to myself, "Okay, what would have happened if we'd stayed together? Would our different backgrounds have made a difference?"

'The worst thing, after Roger being killed, of course, was that he had always said to me, "The one thing I actually fear more than anything else is being burned alive." He didn't have nightmares about it, but he used to wake up every now and again saying, "This is what I just dreamed." Which is a bit spooky.'

Jordan, who together with Tony Trimmer, Peter Williams and James Hunt had been a pallbearer on 3 August at Saint Gabriel's Church in Leicester, and when Roger was cremated at Gilroes Crematorium, confirmed that story. 'Roger said to me, "If I die in a racing car, Nick, I don't wanna be burned." And that is absolutely true.'

Jacqui continued to go to motor races. Phillips took her to Pau one year, deliberately choosing somewhere that had no history for her. Fellow *Autosport* writer and

Tom married Fenella Warwick-Smith, whom he had met in 1973, at St Bartholomew's Church in Otford on 5 April 1975. They had their honeymoon in Malaga, to fit in with the Spanish Grand Prix later that month.

friend Chris Witty was there too. 'I couldn't go to a circuit I'd been with Roger, but I had to do it, I had to lay a ghost. Ian and Chris were fantastic. The three of us drove down. The days at the races were very different for me, I must admit. But I felt I had to do it.'

It was worse when, inadvertently, she found herself back at Zandvoort almost 20 years later. 'My husband, Derek, was involved with a Dutch company. We were in Amsterdam. And being there was fine. Then somebody suggested going down to the beach. The guy who was running the company over there didn't know anything about my history, and too late I suddenly realised where we were going. According to Derek, when I realised that I dug my nails into his palm so hard his hand was bleeding. I just kept thinking, "I've got to get through this. I can't make a fuss." If I'd known to begin with where we were going, I probably wouldn't have gone, but going there probably *was* a good thing.'

She attended the memorial ceremony at Donington, 30 years on, but admitted, 'I just couldn't bring myself to go into the museum.' Three of Roger's cars remain there on permanent display.

Another attractive quality, according to Jacqui, was Roger's determination. That was tested to its limit at Rouen in 1973 when his friend Gerry Birrell was killed during practice in a horrible accident on the fast descent to the Nouveau Monde hairpin. There were protests over safety from many drivers, and the organisers erected makeshift chicanes to placate them. Jacqui smiled quietly at that recollection. 'Roger said, "I'm not going to protest. I don't care if I'm the only one on the grid, I'm going to be there. I want to be in that race and I want to win." And Gerry had been one of his great mates. Basically, Roger had the killer instinct, which I think you've got to have, and which, with the best will in the world, some of them don't have.'

So did she think he could have made it all the way? 'I think so, yes. If he didn't it wouldn't be because he didn't try, or because he didn't have the determination. It's rather like... this may not be a good analogy but it is to me: Tim Henman is a good tennis player, but he will never, ever win Wimbledon – because he doesn't have the killer instinct. Roger always had that. Not so much off the track, where he was wonderful company, but on it he was there to win. End of story.'

Of all the places that two such fundamentally shy people should meet, a discotheque had to be the most unlikely for Tom Pryce and Fenella Warwick-Smith.

Nella came from a well-to-do family who lived in a large house in Otford. Her father, Miles, was the managing director of the London Rubber Company.

'In 1973, I'd gone to this disco with some friends and so had Thomas,' Nella recalled in 2006. 'He came over and asked me if I'd like a drink, and we got talking. When I asked him what he did, he said he worked with cars. He never said that he was a racing driver, and I thought that was rather nice. He was quite shy. I always thought that was very attractive, and that people who were quite shy often had more to them, hidden away. I was painfully shy myself then.'

Jorge Koechlin was with Tom when he met Nella. 'The disco was in The Mill, a very nice posh pub in Otford. Thomas was very shy and I wasn't, and there were these two nice young girls there. I said, "Let's see what we can do here." It was Nella and her sister Penny. Thomas took a clear liking to Nella, and I to Penny. That's how it happened between them.'

Nella was going out with somebody else at the time, but soon acknowledged that this was the real thing with Tom. 'I'm afraid they were very soon dropped!' she admitted with a rueful laugh.

By the middle of the year she was going to races with him. It was a totally alien world for her, but they made a handsome couple. 'When they were together, they looked *together*,' Cledwyn Ashford thought. 'Sounds daft, I know, but you know what I mean? They were very close, but none of this showing off: "This is Tom Pryce." No chance. She would have done anything for her and him to go out quietly for a walk, have a meal, and for nobody to know.'

Nella complemented Tom, and vice versa.

Looking back at old video footage, Tom then had the appearance of a better-looking and smarter Bob Geldof, with his unruly hair, while Nella had the quality of Princess Diana's up-from-under expression in her evident shyness. 'Maldwyn was a very good-looking lad,' Cledwyn said. 'He had film star looks, but he never, ever played on that. That was the last thing on his mind.'

'Nella didn't like racing,' Alan Henry said. 'I always interpreted it that she thought it was a phase he'd get through. I never thought that Nella believed this was going to be something that lasted forever. I always thought she believed Tom would do racing for a bit and then he'd do something else and he'd get away from it. I think it frightened her.

'She was an affectionate, nice girl but very cool. I won't say that she was in any way haughty, but she was very self-contained and independent, and they liked their own company. I think she was ambitious for Tom but protective of him too, in the sense that she didn't really like him racing.'

Nella herself explained her feelings. 'I did distrust racing. It wasn't my world. Put yourself in the horse world, which was my world, and then you are suddenly put into this other world. I could see its appeal, but it was just so different for me; and, don't forget, I was very, very young and very, very shy. I'd just met Thomas. Once we'd got married (in 1975) and I was going to grands prix, we were living together for the

An incognito Tom with Nella in her equine world, and her Shetland pony 'Tomboy'.

first time, and we seemed to spend all our time with these other people who wanted to talk about motor racing all night. It was actually quite boring for me. I just wanted to be with Thomas.'

They set up home together in a beautiful oast house in Ightham, five miles away from Brands Hatch.

'Thomas was quite a calm, steady sort of person,' said Nella, 'good sense of humour, always laughing about things, seeing the funny side. He'd sometimes point someone out to me who was doing something funny without realising it. He was quite shy but he didn't want to have people around him that he didn't like. He didn't suffer fools gladly. And good for him, why should he? He was very easy-going. He didn't really get angry at all. I don't really think he had enough time to show the way he was. He was quite quiet, very self-effacing, not a show-off at all. When he got home from grand prix races he liked to be home.'

In his interview with Henry, Tom said that often when he was away at races all he was thinking about at times was getting back to Ightham with Nella. Theirs was an uncomplicated, loving relationship in which each was sufficient for the other.

'We'd go off for walks, we'd go to the local pub, I would be doing quite a lot of riding. Thomas was very interested in photography, he used to take photographs of the countryside and me riding, that sort of thing. He liked that lifestyle. He didn't want to be out at nightclubs. The first year we were married we had some good friends in London and we used to spend a lot of time up there going out to various restaurants. And then I said to him, "We are spending a fortune doing this and we're always up in London." We'd both really had enough of it so we didn't do it any more. We changed a bit and stuck more with the things we liked doing together, which was basically being in the countryside.'

Nella hit it off straight away with Gwyneth and Jack Pryce. 'When I first met her, she'd had cancer. She was getting over an operation. She's been fine ever since. But she had been very ill, and there she was, running a private nursing home. Thomas took me to meet her, and she teased the life out of me. I was painfully shy with her, and I had a pair of jeans on and an orange jumper with a hole in it, I was quite scruffy. And she said, "Oh, my goodness, couldn't you even have mended that hole? Look at it!" She really took the mickey out of me. I instantly liked her, because she was such good fun.

'They are lovely people, they are still my family and, in a way, I've sort of inherited them from Thomas. He adored his parents. You always wonder what the future holds, and I always used to think that if he loved his parents – and he really looked after them – that's what he would be like with me. He was very generous, and very caring towards them, and I think that's a good indication of what someone's like.'

As his finances improved, Tom had some work done on his teeth – he told people he'd rather sit on the grid at a grand prix than in a dentist's chair – and then sported a tidier haircut. That was Nella's handiwork. 'I always cut Thomas's hair for him. It was very long when I first knew him. He got very annoyed with me the first time I cut it, at home in Wales, and I'd done one side a bit too short and he swore at me. And Jack said, "How dare you speak to Nella like that!" I thought it was lovely, him standing up for me. I've always called him Dad.

'They had farming roots. His mother was born on a farm, and Jack worked on one. They were wonderful people, and it was just so unfair for them to lose both of their children.'

The Pryces became Nella's in-laws on 5 April 1975, days after he had won the Race of Champions. They were married at St Bartholomew's Church in Otford, and took their honeymoon in Malaga just prior to the Spanish Grand Prix at the end of that month.

Nella's distrust of racing bred an irrational fear that her husband might also become a victim of change. 'The thing about motor racing is that it spoiled people. I saw people I knew become prima donnas, and I didn't like that. I didn't want that to happen to Thomas. The constant adulation, the constant attention, can spoil even the nicest people. That's what used to worry me, that he might change...'

Tom, however, was just one of the guys. He was always at his most relaxed with his mechanics, who loved him to a man. 'A lot of the guys you get to meet do change as they go up the ladder,' former Shadow mechanic Trevor Foster said. 'But I'll tell you what, Tom was definitely one that you could have said would never, ever have changed. He was never, ever selfish, and if he walked into a hotel bar and you were there, he'd still always buy you a drink. Always. He'd just walk straight up, even if he'd come back late from a meal and was going to the lift. He'd divert, just have five minutes, and he'd say, "Right, lads, who's having a drink?"'

'I always respected Maldwyn's privacy,' said Cledwyn Ashford, who behaved similarly with footballers Michael Owen and Gary Speed, whom he knew. 'You know, never asked him for tickets to a race, or whatever. You didn't do that; you respected his space and his personality. And yet you knew if you ever did want anything you *could* ask him.'

Keeping fit became more popular in the mid-seventies among drivers. Nella remembers Tom buying himself a bike and some weights, but never using either. 'They just sat in the corner and got covered in dust. That's the way he was; he kept fit by doing what he did. He didn't go off running. He wasn't a smoker, he wasn't a drinker, he wasn't a hell-raiser. He was just a quiet, gentle sort of a person.'

She admitted that she thought long and hard before marrying a racing driver. 'It wasn't a way of life that I liked, and I had to ask myself whether I could cope with it. I mean, a vet would have been quite useful, with my horses! Why didn't he do something else, why motor racing? But if I was going into it, that's what he did and I wasn't going to change it.

'I didn't want to marry a racing driver. That was one of the funny things about it, because Thomas said that's what he always liked. He'd laugh and say, "Ah, these girls who are always hanging around motor racing, trying to pick up drivers! It's refreshing to meet one who doesn't know anything about it."

'I don't think Thomas enjoyed all the travelling. He used to say that he'd be happy if he could just drive the car and not have to go anywhere. But I would never, ever have asked him to stop.

'I always had this recurring dream in which I'd say to him, "Thomas, couldn't you do something else?" and he would say, "Well, no. I don't know how to do anything else. This is what I do." And, of course, in real life it was what he loved. He said to me once, "I can't believe I'm being paid to do something I love doing. I'd do it for free, and they're paying me a lot of money." He was the luckiest man in the world, as far as that was concerned. Maybe that's what made him so nice to be around, because he was very fulfilled in his career.'

Like Mario Andretti, Tom Pryce was put on earth to drive racing cars.

'This is going to make him sound big-headed,' Nella continued, 'which he wasn't, but he once said to me, "I know I'm the best. I know that I can do it." It was just his calm sort of confidence.' It was, of course, the inner belief that all drivers have, expressed in private to the most important person in his world. If anyone other than Nella or his parents had asked Tom to rate himself, he would never have expressed it that way but would simply have said he reckoned himself to be as good as anyone else out there.

'I've often thought since that, with lots of things in life, there are some that some people can do naturally very, very well, and you can see other people struggle like hell to try and achieve the same thing. It takes everything they've got, whereas to some others it's just natural. Thomas just had it, he had what it took. He never doubted himself.'

There was never any need to.

If any woman had been put on earth for Tony Brise, it was Janet Allen. Her father Reg and uncle Dennis had both raced small hydroplanes, and motorsport was in her blood.

Their first meeting was at Rubery Owen Motor Club's dinner-dance in Wolverhampton, early in 1971. They were both only 18. 'I'd gone there with my parents, and Tony had gone there with a friend of a friend of mine and a blind date. He didn't get on with his blind date, and we ended up talking. I ended up sitting on his lap after we'd had a dance, because there was nowhere else to sit. He asked a friend who smoked for his packet of cigarettes and took out the silver lining paper. He gave the cigarettes back and then proceeded to make a daffodil out of the silver paper and presented it to me. I still have that daffodil.

'It didn't happen immediately from there, though, because he couldn't get my phone number. My cousin Richard, whom he knew, wasn't quite sure whether Tony was right for me! It took him three weeks to get my telephone number!'

Jenny Anderson, the Brise family friend, was there the evening Tony got back from the dinner-dance. 'Tony was my first boyfriend. He took me out to the pictures when we were 15, and he was always a real gentleman. We would hold hands, and he'd walk on the outside of the pavement. We went out twice, but we were such good friends that, because of that, he didn't make a great boyfriend. And I don't think I was ready for a boyfriend at that stage!

'I was at the Brises' when Tony got back that night. "I've just met the girl I'm going to marry," he said, and if he was determined to achieve something then he would go after it. He just wouldn't stop talking about this girl. There was no way he could possibly *know* about marrying her, but he was so absolutely sure. It

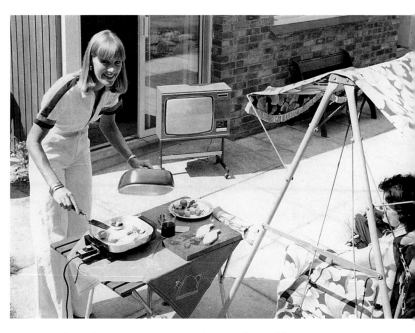

'I've met the girl I'm going to marry,' Tony informed his family, after making the acquaintance of Janet Allen at a Rubery Owen Motor Club dinner dance early in 1971. He was right.

was quite amazing. I remember feeling worried that he might come down with such a bump. But he was determined she would come round.'

'He had a white Escort van with a Formula Ford engine in it,' Janet remembered. 'Shortly after we started going out we were following a friend of his whose Mini broke down. Tony didn't know how I drove, but he jumped out to help this friend and said to me, "Just get in the car and drive it over there, will you?" I was thinking, "Hey, I'm just 18, and he's asked me to get in and drive this car that's all souped up!"'

Tony was still doing his Business Studies degree at Aston University when they met, and Janet got the usual driver's 'racing comes first' vibes. 'Very much so! But bear in mind that I also loved cars. I was an only child, and I think I should have been a boy, because my father bought me a Scalextric and used to take me to races at Mallory Park and Oulton Park. The first car I had was a Mini, which I plastered with Champion and Duckhams stickers. I thought I could burn everyone off at the traffic lights! So when I met Tony I was absolutely on Cloud Nine because he would invite me to go to these races. His friend Martin Miner took me to my first one because Tony had to go back to Kent as his car was kept at his parents' place, in the old piggery. They had a big barn where he used to prepare his car himself. I'm sure that the race was at Snetterton. I'll never forget, because Martin and I arrived, and we were looking for Tony and his car, and Martin said, "Well, there's some bits of it." Tony had already

Young love: Jan and Tony with his Triumph TR6.

spun off in practice and all we could see were bits of red fibreglass. Eventually we found him and he was all right, just gluing bits back together again. That was my first experience, and I thought, "Oh, my goodness!"'

That was the race in which Tony beat local hotshoe Martin Watson by four-tenths of a second on his first visit to the Norfolk venue.

'He worked so hard on the car. When I did go down to stay before a race, my Friday night would be spent sitting up in the barn until three or four in the morning, or even on the Saturday night if things had gone badly in practice. Most nights before a race he'd be working into the small hours to get everything set up.'

John Brise would leave his kids to get on with it. Tony was 18 months older than brother Tim, who in turn was nine years older than Simon. 'But he was always there for them if they needed him,' said Janet. 'He was always popping in and out. He was a wonderful dad.'

If Roger was the tough little fighter who never gave up, and Tom the shy boy who hated the limelight, is it fair to pigeonhole Tony as a stylist who seemed arrogant because he knew how good he was? Janet nodded. 'He was very self-confident.'

And tough enough to make hard-nosed decisions about his career path?

'Yes, he was a businessman as well. I think that's a

fair assessment. He looked at it from a business angle. It's difficult to say; I don't think he would have been cut-throat, but he would have been astute enough to make the right decisions.

'He did his thesis for his BSc on Formula One sponsorship, and he went into it in quite a detailed way. And I think that's what let so many drivers down, because they didn't really know how to handle the business side of it, whereas Tony, I think, was quite astute. And in Nick Brittan he had a very good manager. He was a good choice, though he only took him on a few months after he'd got into Formula One. Before then, Tony made all his own decisions.'

Brittan was a family friend, who had raced karts against John Brise. 'He built the Brisekart I used when I won the European Championship in about 1902,' Brittan laughed. 'John and I were good mates. At home at the time he had two kids, Tony and Tim, rushing around doing what two kids do at that age. Basically I knew Tony before he even began to register me.

'I gave up karting, and John and I went in different directions. John went on to race the Arnott-Bristol and Cooper 500s, as well as stock cars a bit later on. Once he was at this 500 race at Montlhéry and he filled out the entry form. Name: John Brise. Driver: As above. He appeared in the French press, and was mentioned as such by the commentator, as 'Asa Bove'...

'When Tony went Formula Three we had a little chat, a family yarn, and I pointed out this and that, and left them to get on with it.'

Like Tom, Tony would talk things over with his father. 'Always,' Janet confirmed. 'It was very much a family affair, everything would be talked through with Pam and John, and me. It was always sitting round a family lunch table, to discuss it all. It was John who had got him into it and set him up with his karting and then Formula Ford, and John's money that had gone into it before Tony got sponsorship.' He never forgot that.

'Tony had great respect for his father,' Jenny Anderson said. 'They had a very, very similar thought process. I think John wanted to live out something through Tony. It wasn't that he was pushing him so much as he just simply knew what Tony was capable of doing, and encouraged him to expand his boundaries and to achieve that. He was not a pushy dad in the other sense.

'He stepped back a bit after the karting days, but he was there for Tony the whole time. But he was quiet and shy, a man who preferred to be in the background.

'Simon was more like Tony than Tim was. Tony was very serious and thoughtful, whereas Tim was very bubbly and really great fun as a young lad. Tim was the cheeky one. Tony he had a lovely, deep growly laugh. You'd hear Tim laughing all day, but it was really great to hear Tony laugh because it was infrequent.

'Tim lost a lot of his bubbliness when Tony died. He

suddenly had a lot of sadness dumped on him, and later when John died it came back and he had a lot of business responsibility to go with it.

'The Brise brothers were karting since they were little kids, you remembered that at primary school. They were both talented, but Tony was more serious. It was strange, really, looking at him later and thinking, "I've been to school with this chap and I know he is going to be absolutely fantastic."

'Tony was a very caring person. Gary and I broke up shortly before Tony died, and he called to see if I was okay. Initially he had said that he didn't like Gary, that he wasn't the right man for me. Then he and Gary worked together for a while via my brother Bob, and after a while Tony came back to me and said he had changed his mind. That was Tony; he never took an idea on board without exploring it thoroughly first. He was a very interesting person. I'll say to Gary, "Let's do this," and suggest a course of action. And he'll say, "Okay, but let's do it this way." He's looked into every crevice and seen things I haven't. Tony was very like that.'

What Jenny said next further punctured the image of an arrogant and aloof Tony Brise. 'He was vulnerable, he had a soft centre. Not as far as motor racing was concerned, but as a person. There was a person in there who could get hurt. He could bring the shutters up. He would answer people honestly. To him there was just truth or non-truth, as he saw it. If he was deep in thought he might appear to be ignoring people, but he was simply wrapped in thought.'

Janet and Tony were married on 29 June 1974 in Sutton Coldfield, where she lived, 'at St Peter's Church in Little Aston Park, the little church at the end of the road. Our reception was at The Belfry, before there was a golf course there.

'Tony designed my wedding ring. It was yellow gold and shaped like an octagonal nut. He liked designing things. He also made our bed out of steel tubing and painted it. The only problem was he was building it in the spare room and then realised that it was going to be too wide to go through the door so he had to cut it in two and then reinforce it!'

In one of the nicest observations one person can make about another, Jenny said, 'Tony became complete when he met Janet; she made him whole. She is very gentle, but a part of her has the same steel as Tony had. She always looks good, and is very warm and caring. The moment I met her, I saw what Tony had seen in her, and equally I already knew what she had seen in Tony.'

Later, Janet would become very friendly with Tom and Nella Pryce, thanks to the ministrations of Bette Hill, Graham's wife. 'We were the babies of Formula One. I was 22 and Nella was 20. We were both told we had to join the Doghouse Club, and I guess that was the connection. There were the cabarets. We didn't *have* to

do them, but Bette talked us into it: "Come on, you're doing this cabaret. It's great fun, you'll love it!"

'I remember I had to drive to Slough to Sylvia Davis's house for rehearsals. It was every other week for the first six months, then every week coming up to the date. They were quite some rehearsals we did! Nella and Tom lived in Ightham and we were in Bexley, so Nella used to drive up to my house and then we'd go together. So we were very friendly then.'

Often they travelled in the Triumph TR6 Tom had bought Nella as a wedding present. 'It was a lovely green one,' said Nella. 'I was a hopeless driver. He told me that when I left he would run upstairs and from the bedroom window you could see where the road went. It was quite a fun road and I could put my foot down. So he'd go up and watch, and when I'd get back he'd say, "I know you were going too fast, because I saw you..."

'Jan and I used to drive to the rehearsals, and we got completely lost round London. It was quite fun, quite a laugh, but from what I knew most of the people – apart from Jan, Bette Hill and I – were nothing to do with motor racing at that time. They were all a lot older than us. I was very young and very shy, and I'd got involved with motor racing only because I fell in love with Thomas.'

Fate would make Nella and Janet's friendship even stronger in the months to come.

Jan with Tony's Porsche 911 at Brands Hatch, late in the summer of 1975. Argentinian journalist Tony Watson remembers seeing the Brises enjoying a picnic that day and thinking how idyllic their young lives seemed.

CHAPTER 11

Enter the dragon

Tom, 1974

'After I'd won, all I thought was, "Well, at least we'll get the money for the Token to continue." I never dreamt that there would be such a fuss as there was.'

Tom Pryce

Tom Pryce's turn to graduate to Formula One came in 1974, with the newly formed Token team in the non-championship *Daily Express* International Trophy race at Silverstone.

The car should have been Ron Dennis' entrée to Formula One as it was conceived by the Rondel Racing enterprise for Australian Tim Schenken to race, but it came under the wing of Token Racing when, at the end of 1973, financial difficulties arose and the backers, Tony Vlassopulos and Ken Grob, decided to close the operation down. The French Motul oil company had backed Rondel's bespoke Motul Formula Two car programme, for which Tom had driven in 1973, but for 1974 Motul had been lured by Louis Stanley into backing BRM in Formula One. Dennis's graduation was put on hold.

Subsequently, Tony Vlassopulos and Ken Grob formed a small new team to complete the stillborn project. 'Token' was an amalgamation of their names.

Vlassopulos, a shipping magnate (he always laughed when he read of himself being described thus), a barrister at law and one-time Goodwood top commentator, remembered it thus, 'My wife Sue and I used to go to Phelps, a big antiques emporium in Twickenham, and one day in 1970 John Phelps said, "Would you be prepared to ask any of your Greeks if they'd be interested in putting

At his beloved Brands Hatch during first practice for the British Grand Prix, Tom stormed to fastest time round the Kentish track that had become his home.

Tom had plenty to smile about, as he tried the cockpit of the Token for the first time prior to making his Formula One début in the 1974 International Trophy race at Silverstone.

money into motor racing?" There was a young man dating his daughter who was looking for funding. Back then we Greeks controlled the City, so I went to people like George Livanos. They all had fast cars, but all of them with one voice said, "Oxi!" which means "no" in Greek. So I went back to Phelps, quite innocently, and said I was awfully sorry, I'd had no success. And then I committed the fatal error of saying, "So how much is he looking for, anyway?" I didn't even know who the hell *he* was. John said he wasn't sure, but could this chap Ron Dennis come and see me? I said "yes" and it was like one of those cartoon things: whoosh, and there was Dennis outside the door, with Tim Schenken! They came in and presented this thing, and they wanted about £25,000. Cut a long story short, I said okay. Around that time I spoke to Ken Grob. We were already buddies, and one of his conditions was that his youngest son Ian could work for the team. We shared the financial load between us.'

Thus was born Rondel, the Formula Two team run by Ron Dennis and Neil Trundle, for whom the likes of Schenken, Graham Hill, Carlos Reutemann, Henri Pescarolo, Jody Scheckter, Bob Wollek and Tom himself

would race with varying levels of distinction between 1971 and 1973.

'Rondel is a separate story,' Vlassopulos continued, 'but we started on a farm in Cranleigh, then we went to Old Windsor and eventually ended up in what became Graham Hill's Embassy Racing workshop in Feltham. Then, one day late in 1973, I went up to the City on the train from Weybridge station, I picked up *The Times* and there's a story, 'Rondel to build Formula One car'. I couldn't wait to get to the office: "Get me Dennis!"

'I said to Ron, "What the hell is this?" and he said, "Oh, yes, Tony, it's in the workshop." So that was sort of the breaking point, and what I understand is that he had been trying to find money for it with John Hogan. All John had got us was Radio Luxembourg 208 air time, but now he was with Marlboro and Ron was apparently saying to him, "This is what I've done for you, what are you going to do for me?" This was all just too late for me and the rest is history. If we could have got the Marlboro money right then that Ron eventually got, it might have been different. But the bank had rung me to say we were way, way out, and I thought, in fairness to the family, that I just couldn't go on pouring money in, and Ken felt the same.

'So Ron went off to Project Two – we were Project One, and it wasn't until he got to Project Four, being parachuted into McLaren, that he made it all work. Neil Trundle then wrote me a letter, explaining what had

The Token had been assembled hurriedly and, after a feisty showing, Tom's race ended with a spin which was caused by a faulty gear linkage.

been happening. We had to disband the whole Rondel thing, but we took the Formula One car. I said to Ken, "Look, it seems silly if they got that far, why don't we have a crack?" because we had put of a lot of our money into it. So we set Neil up in the garage at Walton, Ray was there, with two guys called Chris Lewis and Alan England, and they finished the car.

'We couldn't get any sponsorship for it, all we had was from ShellSport. They were the only people I could get to come forward on an unknown car. And Chris Meek was involved through Titan Properties.'

'The situation regarding the Token was that I was given the choice of providing the chassis or the mechanical running gear, including the engine and gearbox,' Meek said. 'I chose the latter and reached an agreement with Graham Hill to take over a selected engine destined for Graham's car straight from Cosworth. I believe I still have the block of that engine incorporated as a chassis for a glass table.'

Designer Ray Jessop had produced a conventional car for Dennis, working to a strict budget. The eventual result was called the Token RJ02, a neat and uncomplicated machine distinguished mainly by its unusually curved cockpit surround and beaked nose, and it was beautifully finished in the old green and yellow colours that Lotus had used until the dawn of the era of commercial sponsorship.

Tom got the drive on the strength of his evident promise and the backing from Meek (his mentor), which

helped to secure a fresh Cosworth V8 engine. He could hardly wait for the Silverstone race.

'I went down to see Mald, I think it was on the Tuesday before the race,' Jack Pryce remembered, 'and there was the chassis still on trestles. All of the suspension was being re-fabricated because the tyres were fouling some of the components. I took one look and was convinced it would never be ready by the following Saturday.

'Neil worked five days solid to get the car ready, getting very little sleep. Then it transpired that this poor fellow was the only one with an HGV licence, so he had to drive the car up from Surrey to Silverstone. Mald went with him, and kept punching him in the arm every time he looked like dropping off to sleep!'

Ian Flux remembered things slightly differently and that it was actually Tom who drove the truck. But Cledwyn Ashford thought that Tom might have altered the story about who drove, knowing that Jack would not have approved.

'Token was my first job in racing,' Flux recalled. 'I sort of got thrown out of the BLMC dealership in Cobham which was run by Brian Woodfield. He was a good mate of Tony Vlassopulos and knew I was mad on racing, so he

Tom Pryce, vintage 1974, with Geldof hair and chiselled features. He did not believe in mugging for the camera, but part of his quiet mood captured here was almost certainly lack of sleep due to the battle to get the Token to Silverstone.

suggested I contact Tony. I did, and he offered me a two-week trial. That was my life-changing moment!

'They were working out of a lock-up garage by the rail station in Hersham and a disused house. They must only have set things up a month or so before I bowled up on 1 February, and I spent my first three weeks unpacking boxes of stuff from the old Rondel set-up and erecting Dexion shelving in the house.

'At that stage the RJ02 chassis was finished on the outside, but not quite on the inside. There were five of us: Neil Trundle, Chris Lewis, Alan England, Ray Jessop, and me. That was our complete team, really, apart from Tony and Ken! Since I was the smallest, guess who then got the lovely job of wriggling into the tub, and foaming and tank-taping all the anchor nuts so that they wouldn't chafe against the fuel bags?'

Flux's first meeting with Tom was unusual, insofar as he did not find him monosyllabic. 'It must have been three weeks before the International Trophy. He came to the factory. He had always stood out to me, and we got on from the word go. I said, "Do you want a cuppa?"

And he smiled and said, "That makes a change. Normally I have to do that!"

'We worked for weeks and then ended up doing two all-nighters to get the car ready, and I remember us packing the truck around eight o'clock on the Friday night. In fact, little did Tom know that I'd purchased it only a month earlier from a mate, and that it had been a furniture van. It cost £350 – that was our version of "international" racing!

'We were all so knackered that Tom actually had to drive the truck up to the circuit even though he didn't have the right licence to do that. We were all just too tired; I suppose Tom was the least tired of us. From memory, we arrived at eight o'clock Saturday morning. We had done no testing, and we missed nearly all of qualifying.'

Tom managed only four shakedown laps and started at the back of the 32-car grid with a time of 1m 42.9s. 'He encountered silly problems every time he got in the car,' Fluxie recalled.

'Crikey, was I nervous!' Tom admitted. 'The clutch didn't work and the car had to be push-started – but I did enjoy those four laps. It was fantastic.'

By contrast, local hero James Hunt, who was by now really beginning to make a name for himself, took pole position for the second non-championship race in a row from Ronnie Peterson's Lotus and Jochen Mass's Surtees after a lap of 1m 16.7s in Lord Hesketh's eponymous new car.

In the race, Tom put in a spirited performance to battle with promising Formula Two star Noritake Takahara in a works-run March 741, until a spin on lap 15 prompted a pit stop to investigate gear selection problems. He retired in the pits a lap later after the linkage had fallen apart. But he had lapped the new car in the 1m 21s, which would have qualified him mid-grid.

'I was determined to pass a few F5000s,' Tom said afterwards. 'I didn't like the sight of those in front of me. We got going pretty well and passed a few people until the gear linkage started playing up.'

Meanwhile, Hunt made himself the Golden Boy of British motorsport by coming back from a dreadful start to catch and pass Mass and then Peterson. The blond Swede was generally regarded at that time as the fastest man in Formula One, but Hunt earned his own spurs with a stunning move down the inside at the tricky, sweeping Woodcote corner, and went on to score his and Hesketh's first, hugely acclaimed, Formula One victory. It was another headline-grabbing step in Hunt's career that was fast elevating him to super-stardom. Tom was more than happy just to have made his Formula One début, and to have kept out of the limelight.

'We all loved him,' Flux continued. 'He was instantly one of the guys and he was the first Formula One driver I'd met. Of course I'd seen Jackie Stewart and Graham Hill on television, and I was expecting him to be like that. But he wasn't. However, he immediately engaged me in conversation, and it was like being with a mate down the pub.' Clearly, Tom was more relaxed at this stage with people he perceived to be similar to himself.

Vlassopulos and Grob decided that they would next tackle their first F1 race, the Belgian Grand Prix, which that year was held on the sterile and intensely unpopular Nivelles-Baulers circuit on 12 May as the great Spa-Francorchamps venue was currently spurned on safety grounds. Indeed, someone described Nivelles as 'grand prix racing in a motorway services…'

Considering the conventional nature of the car, the minimal budget and the lack of testing, Tom did a remarkable job to qualify it 20th out of 32 entries, three seconds off Clay Regazzoni's pole time but ahead of established stars such as Tim Schenken, Carlos Reutemann, Jochen Mass and Vittorio Brambilla. More importantly, given what was to come, he was mere tenths of a second shy of the Shadows of Jean-Pierre Jarier and Brian Redman who shared the ninth row of the grid just ahead of him. He was running strongly in the midfield after a couple of pits calls to investigate fuel starvation; unfortunately, the DFV hiccoughed again just as Tom was being lapped by Jody Scheckter. The South African couldn't miss the Token and his right rear wheel clipped Tom's left front. Scheckter carried on to finish third with a buckled rim, but the Token suffered a broken wishbone and Tom crept back to retire in the pits.

'Nivelles was a real dump,' Flux remembered with complete disdain, 'and I remember that whoever booked our accommodation cocked up because our hotel was an hour away. That didn't actually matter on Saturday, though, because we spent the entire night at the track working on the car. We were very conscious that Tom had done so well, so we were all prepared to work as long as necessary on it.'

Later, when Ian Ashley was struggling with the RJ02 at another venue and had failed to qualify, Schenken – perhaps a little unkindly – said he was surprised that the car was not further up the field. 'If Tom Pryce was driving it, it wouldn't be wanking around down there,' he told Flux in his typically forthright Australian manner.

Curiously, Tom's performance in Belgium was not impressive enough for the Automobile Club de Monaco, or Bernie Ecclestone (depending on whose version of events you accept), and Token was refused an entry to the prestigious grand prix round the streets of Monte Carlo. Instead, Tom was obliged to take a step back after Tony Vlassopulos offered him a ride in the Formula Three race that supported the Formula One event.

On his grand prix début at Nivelles, Belgium, Tom startled the Formula One world by qualifying the unfancied Token RJ02 a remarkable 20th in the 32-car field.

In the race at Nivelles he was running strongly until the engine began to cough; as the car stuttered it was brushed by a passing Jody Scheckter, breaking the left front wishbone and forcing Tom into retirement.

'I was so disappointed,' Tom admitted to Alan Henry, 'but Tony gave me the opportunity of driving one of the Ippokampos Formula Three Marches. I must admit I wondered whether I was doing the right thing, because Chris (Meek) kept telling me that I'd got no alternative but to win. I realised that it might harm my chances in the future, but there were a lot of potential sponsors going to Monaco who they thought might back the Token, so I went ahead and did it.'

'He was very concerned about that,' Jack confirmed. 'He said he would be expected to win. "And if I don't, I'll be finished in Formula One."'

It wasn't just Meek who was adamant that Tom had to win. Vlassopulos had made it very clear that that was the minimum requirement of him.

'We had the Token, and I also had Ippokampos,' Vlassopulos explained. 'That's a seahorse, that's what it means. That was part of the shipping deal that we had with Elias Kulukundis, known as Farouk, of the Kulukundis family who were then in charge of Burma Oil Tankers. We had put a team together and again Ken was involved because his good friend was John 'Buzz' Buzaglo. But the first driver we put into it was a friend of my shipping partner Steve called Johnny Gerber – he had won the Formula Ford Festival. Buzz was a nice

man, and was the lead driver. They were pottering around, and I wasn't taking a great deal of notice so long as they were getting exposure.

'We'd done very well with the Token in Belgium, and I said to Bernie, "I'll bring it down to Monaco," but he said, "No you won't. I don't want it at Monaco." I went off with my tail between my legs, and I just thought, "That's silly." Then I had an idea: "Tom's not doing anything that weekend, I'll throw Buzz out of the Formula Three car and put Tom in."

'In a line of all the drivers I've met, I would put Tom alongside somebody like Ronnie Peterson. Very quiet, very efficient, very polite, not an extrovert of any sort. Not a guy who would make a big scene. I said to him, "Tom, I want you to go to Monaco, for the Formula Three race. I will provide for you anything that you want, *anything*. I'll have a plane standing by, so that if there are any parts you need... if you break anything, we'll fly it down from the March factory. But there's one condition: you've *got* to win. You *have* to win. I can't go there with you, and lose this race. You're a Formula One driver, mate." And he was a *fantastic* driver.'

There's nothing like putting somebody under a little bit of pressure. But Tom just shrugged, and told Tony V, 'All right.'

'Then Ken Grob phoned me up,' Vlassopulos admitted with a chuckle. 'I was sitting in the kitchen, and I remember that he said, "Tony, we as a family think you are a shit! You've taken Buzz out of the car." And I said I had done it for a reason, because I was going to win that race. And he said, "Well, we still think you're a shit. You

shouldn't have done it." They were just friendly with Buzz; none of their money was in Ippokampos, that was Burma Oil Tankers money.'

As usual the grand prix-supporting race for Formula Three cars was split into two heats and a final. Tom won his heat with relative ease in the Ippokampos March 743, setting fastest lap and outrunning Tony's Ford Pinto-powered converted Formula Atlantic Modus by 15.8 seconds after Tony had fought his way through the Italian opposition. Sandro Cinotti was a further six seconds adrift.

But there was almost a drama for Ippokampos before the start of the heat, which could have threatened Tom's complete weekend. And it came from their fellow Britons at Modus.

'Neil Trundle was running Tom,' said Nick Jordan. 'We were third on the grid, I think. We'd basically cobbled the car together for Tony to run. The rules stated that you couldn't use outside assistance to start the car on the grid, and I'd read the rule book, and Neil was standing there with a mechanic with the jack plug ready to give it the jump start. Those Pinto engines were bitches to start. What I'd rigged up back in the factory was an extra six-volt motorcycle battery so I could wire it through to give 18 volts at the starter motor. Now Neil is a fantastic guy – I was recently at his 60th birthday party, and he and his wife Pam are lovely. But, back then, I walked over to him and said, "Neil, do not use the jump battery." I explained it to him and I didn't need to, but I did it as a matter of courtesy. And he looked at me and said, "You wouldn't protest me,

There was no pressure on Tom at Monaco: all he was told to do was win. On his enforced return to Formula Three he did precisely that in Tony Vlassopulos' Ippokampos Racing March 743, decimating the opposition.

would you Nick, you bastard?" Like that. I said, "All's fair in love and war, we're here to win just the same as you." Neil told his guys and they didn't use it. Their car started and Tom went off to win.'

Their main rival was another Briton, Brian Henton, a tough Derbyshire driver who was driving the works March. Henton won the second heat by more than seven seconds, from Italian Alberto Colombo in a GRD 374, with Renzo Zorzi another four seconds back in his March. Tom's race time was a remarkable 16 seconds faster than Henton's, though Henton's fastest lap was only a tenth off Tom's.

'Another complication had arisen,' Vlassopulos related. 'My company, Ney Shipping, represented the Indonesian state oil company. I chose Ney because I've always been interested in Napoleonic history and Ney was one of Napoleon's finest 26 marshals. In most languages "N" means "no", "niet", "na". The negative in Greek is the exact opposite, so in the City we were known as "Yes Shipping", because in Greek "nai" means "yes"!

'At that time the Indonesian state oil company was owned by General Ibnu Sutowo – he was in our pocket and we were in his – and under my command I had the biggest fleet of "spot" (meaning available) tankers. Anyhow, his son came to Monaco. We'd already given

ABOVE: *Tom with one of the Ippokampos team's Indonesian guests, and the silver trophy he received for winning in Monaco. He gave the trophy to his Indonesian team-mate Hanne Wiano in a gesture of kindness, and just kept the gold and blue glass trophy that Princess Grace gave him for setting fastest lap. Tom obliged happily when she asked him to say thank you in Welsh.* BELOW: *Suddenly popular after his Monaco triumph, Tom made his début with the Shadow team at Zandvoort, where he talks to team principal Alan Rees in the pits.*

him a Ferrari Boxer, and now along he comes with all his mates. We were all at l'Hermitage Hotel, we always were, with suites for everyone. So I said to Steve, "I'll stay with the team and you look after the Indonesians when the racing is on." But he said, "No you won't. I need you up on the balcony while the racing is on." He insisted. There were no walkie-talkies, and they'd be asking hundreds of questions.'

The heats had set up the battle for the final, and to Tony V's intense consternation it was Henton who came around in the lead on the opening lap.

'So I'm giving the Indonesians all this bullshit. We have a wonderful car and a wonderful driver, we're going to win this race. We're up on this balcony, and we come to the final; we are looking down, and on the first lap there's no sign of Tom! First, second, third, fourth, fifth, no Tom. And Steve looked at me, and I was gobsmacked. And then, about sixth or seventh, there he was.

'Anyhow, we go to the second lap and he's about fifth, then history tells you that after three or four laps he absolutely disappeared. He absolutely waltzed it.'

In the end, Tom beat Tony by 21 seconds. After falling foul of Gaudenzio Mantova early on, Henton put his car into the wall at the Swimming Pool after 15 laps. Tony, noticeably, took on and beat the Italians. And only Tom beat him, once Mantova had crashed out.

'I made a bad start, because I missed second gear and a couple of cars passed me. I went up the hill then someone else passed me going down the hill from Casino Square,' Tom told Andrew Marriott of *Motoring News*.

It was the nightmare scenario for a man under the pressure he was under to deliver the win, but it was not just Tom's car control that was spectacular that day. 'I decided not to do anything silly so I was fourth at the end of the first lap. I think Brian was leading with Colombo second and Mantova third. The second lap I thought, "I'll have to pass them this time or they will get away," so I did and it just worked out. I passed two of them going down the hill from the casino, and then flashed by Brian a little later on.

'That was it; I steadily got away and it was easy from there. I had no problems apart from a little bit too much rear brake and a slight overheating problem with the engine at the end. I tried hard almost to the finish because I wanted to have a margin in case I spun.'

It did not go unnoticed that his press-on style earned him another fastest lap, a second faster than he had gone when winning his heat. And that he had given those who refused him an entry in the big race the perfect riposte. Indeed, he gained far more publicity, and far more of a boost for his career, than he ever would have if he had raced the Token. His driving that day bore the stamp of greatness that would have made him a champion.

'At least this race has given me more Monaco

experience and I am looking forward to next year,' he said modestly, adding, 'in Formula One.'

'Pryce like Peterson' said the headline in the Italian magazine *Autosprint*, comparing the style of his victory with Ronnie's back in 1969. But Vlassopulos remembered Tom being totally underwhelmed by his stunning success.

'I went down to the paddock, and people are sticking stickers on our car and having photographs taken, and in all this hubbub, at the back somewhere, there's Tom with his lovely girlfriend Nella, a very sweet young girl. And I went over to him and said, "Tom, what *happened*?" And he said, "What do you mean?" And I said, "Well Tom, what happened at the beginning? Where *were* you?" It was like pulling teeth. "I mean, you were fifth, or something." And he thought for a minute, and then said so nonchalantly, "Oh, missed a gear..."'

Vlassopulos laughed at the recollection and shook his head. Tom was not like other drivers. 'That personified that man. He was the perfect driver. Flamboyant? What are you talking about? You and I are 50 times more flamboyant than Tom was. But put him in a motor car, he'd drive his socks off. He had so much potential. He was a lovely man. But my wife Sue and I didn't really get to know him long enough because, as soon as it all finished in Monaco, and I'd said thank you very much and all that, his new Formula One deal was done.'

Tom Pryce, the man the Monaco organisers had not wanted in the grand prix, suddenly found himself inundated with interest from Formula One teams. March boss Max Mosley was beside him virtually the moment he got out of the cockpit of the victorious 743, talking about a possible Formula One drive at the next race, in Sweden; Alan Rees from Shadow discovered after Sunday's grand prix that he needed to replace Brian Redman; Hesketh Racing was keen to have him partner Hunt at selected races; Graham Hill wanted him in one of his Embassy Lolas; John Surtees and Frank Williams were also interested; Marlboro's Ronnie Thompson was seen talking to Tom, too.

'After I'd won,' Tom said, 'all I thought was, "Well, at least we'll get the money for the Token to continue." I never dreamt that there would be such a fuss as there was.' Vlassopulos points out that there was no direct connection (apart from himself) between Token and Ippokampos, but Tom meant that his success might encourage companies to sponsor him in the Token.

'I took a lot of calls for him,' his landlady Red Webb recalls. 'From Lord Hesketh, Colin Chapman, Graham Hill, Louis Stanley, all of them.'

Before his Formula One future was finally settled, however, he had another chance to leave his mark on Formula Two. Garage owner Chris Marshall's Baty team was to run James Hunt in one of Derek Bennett's works-backed Chevron B27s. Baty missed the first few races and wasn't ready to compete until the Salzburgring on

2 June, but there was a setback when Hunt's intended partner, Hiroshi Kazato, was killed in a multiple-car accident at Mount Fuji. Then there was an argument over start money for Hunt. So Tom received a call to drive the car, the week after his great performance in Monaco, and surprised many by qualifying the unfamiliar Chevron on pole position on the Friday with a superb display of on-the-limit driving that yet again served to underline his talent. Despite concerns about understeer, he was also fastest on Saturday morning.

'As I recall,' Jack Pryce said, 'Tom was using a Schnitzer BMW engine and one of their engineers had promised to shave if anyone put one of their engines on pole for a Formula Two race. He had these rather magnificent whiskers, like the driver Harald Ertl, but went ahead with the deal after Tom had done his stuff!'

Bill Harding was in charge of the Baty team then, and remembered that Schnitzer would not give the team a 'demon' engine it had kept in reserve for Hunt. 'But when he saw Tom put the Chevron on pole he suddenly wanted to whisk the car back to the factory to instal it. We said no, please leave it. But they did change the

It was at Dijon that he really made his mark in Shadow's smooth DN3, challenging aces Niki Lauda and Ronnie Peterson for the fastest time in practice.

engine and then of course there was a problem. It would have been better if he'd just left it alone. But Tom's performance there was a real eye-opener. The amazing thing was that he just wanted a steering wheel and he'd drive the car. That was all he was interested in.'

Thus far, the season had been dominated by the BMW-engined works March 742s of Hans Stuck and Patrick Depailler, so Tom's performance in the BMW-engined Chevron brought some welcome change. He led from the rolling start, but after three laps his charge was stymied by a fuel pump problem which over-pressurised the Kugelfischer system and burst an injector pipe, and the victory ultimately went to upcoming Frenchman Jacques Laffite in a BP-backed March.

In that same race, Hong Kong-based entrepreneur Bob Harper had entered two Chevrons, after switching allegiance from March. One was driven by Zandvoort hero David Purley, the other by seasoned Formula Two star Dieter Quester. Purley had been second at Salzburgring, but Quester never got on with his car; come the race in Karlskoga he had pronounced his B27 undrivable.

Tom had taken fourth place overall in the wildly oversteering Baty Chevron at Hockenheim after qualifying fifth, then finishing fourth in the first heat and fifth in the second after a last-lap moment in a sudden rainstorm enabled Laffite to slip ahead. Angered by Quester, Chevron boss Derek Bennett then quickly slipped Tom into the Austrian's seat. He promptly qualified the 'undrivable' B27 on the second row for the slipstreaming epic round the Italian speedbowl at Enna, but then had one of the few serious shunts of his career in the race. It was a major one as the car went end-over-end over the barriers and landed up in the reeds alongside the infamous lake which, legend had it, was populated by poisonous snakes. The chassis was a write-off, but Tom escaped unharmed and was more worried about the reptiles. Greg Field was a mechanic with Harper at the time, and remembered the incident well. 'The car ended up in the water, and Tom scrambled out and stood on the engine so no snakes could get him!'

Tom had one more race in the car, at Mugello in Italy, and there he realised much of his promise as he finished third.

'We all loved Dave Purley, because he was a man's man,' Field said. 'But Purls really had no idea about racing outside of the driving. When Tom arrived in the team it was a refreshing change. I don't mean that nastily to Purls, but Tom knew all about racing and he was the complete professional. And he could certainly drive! I

Look at the angles of the tyres, and you begin to appreciate the speed Tom is coaxing from the DN3 round the swoops and dives of the French track.

remember watching him through the last corner in Mugello, which is a long, really challenging right-hander. He was sliding the car all the way through it. Magic...'

After that, a clash of tyre contracts kept Tom out of the formula; the Chevron ran on Firestones, and Tom's new Formula One Shadow was on Goodyears...

He would reappear later in the year when French-speaking American Formula Two team owner Fred Opert entered him in one of his B27s in the prestigious Trois Rivieres Formula Atlantic street race in Quebec that would later make Gilles Villeneuve famous. Driving in place of Jean-Pierre Jarier, alongside French veteran Jean-Pierre Jaussaud and Jose Dolhem, the brother-in-law of another upcoming French racer Didier Pironi, Tom was his usual spectacular self before crashing with brake problems while fighting for third place.

He also had a few tests in a Mazda RX-3, attempting to track down a misfire for an injured Barrie 'Whizzo' Williams. Tom did 50 laps in the car at Goodwood, which included briefly putting it through a hedge; Williams was only interested in knowing if the misfire had been cured – it had! Tom later lapped Silverstone in the car at class lap record pace.

Back in the Formula One world, journalist Alan Henry played a role in the drama of Tom's new deal, flying to races across Europe bearing letters from Alan Rees at Shadow. Meek, who was still effectively managing Tom's career at this stage, was resigned to his driver leaving Token; he had no intention of standing in his way, but wanted him to take up the Hesketh offer. So did Tony Vlassopulos.

Though Hill, Surtees and Williams were still chasing him, Tom's choice had distilled to one between Hesketh, which was very keen, and Shadow, which came into the picture later.

'March never really pursued it,' Tom said, 'Frank Williams mumbled something to me that he'd like to talk to me after the Formula One race, but I suppose he was too busy afterwards. Later the following week I had a 'phone message to say Embassy Racing was trying to contact me and they would ring back, but they didn't.'

Shadow was a relatively new team, having raced in the North American CanAm sportscar series since 1970 before entering Formula One in 1973 with mixed results. There had been signs of great promise with the new DN3 earlier in 1974 in the hands of the popular American driver Peter Revson, but he had been killed in the new car following a suspension failure while testing at Kyalami in South Africa in March. His replacement was the doughty British fighter Brian Redman, who did only three races before deciding that he did not care for the atmosphere in Formula One and preferred to dominate Formula 5000 racing in North America. Swedish driver Bertil Roos, a star in Formula Atlantic, made an unconvincing Formula One début in his homeland. At the time Shadow was also estimated, via its sponsor United Oil Products, to have one of the biggest budgets in Formula One. And it was offering Tom the remainder of the season.

Hesketh, meanwhile, had also entered Formula One in 1973, and with James Hunt driving, Lord Alexander Hesketh's modified March 731G had become the surprise of the season. In 1974, Hesketh had his own car designed by Dr Harvey Postlethwaite, and it was again proving highly promising in Hunt's capable hands; indeed he had just won the International Trophy race at Silverstone. But Hesketh's offer was only four to five races in 1974 as number two to Hunt, followed by a two-year deal.

The day that Flux best remembered in his brief time working with Tom came when Token had a rare test run at Goodwood, after Monaco.

'I remember it because there we were, focused on our test programme, and Hesketh and Shadow suddenly flew in with their helicopters! I think they appeared within half an hour of each other, Hesketh first. I think it was after lunch. Tom did a few laps, then came in and Hesketh's Bubbles Horsley rushed over. Ray said to Tom that he had better go and talk to him. After 10 minutes or so, Tom got back into the car and did another handful of laps, and then it was Alan Rees of Shadow wanting to talk to him. He did another half-hour in the car, and we tried some different front wings, and then it was the end of the day. Tom said that he had to go and talk to Bubbles and Reesie again, and that was the last we saw of him at Token…'

Vlassopulos remembered, 'I said to him at that time, "I'd very much like you to go with Alexander (Hesketh). I think you should go with a British team."

Subsequently Vlassopulos would agree a deal through Ippokampos to pay Hesketh £5,000 a race, and the Hesketh carried the little green seahorse on the front of the cockpit. 'Tom was totally contracted, in fairness, to Chris Meek, but he wanted Tom to go to Hesketh, too. One time we were testing the Token at Goodwood and all these helicopters started appearing in the sky: Alan Rees with Jackie Oliver from Shadow, Bubbles Horsley from Hesketh. All of us wanted him to go with Alexander, but I didn't realise Hesketh was losing so much money on his racing at that time.'

'I had reached an agreement with Alexander Hesketh for Tom to drive his car, this was my option at the time,' Meek explained. 'Tom was persuaded by Alan Rees and Jack Oliver to ignore my contract. Shadow at no time made approaches to me, they just rode roughshod over all I had done for Tom.'

There had never been any question of Tom racing at the Swedish Grand Prix at Anderstorp because of his prior commitment to Baty. That was why Shadow ran Roos, as negotiations with Tom and Jack Pryce

continued. After a period of contemplation, spent mulling things over carefully with his father, Tom finally opted to join the Anglo-American team, and signed a six-month contract. His relationship with Meek suffered as a result, but Tom knew his own mind. Hesketh Racing, with its yacht in the Monte Carlo harbour, the Champagne and parties, would have been a complete anathema to such a self-contained man and, besides, Hunt was the team's star. 'I eventually told him (Meek) that I thought the Shadow drive would be the best idea and that I didn't agree with him,' Tom told Henry. 'We haven't exactly spoken much since then.'

He felt guilty about leaving Token, and said, 'I feel the same as if I'd left anybody halfway through. I feel really bad about it. I had it on my conscience when I was making my decision.' But he knew he had to leave, that the really big chance had arrived. Token had confirmed entries for some grands prix, but not yet all. 'What was I to do?' he reasoned. 'I don't want to be sitting around and thinking how nice it would be if we were there, if only I'd taken those offers… I'd be there whatever, I had to leave.'

Rees was convinced he had found his man, having gone after him for precisely the same reasons he had hunted Ronnie Peterson to join his fledgling March company back in 1969. 'I know what's involved to win that Formula Three race at Monaco,' he said, 'and I know that Tom is good, just like Ronnie was in 1969.' This was high praise indeed, given Peterson's status in Formula One at that time.

'The Monaco race was the key,' Rees added. 'You were aware of what he was doing but that was the clincher. I always thought that was quite difficult, not being in the formula any more as a regular driver, and then going to a major race like that and just cleaning up. He hadn't been in Formula Three for two years. I know it's less power and people might think it's easy to go back down like that, but it's not, actually – unless you are a very good driver. Most people have got to get into the swing of it, go testing and all that sort of thing. But Tom just went down and did it. And did it easily.'

His first outing with Shadow was a test session at Goodwood. 'They spent the morning bedding everything in, just tooling around,' Jack Pryce remembered. 'The serious stuff, the blue smoke stuff, came after lunch. Mald was very quick. James Hunt liked to tell people that he had the unofficial lap record round Goodwood in the Hesketh, but locals who were timing there that day told me that Mald had gone faster still.'

The first race with his new team came at Zandvoort for the Dutch Grand Prix in June, where he immediately distinguished himself by qualifying 11th, only four-tenths off established team-mate Jean-Pierre Jarier. Within laps of trying his new car round the seaside track, Tom was opposite-locking happily through the Tarzan hairpin. Unfortunately, he got no further than

After impressing so much in practice, Tom had a less satisfactory British Grand Prix at Brands Hatch, the Shadow fading from a possible fourth place finish due to gearshift problems caused by a chassis failure.

that corner at the start. Hunt had qualified his Hesketh sixth but made a tardy start and was engulfed as the field headed into Tarzan. Trying to minimise the damage, James inadvertently moved over on Tom and left the Shadow sat on the side of the road with its right rear wheel at a drunken angle.

If anyone doubted Tom's inherent talent, he silenced them when the French Grand Prix was run at the undulating Dijon-Prenois circuit on 7 July. This was the sort of performance Michael Schumacher would later be praised for, long before Schumacher was out of short pants. Niki Lauda and Ronnie Peterson were the two acknowledged fast men that year, but in Saturday's first qualifying session Lauda was the only man faster than Tom, who lapped his Shadow in 59.11s compared to the Austrian's 58.79s best in the Ferrari. Observers returned to the pits with lurid tales of the black car being bounced over kerbs, especially in the section behind the pits, but though some protested that he was using rather more of the circuit than he was entitled to, everyone else took the view that whatever shortcuts Tom might be taking were legitimately available to one and all. It was simply a matter of him driving his heart out, the only way he knew how. The performance left him on the front row with Lauda, until Peterson squeaked his ageing Lotus 72 round in 59.08s in the afternoon to pip him by three-hundredths of a second. Tom's sensational run remained the talk of the day, but as usual he couldn't understand what all the fuss was about.

Incredibly, Tom again collided with Hunt, and again his race failed to go beyond the first lap. The problem began when there was an inordinate delay as cars were held on the grid. Tom admitted to Henry that he had one eye on his water temperature gauge and was caught ever so slightly on the hop when the flag fell. The

Shadow refused to pick up cleanly, and Carlos Reutemann's Brabham brushed it from the right-hand side as the Argentinian came between the DN3 and the pit wall. The impact tweaked the steering wheel out of Tom's hands and shoved the car sideways, just as Hunt was making a brilliant start from the fifth row. Black car met white; the Hesketh's monocoque was torn open and James was an instant retirement, while Tom crept round half of the lap before yielding to serious suspension misalignment.

As the season continued, however, with the British Grand Prix at Brands Hatch in July, he continued to prove his mettle. After Dijon there were quiet expectations of fireworks from him on his home track, and the moment practice began on the Thursday Tom did not disappoint. He spent the morning fighting the Ferraris, and ended the session a tenth of a second faster than Lauda with 1m 21.4s. That was three-tenths better than Regazzoni and half a second up on Reutemann and Hunt. Jarier in the other Shadow lapped in a leisurely 1m 23.1s. The reward for Tom's efforts was 100 bottles of Champagne, traditionally offered by the London *Evening News* to the fastest driver in the first official practice session for the race.

Subsequently Lauda and Peterson ended the day fastest on 1m 20.6s, while Tom was still up at the sharp end with 1m 21.3s. He took a second off that on Friday, to take fifth on the grid behind Lauda, Peterson, Scheckter and Reutemann.

There was an episode in practice when he appeared in the paddock with black tape covering his name and blood group on his overalls. 'They were all a bit scared that Chris Meek might try to have a writ served on them,' Jack Pryce revealed. To be fair to Meek, however, he had made it clear to Tom, who in turn made it clear to the press, that he was not going to stand in his way even though the contract they had allegedly guaranteed him 90 per cent of Tom's future earnings.

'I was unlikely to sue him for breach of contract,' Meek said in 2006, shortly after unveiling a bronze statue of Sir Stirling Moss at Mallory Park. 'In the end I spoke to Tom and his father and made my dissatisfaction clear, but agreed to take no legal action and wished Tom all the best for his future. As a direct result of that experience, I decided not to involve myself further in this high profile sponsorship. I downgraded to helping a few others in lower categories.

'With regard to his management contract, not one penny of his income was allocated to me. The sole purpose of the contract was to finance and guide him to the best route of becoming F1 World Champion.'

There was another small measure of concern when Hunt sat alongside him on the third row with an identical time. Surely they could not get together for a third consecutive start? Thankfully, they didn't. Hunt made a slow start and Tom ran seventh in the early going, behind Lauda, Scheckter, Regazzoni, Peterson, Reutemann and Emerson Fittipaldi, while fending off Stuck, Jacky Ickx and Mike Hailwood. After gradually dropping his pursuers he hauled in Reutemann and Fittipaldi. After 20 laps he was running nose to tail with the Brazilian's McLaren. He moved up to fourth as Peterson, Regazzoni and Reutemann dropped back, and was about to embarrass Jarier by lapping him when the Frenchman headed for the pits to investigate a handling problem. Shortly afterwards, Tom himself ran into trouble, being able to engage only fourth and fifth gears. A rear chassis tube had broken and was interfering with the gearshift, and gradually he faded to finish seventh. But he had certainly made his point. He was fast in races, as well as in practice sessions.

There was a major fillip to offset the loss of his first championship points: despite another approach from Lord Hesketh regarding 1975, on Friday he had committed himself to a new two-year contract with Shadow.

He finally scored that elusive first point after a gritty drive at the old Nürburgring in the German Grand Prix in August where he qualified 11th, ahead of Hunt, John Watson and Jarier, and finished sixth on his first visit to the world's most challenging race track. It was only his fifth grand prix.

Things went a little downhill thereafter. He spun out of the Austrian race, finished two laps down at Monza, broke the engine in Canada, and was not classified in America after pit stops for a new nose and then for attention to a misfire. But he had done enough in a car that was not always consistent, and with a team that was still learning its way, to prove that he deserved his place. Enthusiasts began to acknowledge that another star had arrived. Tom was the quietest and most reticent man in the paddock until he climbed into his car, and that was when he let his driving speak for him. As Bob King had said, he came alive in the cockpit. People who knew what they were talking about said he had the same natural flamboyance and car control as Rindt and Peterson.

One such man was Alan Rees, who had worked with Jochen (as team-mate at Winkelmann Racing in Formula Two) and with Ronnie (at March Engineering). 'They all had the same driving style,' Rees said. 'Jochen and Ronnie were different personalities. Ronnie's was closer to Tom's. Jochen was very clever, very smart and worldly wise, whereas the other two just wanted to drive racing cars. They weren't particularly analytical in their driving, they just got on with it. Tom was a bit naïve. I got on with Jochen very well, but I was running the team he was in, I was in his inner circle.'

Rees' Shadow partner Jackie Oliver, who was replaced by Rindt at Team Lotus for 1969, interjected, 'Tom was nice while Jochen could be a nasty piece of work except with people that he liked. He was black or white on everything. Tom was very engaging, a nice guy.'

'Tom really was a super guy,' echoed Trevor Foster, who was then working as a mechanic with Shadow. 'It's hard to evaluate the two characters of Roger and Tom. Roger was far more of a lad; on the grid you could talk to him, but he used to get this sort of glazed look of concentration, whereas Tom'd be sitting there, even at the grands prix, and you could talk even with two minutes to go. They approached it in slightly different ways. They were different characters, but in the way they approached it overall they were the same; never overawed by anybody. Tom was very open in his praise of people, but I don't think he ever thought he was as good as Ronnie Peterson. He never wanted to be a high-profiler, he really just wanted to turn up and drive the car, do a good job and go.'

Tom's view of all this was simple, and typical of his modest nature. 'Ronnie's the best driver in the world, everyone knows that,' he told Alan Henry. 'Just think, if I could lap within a few tenths of his time in the same car... Just think what it would do for my driving. I really admire Ronnie; to me, he's simply the best.'

Tom finally scored his first World Championship point with a gritty drive to sixth at the Nürburgring, in only his fifth grand prix outing. Again, the attitude of the Shadow in the Karussel tells its own story of boldness and commitment.

CHAPTER 12

Atlantic wings

Tony, 1974

'After that it ended up a little fisty. We ended up in this little toilet, I was dragging Alan (Jones) off, and he had this Irish guy and he's banging him against the wall, "I'm gonna smack you around..."'
Nick Jordan

While things were very much happening for Tom Pryce as he established himself as a potential star of the future, Tony Brise was left feeling a little disillusioned.

The plan had been to graduate to Formula Two with a Ford-engined March 742. And he told *Motoring News* why in no uncertain terms. 'The reasons are simple,' he said, explaining why he wasn't interested in either Formula Atlantic or Formula 5000, the next steps up the ladder from Formula Three. 'Formula Atlantic is a restricted formula and I don't believe in restrictors, having had enough trouble already in Formula Three. I don't see the point in a formula where you have to put money down and pay for rebuilds just to prove that others aren't running with "bent" engines. And there still are not any regular grand prix drivers in Formula 5000, which is the main reason why I prefer Formula Two.'

He was gracious enough to admit that he would consider any Formula 5000 offers, but was outspoken again when the subject of sportscar racing was raised. Asked if he found the idea appealing, he responded

Compare the frontal area of Tony's Formula Three-derived March with that of Stephen Choularton's following Formula Atlantic version, and the aerodynamic advantage Tony enjoyed from updating his 1973 racer is clear. Running the Formula Three car with an Atlantic engine, he scored a conclusive victory in the third John Player Atlantic Championship round at Silverstone early in 1974.

trenchantly, 'The answer to that is a resounding no! I think that long-distance racing is extremely boring; to me a sprint race is the nearest to perfection that you can get, you have to be able to be absolutely right all the time.'

He was also scathing about the sacred cow of endurance racing, the 24-Hour classic at Le Mans. 'I see no point in making motor racing more dangerous than it is already. I definitely ally myself with the so-called "Armco men", and don't see the point in running races with such a great speed differential – a large accident involving perhaps spectators, doesn't do motor racing any service and I am against races of this type.'

Tony, it was clear even at that stage of his career, was a purist who was aiming for the pinnacle of the sport.

Unfortunately, the March plan never got off the ground. 'It's funny the way things happen,' he told Nigel Roebuck. 'There I was, at the beginning of '74, with no drive, no sponsor and, apparently, no prospects. I thought I had all the right credentials: I'd won the John Player F3 Championship and the Lombard Championship in '73, I'd been winning races fairly consistently, and yet no-one wanted to know.'

It cannot have helped that several of his Formula Three rivals had graduated to Formula One before he did. Rikki von Opel's family wealth had financed the move, with Ensign, the previous year. Then Essex-based Richard Robarts, who had won some Formula Three races in 1973, first with a GRD, and then a March sponsored by the Myson central heating company, had also made the jump. He would be partnering Argentinian hotshoe Carlos Reutemann in one of Bernie Ecclestone's Brabham's, courtesy of Myson.

There were some who drew pleasure from Tony's obvious discomfort and disappointment, for his habit of saying what he thought did not suit everyone. These were the people who perceived him as arrogant, but, unless you took the trouble to get to know him, it was not surprising that he did not always come across well to everyone that he encountered.

The problem with the March deal was money. Max Mosley was very pleased that Tony had snaffled the John Player title away from Alan Jones and GRD right at the last moment, since his success in a March 733 would surely generate lucrative sales for the company's new 743 model, and he wanted him in the Formula Two team. But there was £25,000 to find. Tony mentioned it to as many journalists as possible in the hope that they could publicise his plight, but somehow the general perception was that the deal was done, and the money side was overlooked. Everyone assumed he was safe in the seat.

'We never did find the money to run the car, although everyone thought the deal was all signed and settled. When we realised that we weren't going to be able to do Formula Two, we looked around to see what alternatives there were. I'd done two seasons of Formula Three and there seemed no point whatever in a third; I mean, I'd won pretty well everything, and I wasn't going to gain anything in terms of experience.'

The depressing answer was that there were not many answers at all. There had been rumours that he might make his Formula One début at the Race of Champions in the very Hesketh-run Surtees TS9B in which James Hunt had made *his* début; but, besides money, the car had already reportedly been sold to New Zealander Neil Doyle and converted to Formula 5000 specification. So, despite all his misgivings, it was Formula Atlantic or nothing. Putting a brave face on it after his earlier comments, he said: 'It seemed to be the answer; in terms of power it was a step up and, being a UK formula, it was relatively cheap. We didn't have much money to play with.'

He did, however, still have the March 733. A Holbay BDA Formula Atlantic engine was installed, together with a revised nose to generate more downforce. But, complete with skinny Formula Three wheels and tyres, he ventured off to Silverstone for the third round of the John Player Formula Atlantic Championship that supported the *Daily Express* International Trophy race.

He encountered numerous 'new car' problems in practice and only lined up eighth on the grid. Then he made a slow start after the clutch failed leaving the startline, and spent a long time getting heat into his tyres in the cold conditions. But once he hit his stride he annihilated his opposition as he passed car after car to take the lead with four laps remaining.

Rival Peter Wardle remembered the race 32 years later. 'He pulled a good stroke there before the regulations were amended. That was when he ran his Formula Three March 733 with Atlantic engine, and won easily. His tyres were narrower so they warmed up faster in the cold weather. He had far more grip than anyone else, and he looked brilliant! They changed the regulations not long after that...

'He was a very different character to, say, Tom Pryce. A little bit arrogant, but it was down-to-earth arrogance not obnoxious arrogance. He knew he was good. I thought he was a nice lad.'

Others were captivated by the performance, leaving a happy Tony feeling more than a little bemused by all the fuss. It was, after all, no more than he had being doing for several years, but suddenly people were now taking an interest.

'It really was amazing,' he told Roebuck. 'All those Formula Three wins seemed to mean nothing in comparison with that one race at Silverstone.'

And, musing on how capricious Fate can be in racing, he went on, 'You do get bitter about it sometimes, because there you are, plodding your way up through the formulae, with everybody telling you you're doing the right thing, and that's the way to go. And then someone comes along and does the right drive at the right time, and suddenly he's the man of the moment, getting loads of offers, and he's made it. With me, it all happened after that drive at the International Trophy meeting. That win brought me a works Formula Atlantic drive, which, in turn, allowed me to win a lot of races. I'm quite sure there are a load of people in Formula Two and Formula 5000 who feel resentful about it, who reckon they'd got higher up the ladder than I had, and yet had not been given the chance. And I can't really say I blame them.'

His spirits were lifted when Teddy Savory, the founder of the emergent Modus marque in Watton in Norfolk, approached him at the next race to offer him the works seat in his Formula Atlantic team. Several teams had expressed interest, but Savory was an enthusiast who had himself raced saloon cars, and Modus was an offshoot of his successful building and farming group. Tony liked him, and his M1 car had good pedigree having been designed by Swiss Jo Marquart, who had an excellent reputation forged from his previous work with McLaren and GRD.

'I took something of a chance,' Tony admitted to Roebuck. 'This was a new team, an unknown quantity. It had two things going for it – Teddy's tremendous enthusiasm for racing and Jo Marquart's ability as a designer.' Nevertheless, a lot of work would be needed to massage the Modus into winning form. He lost one race when the rear wing collapsed and another, at Mallory Park, when he was challenging John Nicholson for second until the gear linkage went awry.

'We tried all kinds of things with the Modus: long wheelbase, short wheelbase, big wings, little wings, big tyres, little tyres... We learned a tremendous amount, believe me,' he told Roebuck. And he worked particularly well with Nick Jordan.

'When they banned the Formula Three-based car and said you can't run eight- and 10 inch wheels any more, and that you had to run 10s and 14s, everybody was more or less the same,' Jordan said. 'And he still was able to do it. We had a lot of development things such as little wings and skirts forming a little 'v' right under the monocoque.

'Tony would ring me up on a Monday, "I've been thinking; can we move the engine forward?" So you'd go downstairs, and Jo and I would figure that you could move the oil tank there and the engine could thus go forward two inches, and I'd ring Tony back, "Yeah, we can do it." He'd say, "Okay, just do it. I think it'll work. But keep the same wheelbase." So we made a spacer and a longer clutch shaft. We could do that in three days. Wide track, narrow track. We went testing one day to Brands Hatch, ran the narrow rear track all morning and he was ace at Brands; did a set-up, he did a time, and would say, "That's what I can do with this." At lunchtime I had everything ready, bolted the wide track on, three inches wider overall, bump-steered it all, all set up, and within

The Silverstone success led to a deal with Modus, for whom Tony raced the M1 Formula Three car to a strong second place at Monaco behind dominant victor Tom Pryce.

five laps he'd equalled the same time as he'd done after 50 in the morning. He ultimately went another three-tenths quicker. He came in later in the afternoon and said, "Just give me a little bit more front dam, another quarter of an inch on that." He had a very sensitive feel. And he went out and did a time, and then came back in and said, "Leave it. Just prep it for the weekend, that's what we're gonna race." He'd got to that level.'

But the big problem, as Tony noted, 'was engines again, I'm afraid; we just weren't getting enough power.'

Eventually, the penny dropped at the British Grand Prix meeting at Brands Hatch, where he had a driver called Rudi Gygax as his team-mate in a hired M1. 'On the straight he was pulling a ratio higher plus 400rpm more! And yet he was more than five seconds slower on lap times. There had to be a message there somewhere. We were very short on power. At that meeting, two of my Holbays came unstitched and we came very close to lifting the Nicholson out of Rudi's car, but it didn't quite happen!'

Towards the end of a tough season he began to get some better engines and then the Modus began to fly. At Phoenix Park in September he finished second to Dave Morgan's Chevron in the wet first heat. It was still wet for the second; he leapt into the lead and was heading for victory when the oil tank union's weld broke due to vibration and seized the engine. 'That was quite funny,' Jordan recalled. 'Dave could stick with Tony round the corners, but on the straight we had the little F3 wheels and tyres, and Tony'd pull away.'

Once carburetion issues had been sorted out, Tony scored his and Modus's first Atlantic win in the Leinster Trophy race at Mondello Park, where the post-race celebrations took a turn for the worse as Anglo-Irish relations deteriorated.

The real turning point came a week later, when Atlantic's Irish tour fetched up at Mondello Park for the Leinster Trophy.

'We were running the Holbays,' Jordan continued, and were testing at Mondello, all pounding round. Those were the days when you'd arrive a few days before. "Ah, we'll just get the sheep off the circuit, and you can go and drive there. You'll be all right!" Tony had a pick-up problem in the first hairpin, there were a lot of carburetion problems in those days. And John Nicholson, bless his soul, came over and said, "I can see you've got a bit of a carburetion problem there, I'd like to have a look at it for you, if you don't mind." "That's very kind of you John, but you're really the opposition, aren't you?" He was racing the Lyncar against us. He says, "No, no, that's all right." Okay, he was looking to do some more engine work, but even so it was a nice thing to do. It was a sunny day, he put his box of jets and the emulsion tubes on the rear wing, and just changed all the jets around. "You don't want an F15 in there, you want an F12," he said. "Try that." And Tony went out and was immediately three-tenths of a second quicker. We didn't look back.'

That race provided Tony with his first win for Modus. He won the first heat with Alan Jones taking

the second in a March 73B. They met for the 41-lap final, with Tony taking pole because his had been the faster heat. But it was Jones who spurted into the lead, and Tony who had to follow him for the first 33 laps. But then he pounced and pulled away to a 2.6s victory. He broke the lap record along the way, in the longest race ever held at that time at the tricky little track.

'We had a daggy old pit board,' Jordan recalled, 'and there was a Scottish fellow who helped us out at races, name of Frank Williamson, and who worked as a buyer for the Modus building company. And he took this pit board and chucked it into the air in celebration, and it smashed to bits. He says, "Oh well, that's got rid of that!"

'The sequel to that win was we went to some fancy hotel and they had a band for the presentation. They were standing playing the Irish national anthem and Frank, who is a bit of a character, starts to conduct the band. Taking the piss, everyone standing very solemnly. This little Irish fella comes and chucks this glass of what we thought was water but was actually vodka, into Frank's face. Frank says, "Whadda you do that for?" And the other guy says, "Dat was a double vodka." Frank, quick as a flash, says, "Why didn't ye give it me in a glass? I'd have drunk it."

After that it ended up a little fisty. We ended up in this little toilet, I was dragging Alan (Jones) off, and he had this Irish guy and he's banging him against the wall, "I'm gonna smack you around…" It ended up peacefully, and we ended up in the early hours in this hotel and slipped the night porter a couple of quid. There's Frank Williamson and myself, Janet and Tony, and a couple of other people; the fella brought out three or four roast chickens, so we ripped them apart and hoiked into them, about three o'clock in the morning.'

Tony won again at Brands Hatch later that month, beating Morgan, Nicholson and Jones. But the finale at Oulton Park proved a crashing disappointment, literally. He slithered off the wet road going up Clay Hill while acclimatising himself to the conditions, and didn't even get to start from the pole position he had earned.

Nevertheless, he finished third in the series despite missing the first two races, with 101 points to Nicholson's 132 and Jim Crawford's 127. He was still dissatisfied, however. Even his smooth second at Monaco in the Modus Formula Three car, an excellent result for a new marque and for an untested car, went all but unnoticed in the excitement over Tom's stunning victory in the Ippokampos March.

It was time for some serious analysis.

Janet denied that Tony was feeling frustrated as others, such as Richard Robarts, got to Formula One before him. 'I really don't think he was. He never showed that. He just knew that he had to keep going and do better. I think he always knew that he was going to get there, so I don't think it worried him. We were friendly with Richard and his wife, and we used to go out and have dinner. It wasn't a problem. He just knew his time would come, and I think Richard had started racing before him anyway.

'I can't remember him particularly worrying about it, I don't remember him being upset about it. But he was worried about where the money was going to come from. However, he'd got Teddy Savory behind him by then in Atlantic, and there were people starting to get interested in him. He was aware of that.'

He was also very well aware of what his detractors thought of him, and there were plenty of them; people who still saw his self-confidence as pure arrogance. He had lost no time responding to them in his interview with *Motoring News* the previous year. His views were trenchant, but extremely perceptive.

'I suppose it's because they don't like somebody rich,' he said, 'and they don't like me winning at 21, probably because the English temperament demands adulation for the underdog. Also, a lot of journalists are very bigoted and if I say I am not in favour of baulking or something, they tend to think that I'm a big ****. As far as the drivers are concerned I think that is because I am successful and on the way up; after all, nobody has shown such consistency as me this season (1973) in Formula Three.'

That winter he started up his own business as the official importer of Bardahl oil into the UK. But he also invested a great deal of time in some achingly candid self-analysis, as he explained without flinching to Roebuck.

'What had I done?' he questioned. 'Well, I did a

season of Formula Ford, won a championship and more races than anyone else that year. I did two years of Formula Three, won two championships in 1973. I won a Grovewood Award. I did Formula Atlantic, with a new team, competing in only half the races, and still finished third in the championship. So what's wrong? It can't be my results, so it must be something else. I looked at the magazines. A lot of people had said that I was inconsistent. So, okay, I admit that on very rare occasions, you get to a meeting and you just don't feel that you are going to be quick that day. It doesn't happen often, of course.'

And he made what, in retrospect, seems a remarkably bold and tough decision.

'I decided that 1975 was going to be my make or break year. You can't go motor racing for ever – if you're not successful, all you do is drag around the place, conning money from people here and there, and generally becoming a bum. Teddy Savory has always had a principle about not drinking anything for 24 hours before flying his helicopter, so I decided to adopt the same policy towards racing. I decided that I would not go out late on any night before a race. I approached the whole thing much more calmly.'

Whatever talking to he gave himself, Tony Brise could have had no way of understanding just how successful his new regime would be, in the short time that he had left.

After the post-race fuss at Mondello Park, Tony relaxed by taking a different kind of pole position.

CHAPTER 13

Shadow boxing

Tom, 1975

'I'm not saying that he was an Andretti, but there was an element of him being a somebody when you met him. You thought, "This bloke's a bit special."'
Alan Henry

Greatness seemed just around the corner for the Shadow team from the moment that Tony Southgate's elegant new DN5 took to the track. The DN3 had shown flashes of promise, but the team was hurt by the death of Peter Revson and compromised by the search thereafter for his replacement. Following the failure of a titanium component in Revson's front suspension, Southgate had cut back on the material's use and the DN3 had become heavier. Jean-Pierre Jarier also felt that its aerodynamics limited straightline speed, and reported that it oversteered in high-speed corners (perhaps another reason why Tom had, at times, starred in it) and often overheated. Now the team had regrouped and redesigned and was ready to push forward again.

After testing the new DN5 (the DN4 was a CanAm machine) at the Paul Ricard circuit in the south of France, Jarier knew that they had a winner on their hands. Having had so much input into its design brief, the Frenchman understandably felt an affinity with it, that it was *his* car. Tom only drove the DN5 briefly but even before the first race, the Argentinian Grand Prix on 12 January, a political situation arose which made it seem possible that he would never get to race it.

At the London Racing Car Show, earlier that month, it emerged that talks had been under way for some time

Pete Kerr, Tom, Jean-Pierre Jarier, Alan Rees, Tony Southgate and team owner Don Nichols are all smiles after the new Shadow DN5's first blistering test laps of the Paul Ricard circuit early in 1975.

Part of the reason why Tom was reluctant to leave was his relationship with the Shadow team personnel, especially team manager Alan Rees (far left).

team chief could offer Ronnie the prospect of nothing better for 1975 than another warm-over of the Lotus 72. A new car, the 76, had failed miserably in 1974 and its successor, the 77, was still on the drawing board and was now unlikely to appear until later in the year at the earliest. The 72 had been ground-breaking when it first appeared in 1970, with its revolutionary wedge shape, side-mounted radiators and torsion bar suspension, and won World Championships that season for Jochen Rindt (posthumously) and Fittipaldi in 1972. But it was now very long in the tooth, and its competitive edge had been blunted by changes in the regulations and tyre technology, as well as by progress other teams had made. Alan Rees knew that Peterson was unhappy, and the possibility of persuading 'SuperSwede' to join his team was simply too good to miss.

All Tom could do was maintain a dignified silence even though the situation, especially when he got to Argentina, was uncomfortable. Maths of three into two clearly did not favour him, and the deal was for him to be swapped for Peterson with John Player Lotus. Shadow believed it could afford the expensive Swede, while Chapman believed he was getting a cheaper driver with a similar level of talent, plus a cash payment to sweeten the pot. From Tom's point of view it was hardly the most flattering deal, nor the most propitious, given Lotus's financial problems. He could have been forgiven for feeling like a pawn on a chessboard.

Lotus team manager Peter Warr emphatically denied that Peterson would be leaving, but said, 'I would be foolish to think that no teams had spoken to Ronnie during the off-season. But as far as I'm concerned, Ronnie and Jacky (Ickx) will be driving for me in Buenos Aires.'

Peterson's reaction was simple, if slightly bemused, when Alan Henry suggested he would be moving. 'Oh, am I?' Rees, meanwhile, said he was in no position to say anything but confirmed that his drivers would be Jarier and Pryce.

The rumours persisted, however, that Shadow team owner Don Nichols was impressed with the idea of signing Peterson, who was a close friend of Rees's since driving a Rees-run Winkelman Brabham in Albi's Formula Two race back in 1969, and then running together at March. At the same time, Chapman was known to have been keeping an eye on Tom's progress throughout 1973 and '74 so, to some, the swap scheme appeared to dovetail nicely.

'I remember having talks with Alan Henry about it, and being very worried,' Nella said. 'Lotus had a history of accidents, wheels falling off. And I thought, "God, he can't go and drive for them. Something's going to happen." Thomas was very loyal, too loyal perhaps. And at times I think they took advantage of that. I suppose it's only natural that they later tried to hold on to him. Reesie might have said, "Tom, you're surely not going to

to lure an unhappy Ronnie Peterson away from Lotus, to join Jarier at UOP Shadow. Though he had won three races with Lotus in 1974, the team was clearly not the force it had been in 1973 when the swift Swede had first gone there. He had proved quite convincingly that season that he was quicker than Emerson Fittipaldi, but upon leaving the team for McLaren in 1974 the Brazilian had taken a second title. Ronnie was beginning to think he was running out of time, and knew that Colin Chapman faced serious budgetary restraints. Sponsor John Player had been obliged to cut back its financial contribution to Lotus because of the state of the economy and through indirect pressure from the Tobacco Advisory Council. This meant that the Lotus

leave me now?" And Thomas would have said, "No, no, I'll stay with you." That was Thomas. He was like that.'

'I don't really want to go,' Tom said now, clearly rather bewildered by all the political wrangling. 'I like everybody here.'

Everybody liked him, too, not the least because of his loyalty. 'He was always happy to stay,' Rees said, years later. 'He had a strong sense of loyalty. Too strong. Tom was going to get a good deal, anyway, because Chapman was pretty interested in him. It seemed to suit both sides. It would have suited Tom, too, although perhaps he wouldn't have appreciated it at the time. He would have gone to a better team, not at the time, maybe, but overall he'd have done well out of it.'

There were other, unseen, factors at work in the background. Nichols was doing everything he could to woo the Matra aerospace company into returning to Formula One as an engine supplier, and having both Peterson and Frenchman Jarier aboard was seen to be a potent sweetener. And he also wanted a topline name for his Formula 5000 programme, with a modified version of the DN5 design called the DN6, which would run in the United States that season.

At the same time, heavy-hitting American entrepreneur Roger Penske, whose team had made a return to Formula One at the end of 1974, was also chasing Peterson's signature, and the other American team, run by Vel Miletich and Indianapolis legend Parnelli Jones, was considering seeking a partner for their own ace, Mario Andretti. Peterson was also the choice there.

By the time the circus moved to Interlagos for the second race of the year, the Brazilian Grand Prix on 26 January a fortnight later, sharp-eyed journalists spotted a Shadow DN5 with Peterson's name on the cockpit sides...

Straight away in Argentina, Jarier proved that Southgate's new DN5 was the class of the field. He took pole position by half a second from Carlos Pace's Brabham BT44B, but while doing a practice start out of the pits on his way to the grid, he suffered failure of a brand new crownwheel and pinion that sidelined him from the race. Fittipaldi won. It transpired that all of the teeth on the crownwheel and pinion had stripped off, after being manufactured from the wrong material.

At Le Mans in June 1974, Jarier had injured a wrist in a minor accident. He had largely kept the incapacity to himself for fear that it might jeopardise his position within the team, and had only begun to regain his true form in the final races of the year. Now he had arrived at what should have been his moment of destiny in Formula One. In Brazil, he simply left his opposition for dead in qualifying to take another dominant pole. In the race he calmly bided his time as Carlos Reutemann made a superior start in his Brabham, then outbraked the Argentinian and opened up a commanding 26s advantage until the fuel metering unit jammed on the 33rd lap,

handing victory to Reutemann's team-mate Pace. Jarier's fastest lap was a second quicker than next fastest man Mario Andretti. It was small wonder that Peterson, a lowly 15th for Lotus, was so keen to jump ship.

Almost overlooked in all the excitement over the new car, if not in all the hoopla about possible driver changes, Tom just quietly got on with the job. He had to make do with a DN3 at both races, modifications to which centred mainly on a splash of colour on its wings to brighten up UOP's black livery. In Argentina he was 14th on the grid alongside Jochen Mass in the second McLaren, nearly three seconds slower than his team-mate. He was running 10th with two laps to go when the transmission failed, leaving him classified 11th. In Brazil he started 14th again, three and a half seconds off Jarier. He made a bold start but gradually fell back with poor handling as the front tyres went off and understeer built up. He crashed out on the 32nd lap after running no higher than 11th.

He was not completely inactive on the political front, however. Chapman had told the media prior to that race, 'Tom has been up at our racing factory and looked around, liked the people and set-up, and we like him. Only details are to be sorted out – he could be in our car this weekend in Brazil.'

But Tom's London solicitors issued this statement on his behalf at the same time: 'Lotus could not match my present financial arrangements with Shadow so I will be staying put.'

While Jarier starred in the new DN5 in Brazil, as second driver Tom had to rely on the old DN3. He crashed it after 32 laps.

Peterson to leave Lotus?

UOP-Shadow deal discussed

DRAMATIC negotiations to secure Ronnie Peterson's release from his Lotus Grand Prix contract have almost certainly been under way for the past fortnight or so. There seem to have been some serious problems concerning the Swede's 1975 commitment with Colin Chapman's team and intense behind-the-scenes activity is under way in an effort to secure his services for the works UOP Shadow team. What's even more surprising is suggestions that recent Shadow recruit Tom Pryce may be "traded" for Peterson in some last-moment switch, possibly even before Sunday's Argentina Grand Prix at Buenos Aires.

Both teams are remaining tight-lipped on the subject, along with Peterson who was due to fly to Argentina last night (Wednesday). The basis of the problem seems to surround the cut-back in John Player's financial support for the Lotus team, a sum which is known to have been reduced as a result of economic stringency and indirect pressure from the Tobacco Advisory Council. "We've all had to make economies with the economic climate as it is" Lotus Racing Manager Peter Warr told us on Monday, "and one of the areas we've had to look at is drivers' retainers. We've tried to co-operate with Ronnie and Jacky on this subject to see if there's any way in

which they can help us in reducing expenditure. And saving thus made means we've got more to spend on the racing cars and, indirectly, improve their chances of success or glory or whatever motivates a driver."

Emphatically, Warr denied that Peterson would be leaving but he did add "I'd be foolish to think that no teams had spoken to Ronnie during the off-season. But as far as I'm concerned, Ronnie and Jacky will be driving for me in Buenos Aires." Peterson declined to comment, his only remark to us being a slightly amused "Oh, are I?" while Alan Rees simply told us he was in "no position to say anything. My drivers will be Jarier and Pryce."

It's nevertheless known that Shadow boss Don Nichols is extremely impressed by Peterson and the blond Swede has been a great friend of Rees ever since he drove a Winkelmann F2 Lotus at Albi in 1969. Pryce was a driver under Colin Chapman's scrutiny during 1973 and '74 and it would probably dovetail well with Shadow's plans to exchange his contract for Ronnie's in addition one assumes, to a substantial payment to Team Lotus. For Pryce the prospects offered would be equally attractive as in his Shadow position, while Peterson would doubtless find financial satisfaction as well as a great rapport with Rees. In addition, with Jarier or the strength there would still be the hope, albeit slender, of a Matra tie-up and Nichols is known to be impressed with the idea of such a car handled by Peterson.

Even if the deal is not arranged before the two South American races, there is a chance that it could be organised before South Africa or the European season. One thing is for sure, although nobody is doing any talking off the record, some pretty high-powered negotiations have been in hand for some time between the two teams.

Underlying tensions were caused in the team by persistent rumours of a swap in which Tom would be traded to Lotus in return for Ronnie Peterson. This clipping, written by Alan Henry for Motoring News, was right on the money.

Ultimately the swap deal with Peterson came to nothing, even though, according to Rees, at one stage it was all done bar the final rubber-stamping. 'What happened was that John Logan, the president of UOP, didn't want to do it right at the last minute. Obviously, when you do these deals, you negotiate it all out and then you tell the people at the top what you are doing. And that's why it all happened – or didn't happen! – at the last minute. When we told him what we were proposing to do, what we had all but agreed to do, he didn't like what had been done and he said, "No."' Since UOP was paying Shadow's bills, Logan's word was final.

From Tom's point of view, it was undoubtedly for the better. Henry had his doubts that he would have benefited quite as much as others believed from a move to Lotus. Chapman had enjoyed a deep relationship with Tom's childhood hero Jimmy Clark, which was based on friendship and genuine respect. Since Clark's death, however, Chapman had changed and his relationship with Jochen Rindt was always fractious. Chapman had a poor reputation for handling drivers. Henry was very close to Tom, and his parents still remembered the friendship 30 years later. 'Tom was

immensely serious about motor racing,' Henry said. 'It's very difficult when a bloke is a good friend actually to get a measure of just how committed he is to it. He was, after all, a very quiet person. But if he had turned up at Lotus when there was a 78 or a 79, he'd have been Chapman's darling. If he'd gone there when they had their backs to the wall with that old 72, he'd have been broken by Chapman and would have ended up like Bob Evans did with the troublesome Lotus 77 a year later; if Evans had come along a year later than he did it might have been all so different for him.'

Jack Pryce remembered one time at a race in 1974 when Tom was sleeping in the back of the Shadow truck and a woman poked her head in. 'She asked him if she could speak with Tom Pryce. Mald told her that he wasn't around, and she disappeared... It wasn't nastiness, he would just rather avoid all the fuss of fame.'

'His quietness was a by-product of his shyness and the fact that he really did come from a country boy background,' Henry continued. 'I think that he had a gentleness about him that reflected in the way he drove a racing car. I always thought that he had the star quality, to a lesser extent, that radiated off a driver like Mario Andretti. I'm not saying that he was an Andretti, but there was an element of him being a *somebody* when you met him. You thought, "This bloke's a bit special." Perhaps if he'd been around 10 years later he wouldn't have been pushy enough to get as far as he got in the seventies. I think his only disadvantage was that he wasn't assertive enough.

'Reesie understood Tom, which is why Shadow was ultimately the best place for him. I always felt that Reesie understood Tom in a way that Jackie Oliver didn't, in a way that Don Nichols didn't. I think Reesie was always clever with racing drivers in that respect.'

Now, after all the fuss, Tom duly stayed with the team, and his ultimate fate was settled. In an interview for *Autosport* with Chris Witty in February, Rees explained why he thought Tom needed more mileage and why, initially, he thought Tom would not be able to do with a DN5 what Jarier had been doing.

'I think that what you've got to remember about Tom is he came into Formula One racing in the middle of last year. He has done a lot of good things already which, when you compare it with Ronnie, who's in his sixth season, you can obviously see that without a lot of experience that Ronnie's got, Tom won't be able to make the same use of the car as Jean-Pierre. Not yet, anyway.'

And he further explained why Tom's performance level had dipped in the latter part of 1974.

'If you take the races one by one, the only circuit he's ever known to this day in Formula One is Brands Hatch. That's the only circuit he's ever gone to with as much knowledge as the other drivers. He was fastest in the first session, fifth overall by the end and he put up a tremendously smooth performance following Fittipaldi

around for about two-thirds of the race before he started having trouble. But if that hadn't happened, indications are that he would have followed Fittipaldi home in third place.

'Every circuit he goes to is a new one. At Dijon we went testing for two days before the event and it's generally a slow circuit which suits us. Tom had a whole day at the circuit. I think in those days, because he was so new, we didn't really know much about him and about his style. So he tended to get perhaps a freer hand to drive the car the way he liked than he gets now. He put on a tremendous display in practice but, at the same time, he couldn't keep any tyres on his car, and that's not the way to go grand prix racing. He had to start on hard tyres, which would have put him at a disadvantage.

'From that point on, when we started to discover how he drove, and what were his good points and perhaps what were his weaker ones, we started to try and mould him as a driver. I don't think he shows any less ability than he did in the middle of last year and what I'm waiting for is when he starts going back to some of the circuits that he raced on last year.'

Presciently, Rees ended the interview with the comment, 'Maybe, when Tom gets more experience, he'll be in the same position as Jean-Pierre. They're both excellent prospects.'

It was not until he got to South Africa for the third race, in March, that he finally got his hands on a DN5, but that coincided with a downturn in the team's performance. No matter what they tried, Southgate, Oliver and Rees could not massage South American performance out of their cars. The DN5 was ill-suited to the track, slow on the long main straight, and both Tom

ABOVE: *Tom finally got his hands on a DN5 for the South African Grand Prix, which unfortunately coincided with a decline in the team's fortunes due to aerodynamic shortcomings, as it struggled to match its South American performances.* BELOW: *At Brands Hatch in March it was a different matter altogether, as Tom celebrated by taking a dominant pole position for the non-championship Race of Champions.*

and Jarier struggled. The latter qualified 13th, Tom 19th. He was going backwards, even with the new wonder car. Tom caught and passed his team-mate on the 16th lap and went on to finish ninth; Jarier's car broke a couple of exhaust pipe primaries early on, and blew its engine after 37 laps. Shadow went back to Europe with its tail between its legs – but good news was just around the corner. The non-championship races were still a popular means of adding mileage in those days, and Don Nichols entered two cars for the Race of Champions on 16 March at Brands Hatch – Tom's circuit.

He was unstoppable in Friday's cold and damp practice session, slithering the DN5 round with complete abandon to take pole position with a lap of 1m 34.9s. Jody Scheckter, the winner at Kyalami 15 days earlier, was next in his Tyrrell, a second adrift with 1m 35.9s. Jarier, third on the grid after struggling with brake problems, lapped in 1m 37.3s.

Behind them lined up drivers of the calibre of 1974 event winner Jacky Ickx, Peterson, John Watson, Mark Donohue and reigning Champion Fittipaldi.

For all that he was a shy boy from Ruthin, Tom did not suffer fools gladly, and he was very wary of national newspaper writers. One in particular really irritated him at Brands. He told Henry, 'I had some bloke come up to me and start asking me how I did it, after I'd set pole position. What can you say? I always find myself getting a little short with them, although I sometimes wish that I hadn't been so harsh a few minutes later!'

Race day started with typical March weather: a biting wind, damp patches and the odd flurry of snow. Such was the confusion that only Tom, Scheckter, Ickx and Peterson of the front runners opted to stay on slick tyres at the start.

Ickx jumped it, shooting between Scheckter and the two Shadows before they even moved, while Tom only got away fifth from the traditionally difficult right-hand side of the upward-sloping track. Scheckter, angered by Ickx's move, grabbed the lead at Bottom Bend and quickly pulled away. He had four seconds' advantage as they crossed the start-finish line.

It was soon apparent that wet tyres were the wrong choice. Jarier pitted for slicks at the end of lap two, promoting Tom a place, and a lap later he moved up another one as he blasted by Peterson. Another lap later, Ickx was also history. Now it was just Tom versus Scheckter, the South African 12 seconds ahead.

For a while they traded fastest lap, but then Jody began to get into lapped traffic, and Tom quickly started to slash the deficit. By lap 16 he was only five seconds

At the start Tom threw away the advantage of pole with too much wheelspin, as Jacky Ickx jumped the gun from the second row to slip alongside Jody Scheckter and into the lead.

down, by lap 20, three and a half. He was charging, setting the fastest lap in 1m 21.1s. It was only a matter of time before the sheer force of his drive took him past the Tyrrell. By lap 25 they were nose to tail, again after Jody had trouble with backmarkers. As they sped through Clearways at the end of that lap, the Cosworth DFV in Scheckter's car coughed and spewed a cloud of oil smoke. It was over. As the South African pulled into the pits to retire, Tom swept majestically into a lead he never surrendered. Three years after he had dominated the Formula Three race at the same meeting for Royale, he had won his first race in the big league. That day he became the first – and thus far the only – Welsh driver to win a major international Formula One race. After vanquishing Peterson, Watson finished runner-up, more than half a minute behind.

'Tom was possessed of a very natural and huge talent,' Watson said 30 years later. 'I first spotted him

Having caught Scheckter, Tom swept into the lead when the South African's engine failed and was never thereafter challenged on his day of days.

while I was at Brands Hatch standing at Bottom Bend on the run in to Surtees, when Tom was racing in Formula Atlantic. Mike Earle and I were watching the race, and Tom's ability stood out by a country mile. The guy had huge amounts of natural ability, and he came from an entirely different background to, say, Tony Brise, a much softer, rural, family-orientated background. Tom was maybe more like me than Tony was. We were more of a kind.

'We spent a bit of time together because we both did Formula Two in 1974 and travelled round a bit together. We'd have supper together. The thing I noticed about him was that he wasn't a very worldly man when he came into international motor racing. When he started going out with Nella, she was more worldly. I remember one time in Italy having dinner, and what Tom wanted was chicken and chips. And there in Italy you had the choice of the most incredible food, but that was all he wanted because he hadn't grown enough yet to enjoy and understand it. It was one of those memories that stuck with me.

'Then the next big step was when he won the Race of Champions. I remember I passed Ronnie in the Lotus

and Chapman was so pissed off that one of his cars was overtaken by a Surtees that he just didn't want to know. He couldn't deal with it.'

When he had won the Formula Three race in 1972, Tom found that backing off too much when in the lead risked losing concentration. Now he told *Autosport*'s Pete Lyons, 'I had to drive hard at first, but as soon as I was in the lead I backed off, straight away. I was able just to watch my pit signals and know that if a challenge came I had something in reserve. It was a nice feeling, but I don't think it taught me much.

'Mind you, in Formula One that's been the only time I've been in that position, and I must say that I could see a danger of losing my rhythm and perhaps some of my concentration. I felt I had to keep concentrating hard even though I wasn't trying as much as before, so that I could quickly get back into my rhythm if the challenge ever did materialise from behind.'

It never did. That day he was truly in a class of his own, giving the clearest indication yet of the sort of form rivals could expect of him in a well-sorted car on a circuit he knew intimately.

He gave his own account of the success to *Motor*'s Mike Doodson: 'I'd just dropped the clutch when Jacky Ickx shot past me. My side of the grid was very wet, so that made a big difference. Several others went past me, too, including Ronnie Peterson, but I passed him before the end of the first lap.

'Ickx then held me up for almost two laps, but I made a bit of an effort to overtake him, and then I was in second place behind Jody. At this stage I was making a few mistakes: I was trying to take a wider line around some of the corners, but it was still very wet and slippery for slicks off the line, so I was sliding up the kerbs.

'It took me a couple of laps to gather myself up again. Jody seemed to be going very well, but there were only a couple of places where he had any advantage over me. My Shadow was putting its power down very well and I felt very confident.

'Then, just as I'd got him in my sights, Jody's engine blew and he pulled into the pits. That left me with the lead, and it was difficult to concentrate on staying there without making any more mistakes.

'I always wanted to win a Formula One race at Brands, which is my home circuit. Now that it's happened I feel really good. So do the UOP people: they say it's a rare and wonderful thing the Stars and Stripes was played at a Formula One race.'

It was a good meeting for Cledwyn Ashford too; he found a paddock pass and was thus able to join Jack in its exclusive confines. Jack's great memory of that day, his son's victory apart, was of watching him and Ronnie, and their hand-sawing mastery of the slippery conditions from the inside of Clearways.

On 13 April, just over a week after his wedding day,

Tom is joined on the rostrum by 11th placed David Purley, who won the Formula 5000 section in his Chevron B30.

Tom was unable to repeat the success in the other non-title race, the *Daily Express* International Trophy race at Silverstone. He qualified fifth, but after another poor start the aerodynamics of the DN5 militated against another strong recovery drive on a circuit with long straights and few medium-speed corners and Shadow had to be content with ninth place after a race-long chase after Carlos Reutemann's Brabham. Niki Lauda, the World Champion-elect, won.

For Tony, 1975 began with another bout of disillusion; it was becoming as familiar as singing Auld Lang Syne on New Year's Eve. The plan initially was for Teddy Savory's Modus operation to move up by building a Formula Two car for Tony, powered by John Nicholson's engines. Everything was geared up, but Tony had to bring £12,000, half of what Max Mosley at March had required the previous year. But again it didn't happen, because of money. 'Ted had a contract with Tony and he was quite hard with him,' recalled Nick Jordan, who would have built up the car. 'Ted said, "You come and you do it with us; I'll put this much in but you have to find 12 grand."

'I remember Tony sitting up in the office with Jo Marquart, saying, "I can't really get the money, Jo. Ah well, I won't be doing it." It was quite tough for him. So I went to have a bite with him down the café, and I said, "Tony, I'm gonna tell you what we're going to do here."

And he says, "Well, I don't want to do Atlantic again." I says, "Look, look at your future. You're not going to do Atlantic again, where else are you gonna go? Sideways, to sportscars or whatever, back to Formula Three? Atlantic is where you can win it. Johnny Nick will do the engines; get your Holbay engine updated by him, we've got a car here this year with some updates on it, which we can piece together, we've got the little truck; I'll look after the car, and we'll wax them. And if you win races that will give you the credibility to go forward. Just go and eat humble pie with Ted. Just tell him, "Look, I haven't got the money for that, but how about if we do this…"'

'So he then rang Ted up and said he'd had an idea. And later, Ted phoned me and said, "I'll tell you what we're going to do… We've got the engines here, you look after the car, we'll stay in Atlantic. It's a brilliant idea…" I just smiled and said, "Oh, great, smashing."'

They updated the Modus M1, reskinned the monocoque, did some aerodynamic work, and headed for the first race at Mallory Park. It was wet. 'The opposition wasn't that great at that time, I'll admit that,' Jordan said. 'Tony got a lead out to 18s and I said, "He's going to drop this." Sure enough, he did drop it, at Gerard's. And he came back with a piece of brake disc in his hand, and he said, "That's what caused the accident, it broke."

'And I said, "Oh, is it really? *It* broke? Well, first of all, you shouldn't be braking at Gerard's, so if you braked you were wrong. The second thing is, this crack is all grey, it's all new, so it wasn't cracked otherwise you'd have rust marks in it. You dropped it, and this is the damage." In fact, the car nearly went over the bank. Jo Marquart was livid. Tony got a huge bollocking.'

Interestingly, Tony remembered things in a different way when he did an interview with Nigel Roebuck in *Autosport* later that year. Admitting to a spin he said, 'I still managed to win, but afterwards Jo Marquart said, "Look, you finished last year with two shunts and now you start off this year with a spin. Now that's wrong." So then I had even more soul-searching, and after that we won six on the trot, fairly comfortably, too.'

That last bit was correct. Just as he had been at times in Formula Ford and Formula Three, he was once again the man to beat after six dominant on-the-trot victories at Brands Hatch, Snetterton, Silverstone, Brands Hatch, Silverstone and Oulton Park. And all while dovetailing it with his Formula One commitments.

Ian Flux remembered Tony demonstrating the Embassy Hill at Mallory Park in August. 'There was one

Tom savours a superb victory. That day, 16 March 1975, he became the only Welshman ever to win a Formula One race. That record still remains.

hell of a crowd, as it was Bay City Rollers Day. We bowled up with a Transit and the Hill on the back of a trailer, and couldn't believe the traffic jam to get in, we were almost too late. We'd underestimated the power of the Radio One Roadshow! Tony did 10 laps in the car, I think, just demonstrating it. He was overawed by the thousands of people there that day.'

At the end of the year he faced very tough opposition from former Formula Three racer Gunnar Nilsson, who had switched to driving a Chevron for Ted Moore's Rapid Movements team. At his beloved Brands he had even spun out of third place chasing the Swede and Lola driver Nick May.

'The Chevron was quick and Gunnar was fantastic, a lovely guy,' Jordan said. 'He was good, a bit like an Alan Jones. You know, gritty. *hard*. No question about it, he was one of the best to come out of Sweden. Same level as Tony. Ronnie was pretty laid-back, and if you lit a fire under him, he'd do it. Gunnar knew he had to do it every time – that was the difference in their mental approach.'

Jordan had no doubts about his own driver, either. 'At Silverstone, at the support race to the British Grand Prix, Tony was dicing for pole position and a misfire developed and blew the centre out of a plug. I'd seen all the powder, whipped the engine cover off, put a new plug in, and he said, "How long have I got?" There was about seven minutes left; on the grand prix circuit about enough for his warm-up and two laps. That was it. He was about four or five tenths off pole. He went out and got pole by about two-tenths. He switched it off as he came into the pit lane, undid his belts, got out and started to undo his helmet. And I went round the back with him and said, "How was it?" And his face was drained, white, and his eyes were out here. He'd *been* there. And he said, "Jesus, I don't want to have to drive that thing like that all the time. I was *so* close to losing it at Club!" But it showed the mettle of the man. Good drivers can always get that last bit. Senna could. Schumacher can. They've made their mind up.'

Tony did not win any of the final five races – his best results were two thirds and a sixth. Instead, two fell to Jim Crawford, one to Richard Morgan, one to Ted Wentz and one to Nilsson, who also dominated the final Southern Organs championship rounds. But he had done enough to win the John Player International Atlantic title with 150 points to Crawford's 125. 'I'm very relieved,' he admitted to Roebuck, 'because I believe that, if you are going to make it, you only have so many years in which to do it. Otherwise you get known as the 'King of the Club Racers', and that's as far as you will go.'

Long before the season was over, however, things had finally begun to happen elsewhere for him. The long wait for Formula One was over.

CHAPTER 14

Breaking through

Tony, 1975

'Tony had been pretty devastating in Formula Atlantic. It was obvious to me that the guy was a little bit special.'
Frank Williams

The Formula One circus moved on to the daunting Montjuich Park street circuit for the Spanish Grand Prix on 27 April. Nobody knew it as the field assembled in the paddock, but this would become one of the most infamous races in the sport's turbulent history. Among the drivers there was a new face, in one of Frank Williams's cars. His regular pilot, the cheerful Frenchman Jacques Laffite, had a clashing Formula Two engagement at the Nürburgring that took precedence. While looking for a suitable replacement, Williams's eyes fell on Tony Brise.

Whereas Roger had enjoyed the support of Tom Wheatcroft from an early stage of his career, and Tom had that fairytale jump to Shadow after his stunning victory in Monaco's Formula Three race, Tony had been forced to go the long way round, a victim of Formula One team managers' incomprehensible myopia.

Alan Henry thought, 'Tony had a bit of edge to him and was quite an argumentative lad. The Brises, that Dartford brigade, were a tough bunch...' Yet nobody had appeared to want Tony. In contrast to Tom, he was much more outgoing, a brash young man who appeared fully aware of his own talent. Some perceived that purely as arrogance, but it was more a blend of complete confidence in his startling ability allied to his disappointment in being overlooked for so long.

Autosport's Nigel Roebuck had already met him on a couple of occasions. 'I thought he was cocky, more than

On his début in Spain in April 1975, Tony took to Formula One with complete ease, prompting Frank Williams to suggest he would have gone on to become 'an English great'.

Tony spurted into the lead of the second John Player International Atlantic Championship round, at Brands Hatch in March, and was never challenged again.

arrogant,' he suggested. 'Very cocksure, strutting about. But he should have been in Formula One at the same time that Roger and Tom came in.'

Despite his many victories in karting, Formula Ford, Formula Three and Formula Atlantic, Tony still nearly didn't get this chance. Williams initially considered Formula Two driver Giancarlo Martini, but fortunately changed his mind. Tony tested the Williams FW03 at Goodwood, lapping in 1m 11s within 20 laps. 'The step from Atlantic to Formula One didn't feel as bad as the move from Formula Three to Atlantic,' he told journalists. 'In fact, it felt very good!'

Unlike many similar deals, this was not one in which the driver had to bring money. Tony had finally got there on merit, at the ripe old age of 23. But he was only able to accept Williams's offer because there was no clashing Atlantic race that weekend. Modus boss Ted Savory released him especially so he could take up his big break.

'Tony had been pretty devastating in Formula Atlantic,' Williams recalled. 'It was obvious to me that the guy was a little bit special.'

The weekend began badly, however. Even before practice started it transpired that steel barriers had been incorrectly installed all around the circuit. In some cases the bolts were merely finger-tight; in others, they had been omitted altogether. The teams and drivers threatened to strike, the only thing preventing that ultimate rebellion being the fact that the paddock was located within the old Olympic stadium. It would have been the easiest thing for the rattled organisers to lock those gates, trapping the Formula One circus and holding it to ransom. In the end, the teams organised themselves and everyone set to with spanners, and nuts and bolts, making the barriers as safe as possible.

The resultant tense atmosphere was hardly conducive to a Formula One début, and the nature of the track was most definitely not for the timid. Montjuich Park snaked and slithered through the streets of Barcelona, often with sheer drops the other side of low walls. None of this bothered Tony in the slightest. Niki Lauda put his Ferrari on pole position in 1m 23.4s, James Hunt was third for Hesketh in 1m 23.8s, Tom eighth for Shadow in 1m 24.5s. Tony put the ageing Williams 18th on the grid in 1m 26.4s, with American star Mark Donohue for company. He was close behind other stars such as Jody Scheckter, Ronnie Peterson, Carlos Reutemann and Jacky Ickx. And his team-mate Arturo Merzario, who was significantly more experienced, was only 25th. The little Italian would start on the last row.

The problems continued on the opening lap. Mario Andretti tapped the back of Clay Regazzoni's Ferrari, knocking it into the Swiss driver's team-mate, Lauda. Patrick Depailler's Tyrrell lost a wheel in the incident. Two laps later, Alan Jones's Hesketh was taken out by Donohue's Penske after the American slid off on oil from the broken engine in Scheckter's Tyrrell.

Hunt crashed out of the lead after six laps and Andretti took over in his Parnelli until its suspension broke, a legacy of the first lap incident. From lap 17, the German driver Rolf Stommelen settled into the lead in his Embassy Hill, chased by Brazilian Carlos Pace in a Brabham.

Graham Hill was a motorsport legend, a god to many. From humble beginnings he had inveigled himself into a job with the emergent Team Lotus, and after parlaying that into a series of drives had become World Champion with BRM in 1962. Six years later, nearing 40, his resilience and reliable speed kept a shattered Lotus together in the terrible aftermath of Jim Clark's death at Hockenheim; after a three-way fight with former BRM team-mate Jackie Stewart and 1967 Champion Denny Hulme, Hill won a second crown. A serious accident at Watkins Glen in 1969 left him with broken legs but, though he recovered and raced again with typical determination and courage, his greatest days were behind him. He won the *Daily Express* International Trophy race at Silverstone in 1971, after Stewart and Pedro Rodriguez had met misfortune, and won Formula Two races at Thruxton that same year and Monza in 1972, when victory with Henri Pescarolo and Matra at Le Mans combined with his World titles and '66 victory in the Indianapolis 500 to make him the only man ever to win the triple crown of the World Championship, Indianapolis and Le Mans. But by the end of 1972, it was clear that his illustrious and long-running career was winding down. A second season of Formula One with Brabham had not been successful and new owner Bernie Ecclestone was more interested in the swift Argentinian Carlos Reutemann. It was apparent there would not be a place for Hill there in 1973, so he salvaged his famous pride by forming his own team. Embassy Racing with Graham Hill bought one of the new Tony Southgate-designed Shadow DN1s, which would run in competition to the UOP-sponsored works cars for Jackie Oliver and George Follmer. That first season was a disaster; the car was fragile and Hill never featured. For 1974 he commissioned Lola to build him a new car on an exclusive basis, and there were greater signs of promise as he ran Guy Edwards, Peter Gethin and Stommelen at times in a second car.

Hill sought greater independence, and harboured aspirations of becoming a constructor in his own right like his old rivals Jack Brabham, Bruce McLaren and John Surtees. In October 1974, he took on a designer called Andy Smallman, a quiet 24-year-old who hailed from Stafford and served his apprenticeship at the famous Vanden Plas coachbuilding company before joining Race Cars International in 1970 to work on its ambitious Nemo Formula Three car. He then joined Lola Cars where he worked on its unloved T260 CanAm racer that Jackie Stewart campaigned in 1971, together with various other sportscars for the Huntingdon marque and some of its successful Formula 5000 designs, before heading for Don Nichols' Advanced Vehicle Systems Shadow operation for 1973. He cut his teeth in Formula One working on the DN1, DN3 and DN5 cars, and the DN2 and DN4 CanAm

machines, before attracting Hill's attention. There was little time to create a completely new car, but Smallman went through the Lola T371 and made so many minor but significant improvements that Hill felt justified in rebranding the machine under his own name after its début in the 1975 South African Grand Prix. Stommelen had shown promise in the car in the Race of Champions, and now here it was, leading a grand prix for the first time.

Further back, Tony had made a good start. Moving up from his 18th starting position to 15th at the end of the first lap, he made another place when Tom dropped back from ninth in the lap three mêlée, and continued to make steady progress as he was chased by François Migault in the other Embassy Hill and the recovering Pryce. By the 20th lap he was running sixth, in a points-scoring position, when he and Tom had a collision at the hairpin. Tom ran into the back of the Williams and both of them spun. Tom had to bump-start his Shadow down the hill; Tony had to make a pit stop to check for damage and dropped back down to 12th. Tom would pit three laps later, for attention to a damaged nose and exhaust.

Then came the terrible accident on the 26th lap when the rear wing support on Stommelen's car broke as he crested the rise beyond the pits. This was one of the first occasions in which carbon fibre had been used as a support for the rear wing and, according to team insiders, the component had already developed a crack

The dominant victory proved to be the first of six consecutive triumphs in his Modus, which helped to secure him the 1975 title.

and been drilled to prevent the fault from spreading further. Robbed suddenly of all of its rear downforce, the Hill swerved hard into the barriers on the left-hand side of the track before bouncing into the air as the road sloped downwards. Pace closed his eyes and ducked beneath, but damaged his car in the process and was forced to retire. Stommelen's errant Hill landed atop a guardrail on the right, and slid along it until coming to rest by a marshals' post, where some spectators were standing in a prohibited area. They included a Spanish fireman and an American photographer. Four of them were killed. Stommelen was left slumped in the wreckage, suffering from broken legs, a broken wrist and several fractured ribs.

Roebuck who, at the time, was also working on Embassy's behalf for the team, recalled that fateful day. 'Quentin Spurring of *Autosport* was way ahead of his time with the deal he organised with Embassy, whereby he and I ran the Embassy Racing Club for punters, similar to the sort of thing Ron Dennis is now doing with McLaren.

The graduation to Formula One finally came courtesy of Frank Williams, who invited him to test an FW03 at Goodwood prior to standing in for Jacques Laffite in the Spanish Grand Prix.

'After the accident the Guardia Civil was just lashing out at anyone and everyone, and there was complete bedlam. The gutters were awash with fuel from Rolf's car, and all it needed was for somebody to drop a fag end... Luckily there was no fire, but the crowd was in such a mood that Quentin ran the gauntlet getting back to the paddock. At the accident scene he was quickly advised to get rid of his Embassy jacket.

'It was just unforgettable, seeing Rolf still slumped in the wreckage of the car at the top of the hill, conscious and staring straight ahead, and clearly in huge pain. And under the monocoque there was a body, and the place was strewn with wreckage. It really was the scene from hell, with a total absence of control.'

Amid the chaos, officials were finally prevailed upon to end the debacle prematurely. In the ensuing pandemonium, Jochen Mass had inherited the lead in his McLaren. When the race was red-flagged after 29 laps, the German was declared the winner from veteran Jacky Ickx in a Lotus and Reutemann in the other Brabham. Tony was seventh, two laps down, behind Jean-Pierre Jarier, Vittorio Brambilla and Lella Lombardi. The Italian woman became the first of her gender to score a championship point (actually, half a point as the race had not gone beyond half-distance). Before his brush with Tom, Tony had been running ahead of all three of them, and close behind Reutemann. The tragic circumstances surrounding his début overshadowed what he had achieved that day – he was well used to such vagaries of Fate by now – but Tony Brise left nobody who really examined his drive that day in any doubt that Formula One was where he truly belonged.

'Looking back on Spain,' Roebuck said, 'in practice the two blokes for sheer bravery were Wattie in the Surtees and Brise in Frank's car; and that was his first drive! I was just so impressed, because that's a bloody daunting place to go for your first grand prix. I was just so impressed by his confidence.'

Janet stayed at home for her husband's Formula One début, for the most prosaic of reasons. 'I was a personal assistant for PA Management Consultants, working in Sundridge Park in Bromley, and we couldn't afford it, really. I think the chance in Spain came quite suddenly, and he was off.

'As the race had been stopped prematurely, Tony was straight on the phone to me to tell me what had happened,' Janet remembered, 'because he knew it would be on the news and that I would be worrying about him.'

They had their small house in Bexley, a stark contrast indeed to the rented house in St George's Hill where Jenson Button found himself living during his first season in Formula One in 2000. Thus have times changed at the top of motorsport.

The paddock at Montjuich Park was the old Olympic stadium, and the fact that the teams could thus be locked in and held to ransom created further ill-feeling on a weekend noted for its tense and dangerous atmosphere. In the end, its events would prove pivotal in Tony's career.

'My father helped us with the deposit for the house and we had a full mortgage on it,' said Janet. 'I had to work and Tony was working for his father still, in the garage business; John had the Montessa dealership and a kart shop. Tony was importing Bardahl oil into the UK, so he had plenty to do. As soon as he got back from Spain he was straight back to work.'

Monaco was the next race on the calendar, and Tom went there brimming with confidence after his performance there in Tony Vlassopulos's Ippokampos March the previous year. The Shadow was perfectly suited to the track, and by the time qualifying was over only Niki Lauda's Ferrari 312T, with its smooth flat-12 engine, was ahead of Tom and Jarier on the grid; the Austrian lapped in 1m 26.40s, Tom in 1m 27.08s and 'Jumper' in 1m 27.25s. Tom had suffered severe toothache in Thursday's first practice sessions. But it had subsided on Friday and he was quite outstanding as he threw the black DN5 around the narrow streets of the Principality as if he was still in the Formula Three car. Afterwards he was so happy that, related Tony Southgate, 'it was like being with a 16-year-old!'

Former Baty team manager Bill Harding was in Monaco, but didn't have a ticket. 'In those days you could usually find somewhere to watch. Tom was sitting in the Shadow, ready to go out, and when he found I didn't have a ticket he insisted I take his driver's armband.

I was thus able to go anywhere and it completely confused all of the French because I had the right pass but obviously wasn't a Formula One driver! That armband remains one of my most treasured possessions.'

It began raining before the start and, according to the Shadow designer, Tom was duped by his team-mate into starting in second gear to avoid wheelspin. Lauda, Jarier, fourth-fastest Peterson and fifth man Vittorio Brambilla all outdragged him off the line. But the Frenchman's ploy backfired when he creamed his DN5 several times on the opening lap and retired; first, he brushed a barrier in Casino Square trying to outbrave Lauda, then he hit the chicane and punctured two tyres before finally clouting the wall hard at Tabac.

Tom moved up to chase Lauda and Peterson, passing Brambilla at the Station hairpin that same lap. The three of them pulled away from Scheckter and ran in a race of their own. After 10 laps only 1.7s separated them, and Tom was clearly revelling in the broad powerslides on the wet surface that made him the crowd favourite. The

Early in the Spanish race, Tony leads fellow débutant Alan Jones, in a Hesketh 308B, and experienced American Mark Donohue. François Migault and a delayed Tom follow.

track was drying, however, and after damaging a front wing after a brush with a barrier, he pitted for slick tyres on lap 21, having lost places to Scheckter and Fittipaldi two laps earlier after a brake bias problem created even more serious oversteer. The stop included replacement of the damaged nose, and that dropped him to the tail of the field. He was running 12th when John Watson repeated a practice spin near the swimming pool on the 37th lap and blocked the track; Tom chose to spin backwards into the barriers rather than run into the stricken Surtees, but now the replacement nose and rear wing were damaged. He was still struggling with the brake bias, and at Portier two laps later he got caught out and spun. This time he had to pit for good. There were elements of inexperience to his drive, but few who watched it were unimpressed by a performance that once again confirmed his world class.

Despite *his* stunning performance in Spain, Tony seemed destined to wait again for his reward, as he had yet to

crack Formula One permanently. There had been a chance that a Formula Two race in Jarama would clash with Monaco, necessitating another stand-in job for Laffite at Williams, but eventually the Spanish race was cancelled. So instead, like Tom the previous season, he was obliged to go back to Formula Three for another roll of the dice in front of the team managers who mattered. Teddy Savory had a car for him to drive. Once again it was the Formula Atlantic Modus, converted to Formula Three specification with smaller wheels and tyres, and a Neil Brown twin-cam engine.

As usual, there was a closely matched field vying for honours in the Principality. All of them were aware of what victory had done for Tom in 1974.

The first heat was won by Larry Perkins, a tough Australian racer nicknamed the 'Cowangie Kid' after his birth place. Driving one of Ron Tauranac's chunky Ralts he beat Sweden's Conny Andersson in a March and Belgian Patrick Neve in a Safir originally designed by Token creator Ray Jessop. The second heat belonged to Italian Renzo Zorzi in a year-old GRD-Lancia from Brazilian Alex Ribeiro in a March and Swede Ulf Svensson in a Brabham BT41 after Tony had been forced into the pits to have a loose plug lead reattached.

'I'd put a new set of plugs in,' mechanic Nick Jordan admitted. 'Fatal mistake. Should have left it. And he had a misfire and went backwards. He'd qualified second or third, was one of the favourites to win it. He came flying into the pits, off with the engine cover; I saw what was wrong, rammed the plug lead back on, and he went out again. And I was sick, literally. I spewed up in the corner. I knew I'd made a dreadful mistake. I was very emotional about the whole thing, took it very personally. I said, "I've screwed it for the lad."'

It was only later that weekend that Jordan would become one of the few people to know that Tony had already agreed terms with Graham Hill. At the time he thought he had destroyed his chances of making a decent enough impression to attract the big name team managers.

From 17th, Tony pushed his way back to the 10th place he needed to start the final 20th and last. 'We went into the back of the truck, I apologised to him and I was crying my eyes out. I was 28, 29 years of age, and I said, "I've screwed it for you, Tony." And he put his arm around me and said, "Don't worry about it, Nick. The car's fantastic! I'm going to win the race tomorrow."'

It all came down to the final, which Tony would start from the back row of the grid as a result of his problem. He had a mountain to climb. 'At the start Tony was round the corner from the lights. He was standing by the car on the grid, and he was chipper. "I'm going to win this, Nick," he said, "you watch. I'm going to win it, I'll have the lap record, or I'll crash. Don't even worry about it, the car's great. Forget about yesterday." And I felt a bit better about it after that.'

The favourites were Andersson and Perkins, but Andersson helped everyone by jumping the start and

But for this clash at the hairpin with Tom, Tony's début could have yielded fourth place instead of seventh.

Jack Pryce sent this postcard from Monte Carlo to Cledwyn Ashford's parents. The message said: 'It's just like home, raining, but you should have seen my driving from Nice to Monaco!! Gwyn has not got much to say about the pilot?'

removing himself from contention by incurring a one-minute penalty. That left it a straight fight between Perkins and Ribeiro, who would play a leading role in what followed. Ribeiro smiled at the memory and remembered every detail 30 years later.

'Tony and I knew each other beforehand. We met on my very first race in England. I was the Brazilian champion in Formula Ford and I rented a Formula Three car to do two races in England at the end of the season. He was the big name in '73. It was the year that he blew everybody off. He was the champion, and I was on my first race. It was wet and I think when he came to lap me – I was far behind, still learning – I don't think I saw him for some reason, and he was pissed with me afterwards. I had blue overalls and he came over, grabbed them and shook me. "You know what this means? Blue? Blue flags?"' Ribeiro laughed at the memory. 'But I didn't have any deliberate intention to spoil his race. I just never saw him.'

At Monaco, however, he most certainly did see the tall Englishman as they engaged in battle towards the end of the final.

'I was in the pit in Monaco watching,' Janet Brise remembered. 'And Graham Hill came in during the race. I just remember going, "Ahh, it's Graham Hill!" and getting my camera out. I actually got a photograph of him, standing in our pit. I was just *so* excited.'

'In the race there was Ken Tyrrell, Graham Hill, Frank Williams, all around our pit,' Jordan remembered,

Realising so much of his potential, Tom chases race leader Niki Lauda and Ronnie Peterson down from Casino Square to Mirabeau when the Monaco Grand Prix was at its wettest.

'and I'm thinking, "What's this all about, then?" And I'm doing the pit board: fourth, third, second... then on the last lap it was Tony and Ribeiro.'

'What happened was that I was second in my qualifying heat, which put me on the second row,' Ribeiro continued. 'There were two heats. In the first heat, Larry Perkins won it, and in the other, Renzo Zorzi won, with me behind.' Zorzi was a relatively unknown Italian racer, who worked as a tyre test technician for Pirelli.

'I got the jump in third place at the start of the final and at Mirabeau I overtook Renzo, so I was second behind Perkins. But I couldn't keep up with him and he started to pull away. I was trying very hard but my March was not as good as his Ralt so I was losing him until he crashed all by himself.'

Perkins just pushed too hard and shunted his car into the barriers, while further back Tony had settled into a rhythm and begun charging through the field.

'Tony had that problem and had to start the final from the back of the grid. But I knew he was blood fast!' Ribeiro laughed again. There were no car-to-pit radios back then, of course, just pit signals. And Alex had developed a reputation as a bit of a wild man at times during his career, especially when put under pressure.

'As soon as I got on to the lead I start to be very cautious, because I had been involved in so many accidents that year. They were blaming me as a crazy, so I was driving a very conservative race. Renzo was following me, and I knew he was not a brave heart. So I was setting the pace to make sure I would finish the race. Five laps to the end I saw Tony in my mirrors. I thought, "Blood hell!" He came through the whole field, going faster than he did in qualifying. The main reason, I think, was that nobody challenge him, they all wave him through!

'I think he was fourth already when I could see him in my mirrors. Then I start to give it the big wellie again. I figured he would have some trouble to overtake third and then second, and that he would catch me by the end, but anyway I would be okay by then. But in one lap he overtook both Patrick Neve and Zorzi. They both wave him through!'

It wasn't quite that simple. Tony was fighting every inch of the way, and Neve certainly was no pushover even if Zorzi was.

'I said, "Well, now it's with me, and I'm not going to let it go for nothing in this world!"' Ribeiro continued. 'The only guy who gave him a challenge was myself. He was much faster than me on the corners. That March

Back in Formula Three for Modus at Monaco, Tony was walking his heat when a plug lead came loose, much to the distress of mechanic Nick Jordan.

with the long nose was a pig to drive. And his Modus, and the Ralt, were better at Monaco than the March because of their short wheelbases. But I had a good engine, so I had a good peak going out of the corners, which helped me. Then I start protecting; I was always on the inside. Then, although I had to go slowly in the corners, once I gave it the wellie I could pull away, and he would catch me again in the next corner. Because I was defending it was making it even easier for him to be on my shoulders, so I was saying. "How long can I stand it? It's up to him." I was determined to not let him go by for any price in this world. And he was a charger as well, so in the end I closed the door at Mirabeau and he put his right wheels on the pathway, where they had put some nice kerbs so he could actually drive on them, and he went there.'

In other words, Ribeiro had Tony off when he tried to dive down the inside of the March. The kerbs had been chamfered since the 1974 race, when James Hunt had forced Hans Stuck up the previous sharp-edged kerb on the run down the hill from Casino Square and sent his damaged March slithering helplessly down the sidewalk before it crashed at Mirabeau.

'By the time Tony went there, there was not enough room for his car and his left front wheel hit my right back wheel and did the effect of this (Ribeiro demonstrated a turning, lifting action), and so he went

ABOVE: *Having just scraped into the top 10 in his heat, Tony had to start the final 20th and last. Racing on the limit, he put in the drive of the race.* BELOW: *This is the snapshot Jan took as Graham Hill suddenly turned up in the Modus pit to discuss things with owner Teddy Savory, and to watch Tony race. Little did she know then how quickly things were moving for her husband.*

ABOVE: *The denouement was set up as Tony moved ahead of Renzo Zorzi and Patrick Neve to chase Alex Ribeiro for the lead.* BELOW: *Going round the Swimming Pool on the penultimate lap, Tony was right with Ribeiro, and the Brazilian's eyes were glued to his mirrors.*

up in the air. He landed on my top and I had a mark of rubber on my helmet.' He laughed again. 'Then I give it the big wellie to see if I could become untangled. That's why the pictures show me sideways, because I was giving it full throttle trying to get away! But in the process the bottom of his chassis broke the distributor of my engine, and in any case then I was up against the inner wall, so we were stuck. The marshals came and pulled him off, and his car was okay and he finished, but I had to leave my car...'

Meanwhile, an astonished Zorzi, who was not that far behind and had enjoyed a grandstand view of the altercation, simply drove past them both to score a disbelieving victory in his year-old GRD. Neve finished second, with Svensson third. Tony was unplaced and very angry.

Ultimately he finished 11th. 'I got the car back, and as I was driving it round to the pits, with the radiator leaking away, the crowd was cheering like mad because they'd seen a motor race,' Jordan chuckled.

'That night I was in the Metropole Hotel and Tony says to me, "It was a good race. The car was great." And one of the things I'll never forget was that Neil Brown was there, and he asked Tony, "How was it?" And Tony said, "The car was fantastic, Neil." And Neil says, "How was the engine?" expecting the same, and Tony says, "Neil, the engine was complete crap." I felt for Neil, and even now I joke with him about it.

'That night Tony came up to me, and he was dressed up in his bow-tie and all – they were going out to the tennis club for dinner with Bette and Graham. Us guys were going out on the piss. And he paid me, like, 500 francs, about 50 quid, and said, "Go and have a proper drink with the lads. I really appreciate all your effort." And then he said, "Come over here, I want to show you something." He put his arm around me, dipped into his inside pocket, and pulled out a cheque from Embassy Hill. I'm not sure how much it was for: £25,000, £35,000, £50,000, I can't remember now, but around there. There were big numbers on it, I remember that. And he said, "The house is paid for, I don't have a mortgage now. I can afford to live."

'He had done the contract the day before, and that's why, when I was so upset he was okay because he already had the cheque. That's the absolute truth, may God strike me as my judge.'

Janet had an after-race recollection, too. 'After Monaco Tony was invited to Walter Wolf's 'castle', for want of a better word. Danny Sullivan was with us, because we'd all driven down to Monaco together to save money; we shared the expenses. So when Walter said he wanted Tony to come up to the castle for a meeting, I just remember Danny and I walking round the garden because we were just sort of left out there to hang around for an hour, an hour and a half.

ABOVE: *As Tony's Modus mounted Ribeiro's March, a disbelieving but grateful Zorzi slipped his GRD Lancia through to take victory.* RIGHT: *Though he never forgave Ribeiro, Tony had a consolation prize in his pocket as he left Monte Carlo. Later he, Graham Hill and mentor Teddy Savory posed for press photos when it was announced that he had joined Embassy Hill.*

Walter was offering Tony a drive, but he never took him up on it.'

There was another postscript to the Monaco story.

'We never said anything to each other, Tony and me, about that race,' Ribeiro said. 'The next time I met him was in Brands Hatch later in the year. He was driving in Formula Atlantic and he won the Atlantic race and I won the Formula Three. At the end of the day all the winners went on a lap of the track on the back of a car. I said, "Hello, Tony," and put my hand out, and he said, "I'm not going to shake your hand."' Tony did not forgive such things easily. Ribeiro was still amused by the incident three decades later. 'So that was that. He never talked to me again. He was a fantastic driver. He was a big-head guy, but a fantastic driver. He knew how good he was, no doubt. He was a great, great driver.'

CHAPTER 15

Hard chargers

Tom and Tony, 1975

*'He was a very good, likeable guy.
There was no way he was arrogant.
Not at all. All of us liked him, and he
was good to us. A superb guy.'*
Jerry Bond

At last, it seemed, the right people in Formula One had begun to share Alex Ribeiro's view of Tony Brise's talents. He might not have won the Monaco Formula Three race the way that Tom had the previous year, but his drive through the field was sufficient to at last make Formula One team owners sit up and take notice.

'He was different to everyone else around him,' said Frank Williams, who revealed he'd been keeping tabs on him for two years in Formula Atlantic. 'He did a bit of testing for us at Goodwood before the Spanish Grand Prix, and we had an oil system problem and lost an engine. It wasn't his fault, it was a Williams lack of knowledge problem. But he was very quick. At home in an unfamiliar car, immediately. Good communication, he understood the car. He was ahead of the game, he wasn't flustered.

'It was obvious that, if we'd got him, he would have done a lot for Williams and would have pulled us right up. But Graham beat us to it. He had a better deal to offer. It was for us a very short-lived possibility to sign Tony. But the guy was very talented, very easy to get on with and this arrogance thing never came over to me. I'm not being charitable, I never had a problem with him in the brief time we worked together. He would have been an English great, I don't have any doubt about that. The talent was certainly there.'

Graham Hill agreed, and with Rolf Stommelen still on the injured list after Barcelona, he had the backing

Tony, ready for action in the Zolder pits.

ABOVE: *Team manager Ray Brimble and Graham Hill prepare for their new driver's début with Embassy Hill in Belgium.* BELOW: *Having qualified a brilliant seventh, ahead of reigning World Champion Emerson Fittipaldi, Tony came down to earth with an early spin in the chicane on the third lap.*

from Embassy to attract Tony. After all the heartache, he was finally a full-time Formula One driver.

His precocious talent would immediately lift the Embassy Hill team. But he got off to an inauspicious start when he was late for his seat fitting at the former Rondel Racing workshop in Mount Road, Hanworth. Hill's staff were a tight-knit, happy unit, managed by Ray Brimble, who had earned his spurs with Shadow in both CanAm and then Formula One, before joining in 1974. Besides mechanics Alan Howell and Preston Anderson, most of them had nicknames: designer Andy Smallman was known as 'Pencil', mechanics Steve Roby, Alan Turner, Jerry Bond and Gerd von Aachen were 'Abo' (he was Australian), 'Moby', 'Chat' and 'Schultz', respectively. Then there were fellow employees Terry Richards, buyer Mike 'Body' Young, storeman Mike 'Truffler' Connors, secretary Liz Morse, John Love, truck driver Malcolm 'Little Man' Allen, van driver Frank Le Sevleaur, workshop cleaner Charlie 'Sir' Woods and office cleaner Helen 'Ajax' Ben. They fraternised regularly. On the wall they had a 'Brownie' graph which recorded the points total of anybody who had unwisely indulged in some 'creeping', or had screwed up in spectacular fashion.

When Tony turned up late, the mechanics took suitable revenge to initiate him into the team. 'Everything was foamed up and the fitting was done,' recalled Ian Flux, who had switched over from Token,

as he described the process by which chemicals were mixed in a large black bin liner on which the driver sat in the car to form the shape of his seat. 'But you stuck to the foam in those days, and Steve Roby and the lads just left him in the car while we all went off to lunch...'

Janet Brise laughed at that recollection. 'That's right! I'd forgotten about that. I remember him coming back and telling me, "Those rotten things, they went off and left me!"'

Surviving members of the team said they came to love working with him. 'Everyone got on really well with him,' Jerry Bond remembered. 'I knew him before he got to Embassy Hill, because I'd been working for Frank Williams when Tony made his grand prix début. He was very good, a likeable guy. There was no way he was arrogant. Not at all. All of us liked him, and he was good to us. A superb guy.'

Nigel Roebuck said, 'I can remember talking to Graham about Tony after he'd done the deal, and he said, "He's a bit pleased with himself, isn't he?" But Graham being Graham, he was thinking that was probably good because he was certainly not going to be overawed by anything, and he never was. And actually, the more Quentin Spurring and I got to know him, the more we liked him.

'Graham was very impressed with him in Barcelona. I remember him talking about it. It surprised me that it registered with him, because Graham was absolutely at the centre of all the controversy that weekend. He was really the guy that kept them all under control, because guys like Niki (Lauda) and Emerson (Fittipaldi) were getting almost hysterical.'

To Flux, Hill was an aloof presence who only turned up for the regular post-race debriefs each Tuesday or Wednesday, as he concerned himself with running things from his Shenley office inbetween times. 'Everyone was invited to the debriefs. We'd discuss what went wrong and what needed putting right. Invariably the fabricators would make the bits and wouldn't see Graham for a week, then he'd come in and say, "What are you making? I didn't mean make it like that. Chuck that in the bin!"'

Brimble was relatively inexperienced but popular, and so was Smallman. His GH1 had shown tremendous promise until Stommelen's accident in Barcelona. Now everyone thought that, in Tony, they had a driver who could get them back on their feet.

He briefly tested the old Lola, at Snetterton, Afterwards it was taken to the Modus factory, as Hill

He soon bounced back in Sweden. Here he follows Jody Scheckter, Mario Andretti, Emerson Fittipaldi, Jochen Mass and Mark Donohue. He would take some of these star scalps before the race was over.

was very friendly with Teddy Savory. Nick Jordan remembered, 'Tony said to Graham, and to myself and Jo (Marquart), "Why can't we make this car handle like my Formula Atlantic? That's a sweet car." And he added, "I can win championship points if it's like that, I know I can." He was so determined.'

Jenny Anderson had this to say, 'Tony was special. We all of us believed that he had a very rare talent, and that he had enough to make it to the top. He was a clever man, along the lines of Jackie Stewart. He calculated everything, he would think everything through very deeply. He would spend hours talking things over in the workshop with my brother Bob, and on the track he was always thinking about his driving. Racing was his life, he became the full person when he was in the car.'

When he made his début for the team at Zolder for the Belgian Grand Prix on 25 May, Tony lost no time proving that. Unquestionably the Hill GH1 was a better car than the Williams FW03 or the Lola T370, and he celebrated his graduation in stunning style. Just as in Spain, he had never seen the track before but showed his class to qualify on the fourth row of the grid, seventh fastest and just ahead of reigning World Champion Fittipaldi. Lauda put his Ferrari on pole position with

A damaged nose wing generated some pretty serious understeer, but Tony only lost fifth place in Sweden when fifth gear refused to engage. Sixth place earned him the sole F1 championship point of his career.

1m 25.43s, then came Carlos Pace, Vittorio Brambilla, Clay Regazzoni, Tom, Carlos Reutemann and Tony on 1m 26.22s. It was a brilliant performance, given that the GH1 vacillated between oversteer and understeer. 'This seems a rewarding circuit to get right,' Tony said nonchalantly. Team-mate Francois Migault, a French journeyman, qualified his Hill 22nd, almost three and a half seconds slower.

Tony made a good start to maintain seventh place, losing a place to Jody Scheckter but beating Tom in the rush to the first corner. But then he pushed a fraction too hard and spun in the Paddock chicane on the third lap. It took him a long time to get the stalled Cosworth DFV restarted, and only then after advice from a mechanic who ran down to the stricken car. After 18 laps he had to call it a day when the engine blew.

Tom drove well to qualify fifth at Zolder. But he made another indifferent start, caught up a place after Tony's spin on the third lap, and then was passed by Fittipaldi on lap 14. He lost two more places to Patrick Depailler and Ronnie Peterson on lap 21, but moved up again when Ronnie crashed and Pace faded on lap 49. He then took another place when Brambilla pitted five laps later. Regazzoni pushed him down to seventh on lap 62, but he grabbed the final point after repassing Fittipaldi on lap 67. Jean-Pierre Jarier spun off after 13 laps.

The Shadows were quick in Sweden, too. On the Anderstorp circuit, Jarier took third place on the grid, Tom eighth. But if anything highlighted the costliness of Tom's flamboyant driving style, it was the eight-tenths of a second gap between them. While Jarier looked smooth and slow, Tom was still throwing his DN5 around with his usual gusto. He put writer Pete Lyons in mind of Peterson at the same circuit in 1973, but though he looked quicker than Jarier, he wasn't. 'Near the end of one session,' Lyons wrote in *Autocourse*, 'Tom did two laps at such extreme angles and with his foot so hard down that the blue smoke was left hanging in the air all through the Karusell; jab on the brakes and pitch into the following right angle before the pits and boot it hard again, and the back wheels absolutely dissolved in blue smoke and left black rubber streaks for 100 yards.'

Lyons was so fascinated that he investigated further, convinced from watching him that Tom had to be fastest by far. 'Umm, let me see…' Shadow team manager Alan Rees said. 'Yes, that was when his rear tyres were worn right down to nothing. Those were about the slowest laps that he did…'

Literally, all his great talent was going up in smoke.

The car also had a problem with its rev limiter and was handling horribly, and Alan Henry recalled an amusing moment which occurred during practice when Tom got the final corner wrong. 'I saw him make a pit stop in which he didn't seem to do anything, he barely even stopped before pulling away again. When I asked

ABOVE: *Earlier in the year there was talk of a swap between them, but in the wet at Zandvoort Tom kept his Shadow ahead of Ronnie Peterson's Lotus.* RIGHT: *A great reflective portrait of Tom, showing off Nella's hairdressing talents.*

him what had happened he sheepishly admitted that he'd overshot and could only go down the pit lane, so he pulled into his pit to hide his embarrassment!'

Tom's style was extremely popular with spectators but drove Rees mad, and he was continually exhorting him to calm down so he could go faster as a result. Tom was not convinced.

His race fell apart on the opening lap when he had to pit after the throttle had become jammed with dust thrown up in traffic in the third corner. He rejoined in time to run in second place on the road (a lap down) behind leader Brambilla and ahead of real second-place man Depailler. Jarier's race ended with a blown engine after 38 laps when he was running second; Tom spun on lap 53 after climbing back up to 11th. Once again the Shadow was oversteering horribly and his efforts to maintain his speed only exacerbated the problem until

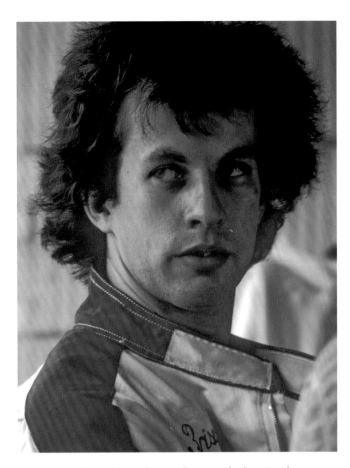

Tony Brise, Grand Prix driver, photographed at Zandvoort.

finally he got caught out, locked up the rear brakes, and half-spun at the chicane. The clutch would not disengage, so he was out.

This time there would be no storming performance from Tony in qualifying. Despite trying both chassis, he was plagued by engine trouble in his race car and a persistent misfire when he took over new team-mate Vern Schuppan's. New magnesium bell-housing castings kept cracking and a damper detached itself. He qualified only 17th, almost three seconds off Brambilla's pole time of 1m 24.630s. (Years later, March co-founder Robin Herd admitted that Brambilla's time had been achieved by him swinging his pit board across the timing eye a while before the Italian's car actually crossed it – so the real pole should have belonged to Depailler's Tyrrell).

In the race, however, Tony made the Hill come alive with a magnificent drive. He made one place on the opening lap after Tom made his pit stop, and then stayed right behind Spanish Grand Prix winner Jochen Mass's McLaren for the next 32 laps until Mass pitted. By now Tony was 11th, which became 10th as Jarier's engine broke, then ninth when Pace crashed out of second place. Tony then moved ahead of American

CanAm champion Mark Donohue's Penske on lap 45 and Peterson's ageing Lotus 72 on lap 47. When John Watson's Surtees dropped back, he moved into the points on the 56th lap, and up to fifth on the 60th when he overtook Fittipaldi. Every move was forceful yet clean-cut, and these were top-line scalps he was taking. He seemed destined to score two points when the Lola agonisingly lost fifth gear; Tony left the car in fourth and paid the penalty for the handicap as Donohue was able to repass. It was galling, but he earned his spurs as he scored what was to be the sole championship point of his brief Formula One career.

Photojournalist Jeff Hutchinson has never forgotten watching him in practice and the race at Anderstorp. 'I saw him ding a front wing on the first lap, and it bent down and started to wear away where it was touching the track, but he still passed half the field and should have finished fifth. He really deserved that place. It was a brilliant drive that proved once and for all what ability he had.'

At the Dutch Grand Prix at Zandvoort Tony had yet another new team-mate, his former Formula Three sparring partner Alan Jones, the tough Australian who had also made his grand prix début in Spain driving a private Hesketh. But whereas Jones lapped his understeering GH1 in 1m 22.01s for 17th place on the grid, detection (at last) of a loose wire, and thus a cure for an irritating and persistent misfire, gave Tony a car that enabled him to repeat his Belgian form. He lined up seventh on 1m 20.94s. Lauda was on pole, from Regazzoni, Hunt, Scheckter, Reutemann and Fittipaldi. His fourth grand prix, and he was a hair over half a second off fastest time in a hitherto unfancied machine.

Meanwhile, Tom was only 12th for Shadow, two places adrift of Jarier.

The start of the race was delayed because of a heavy rain shower, which prompted an acclimatisation session. By the time teams gathered on the grid it was beginning to dry out; but just as everybody began dithering about tyre choice another light shower prompted them all to go for wet tyres. The rain had stopped by the time the race started, so it would be only a matter of time before tyre changes were necessary. In the meantime, the conditions would create a fantastic race.

They were, of course, tailor-made for Tom, who rocketed up to sixth behind Lauda, Scheckter, Regazzoni, Hunt and Mass. Tony made an indifferent start, dropping back to 11th before losing another place to Peterson on the fourth lap.

A lap later Tom swept by Mass and moved up to fourth on lap seven when Hunt bravely became the first man to decide that slicks were the answer. It was a move that would win the blond Englishman – and Hesketh Racing – his first grand prix. Scheckter and Tom stopped on the 12th lap, Regazzoni the 13th and Lauda the 14th.

Tony's relationship with Embassy Hill clicked straight away. His talent behind the wheel geared the team up another notch.

By the 15th, Hunt was leading from Lauda and Jarier, who had stopped two laps earlier than Tom and jumped by Lauda on lap 16. Tom was now seventh and throwing the Shadow around with his habitual abandon. Tony, who had rocketed up to fifth behind Tom by lap 12, was back in 13th after a slow stop.

The order of the top seven remained Hunt, Lauda, Jarier, Scheckter, Fittipaldi, Regazzoni and Tom for the next 16 laps, when Regazzoni overtook Fittipaldi. Then Reutemann found a way past Tom on lap 39. Engine failure for Fittipaldi on lap 40 moved Tom back up to seventh before Peterson edged past him on lap 42. Two laps later, however, Jarier was out after a punctured tyre had thrown his Shadow off the road, so now Tom was seventh again. On lap 56 Mass took his McLaren past the Shadow, but Tom moved temporarily back to seventh as Pace faded on lap 62 before repassing next time around. Tom now had an Embassy Hill chasing him hard after Tony had staged an excellent recovery. Tom got back into the points when, first, Scheckter pitted on lap 68 and then Peterson's Lotus ran out of fuel on lap 69. Yet again, Tony just missed out, and admitted that he had mistimed his pit stop.

'I should have come in sooner, because by the time it was drying my rear tyres were really going off,' he conceded. He was also having to pump the brakes, but at one stage of the race Embassy Hill number 23 was lapping as quickly as Hesketh number 24. On this day that was the car on which most eyes were focused, as Hunt drove a fabulous race and demonstrated remarkably improved maturity to hold off a challenging Lauda to the flag.

Roebuck said, 'In the opening laps what I remember most was Tony coming into Tarzan and waving behind Jones because he was trying to lap him. And this was less than 20 laps into the race! And you think how Jonesy came to be regarded... Tony absolutely annihilated him, to the point where, after the race, Graham was starting to think about Jones, "Jesus, have I done the right thing here?"'

Andrew Marriott rubbed his hands at the memory and chuckled. 'Oh yes! Tony was ready to lap Jonesy! That was brilliant, but people so easily forget that.'

For his part, in response to a letter from reader Phil Pyne published in *Motor Sport* in April 2004, posing the question, "Do you think Tony was good enough to win the title?" Jones, the 1980 World Champion, responded, 'Yes, absolutely. He was very talented, an extremely gifted driver. There is no doubt in my mind that he could have gone on to be a World Champion.'

'He was conceited,' Quentin Spurring thought. 'That was the first thing that came to mind. And when Nigel and I were at *Competition Car* in 1973, we received a press release from Tony when he got his degree. After that, whenever we mentioned him – in race reports, results and championship tables – he was Tony Brise, BSc. He was just naïve in a way, looking for a paragraph in the press. But he was a bloody good race car driver, and he was going to be World Champion. He was clearly together, and he was going to make it work. I thought he was terrific.'

The French Grand Prix at the ultra-quick Paul Ricard circuit in July finally saw a change in Tom's driving style. And what a difference it made! On his home ground Jarier was the quicker, lapping a

With only two grands prix under his belt, Tony was already making his presence felt.

Shadow that now worked on fast circuits, too, in 1m 48.44s to take fourth place on the grid. But Tom was right behind and his 1m 48.48s left him sixth, one row behind.

In his interview with Alan Henry for *Motoring News*, he explained, 'I really love throwing the car about. I'm never happier than when it's nicely out of line and I've got plenty of opposite lock on. I feel really exhilarated, I *enjoy* it. But Alan (Rees) kept on telling me that I must drive smoothly, without all that fuss. I was knocking out the tyres in South America at a terrific rate, and by the time we got to Ricard Alan was watching me in practice on the corner before the pits, and hauling me in if I did much more than brush the rear wheels against the kerb. I felt so frustrated, but I tried to drive round smoothly. Although it felt *so* slow, I found myself recording faster times.'

Rees explained why he wanted his driver to calm down. 'It wasn't the quickest way. Perhaps for him it

was, but if he could modify that without compromising his style, just not being quite so sideways, he could be quicker still.'

Rees denied that he had to bully Tom into driving more smoothly. 'I'd just point out to him that there was a better way, without trying to make him lose the central style of his driving. I'd say, "Tom, that's okay, but not as much. If you can just keep the car a bit straighter, that's going to be reflected in the lap time."'

Jackie Oliver, Rees' partner at Shadow, explained why many drivers of that era liked oversteer. 'On those cars the weight distribution was more to the rear than the current cars, and tyre width was proportionately greater to the back than the front, so the Goodyear tyres would take a lot of slip angle. So, although you could gain time by being tidy, you didn't lose as much as you would do in another era, by hanging the tail out. Hanging the tail out then, there was security to it because the car would take that and wouldn't suddenly

get away from you, and a lot of people used to do that. Tom had a lot of car control, so to run it at a slip angle of 15 degrees was very easy for him.'

Sadly, Tom's new-found smoothness barely showed in the race, as he retired after two laps. The clutch had been malfunctioning on the warm-up lap, forcing the DN5 to creep on the grid even when he had the pedal right down. Holding the car against the brakes before the start left the clutch fried, and by the Esses on the first lap he had dropped to last. He managed to massage the clutch back into some semblance of life, but then the gearbox broke under the strain. To compound Shadow's disappointment, Jarier could only manage eighth by the flag as his rev limiter turned itself down to a crippling 9,500rpm.

At Embassy Hill, Tony again out-qualified Jones.

Tony was sensational in the wet stages of the Dutch Grand Prix, threatening to lap team-mate Alan Jones in an identical car.

At Paul Ricard, Tony was again on great form, vanquishing Mario Andretti at one point and finishing seventh after setting the sixth fastest lap.

This time he was 12th fastest, after a switch to revised rear suspension cured problems with the rear tyres blistering. He recorded 1m 49.21s late in qualifying and believed he could have gone a lot quicker, whereas Jones was stuck down in 20th place on 1m 51.02s. Lauda was on pole again, with 1m 47.82s.

By lap seven Tony was running eighth having passed Brambilla and Andretti in the Parnelli, and benefited from Tom's demise. That became seventh as Pace made a pit stop on the ninth lap, and there he stayed until Andretti was able to make his car's superior aerodynamic performance work for him on the long Mistral straight to regain a position on the 29th lap. Tony regained seventh when Scheckter dropped back two laps later. Subsequently Depailler passed him on the straight, but when Jarier faded Tony was able to pass the Shadow to finish seventh for the second consecutive

race. Missing out on a point again was frustrating, but he set the sixth fastest lap.

A fortnight later came the British Grand Prix at Silverstone. Tom had already set an unofficial lap record for the circuit in 1m 16.2s during a test in June. Now, on a track modified by a chicane at Woodcote – following the first-lap débâcle in the '73 race – he turned on a perfect performance to take his second pole position of the season in front of an appreciative home crowd. To this day he remains the only Welshman ever to have started a grand prix ahead of the rest of the field. And he had achieved it without use of the Shadow's clutch as the mechanism was misbehaving, and with precious little of his trademark oversteer. Rees's counsel had paid off. Having carefully scrubbed in a new set of tyres he put in one lap of 1m 19.4s and followed it with 1m 19.36s, which was sufficient to settle the issue. Pace, on 1m 19.50s in his Brabham, got the closest.

'I was behind a couple of cars on those laps,' Tom told Lyons in *Autocourse*, 'so maybe I could possibly shave off

One of the things that exasperated Alan Rees was Tom's sideways style. In Sweden (above) and France (right) he was spectacular but slower than he could have been, and it was at Paul Ricard that he finally tempered his penchant for opposite lock and went quicker as a result.

a tenth, but it was pretty well the fastest I can go. I'm not going to have them change a thing on the car.'

While Tom was starring, a poignant story was unravelling elsewhere in the pit lane. After 17 years in Formula One, Graham Hill had finally decided that it was time to stop driving. Earlier in the season the former double champion, Le Mans winner and Indianapolis 500 victor had failed to qualify for the Monaco Grand Prix. In his prime he owned the streets of the Principality, having won the race five times, and it would not be until 1992 that Ayrton Senna would equal that, before beating it in 1993. That failure hurt Hill deeply.

'People didn't realise he was an incredibly shy man, really and truly – and proud,' his wife Bette said. 'He made himself be the clown. It wasn't unnatural for him

One immediate result of Tom's newfound calmness was his first pole position – the only one for a Welshman in a grand prix – at Silverstone.

to be humorous, but I sat next to him at dinners where he was giving the speech, and he never ate a thing. He was so nervous beforehand. He never made a note, and never ate. Then he'd get up and floor them with his opening sentence. So he had them in the palm of his hand and that made him feel comfortable, and he could go from then on. Failing to qualify in Monaco really did hurt him, because he knew it was the end.'

Roebuck told the story in a slightly different way. 'With Rolf (Stommelen) out of action after Spain, Graham had to do Monaco himself. He had pretty much made up his mind that he wasn't going to drive again. Ah, it really hurt him that he didn't qualify there. I had mixed feelings about Graham, having worked with him, but that was an awful thing to witness.'

Flux remembered that race in the Principality. 'We had to meet Graham outside the hotel and walk down the hill to the start after he hadn't qualified. The thing that stayed with me was the really great reception he got from the spectators. He did an awful lot for British motorsport.'

That weekend at Silverstone, Hill toured round for a slow lap in one of his white and red Embassy Hills, his

long mane of hair flying in the breeze as he waved to his appreciative public. When he got back to the pit lane, he was no longer a Formula One driver.

'I was very emotional about that,' Bette said, even though she was one of many who wanted him to stop. 'It was the total end of an era. He said to me: "Are you crying?" And I said: "Yeah, I am! I think it's very sad that you are giving all this up." I wanted him to stop before he started his team, but didn't have the guts to say it.'

In Tony, Hill had found not just the means of withdrawing gracefully, but also of moving his team forward. But, more than that, Tony would prove a rallying point for the mechanics, a justification for all the late nights, a skilled artist whose talent would let them generate new pride in themselves.

'Tony? No, we couldn't have had a better driver,' Bette agreed. 'But Graham should have just managed another team. He should have been in motor racing, not for himself, but for other people really. Because he was so dedicated and determined, he had a lot of guts. He was very good with young people – he was with Tony. They gelled brilliantly together. They were like son and father. That is what he should have done, he shouldn't have built something that was going to be a great big hassle. Pity...'

Tony put the Hill 13th on the grid, just over a second slower than Tom's pole time. Jones was 20th.

Janet Brise recalled that getting to the circuit on race day was a drama. 'Tony was so laid back that we would always be catching flights by the skin of our teeth. That morning we were driving to Silverstone (as one did in those days!) and got stuck in the traffic. Tony was running late for the morning warm-up so he suggested that I drive and he would change into his overalls, ready to jump into the car when we got there. Not an easy thing to do in a Porsche! The traffic was really bad but Tony spotted Clay Regazzoni coming along on his motorbike. The next thing I knew he was out of the car, had flagged him down, hopped on the back of the bike and was gone!'

The opening laps of the race were a dogfight, with Pace initially leading Tom and the Ferraris of Regazzoni and Lauda, with Hunt, Scheckter, Andretti and Fittipaldi all in there battling away. Regazzoni took the lead from the Brabham driver on lap 13 and soon opened a lead of three seconds thanks to the potency of Ferrari's latest flat-12 engine. Tom also confidently passed the Brazilian on lap 17, and when Regga toured into the pits at the end of lap 19 after sliding into the wall at Club, Tom led a grand prix for the first time. He stayed there on lap 20, too, creating another first for Wales. But, as Regazzoni had already discovered, this would be a race ruined by the capricious British weather. On lap 21, Tom was the first to encounter a pool of rain at Becketts. The Shadow twitched and slithered off into the catchfencing. A pole struck his helmet and left him momentarily stunned.

'Actually,' he told Henry later, 'leading wasn't too difficult. I could see Niki behind and also that Jody was pressing the Ferrari. I was driving pretty quickly, but I knew I'd got a little in hand. It's always a little easier to lead early because the pressure doesn't come on fully until the closing stages.' He paused, before adding wistfully, 'I wish I'd been around in the closing stages...'

'The shunt was down to his lack of experience,' Shadow designer Tony Southgate said. 'But, what the hell, you're leading, you come across a wet patch after the rain... We accepted that – it was his apprenticeship.'

It was a sad end to a wonderful drive – the only time, it would transpire, he would lead a grand prix. But Tom was hardly alone that bizarre day; later, Jim Crawford, Hans Stuck, Jean-Pierre Jarier, Wilson Fittipaldi, Dave Morgan, John Nicholson, Brian Henton, John Watson, Patrick Depailler, Jochen Mass, Mark Donohue, James Hunt, Jody Scheckter and Carlos Pace – 14 drivers – would all do likewise. So would Tony.

Another good start catapulted him to 11th at the end of the first lap. Then he passed Brambilla, Reutemann and Andretti to run eighth, all the while closing on the leading septet. He was the fastest man out there until a loose right rear wheel nut forced him into the pits on the 12th lap. That dropped him back to 22nd, right behind Andretti who'd had to pit a lap later for a new

ABOVE: *In the actual race Tom scored another first, being the only Welshman to lead a grand prix, before sadly getting caught out by a rain shower at Becketts. He would not be the only driver to slide off the road.* BELOW: *Tom did not rate Alan Henry's qualities as a driver after the journalist tested his DN5 at the venue later in the year, but greatly admired his friend's skills as a reporter.*

At the British Grand Prix, as Graham Hill finally announced his retirement as a driver, he found in Tony the means to step gracefully from the world stage.

nose after a brush with Jarier. Tony stopped again six laps later, this time being the first to switch to wets as the overcast sky yielded to rain. A rash of stops followed, but Tony had by now lost too much ground. Then the track began to dry again so that Fittipaldi and Hunt, who had stayed out running gingerly on slicks, moved back up. As the race neared the 45-lap mark the skies darkened again, and it began to rain at Stowe and Club corners. On the 55th lap Tony was following right behind Regazzoni's Ferrari as they went through Club, but the Hill refused to take the corner and slithered off the track and into the catchfencing. A support pole hit him sufficiently hard on the head to rip off his Griffin helmet and knock him out. Fortunately, like Tom, he did not sustain lasting injury. Fittipaldi stayed on the track to be declared winner of a farcical race.

'Graham came over to the pit wall and said that Tony had been taken to the medical centre,' Janet remembered, 'and that we had better get over there. It wasn't far to walk but there were crowds of people everywhere and they were all trying to get Graham's autograph. He very politely said: "This is not a good time now, can you let us through please?" When we got there Tony was conscious and smiling but they wanted to admit him to the John Radcliffe Hospital in Oxford for head x-rays and they also thought he might have concussion.

'I said I would go with him in the ambulance but went to give the car keys to my parents so that they could take the car. On the way I bumped into Teddy Savory who offered to take Tony to hospital in his helicopter. By the time we got back to the medical centre Tony had already left by ambulance, so Teddy said he would take me. I arrived at the hospital about 45 minutes before Tony and at least was able to do all the form filling. They kept him in overnight but, other than an enormous black eye and hurt pride, he was fine.'

Neither of the Shadows was particularly quick round the 14.1 miles of the Nürburgring, at the German Grand Prix. Jarier was 12th fastest, Tom 16th. Tom's race car had a poor engine, but after switching to the spare DN5 he said it didn't handle anything like as well as his original chassis. Tony out-qualified Jones by almost eight seconds! He was 17th, Jones 21st. Tony, however, had had a scare in practice when one of his tyres punctured and he crashed his race car, forcing him to take over the spare for the rest of the weekend.

Jarier ran ninth initially with Tom 13th and Tony

14th, but they all moved up a place when Fittipaldi pitted at the end of the second lap. Then it was Brambilla's turn, moving Tom and Tony up another one. The two Britons chased up the field, and when Jarier punctured on the seventh lap while running seventh, they were sixth and eighth. Depailler's demise on lap nine promoted Tom to fifth, and then Ferrari suffered a body blow on lap 10 when leader Lauda pitted with a punctured front tyre and second-placed Regazzoni, who had been setting lap records after a poor start, suffered a broken engine. Now only Reutemann and Hunt separated Tom from the lead with four laps to go. This became second place a lap later when the Hesketh suffered broken drive pegs on a rear wheel hub, but within the Shadow's cockpit Tom was already feeling intense pain.

Fuel had been leaking from a loose filler cap for the previous four laps, and he was sitting in a bath of it. It was also getting into his eyes and mouth, at one point prompting him to brush a barrier at Metzgesfeld as he fought to clear his visor. For a while he clung on to second place, but as the fuel began to eat into his skin he was forced to slacken his belts so that he could hoist himself up in the cockpit for modest relief every so often. Unable to go full-speed over the 'Ring's numerous humpbacks, he gradually but inevitably lost ground. Jacques Laffite pushed past him on lap 12, and on lap 13 a recovering Lauda also moved ahead, demoting him to the fourth place in which he finished. Five years later, the world heard endlessly of Nigel Mansell's similar problem in his Formula One début in Austria, but Tom made no fuss at all about his gutsy drive and few even knew of his predicament until Shadow personnel told them afterwards.

'That was typical Tom,' Trevor Foster said many years later. 'His skin was totally burnt and blistered. He was in serious trouble, no doubt about it. But he just wouldn't let anybody down.'

His courage earned him the Prix Rouge et Blanc Jo Siffert award for grit and determination.

Just when Tony seemed well placed for points, running seventh right on the heels of Laffite's Williams (and thus a contender for second place), a rear suspension radius rod tore itself out of the Hill's chassis and, for the second race running, and the second time that weekend, he crashed out. There was some consolation for Hill, however, as Jones brought his GH1 home fifth in what would be his last race for the team.

A dry road at the Osterreichring in qualifying for the Austrian Grand Prix on 17 August suited neither Shadow, and once again the team's two drivers were virtually inseparable as they lined up 14th and 15th on the grid, two-hundredths of a second apart with Jarier just ahead. This was particularly interesting, as Jarier was giving the unique Matra-engined DN7 its début as Tom, still saying nothing about the discomfort of his yet-to-heal Nürburgring burns, stuck with the Cosworth

Tony kept his powder dry in qualifying, but was a sensation of the early laps as the fastest man on the track at Silverstone.

car. Rolf Stommelen was back in the Hill team for the Austrian Grand Prix, replacing Jones, but Tony reconfirmed his status by out-qualifying the German by almost two seconds and nine places. They started 16th and 25th, respectively.

To Tom's delight, before the start the weather took a turn for the worse. However, everyone had been sobered by the accident to Mark Donohue in the morning's warm-up session when his Penske crashed heavily into an advertising hoarding due to a puncture. The likeable American had been taken to hospital.

The start was delayed as rain poured down, but eventually there was nothing to do but get on with it. Tom could barely wait. Lauda led initially before being overtaken by Hunt. But the hero of the hour was Brambilla who assumed the lead from the Englishman on the 19th lap when Hunt was inadvertently baulked by his own team-mate Brett Lunger. Behind them, Tom was 14th at the end of a spray-spoiled opening lap, and then got his head down. Within two laps he was up to 12th; in two more, 10th, with Tony thirsting after him in equally aggressive style. Tom overtook Regazzoni on lap six, and soon Tony followed suit, the two Britons

putting on a fabulous display of car control in conditions that had already accounted for men of the calibre of Mario Andretti and Hans Stuck.

They were eighth and ninth by lap 13, but that proved unlucky for Tony. At one stage he had set the race's fastest lap, but the Hill had lost a balance weight from a front wheel and the resultant vibration became so serious that he was forced into the pits a lap later. He resumed 17th and finished a disappointed 15th, a lap down, although once again had shown his mettle.

Tom, meanwhile, was still forging ahead. On the lap that Tony pitted he overtook both Depailler and Fittipaldi and was now running in the points. But he was not finished yet. Making up for the moment of rashness that had seen him slide off at Silverstone, he took fifth as Peterson pitted on lap 22, then passed Lauda – the World Champion-elect – two tours later. When Mass slid his McLaren off the road on lap 28, Tom was on target for the podium again. Only Brambilla and Hunt were still ahead of him. But by lap 29 the conditions had deteriorated so much as darkness moved over the mountains that the organisers prematurely ended the race

ABOVE: *Tom made a one-off appearance in a sports car, his first since Formula 100, when he shared this Gelo Racing Mirage with John Watson at the Nürburgring.* BELOW: *On the podium in Austria James Hunt ponders the antics of team-mate Brett Lunger, Vittorio Brambilla looks dazed after scoring the only grand prix triumph of his career, and crashing as he crossed the line, while Tom contemplates what might have been had the race run its full distance.*

by waving the chequered flag. To celebrate, Brambilla
crossed the line waving to his pit crew – only to
promptly spin and dislodge his March's nose on the pit
wall! There was talk of a restart, until March boss Max
Mosley pointed out that in order to do that they should
have shown the black flag as well as the chequered flag.
At the age of 37, the 'Monza Gorilla' had won. To
Shadow's frustration, Hunt had actually been coming
into the pits that lap as his Hesketh was running on only
seven of its eight cylinders, but saw the chequered flag
being waved at the very last moment and was able to
change his mind. Nevertheless, third place was a superb
result for Tom, even if he only got half of the four points
he deserved as the race had not reached the 60 per cent
mark. It was also further indication that, like Hunt, he
was maturing nicely.

On 24 August, the curiously named Swiss Grand
Prix, the third non-championship race of the year, was
held – at Dijon-Prenois in France! Motor racing had
been banned in Switzerland in the wake of the Le Mans
disaster in 1955 in which more than 80 people were
killed when Frenchman Pierre Levegh crashed his
Mercedes-Benz into a crowded tribune. But an
accommodation was reached between Dijon and the
Automobile Club de Suisse to stage a 60-lap event that
attracted 16 cars. All the teams had been saddened,
however, when it was learned that Mark Donohue, hurt
in the race-morning crash in Austria yet able to hold a
lucid conversation with, among others, Emerson
Fittipaldi, had succumbed to his injuries two and a half
days later. Frighteningly, his death was put down to the
blow on the head he had suffered. Tom and Tony
had much to ponder after suffering similar accidents
at Silverstone.

Jarier took pole position by a whisker from Fittipaldi
and was walking the race with an attacking drive when
his Shadow's transmission broke on the 24th lap.
Victory thus fittingly went to 'local' hero Clay
Regazzoni in the Ferrari.

Tom had an unusually subdued meeting, qualifying
only eighth, well off his 1974 form at the swooping
track, and racing home seventh. His qualifying lap was a
second slower than 'Jumper's', as was his fastest race lap.

The Italian Grand Prix at Monza on 7 September,
brought Tony his best-ever qualifying position as he
lined up in sixth place, more than three seconds faster
than Stommelen. That day the Hill was markedly better
than the Shadows, as Jarier qualified the Matra car 13th
and Tom, his Cosworth mount, 14th, one-tenth of a
second behind.

Raceday was a disaster for Hill, however, as Tony
made a disappointing start and dropped to ninth by the
end of the opening lap. Going into the first chicane at the
start of lap two, Scheckter missed his braking and ran up
the escape road, and inevitably that affected the flow of

Tony's sixth place on the grid at Monza was negated by a poor
start, and then this tangle with Andretti at the first chicane.

those following closely. Mass bounced heavily over a kerb
and Reutemann momentarily became airborne doing the
same thing; Fittipaldi and Hunt made it through but
Peterson's Lotus got tailgated. Behind the Swede, Andretti
and Tony tangled, and the game was over.

Almost unnoticed in the drama, Tom had worked his
way from 15th to seventh by lap four. That became
sixth when Depailler dropped back on lap 16, and after
fighting over fourth with Reutemann and Hunt he
grabbed fifth from the Hesketh driver on lap 27 after
James had spoiled his entry into the first chicane. The
Englishman reversed that, however, when they came
upon his team-mate, the bearded Austrian journalist
Harald Ertl, who circulated for many laps with the
Reutemann-Pryce-Hunt trio; after Hunt had repassed
the Shadow, James pulled away from Tom. Typically,
Tom did not criticise Ertl for racing men trying to lap
him, and was happy with another point. Instead, he told
Lyons, 'No, he drove really very well! I couldn't get by
him because I'd ruined my brakes early on – and two
laps from the end I started to run out of petrol anyway.'

The Italian race provided Roebuck with further
insight into Tony's true character, too. 'The thing about
him that I liked the most was that, even in 1975, he
never gave safety a thought. It just wasn't on his radar
at all. He was going to new places all the time. He
absolutely adored the Nürburgring, and he thought
Monza was out of this world. He loved everything
about it; he was like a kid. I remember after first
practice there and he'd been out for the first time, he

was literally just like a child in a toy shop. It was just sort of "Wow, I'm at Monza!"

'That was the overriding thing that got me about Tony, his enthusiasm. He was a massive fan. It really meant something to him to be at Monza. And, from not having known him at all but only having heard about him, I wouldn't have suspected that. On the face of it, he was going to be one of these hard-faced, "Don't give a damn about the past, all I'm interested in is getting on and making money" types. And that's not at all how he was.'

Roebuck made another observation. 'There was another little thing concerning how confident he was on the outside. I remember we were at a race and there was some function, a race organisers' do or something for Embassy. And in the paddock he sort of said, "Can I have a word?" And whatever this do was, he said, "Do I have to wear a tie? Only I haven't brought one..." He

Graham Hill was rather more impressed with Tony's driving abilities than his prowess with a golf club, when they played in a celebrity match at Watkins Glen.

obviously didn't want to ask Graham or anyone else. And again you find yourself thinking, can you imagine anyone around today even thinking of wearing a tie? "I'll wear what I want." So he was this mixture of ultra-confidence, almost cockiness in his job, on the outside; but in some ways he was still really just a kid.'

Janet remembered her husband signing autographs at the Italian track. 'In those days they weren't all cushioned, and stuck in a motorhome. He was sitting on the back of a trailer and I was with Bette. She said, "Give me a pen," and she got her book and went and stood in the queue. And of course he was signing this book, and then he looked up and saw it was for Bette! He was just so busy signing away, and it was lovely.

'It was very, very exciting, especially with all these names that you knew so well: Lauda and Scheckter and Andretti. And sometimes he was blowing a lot of them off.'

Shadow staged something of a comeback in qualifying when the circus went to Watkins Glen in upstate New York for the US Grand Prix on 5 October. Jarier was back in a Cosworth-engined DN5 and put it fourth on the grid; again, Tom was close behind in seventh, two-tenths adrift. Graham Hill, meanwhile, had decided to focus all his team effort on just one car for Tony in 1976 and now entered only one in America. Tony found it less than ideally suited to the sinuous Glen and qualified only 17th. Again, he had a short race, running 13th behind Lotus driver Brian Henton until the latter spun in front of him on the sixth lap. Tony couldn't avoid him, and the Hill lost its right rear wheel as he tried unsuccessfully to jink around the stricken 72.

Tom's race was equally miserable. He made a terrible start and fell to 14th but had recovered to ninth when he had to make a pit stop on lap 11 to investigate a serious misfire. That dropped him back down to 14th again and a further stop on lap 26 in which a faulty distributor cap connection was discovered delayed him further. He was eventually too far behind to be classified.

Thus the season ended. At Shadow, Tom scored eight World Championship points and was rated 10th overall. Jean-Pierre Jarier, who was often unlucky, scored only one and a half for 18th place. The Frenchman scored two pole positions, giving him two front-row starts, while Tom had one pole but also started from the front row in Monaco. They were, by and large, pretty evenly matched as far as performance was concerned, but Tom seemed better able to bring his cars home. In Tony's case he had some good team-mates in Alan Jones and Vern Schuppan. But the combination of his talent and the Hill team's inability to run two cars at the same level left him head and shoulders above them, even though his sole championship point left him 19th in the overall ratings.

Tom had also joined wealthy German industrialist George Loos's Gelo team in sportscar racing in an ex-Gulf Mirage GR7, but team-mate John Watson crashed the car after the brakes locked when they were on for a top-five finish at the Nürburgring.

At the end of the year, *Autocourse* rated Tony ninth, Tom 11th, a place ahead of Jarier.

'Here is a story of someone who deserved to be in Formula One some time ago,' editor Mike Kettlewell suggested. 'Kent's Tony Brise, aged 23, rose to the top in British club racing but nobody wanted to know. Fortunately, some excellent drives in Formula Atlantic races in front of the Formula One circus netted him a guest drive for Frank Williams in Barcelona. That was enough. His intelligent and confident approach quickly brought him a regular drive for Graham Hill, and Graham found in Brise an excuse to retire gracefully.

'The 1976 season should see Tony Brise a regular front-runner in Formula One. He may even win a grand prix. And should he maintain progress he may even be World Champion one day.'

And of Tom, he said, 'Excellent entertainment value, that was Tom Pryce. "Was" is the word, for when he realised that his spectacular style was not exactly conducive to obtaining good results he calmed down, and was still fast.

'Pryce won the Race of Champions in great style, but afterwards had to be satisfied with place results despite many excellent practice performances, notably at Silverstone. The 26-year-old Welshman really deserved better luck, as did his team, UOP Shadow.

'Next year, perhaps?'

Not with UOP, however. At the end of the year Shadow received a body blow when Signal Oil took over UOP, and management changes ousted John Logan as chairman. In his place came James V. Crawford, and almost inevitably the first casualty was the Formula One budget. Within five days of taking control, Crawford axed it. At the time UOP's spend was calculated at more than a million dollars a season, which made Shadow the next best financed team after Ferrari. Now, liquidity problems elsewhere within the UOP conglomerate had obliged greater financial prudence. Shadow's days of financial security were over.

Tony had an unhappy time in his last grand prix, at Watkins Glen, being eliminated early after colliding with Brian Henton when his fellow countryman spun his Tyrrell in front of him.

CHAPTER 16

Isn't life great?

Tony, 1975

'Tony had a lot of talent, for sure,
Yeah, I rated him. Tony was good, he
showed that. He would have been a
force to be reckoned with, no question.'
Mario Andretti

As if competing in both Formula One and Formula
Atlantic were not enough, Tony also did a few races in
Formula 5000 for Theodore Racing, a British team
whose Lola T332 was run by veteran Sid Taylor on
behalf of colourful Hong Kong entrepreneur Teddy Yip.
The first was at Brands Hatch on 25 August, where he
took pole position in the highly competitive car and
dominated the race in majestic style after passing
Champion-elect Teddy Pilette on the eighth lap.
Unfortunately, he picked up a slow puncture and was
passed five laps from the end by Embassy Hill team-
mate Alan Jones in a RAM March.

Next time out, on the streets of Long Beach in
California on 28 September, he was simply awesome.
This was the first-ever race to be held on the newly
inaugurated circuit, and right from the start it was clear
that the two-mile track round the downtown streets was
not going to be the point-and-squirt, on-off animal that
sceptical drivers had feared.

Mario Andretti, who would go on to be World
Champion in three years' time, was driving a Lola T332
for the Viceroy-sponsored team run by Vel Miletich and
Indianapolis veteran Parnelli Jones, and teamed with
fellow American racing star Al Unser Snr. Affable
Englishman Brian Redman, who was shooting for his
second straight USAC/SCCA Formula 5000

In August 1975 Tony made his Formula 5000 début at Brands
Hatch. Here he leads Mike Wilds, Teddy Pilette and Alan
Jones out of Druids early in the race.

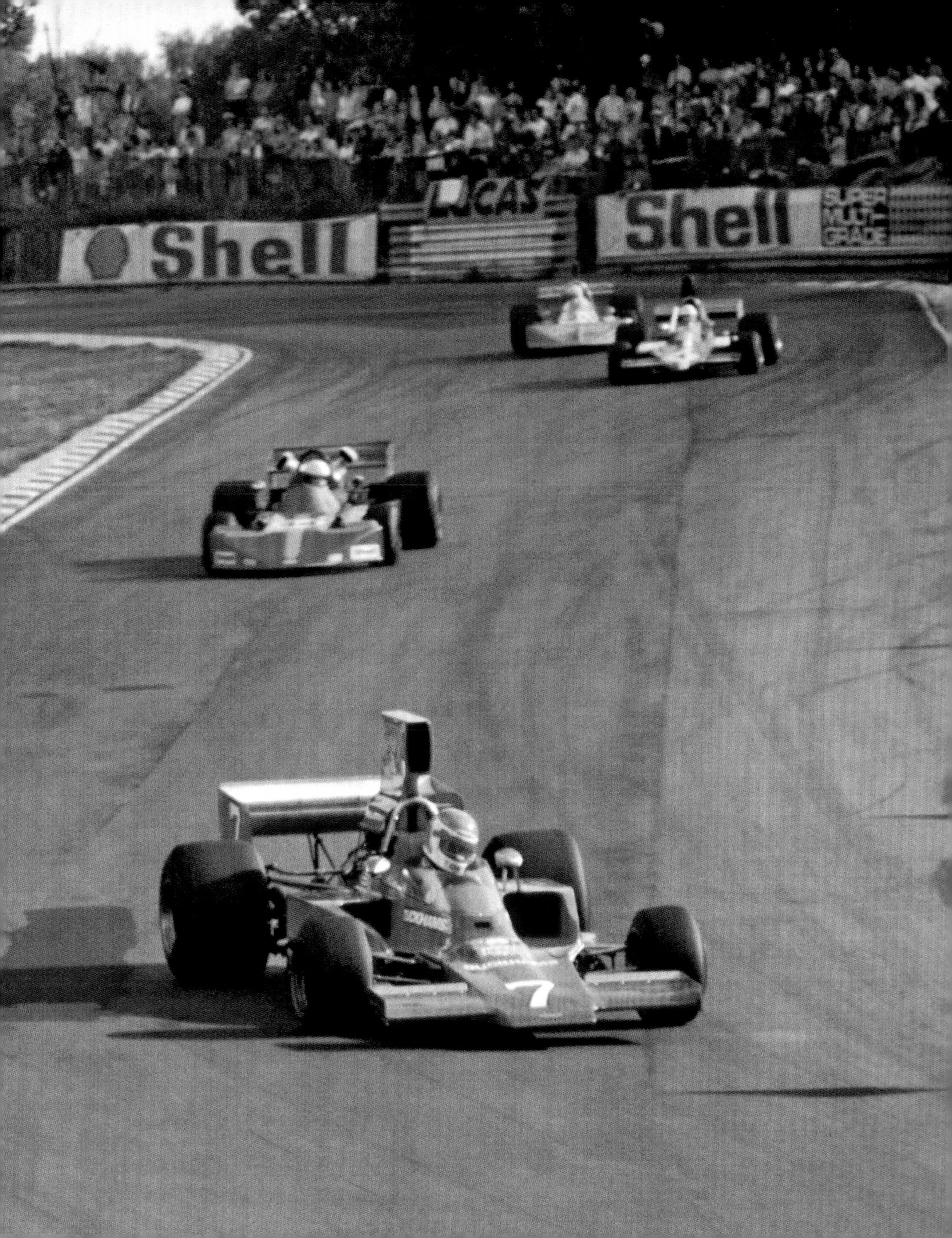

LUCAS
Shell
Shell
SUPER
MULTI-
GRADE
7

Polesitter Ted Wentz, Tony, Dave Morgan and Matt Spitzley await the off at Brands Hatch, for the April Formula Atlantic clash.

Championship title, was in the immaculate T332 prepared by the duo of Lola importer Carl Haas and Chaparral-building legend Jim Hall. Redman and Andretti were the cream of the series that year, two seasoned professionals who had done their time in Formula One and knew exactly what they were about. Unser was no slouch either, despite his relative lack of road racing experience.

It was Unser who set the pace for most of the 45-minute qualifying session, until Andretti just squeaked under his time to claim his sixth Formula 5000 pole of the season. Mario lapped in 1m 21.297s, Al in 1m 21.948s.

People in Europe knew about Tony, of course, but not the Americans. He soon put that right. Straight away he was clean, neat but forceful, and then he really opened everyone's eyes when he lapped in 1m 22.036s to beat Redman, whose best was 1m 23.604s, to take third on the grid. What made this excellent performance all the more impressive was that he had missed most of

the first session on Saturday, when everyone else was busy acclimatising themselves to the challenging new track, after a driveshaft yoke broke up.

While others sweated their way around, Tony's class showed through as he told Gordon Kirby, 'Driving the Lola is very easy. You're going so slow most of the time anyway, and the steering's very light.'

Such matter-of-fact comments were another reason why some people still thought Tony arrogant. But not Annie Proffitt. Once a racer in her own right, she was now a respected motorsport writer on the North American continent and that season was working for different teams as a timer in the Formula 5000 series. She met Tony for the first time in Long Beach, and took to him at once.

'I liked him immediately,' she said. 'Drivers are a strange lot, but I figured if he was good enough for Graham (Hill) he was good enough for me. And he showed me everything out there on the race track. He was not only quick, he was tidy, which to my mind is a fabulous thing. Tony came across as a good fellow, as a very studious driver. Anyone can be quick, but I just liked the fact that he was quick and tidy at the same time. That absolutely amazed me. And he was a complete person. I didn't feel that he was arrogant at all,

but I do think he was confident. Brian Redman was quite entranced by him, as I remember. Mario was impressed, too, and he isn't easily impressed by anyone.'

Alongside Tony sat Englishman Jackie Oliver in the first of the works-entered, Dodge-engined Shadow DN6s. He also lapped in 1m 22.036s, while Tom, who was making his Formula 5000 début in a luridly painted sister car, was fifth on 1m 22.799s; Redman lined up sixth. Behind this sextet were drivers of the calibre of England's David Hobbs, South Africa's Jody Scheckter – making a rare Formula 5000 reappearance after starring in the 1973 series against Redman – New Zealand champion Graham McRae, fellow countryman and Formula One star Chris Amon, and Australian Vern Schuppan.

The race was divided into two 12-lap qualifying heats with the overall victor to be determined in a 50-lap final. Overnight Tony's team changed the gearbox and lowered the rear ride height to improve traction.

Andretti led the first heat until a locking brake forced him to run wide in the first corner. That enabled Tony to grab the initiative, chased hard by Tom and Schuppan. Mario quickly pushed back past Schuppan and then Tom, and was chasing Tony by the fourth lap. For a couple of laps Tony maintained his six-second lead, pushing the red Lola round in neat slides that had

Above: This resulted in the fourth of Tony's six wins, the Modus driver proving unstoppable. Below: Winning the John Player International Championship was a fitting payback to Teddy Savory. The Norfolk businessman was a tough taskmaster, but played a key role in helping Tony's career to progress as it reached a critical point.

Tony was headed for an easy victory at Brands when the Sid Taylor-run Theodore Racing Lola T332 developed a puncture, dropping him to second place behind winner Jones.

the tyres chirping, but gradually Andretti reeled him in, setting the race's fastest lap almost a second faster than he had qualified (1m 20.35s).

Going into the last two laps the battle for the lead had become an absolute nail-biter, and they went into the last lap nose-to-tail. Partway round they came upon a backmarker, and as they each found their way by him they went to the final corner tied together. Tony gave the Lola everything it had as they lunged through it, its tail snapping into oversteer and then the front end sliding fractionally wide so that both wheels kissed the wall on the exit. Tony kept his foot planted and maintained his momentum, but Andretti was right beneath his rear wing getting ready to pull out just before the finish line. He was alongside Tony as they sped beneath the chequered flag, but the verdict went to Tony by a

fraction of a second after 16.5 minutes of gripping racing. You didn't beat Mario Andretti unless you were something special.

Further back, Tom held off Schuppan to the finish, but the Shadow lacked rear-end grip and was oversteering so much that even he complained about it afterwards. They were followed in by Elliott Forbes-Robinson and Warwick Brown.

The second heat was a tamer affair that fell to Al Unser from a tussling Redman and Scheckter, with Hobbs, Eppie Wietzes and Amon rounding out the top six.

Because his heat had been two seconds faster, Unser had the pole for the final from Tony; Andretti and Redman shared the second row. The pair of them exploded side-by-side down Shoreline Drive to the tight, right-handed first corner, Unser exploiting the inside line to maintain his advantage. Tony slotted into second place as Andretti cut across Redman to grab third.

Initially Unser opened a small lead, but with Andretti breathing down his neck, Tony was in a hurry and soon caught Al. They touched briefly on the third lap under braking, and that enabled Tony to snatch away the lead, with Andretti following him through as Unser momentarily lost momentum. For a while Mario stayed right with Tony but, bit by bit, the unthinkable began to happen as the tall Englishman simply began to pull away. After 10 laps he was almost three seconds clear of the two red and white cars, and as Tony began to encounter the first backmarkers he doubled the gap in small chunks here and there. But then, as he freely admitted later, he made an error and spun at the second hairpin. 'I just relaxed too a little too much,' he confessed. 'And then I compounded that by booting it too much and spun back round the wrong way.'

He sorted himself out very quickly, but not before the two Viceroy Lolas had gratefully sped past. Tony was not done yet, however. Within a lap he had caught Unser, and then regained second place after forcing the USAC star into a mistake of his own. Unser hit a wall hard enough to prompt his retirement.

Now Tony set off after Andretti again. Mario was the star, and was proud of his reputation that season as the fastest man in the formula; Tony had been an unknown in America only days earlier. Now everybody knew who he was as he closed the two-second gap that Andretti had opened up. Setting the race's fastest lap – a new record – in 1m 19.905s, he closed to within a second, but there the matter appeared to rest. In the cockpit, however, Tony was biding his time and peering through a visor that was smeared with oil; he had only one tear-off, and wanted to wait as long as he dared before pulling it off to clear his vision again.

Finally, he ripped it away, and then pounced on Andretti going into the first corner. They touched briefly, and somehow the American retained his lead. But, at the second corner, Tony tried again, this time outbraking Mario neatly in one of the most impressive manoeuvres the spectators had ever witnessed.

Andretti was never a man to give up, and he kept the Viceroy Lola right behind the Theodore car. He dropped back a fraction here and there, but it was only to choose a better moment to slingshot back beneath Tony's rear wing as he tried every tactic in his thick book to pressure the Formula 5000 rookie into another mistake. It never came. Tony coolly absorbed the pressure and was firmly in control of the situation when Andretti's car suddenly rolled to a halt with suspected transmission failure.

Mario was mightily impressed by his rival's performance that day. They knew one another from Formula One, but there they drove different cars. Here their Lola T332s had largely been similar. 'Tony was strong,' he said. 'Long Beach was the only place where we hurt tremendously. There was a thing about a Weismann diff, and for some reason we were kind of stuck on that. I'd never run a 5000 on a circuit like that, and we should have had a cam and pawl differential in

there. What happens with a Weismann diff when you put power on is that both wheels are driving – it's like a spool. The car just had a terrific amount of understeer through the hairpin. It was probably the only race where in qualifying I felt like I was giving away tremendously.

'Brise came on with Sid Taylor and they had it right. Fact I think Brian Redman did, too. I felt kinda screwed there, didn't feel competitive. But Tony had a lot of talent, for sure. Yeah, I rated him. Tony was good, he showed that. He would have been a force to be reckoned with, no question.'

As you can see from the comments, Andretti was not a man to praise lavishly and without taking into account all the relevant factors, but he was impressed, no question.

So was Tony. It was only some time later that he made a confession to Nigel Roebuck, a close ally of Andretti's, about that race.

'I seem to remember Tony was at Brands the week after Long Beach for a Formula Atlantic race, and I went down to watch,' said Roebuck. 'The thing that had blown everyone's mind at Long Beach was the way he had passed Mario. And it certainly got Mario's attention, and he was super-impressed. And Tony said there that he thought he was passing Al Unser Snr, that was the thing. He said if it had been Mario he'd never have dared to do it! But that was the sort of bloke he was; he was in complete awe of someone like Mario.'

Now Tony had the race in his pocket and was about to create a major upset in the USAC/SCCA Formula 5000 Championship. But, in the rush to do so, many

The passing move he pulled on series pacesetter Mario Andretti was stunning, but later Tony admitted that he had thought it was the Viceroy driver's team-mate, Al Unser Snr, and that he might not have tried it had he realised this was the charismatic but tough Italo-American.

ABOVE: *Tony prepares for the final where, after vanquishing Andretti and Unser in a straight fight, he would be headed for a stunning victory until the Theodore Lola succumbed to a driveshaft failure.* BELOW: *Tom also ran at Long Beach, making his début in a colourful but poor handling Shadow DN6.*

modifications to the Theodore Lola the previous evening, one thing had been overlooked: after Saturday morning's driveshaft failure, only the affected component was replaced. Barely a lap after Andretti pulled out, Tony slid off on the corner leading on to the straight, the Lola's wheels locked. The other shaft had failed, the stress on it exacerbated by the ride height change and the increase in rear-end grip and tyre chatter. A brilliant victory had been snatched from his grasp at the last moment.

Redman went on to take the win, reaping the rewards of his focus on reliability and longevity. The success also clinched him his second championship crown. But the man everybody talked about as they headed for home was Tony Brise.

'That was just amazing,' Janet said, her voice filling with pride. 'I think that was his most exciting race for me to watch. And then the driveshaft broke. I remember watching him at that last corner and he just went straight on instead of going round it. I was thinking, "Oh, God, why have you done that?" because I hadn't realised then that the driveshaft had broken. But it was a fantastic race. I remember Teddy Yip dancing up and down. There was a big report in the paper, "Tony Brise took Long Beach by its horns and shook it" or something like that. Although he didn't win, he was the hero.'

Subsequently he finished fourth in the Monterey Grand Prix for Formula 5000 at Laguna Seca on 12 October, behind Andretti, Unser and Redman, and sixth at Riverside a fortnight later, where the leading threesome was the same. He'd been third in his heat at the first Californian venue, second to Unser at the second. He had also clinched the John Player International Atlantic Championship, repaying the debt he felt that he owed Teddy Savory, the man who, the previous year, had saved his foundering career.

These were busy weeks for him, with the Formula 5000 races, Atlantic and the unveiling of Graham Hill's new GH2 challenger for 1976. And he loved it all, that heady feeling of going to places he had only dreamed of as a boy, racing against – and beating – name drivers he revered, and especially the new-found security of knowing for once precisely what he would be racing the following season. But it might not have been the Hill. He'd had an offer from Ken Tyrrell, which he considered carefully.

'We were at Watkins Glen and he was humming and haaing what to do,' Janet revealed, 'and then he said, "I've made up my mind, and I'm staying with Graham. Better the devil you know, and we do get on so well." But he did agonise over it.'

Tony really liked Hill, and Janet got on well with Bette. 'She was wonderful to me, because she just took me under her wing, if you like. I was the baby of the

Formula One girls, and she took me round all of the motorhomes and introduced me to all the wives. We'd have cup of tea, a glass of wine, a cup of coffee. She also taught me how to do my lap chart. She and I would sit side by side on our little red Embassy stools on the pit wall. I remember one time, though I can't remember which track it was, they got the wrong time for Tony; so both Bette and I took our lap charts up and, because they both said the same thing, they actually gave us the time, which pushed him up quite a few places on the grid. It was a very absorbing thing to do, and if you were worried about someone the best thing was to get involved in dealing with figures. It was all very friendly and we all got on very well.'

Tony had shaken down the new Formula One car at Silverstone, had conducted one full-blown test at the Paul Ricard circuit, near Marseilles, and was due for another. But before he left again for France, John Brise offered his eldest son some wise counsel.

'Tony had been doing all sorts of things, and having a wonderful time,' Pam Brise said. 'And John said to him, "You know, Tony, you are going a bit mad. I think you ought to calm things down a bit."'

And Tony had smiled at the man who had done so much to get him where he was now, and said, 'I know, Dad, but isn't life great…?'

ABOVE: *Nella and Tom were an introspective couple, but greatly enjoyed Alan Henry's company. Thirty years later, Nella had not forgotten the wordsmith's lurid taste in trousers.* BELOW: *The Shadow's heavier Dodge V8 promoted so much oversteer that even Tom thought it excessive. Mechanical problems ended his chances of a decent finish.*

CHAPTER 17

Fog over Arkley

29 November 1975

'The precise reason for the aircraft hitting the ground short of the runway could not be established, but the possibility that the pilot underestimated his distance from the aerodrome and descended prematurely cannot be excluded.

Accidents Investigation Branch

Graham Hill's new Formula One challenger for 1976 was ready long before the 1975 season ended. Tony tested the dramatically lowline car, which was once again the work of Andy Smallman, at Silverstone in October. He liked the Hill GH2, though it had an understeer problem first time out. The team then headed for the sunnier climes of the Paul Ricard circuit in the south of France to put further mileage on the car and to try out modifications that Smallman had incorporated. But it still understeered and Tony could only lap two seconds off his own pace there in July with the heavier GH1.

Nevertheless, the team was upbeat. Behind the scenes Hill had negotiated with W.D. & H.O. Wills to extend his contract with the Embassy brand. The new deal was worth serious money; a figure of £365,000 was mentioned, which was handsome indeed back then.

There was a second test at Ricard, which concluded on Saturday 29 November. This was much more successful. Ian Flux still has the telex: 'GH2 now faster than GH1.'

As Ray Brimble and Graham Hill stand behind, designer Andy Smallman kneels beside Tony in the cockpit of the Hill GH2 at Silverstone. The car had just begun to show its mettle in the second test at Paul Ricard. All of them, together with mechanics Terry Richards and Tony Alcock, perished when Hill's plane crashed at Arkley.

Smallman headed for home with plenty of fresh ideas for what was needed to improve the car still further.

'The car Tony drove in that second Ricard test was actually a GH1.5,' Alan Howell recalled, 'because we grafted the back end of the GH1 on to the new car and it worked much better. I spent most of my time there cutting and shutting the exhaust pipes, as neither the GH1 nor the GH2 sets would fit. We had a few teething problems, but were beginning to see which way to go with the car.'

'Tony was very optimistic about 1976,' Janet confirmed. 'I remember him on the phone to me. We spoke every night in the week before he died, when he was testing in the south of France. He was on cloud nine. "The car is going really well!"'

Together with Hill, team manager Ray Brimble, and mechanics Tony Alcock and Terry Richards, Tony and Smallman boarded Hill's turbocharged twin-engined Piper PA 23-250 Turbo Aztec 'D', registered N6645Y, for what should have been a routine flight home to Elstree, to the north of London. They were in high spirits. Alcock had only joined the team the previous month at Brimble's request, as workshop foreman. He and Richards were normally based at the factory and had accompanied the others to the test on a 'fact-finding' mission. And, in another twist of Fate, mechanic Alan Howell accompanied truckie Malcolm Allen on the drive back to Britain. Howell should have been on the plane, but agreed to go back in the truck so that Richards could take his place.

'Terry played in a band,' Flux explained, 'and that night they had a gig at, I think, a relative's party, which he would miss because of the test. So he swapped places with Alan and went back in the plane because, that way, there was a chance that he would get to play after all.'

It would not be the only poignant twist of Fate that evening.

Hill's party left Le Castellet, where the Paul Ricard circuit was located, at 15:30hrs, bound for an intermediate stop at Marseilles to refuel and for Hill to file an IFR (Instrument Flight Rules) flight plan to Elstree. The estimated flight time was four hours, with an estimated time of arrival of 22:00hrs. Hill also visited the self-briefing unit at Marseilles Marignane aerodrome, where weather forecasts for the London area for the period 13:00–22:00hrs were on display. They took off again at 17:47hrs, and it is interesting to note from the official report into the accident that the plane weighed 2,515kg–155kg above its authorised maximum take-off weight. After an uneventful flight Hill first contacted the London Air Traffic Control Centre at 20:45hrs. Though there were no qualified meteorological observers at Elstree – which, at that time, was a private airfield and thus did not require them – weather reports from Air Traffic Control reported that the wind was calm and visibility was two kilometres. However, at 21:19hrs, Hill

was informed that the visibility at Elstree had deteriorated dramatically as fog crept over the countryside and night fell. It was now down to one kilometre.

At 21:27.18hrs, Hill reported that he was at 1,500 feet, and at 21:27.24hrs was advised that he was 4nm (nautical miles) from Elstree. When he asked for clearance to descend lower, he was advised that such descent was now at his discretion. Nineteen seconds later he was heard to say the word, 'Elstree', on the London Approach frequency, indicating that he believed himself to be in contact with Elstree, though he had not actually been cleared by London Approach to change transmitter frequency.

At 21:28.02hrs, the London Approach controller passed the Heathrow QFE of 999mb (millibars) and informed Hill that he had only 3nm to go to Elstree. There was no reply to that transmission.

According to a report from the Meteorological Office in Bracknell, the weather conditions over southern England at that time featured a very light south-westerly wind at the surface which would produce upslope motions of air over Arkley. As a result, the hill would be completely covered by low stratus, giving thick hill fog and visibility of less than 200 metres.

Just before 21:30hrs, the air traffic controller at Elstree recognised Hill's voice saying, '45 Yankee finals,' and answered him with the aerodrome information and QFE of 990mb, and gave him clearance to land. Hill answered with a brief '45…', which was followed by a click as if his microphone had been released. At this time several witnesses in Barnet reported hearing an aircraft flying very low, of seeing a flashing light in the fog travelling from the east to the west in the direction of Arkley, and then the sound of an explosion in the direction of Arkley golf course. Afterwards it was postulated that, just as Hill made his '45…' transmission, the Piper brushed the top of a large oak tree 458 feet amsl (above mean sea level) on Arkley golf course while on a two-degree descent path. It then clipped another tree before colliding with a large ash at 450ft amsl. That impact tore off the right fibreglass wing tip tank, and a group of adjacent birch trees bore the signs of propeller slashes. The plane scythed off the tops of these trees as it continued to descend. It rolled over the fourth green and clipped the ground with its right wing at an angle of 45 degrees, collided heavily with two willow trees which ruptured its fuel tanks, and then crashed violently in a copse before coming to rest. A fuel explosion then followed. None of the occupants stood a chance, and several of the six seats were torn off their mountings. The official report disclosed that death was instantaneous in each case.

There was evidence that Hill was repeatedly asked by Air Traffic Control if he wanted to divert to Luton Airport, 15 miles further north. He rejected the idea. He was apparently anxious to get back quickly as he was due at a dinner party at his home in Mill Hill in north-west London, only a few miles and a few minutes' drive south on the A1 from Elstree. Some of the passengers' cars were parked at Elstree, and going to Luton would have created complications that Hill did not need. He regarded himself as an experienced aviator, and was adamant that he knew a safe route home. Flying low over Barnet, he believed that he could see the landing lights of Elstree ahead. But he was flying much lower than he thought and the lights that he could see through the thick fog were not those of Borehamwood, which was the closest conurbation to Elstree, but the streetlights on the A1 near Arkley. Unknowingly, he was attempting to land three miles too soon.

Minutes later, in Dorking, Nigel Roebuck received a phone call from his friend Chris Amon. 'There was a snippet on the news that there'd been a light aircraft crash, between Marseilles and England, and Chris phoned me and said, "I think it's Graham." I remember Chris saying, "I can just hear the old story of, 'There's fog, let's go to Luton.' And Graham saying, 'No, the hell with it, the cars are at Elstree.'"'

Brian Pescod, now retired as assistant treasurer of Arkley Golf Club, was there that night. 'We were in the clubhouse, having a quiet drink, when we heard this unusual noise. To begin with we thought it was kids on the roof, and we actually went outside to check. We had just about convinced ourselves that there wasn't anybody up there when, very shortly, two police cars arrived, and informed us that they believed a plane had crashed on the second green. They were very accurate. It really was a filthy night. Not quite one of the old pea-soupers that we used to get, but the conditions were atrocious and they asked us if we could guide them down there. Obviously we knew the place like the back of our hand, even in that fog, and we took them about 450–500 yards from the clubhouse. The plane had taken the tops off a couple of trees and then cartwheeled into a small copse down there. The wreckage was still burning. As soon as we'd shown the police the site, we were politely ushered away. I think we knew almost straight away that it was Graham Hill, because of what the police had told us.'

After retiring from motorsport, Royale founder Bob King had moved into the aviation world, buying and selling planes. Having started Royale in Edgware before switching production facilities to Park Royal, he had long lived in the Middlesex/Hertfordshire area.

'I was at Elstree Aerodrome that night,' he revealed, 'and I couldn't believe it. It was filthy, the most disgusting night. Fog, rain, you name it. We heard that Graham was inbound and, by the time I got home, which was about 10 minutes from Elstree, there had been a big crash on the golf course. Then, by the time I had got inside the house and had turned the

news on, it was "thought to be Graham Hill". We then subsequently learned that there were six of them on board...'

Flux heard about the accident on his way home later that night. 'I went to see a band in Guildford, and I picked up this girl and was giving her a lift back to Cranleigh. The news was on a bulletin on Radio Luxembourg around midnight, which we were listening to in the car. I dropped her off and went straight round to Alan Turner's house. Then the police called him and asked him to go and identify the bodies, so I stayed at his house to keep his wife company.'

Janet Brise had gone out that night with her friend Jenny Anderson. And it was Janet who revealed one of the hitherto unknown twists to the story: that Graham Hill was not even supposed to have been at the test.

'It's just sad that Graham decided to go out as well, because he was shooting at Gleneagles while the team was out there, and then decided halfway through the week that he would go out, too. He wasn't supposed to be there... What happened was that bad weather had delayed the test so Tony and the boys had to stay out there longer. That's why Graham decided that he might as well fly out and see how they were getting on.

'Tony and I decided that, as it was meant to be only a couple of days of testing, I wouldn't go. We'd only just got back from a trip to Hong Kong, courtesy of Teddy Yip, and Christmas was coming and I needed to make preparations. We'd never been apart for more than a couple of days since we got married.'

Graham Hill and Tony Brise: two World Champions who died in the fog over Arkley on November 29.

'That Saturday night I went out for a drink with Jenny. I don't remember why we called into the Brise home. Pam, John and Tim were there and they'd heard it on the news, that a plane had gone down. They thought it was Graham, and I was saying, "Well, it's not Tony because he's coming back tomorrow." I was so sure.'

Janet was certain her husband could not be on board because she knew he had a return ticket with British Airways for the following evening. What she couldn't have known then was that Graham's unexpected arrival had persuaded five team members to change their scheduled flights and come back with him a day sooner. Tony was due to fly back on the Sunday. In yet another surreal twist, Ronnie Peterson should have been aboard, too – but Graham had decided not to give the Swedish star a ride as his foreign passport might have led to delays at customs.

'Tim was on the phone trying to get Tony,' Janet continued, 'and I was saying he's in such and such hotel. Eventually Tim managed to get through to the hotel and they said, no, Tony wasn't there, he'd checked out. And then, I think, eventually the police came round and that's when we learned the truth. It was just awful.'

Jenny remembered, 'I'd spoken on the phone to Tony and he'd said he was hoping to get back on Sunday so we could all go out together. In the meantime I went out for a drink with Janet. I took her back to the Brise house, and since there were so many cars there I assumed they must be having a party and just dropped her off.

'When I got back to our house in Swanley my parents asked me if I had brought Jan with me, and I asked them, "Why?" Then they told me about the television newsflash, about a plane thought to be Graham's. But we knew Tony wasn't meant to be on it. I called Tim and he wouldn't accept it at first. We all clung to the belief Tony wasn't on the plane, and it didn't come out that he was until the next day.

'It was my first-ever experience of something awful like that happening. In motor racing at that time you half expected accidents, but what happened to Tony, and to Graham Hill and the team, was so totally unexpected. I was just a friend on the outside, and even then there was such a feeling of loss. I wanted to go back a couple of days and make it not to have happened. That feeling was very, very strong for a long time. I had to be with Janet afterwards, to help her through it. It was the hardest thing I could ever do, and the last thing I could do for Tony.'

Alan Howell and Terry Richards had tossed a coin to see which of them would go back in the plane. Howell remembers: 'I lost the toss over breakfast that Saturday. Tony Alcock pestered me all day to swap places, but I said that I'd lost so it wouldn't be fair now to change again.

'The car was in a thousand bits in the garage, and while we were doing that the plane went overhead and Graham waggled the wings. I thought, "Bastards, they'll be home in three hours…"

'We were staying at a hotel down at Bandol, and there was such a winding approach to it that we had to park the truck some way back, outside an old shed. A bit later on, the phone in the room rang. It was Madame downstairs: a policeman wanted to speak to me. The shed turned out to be a discotheque, so I went with him and moved the truck to a car park on top of the cliff. The gendarme and I then went off to have a beer in the disco.

'By the time I got back to the hotel Malcolm was asleep. I'd just got off myself, when the phone rang. It was Madame: the police wanted to speak to me again. But this time it was a sergeant in Britain. He told me what had happened, that the plane had crashed and that there were no survivors. He wanted the names of the people on board. I told him to tell me again what happened and he asked who I was and I told him. "You're dead," he said. "I've just called your wife and told her."'

Howell was unable to call home; every time he tried to contact his wife, Frances, their phone line was engaged. 'She was busy telling the world I was dead. Later we saw Nobby Clarke from Team Lotus on the ferry going home. He took one look at me and said, "It's just been on the news, you're dead!" I said, "I'm not!"

'On the ferry over that Sunday, we hit the harbour wall four times trying to get in at Dover, it was such a foul night with high winds and high tide. Eventually we got in after having to go out and tow home a coaster that was in trouble.

'I still couldn't raise Frances, so she was a bit shocked when I eventually walked in the back door…'

'So many times you go over it and you ask, "Why?"' Janet said. 'And then you just have to end up thinking that when your number is up, your number is up. Just to make things even worse, it was reported the next day in *The Times* that I was on the flight, so I had loads of friends phoning my parents, worried sick.'

Photojournalist Jeff Hutchinson was himself a pilot who had taught several racing drivers to fly, among them Keke Rosberg and Heinz-Harald Frentzen. He had also competed in some aerial races, and was scathing in his criticism of Hill's flying protocol. 'The accident happened because he did not reset his altimeter from Ricard's high pressure, and was trying to land visually in the fog at Elstree when he could have made an instrument approach into Luton. He had a party that night and his car was at Elstree, so he didn't want to waste time with hire cars or taxis from Luton. That was what caused the accident, plain and simple.'

Tony Vlassopulos was also hard in his summary. 'We flew with Graham quite a lot in the Rondel days. We called it Hilarious Airways, always had cheese sandwiches halfway down. Once we went to Gatwick, going off to Pau, and I got all the way to the airport and I'd left my briefcase in the hall at home. Poor Sue, my wife, had to deal with Graham while I drove home for it, had to listen to all this ranting and raving, "I'll kill him when he gets back."

'If you want my story about Tony Brise, I think he (Hill) killed him. And that was another piece of stupidity by Graham Hill. Luton Airport was clear – he could have gone there.'

Gentleman Jacques Laffite was kinder in his analysis, admitting that he had had his own aerial adventures during his racing career. Many drivers had. 'Graham made the mistake that everybody does. We fly home, we know exactly where we are, no problem. I was nearly the same in fog at Nevers once. Then we saw the road, the gas station, okay, we are here, we go 90 degrees, past the church, so the airport is there. You can do that nine times out of 10.'

The official 'Aircraft Accident Report 14/76', undertaken by the Accidents Investigation Branch for the Department of Trade, was not published until 3 December 1976. It made several damning findings:

The aircraft had formerly been registered in the United States, but this registration had been cancelled in 1974 following a request by the previous owners to that effect. The aircraft was not subsequently re-registered in any other country, and was therefore unregistered at the time of the accident, though it still displayed its former US registration markings.

On the basis of a Certificate of Registration, which purported to show that the aircraft was still registered in the US, the aircraft was maintained in accordance with an approved maintenance schedule. However, the US certificate of airworthiness was no longer effective after August 1974 when the aircraft ceased to be registered in the United States.

The pilot filed an IFR flight plan for a flight outside the United Kingdom in controlled airspace when he was not in possession of a pilot's licence appropriate to the registration markings on the aircraft.

The pilot flew the aircraft in UK-controlled airspace where instrument flight rules were in force when he was not in valid possession of a valid Instrument Meteorological Conditions (IMC) rating.

The pilot flew his aircraft with passengers on board below 3,000 feet amsl in a flight visibility of less than 3nm when he was not in possession of a valid IMC rating.

The pilot received adequate warning of the visibility deterioration at his destination airfield, Elstree, prior to commencing his approach to land.

The pilot attempted to land at Elstree when the visibility and cloud base at the aerodrome were substantially less than that permitted by his licence. Although the conditions were below the limits set for

public transport operation from that airfield, these limits did not apply to this particular flight.

The aircraft was descending at approximately 330 feet per minute at a normal approach speed when it struck the tops of trees 458 feet amsl, 1nm south of the extended centre line of Runway 27, and 3nm from its threshold. The area where the accident occurred was covered in thick fog.

There is no evidence of any technical malfunction or mechanical failure to account for the accident nor is there any evidence of pilot incapacitation. The reason for the aircraft's descent into the ground could not be established but the possibility cannot be excluded that the pilot was mistaken as to his exact distance from the airfield and believed himself to be closer than in fact he was.

The air traffic services at Heathrow and Elstree rendered what assistance they could to the aircraft, but their actions in no way contributed to the accident.

As to the cause of the six deaths, the report concluded:

'The accident was caused by the pilot attempting to land in conditions of low visibility at an airfield not equipped with the appropriate precision landing aids. The precise reason for the aircraft hitting the ground short of the runway could not be established, but the possibility that the pilot underestimated his distance from the aerodrome and descended prematurely cannot be excluded.'

Graham Hill bought his Piper PA 23-250 Turbo Aztec 'D', registered N6645Y, with his winnings from Indianapolis in 1966. Here he and his wife Bette prepare to head up.

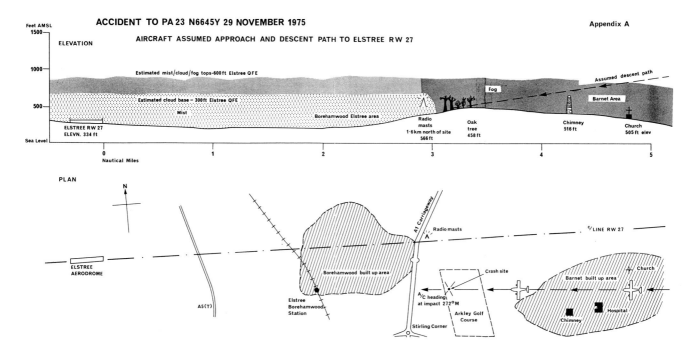

There was no doubt that Graham Hill took chances when he was flying. Many motor racing figures had hair-raising stories of his exploits.

The late Hughie Green, of *Double Your Money* and *Opportunity Knocks* television show fame, was a skilled pilot who flew for the DuPont family after earning his licence in World War Two. 'I remember a time when we were both on a show in Manchester, Graham and I,' he recalled. 'We had both flown ourselves in. It was rough weather that night, cold and snowy, and I decided it might be better to wait until the morning, but Graham was all for leaving regardless of the conditions. And I watched him fire up the engines and then take off straight away. He didn't waste any time allowing them to warm up...'

Tony's manager Nick Brittan had little time for Hill's aerial antics. 'One time, Tony and I were up at my cottage in Norfolk, seeing Teddy Savory on a bit of Modus business. Graham was up at Hethel seeing Colin Chapman, and said if we wanted a lift down to London to meet him at Shipton Aerodrome. It was a tiny strip, and as soon as we slammed the plane door we went straight up. I thought, "Aren't we meant to check instruments or whatever?"

'Tony was learning to fly and was up in the other front seat with Graham, doing the apprentice flier bit. There was a security zone over Mildenhall, the American Air Force base. It was called the Strategic Air Command triangle. Everything went up when the four-minute warning went, that sort of thing. You couldn't fly through it, you had to negotiate two legs of the triangle and go around it. Tony was navigating and told

Graham that, and Graham just smiled. He switched the radio off, gave it full throttle and just flew straight through the triangle. He said it would save 20 minutes. He thought it was tremendously good fun, although you could hear that the radio at the other end was going bloody mad!'

Brittan also remembered how Hill would just sweep in, unannounced, to Elstree Aerodrome. This was then a private airfield that could be used day or night by prior permission only. 'He just went straight in, without a word to the control tower beforehand. He taxied straight up to the hangar, and as we turned into it this guy ran up like Ben Johnson and jumped up on the wing. I'd never seen a white man black in the face before. He actually punched the window and yelled, "Graham Hill, you think you own this place!" Graham just shrugged at him and laughed, and eventually the guy calmed down and left him to it. That must have been four or five weeks before the big business.'

Alan Henry also remembered an adventurous flight with Hill to the Osterreichring. 'There were several of us aboard, and we were generally dozing. I woke up one time and there was Graham sitting down the back with us. Mike Tee asked him who was flying the plane, and Graham told him it was on automatic pilot and that we were flying at 10,000 feet. After a few minutes Mike tentatively asked Graham, "Isn't there a large mountain range... close by?" and Graham very nonchalantly went back to the pilot's seat. All of a sudden we began climbing at a fair old rate...'

Bob King explained the two methods of setting the altimeter. 'QNH (altimeter setting which provides a

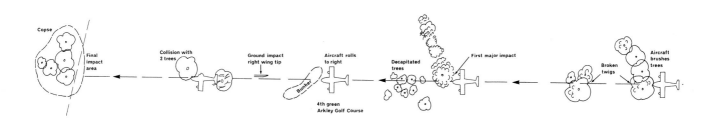

reading above mean sea level) is setting your altimeter so that it's at the airfield elevation, and we were around 330 feet above sea level at Elstree. QFE (altimeter setting providing an altitude reading above the level of a specific airfield) is setting it so that when you land at Elstree, the altimeter would show zero because you were on the ground.' Damage to the Piper was so significant that the crash investigators were never able to confirm whether or not Hill had failed to reset his altimeter from London QNH to Heathrow QFE, but found the left-hand altimeter set to 1,003mb – within 1mb of the London QNH of 1,002, which had been passed on to Hill. The other altimeter was intact, though scorched, and was set between 997 and 998mb which correlated with the Heathrow QFE of 999mb. The report did not rule out the possibility that Hill read the wrong altimeter when making his final approach, or that he had no time in the conditions to consult either instrument.

'Graham wasn't that experienced,' King continued. 'It was absolutely ridiculous that he chose to come into Elstree when Luton were waiting for him with all the instrument landing systems. And the plane wasn't insured and had no certificate of airworthiness. That's pure carelessness. You don't even have the right to kill yourself in a plane, because when you crash you might hurt other people; but when you have another five people in the other seats, that's the bad part.'

Poignantly, Brittan shared another memory, of just what a relaxed air passenger Tony was, how calm he probably would have been even as Hill's Piper Aztec was beginning to brush the trees that would drag them to their death. 'One time Tony and I came back from Switzerland on a Swiss plane, after doing some business for Embassy. We were playing chess on my travelling set when the plane hit a clear air pocket and suddenly, without any warning, dropped 200 feet. It was terrifying, most unnerving. I distinctly remember two things about it: one was me panicking and all the chess pieces on the ceiling; the other was Brise sitting there, in total control. It was a real do, there were a couple of broken arms where people hadn't been wearing their seat belts.

'The thing that was in my mind was, "I'm dead!" And Tony was as cool as a cucumber, no sign of panic whatsoever. Ten minutes later the same thing happened again, exactly the same. Tony was again in absolute control, not even flinching… I thought, "So this is how racers are meant to be." Three weeks later, it was all over…'

The motor racing world was stunned by the tragedy, and mourned the loss of the charismatic Hill and the emergent Tony Brise, together with their less famous team-mates.

'The following week was just horrendous,' Roebuck recalled. 'It was bad enough for Quentin and I, but for Bette Hill there was a funeral a day. I found Tony's infinitely more moving than Graham's. Graham's was at St Albans cathedral, a huge do packed with showbiz celebrities, that sort of thing. Tony's was really quite small. His father's face… it was just stone. He was absolutely wiped out. He wasn't a karting dad, he certainly didn't come to all the races. Put it this way, in a 2005 perspective with their sons racing, he was a Keke Rosberg rather than a Nelson Piquet. And when he was at the races he wasn't

He was so safe says Bette Hill

By ANN KENT and FRANK THOMPSON

GRAHAM HILL, who died on Saturday night when the plane he was piloting smashed into a golf course, was "as safe as houses in the air," his widow said yesterday.

He was not a murderer on the tracks and he certainly was not one in the air," said Mrs Bette Hill at her Hertfordshire home.

She spoke only 17 hours after police telephoned to tell her that her husband's Piper Aztec light plane had crashed in flames on to the snow-covered Arkley golf course, three miles from Elstree airfield, where he planned to land.

Mrs Hill sat talking in the music room of the large detached house which stands in 30 acres at Shenley.

Thorough

Outside the room her 16-year-old daughter Brigitte was in bed and was comforted by a friend. Also at home was a son Damon, 15, and a daughter Samantha, ten.

She said: "I don't know what the future holds for me. It is a bit empty. I suppose I have the children to think about.

"Sixteen years ago I went on ... I have flown in to in with Graham to to Elstree before. It was perfectly all right.

"He used the plane as much as he did his car. He went everywhere in it. The whole family has flown with him. He was as safe as houses. He was as safe as houses to about 10 years and he never, ever took any chances.

"He was so thorough. He used to check on every single

THE TEAM: From the left: Ray Brimble, Hill, Tony Brise and Andrew Smallman. They all died.

Riddle of crash in fog

Continued from Page One

instrument before he took off.

He loved flying. He used to love the rhythm. He used to take up for little aircraft late at night that come and Ro, up for little aircraft which can his way the crash.

Also among those who died with him in the night-flight of Marseille, where he and his racing cars were testing a new car, was team manager Ray Brimble, 31.

Four Brise had just reached the top of the racing driving for them in the next year.

Mechanics

Mechanics for the team, who died with him in the French night, was 29 years old.

Also killed were three younger men who were all members of the Embassy-Hill racing team.

They were racing team manager Ray Brimble, 31, racing driver Tony Brise, 23, designer Andy Smallman, 34, and mechanics ...

ears built to challenge the world's motor racing championship title, was Tony Brise, one of the most promising young drivers on the British tracks, and 29-year-old Tony Alcock, an engineer.

The dangers in private flying

By ANGUS MACPHERSON, Air Correspondent

BY FLYING his own light plane, Graham Hill was 27 times more likely to be killed than if he had travelled on a commercial night.

Hill's smart scarlet and white Piper Aztec.

How a routine trip to France to test a new car ended in tragedy

Hill faced 'touch and go' landing

By MAURICE WEAVER

GRAHAM HILL, who died with his Grand Prix team when his flight aircraft crashed while approaching Elstree Airport in thick fog, was trying a night landing in what other pilots said yesterday were "touch and go" conditions.

FREEZING FOG HITS AIRPORT

Daily Telegraph Reporter

THICK freezing fog blanketed much of England and Wales yesterday causing airport chaos and bringing hazardous driving conditions.

GRAHAM HILL, WINNER WHO HELPED LOSERS

By COLIN DRYDEN, Motoring Staff

GRAHAM HILL, known to millions throughout the world as a world champion racing driver, used his fame to help the less fortunate.

After giving up competitive driving he devoted much time and effort to causes like the Disabled Drivers' Association and the Springfield Boys' Club in the East End.

Experts will study safety of light planes

By Air Cdre E. M. Donaldson, Air Correspondent

THE Civil Aviation Authority, responsible for air safety over Britain, will be studying Saturday night's two similar accidents with particular care to ...

The winner's garland for Graham Hill after his victory in the 1966 Indianapolis 500. He bought an aircraft with the prize money.

Right: Home again with his wife, Bette, and their three children, Brigitte, Damon and Samantha, after prolonged treatment in hospital six years ago when he shattered his legs in a crash in the American Grand Prix.

● The wreckage of Graham Hill's Piper Aztec strewn in a copse at Arkley golf course.

The boy chosen to be champion

A FUTURE world champion ... that was how racing driver Tony Brise was seen by Graham Hill.

HAPPY: Racing driver Tony Brise and his attractive wife Janet

As the national daily newspapers focused their stories on the loss of the charismatic and popular Hill, it was generally left to the special press to remember his team members who perished with him.

Investigators pore over the wreckage of Graham Hill's Piper Aztec, which crashed on the second green at Arkley Golf Club.

intrusive, he was there in the background. And he was so proud of Tony. I don't ever remember speaking to John about this, but I wonder if he'd ever harboured any ambitions to have been that sort of racing driver himself. I saw him racing stock cars when I was a kid. I used to go to Bellevue. He was *so* proud of Tony.'

Alan Henry remembered John Brise that day, too. 'Poor man, he just couldn't take the funeral. He just couldn't handle it.'

Tony's was the first funeral followed, on respective days, by Andy Smallman's, Graham Hill's and Tony Alcock's, Terry Richards's and finally Ray Brimble's. By the end of a horrible week, everyone was completely wrung out emotionally.

'I went to all of them bar Graham's,' Flux said, 'and that was because it clashed with Tony Alcock's. Half of us went to Graham's and half to Tony's. Tony A's was the only atheist funeral I've ever been to. We all sat down, the undertaker eventually came in and said we could stand, then two minutes later he said we could sit again, and that was it. You know, it always winds me up a little when people just talk about Graham and Tony Brise, because there were four others and they were all just as important. There were 14 of us in total in that team, and we were all very close.

'Looking back, at the time you didn't realise how much you were affected by the accident, but later, when you try to remember things about it, you come to realise just how much it did affect you.'

Back then, the dark side of the sport was something few discussed. It was the spectre that walked among everyone who was involved, yet went unmentioned for fear of tempting Fate. Even couples rarely talked about it, as if giving voice to their fears might tempt Providence. Bette once told Graham she didn't know what would happen to the family if he wasn't around, and he told her not to worry. He had it all sorted. She smiled at the memory 30 years later, and said very quietly, with an expression of distant sadness, 'But he hadn't.'

In the space of a nightmare week after the accident, she attended five funerals. She had lost her husband and her children's father, and members of his team who had been good friends. And the aftermath of the tragedy would take her family to a very much lower level of existence. Many people would simply not have been able to cope.

'I don't know how I did, to be honest,' she admitted. 'You just do it. You have to. I went to five funerals and the only reason I didn't go to six was that dear old Tony Alcock was buried the same day as Graham. I did what I did for Graham, and I had three children to look after. Peter Jopp and Jackie Stewart took me to some of the funerals. I said to Nina Rindt that I didn't know how I was going to live without Graham, but you do. And I have.'

Sitting in the cottage in which she lives in Cobham, Surrey, her life rebuilt yet still empty without the man she loved, Bette bore every bit as much of the load visited upon her by the tragedy as the other families who had been touched by it. Perhaps more. 'I still talk to him now,' she said of her husband. "Look at the mess you've got me into." When our daughter Brigitte got married I asked everyone to join Graham and I in a toast to the bride and groom. I can't leave him out of it. He's been so much a part of my life.'

But the legacy that Graham Hill left behind, in the form of the irregularities concerning the plane, meant that, eventually, Bette lost most of her husband's fortune in legal claims.

There was the fact that the plane was no longer registered anywhere, having not subsequently been re-registered after Hill's offshore company, Grand Prix (Bahamas) Ltd of Nassau, had taken it out of the United States. That, while it had been properly maintained, it had no certificate of airworthiness. That, while he had in the past demonstrated the necessary skills, Hill was doing things beyond the remit of the UK private pilot's licence that he held. The equivalent is that if he had been driving a car, Graham Hill would not have held the right driving licence, nor any road tax, insurance or MOT. And his car would initially have been overloaded. Later, it was alleged that one of Hill's advisors had screwed up the plane's documentation – but, by then, it was far, far too late.

'Graham was like an open goal on the business side,' said Vlassopulos, who once accused Hill of losing a potential Matchbox sponsorship deal for 1972 because of the way he behaved during a meeting with the Lesney Board, 'and he seemed to rely on one particular gentleman who I personally thought was crooked in his dealings with me.'

Subsequently the shortcomings of Hill's plane's documentation invalidated any insurance, and Bette faced an avalanche of lawsuits from the bereaved families. The findings of the official report stirred up anger all round.

Janet was in no state to concern herself with financial matters. 'My father took over all of that and explained to me that we, along with the other widows, had to sue Graham's estate as his insurance was not valid. Tony had signed a contract with Embassy Hill Racing for the following year, so the claim was based on what he would have expected to earn in 1976. We settled out of court some years later for only a quarter of that sum. My father wanted to go to court but I was finding the whole thing too distressing as it kept bringing back memories of that terrible night. I just wanted to get on with my life.'

Janet's friendship with Bette would survive. 'We don't see each other very often now,' she says. 'It's usually at a race meeting, but it's always big hugs, "How are you doing?" She's met my husband John. It was just one of those things.'

Terry Richards's widow Linda, who was working as a shop assistant, said, 'I'm bitter and shocked by the report,' while Pat Brimble, left to bring up Ray's two children on her own, said, 'I've known for some time the sort of evidence the report would contain and I hoped it would never be made public.'

With its leader and its number one driver dead, together with the designer and team manager, it was inevitable that Embassy Hill Racing would also become a casualty of the tragedy. There was talk of it carrying on, but that's all it was. There was no sentiment as those who could have kept it going decided otherwise. 'The first thing I remember is how horrible people can be,' Flux recalled. 'Within a week Ford had collected its free cars and Fiat had taken the transporter tractor back. Embassy was committed for 1976, but they said it was Graham Hill's name they wanted and that, without him, there was no deal. Though I stayed on until March 1976, and there were plans to keep the thing running, eventually it all collapsed.'

Such was the enormity of Graham Hill's tragedy that the demise of his team went almost unnoticed. The man was so much greater than his own creation, however promising it had seemed. The nation had lost a hero, the sport its ambassador. In the shadow cast by the great man's passing, it was easy for Tony Brise, Andy Smallman, Ray Brimble, Terry Richards and Tony Alcock to be forgotten outside their own world of racing cars. But never by those who loved them.

'He was doing what he wanted, and he was very happy,' Pam Brise said of her son, many years later. 'And then he never came back. But those few words sustained us tremendously. A lot of my friends said he did more in his short life than many do in a full lifetime.'

When I had written the book *Racers Apart* in 1990, which contained chapters on their respective husbands, I took two copies to the antiques shop Pryce & Brise, run in Fulham by Nella and Janet. Later Janet wrote me a letter in which she said that she had given a copy to Pam, who had told her, 'I will read it one day, when I feel strong enough.' I found it profoundly moving that she still felt that way 15 years on, but then, why ever should she not?

'I think we could have accepted it better if Tony had died in a racing accident,' she said in 2003. 'The way it happened was so stupid and avoidable.'

Johnny and Pam went to most of their son's grand prix races in 1975, but remained quietly in the background, for that was their way. Neither had any wish to try and share their eldest son's limelight, but merely wanted to watch his progress and enjoy their feeling of inner pride. 'You always think these things to yourself when they happen to you in life,' Pam said. 'Why did God choose Tony? A really talented guy who gave pleasure to so many people by what he did? He wasn't a bad example to anybody, he lived his life quietly and kindly… It was a long time before I could justify in my mind what happened to him, before I came out of a little dream world, I suppose. But I did come out of it, in the end. I was never really bitter, but I could never understand why such an accident had to happen to such nice people.'

CHAPTER 18

Shadowing Hunt

Tom, 1976

'That was fantastic! You could do anything with that Stratos, and it was really good to get rid of all my winter frustrations. I only lasted 10 miles, but it was super.'
Tom Pryce

Of the three shooting stars in the 'Lost Generation' who had so electrified spectators in 1972, now only Tom Pryce remained. And the likeable Welshman faced a tough 1976 season. The lead in to it began, literally, with a bang.

Motorsport entrepreneur David Richards hailed from the same town, Ruthin, and knew Tom to speak to and Jack Pryce quite well; Jack laughs today at memories of having occasionally to rein in the town's other upcoming motorsport personality. These were the days when Richards was making a significant name for himself as an international rally co-driver, before subsequently going on to achieve great success establishing Prodrive and running Subaru's World Rally Championship effort, as well as having spells running the Benetton and BAR Honda Formula One teams prior to bringing Aston Martin back into endurance racing in 2005.

Like Jimmy Clark before him with his exploits in a Lotus Cortina on the 1966 RAC Rally, Tom was an inquisitive driver who wanted to try new things, and he hankered after a go at rallying.

'Obviously Tom's exploits in Formula Ford and subsequently Formula One were well known in the area and, although I did not know him particularly well, our paths crossed on a few occasions,' Richards recalled. 'It therefore came about that he and I discussed the possibility of him driving a rally in Wales, which

Tom was on fighting form in the British Grand Prix at Brands Hatch, scrapping with Carlos Pace and Alan Jones.

particularly interested him. The Tour of Epynt took place over the New Year holiday and was one of the few times of the year when he was available to drive. I therefore arranged for Graham Warner of the Chequered Flag in London to loan us a Lancia Stratos, the iconic rally car of its time, and off we went to the Epynt ranges.'

Tom was to start fourth and was, of course, up against stiff opposition from seasoned drivers. One of the favourites was third-placed RAC Rally driver Tony Fowkes, who had learned the Army roads of Epynt by heart. Tom had already tested the Stratos on a 'loose' circuit in Bagshot, and immediately impressed everyone with his confident handling of the car. He also sampled the tarmac course at Chobham; the surface was damp but he was flat out by his second lap. But this would still be a step into new territory.

Autosport journalist Peter Newton accompanied Tom in the Stratos after his first acclimatisation run at Bagshot. In the 25 December issue, three days before Epynt, he wrote, 'If Formula One drivers are all alike, they really are a breed apart. Tom's feel for the car is uncanny and he is already beginning to go really quickly – using the brakes to set the car on the entries, counteracting the understeer as the Stratos fires out of the corners. He is always looking for ways to help the car round. Piles of grading stones, cambers, suddenly everything is flowing past the side windows in that unique and exultant feeling one rarely experiences while being driven in this style.

'He has soon found out that the quickest way to slow down on the loose is to go sideways, but long before the apex he is back hard on the power and the engine note deepens as we rocket wide with power-understeer.'

Tom had a minor off that day before they continued, driving faster than ever.

'Pryce's reactions are staggering,' Newton continued, 'as indeed they would have to be to hold a Shadow in powerslides at comfortably over 100mph on dry tarmac, but this is something again – a cautious glance across at the frenetic arms working at the wheel and the feet dancing on the pedals says it all – and he is grinning, too! The car rushes onward, hurling itself towards the distant line of trees controlled by the remarkable Welshman.

'The revs have not changed at all – 7,800rpm in fourth gear or just over 100mph. The feeling of insecurity is over – the roundabout is upon us: Tom swings in late and hard, and is on the bump-stops of the

After the crash on Epynt, Tom carried on to give fans something to cheer. He said he'd like to have another go at rallying if anyone would trust him with their car. 'He had a lot to learn,' rallying supremo David Richards said, 'but he was very impressive and his ability and reflexes were outstanding. He was just unreal!'

Tom Pryce and David Richards take the hastily prepared Ferrari-engined Lancia Stratos on a demonstration run

Smash ends ace driver's rally debut

Tom Pryce, the Formula One racing driver from Clocaenog, near Ruthin, had a "smashing" time on his rally debut – he "smashed" into a stone bridge less than ten minutes after the on December 27. Co-driving for Tom in a multi-thousand pound Lancia Stratos was another fellow member of Clwyd Vale Motor Club, David Richards, from Llanfair D.C.

The rally is based on that the road surface had changed as he approached the bend and he had lost control of the car. He was unhurt in the crash but David had to have two stitches in his knee after cutting it against the dashboard.

The 1976 season got off to a good start when Tom brought his Shadow DN5 to third place in Brazil. It was the second podium of his Formula One career.

steering lock before we are halfway round. Yet that is as far as the car gets as he forces it to hang there – giant rocks are flashing past the co-driver's door – the return straight is in front of us, the car is riveted to the ground by the astounding traction and we're gone, engine note rising to a screaming cacophony of sound, the sort of sound which sends shivers down the spine. It alters scarcely half an octave with the gear changes.

'The memory of those last laps lives on where the description falls down; the words simply are not there. Tom brings the car back to the paddock, switches off and grins hugely. How did he enjoy it? He is ecstatic, and now he reveals his initial misgivings: "I never thought I could do it, how fast do you think I should be going? I'd like to finish the rally somewhere in the middle order..." The comments are mingled with honest delight and exultation and the car has been tremendous. "How many times have you done this before, Tom?" An embarrassed grin and the unassuming Pryce replies, "Oh never, this is the first time I've ever driven on the loose!" A rare breed indeed; beyond the bounds of comprehension. Tom may not win on Epynt, he may even crash, but I will remember those laps at Bagshot over Christmas, and there will be no need of any coal fires or central heating to keep warm when I recall that afternoon.'

Now, on the tarmac roads of Wales, Tom hit his stride immediately. He was taking minutes off the entire field, including Fowkes, who would eventually win. Then came disaster.

'My wife Karen and I met with Tom and Nella in a little pub near the ranges where we were staying for the weekend, and we went for a drive over the roads to give him an idea of what was in store,' Richards continued. 'As you can imagine, he was pretty horrified by the lack of safety barriers, etc, but, nonetheless, familiarised himself with the Stratos very quickly and we set off on the first stage.

'It was unfortunately on this first one that we came to grief. I remember that, up until that point, he seemed to be fairly in control of things but obviously still finding his way. It was damp and slippery, as it often is over Epynt, and, for Tom, it was quite difficult going round corners at 90 degrees when obviously a Formula One driver works far closer to the margins.

'As we came down the hill towards Fourways Bridge there was some mud on the road and it became very clear that we were not going over the bridge but would hit it or go into the river. As it was, we did both, clipping the corner of the bridge and ending up precariously hanging over the river.'

The car was not badly shunted, suffering mainly damage to the radiator and front suspension. Richards, however, cut a knee quite badly on the dashboard and had to go to hospital for some stitches.

'I always thought that Mald saved Dave from serious

By Spain, however, a combination of new regulations requiring lower airboxes and rear wings to be mounted further forward, and revised Goodyear tyres, conspired to emasculate the DN5.

injury that day,' Jack Pryce said. 'There was a change of surface there and the road was wet. Mald started to understeer and Dave's side of the car was headed straight for the wall at 65 miles an hour. He just managed to jerk the wheel and give the throttle a blip, and that changed its direction.'

That was not quite the end of their day, however. 'It was typical of Tom that, whereas most racing drivers would have put their tail between their legs and gone off home, he realised that many fans had come to see him,' Richards recalled. 'The car was rebuilt over the next couple of hours and we set off for one of the forest stages at Esgair Dafydd in the afternoon so that he could make his appearance in front of the home crowd. As you can imagine, this was extremely popular.'

Tom himself gave an illuminating interview on the subject to *Autosport* Formula One reporter Pete Lyons. 'That was fantastic! You could do anything with that Stratos, and it was really good to get rid of all my winter frustrations. I only lasted 10 miles, but it was super. That's something else you've got to have experience in to do it properly, just as much as in Formula One racing.

You can't just get in there and throw it around like I was; you've got to work at it, and gain the experience in order to get the maximum out of your car. If I get another chance to do some more rallying, I'll take it like a shot, because I thoroughly enjoyed it.

'Mind you, it's very scary. It's much more scary for me to do a rally than to do a grand prix. Going over brows and Heaven knows what. I mean, you get a sense of fear that doesn't exist for me in Formula One. In rallying, I think about it a bit. I think, "Christ, what's the other side of that brow? I wonder if there's a bloody great pothole round this corner which is going to have me off?" I must say I wouldn't like to do it all the time, definitely not. But it was exciting.'

After the event he gave two television interviews in Welsh, and was still enjoying himself greatly as event sponsor Peter Russek presented him with a wooden spoon for the best performance by a grand prix driver.

Back in the Formula One world, and overshadowed inevitably by the deaths of Graham Hill, Tony Brise and the members of the Embassy Hill team, there had been another key event towards the end of 1975. That concerned the defection of 1974 World Champion Emerson Fittipaldi from McLaren to his brother Wilson's eponymous Brazilian-funded Copersucar team which had made its début that season. This had coincided with the financial realities of the sport catching up with Lord Hesketh who, in an emotional plea at Thruxton, had declared himself unable to keep James Hunt in the competitive style to which he had become accustomed. As Hesketh wound down his effort, Hunt serendipitously found himself catapulted into the number one role at McLaren with a realistic shot at the world title. The stage would thus be set for a Hollywood screenplay of a season as Hunt fought tooth and nail to the end with rival and great friend Niki Lauda for the World Championship crown.

Inevitably, Tom was overshadowed by all the excitement that surrounded the Hunt versus Lauda duel and the genuine emergence of James as a title contender and regular race winner. That was how the cards were dealt that year and, far from dwelling on any vagaries of Fate, Tom never let his head drop as he squeezed the utmost out of his Shadow.

RIGHT: *The Shadow was not a pleasant car to drive that season. Frequently, Tom found himself at a loss to suggest improvements. Once in the cockpit, however, he never let his head drop, in direct contrast to mercurial team-mate Jean-Pierre Jarier, who lacked the fire he had shown in 1975.* BELOW: *Oversteer was back in 1976, as a hard-trying Tom demonstrates during the French Grand Prix at Paul Ricard.*

At Brands Hatch Tom spent many laps hounding Gunnar Nilsson, taking fourth place when the Swede's Lotus broke its engine.

One person who was rooting for the Welshman was Janet Brise. 'When Tony was killed, Tom and Nella were wonderful to me. We became very close then. They'd phone and say, "What are you doing? Just get in the car and come down." So I'd go down to them in Ightham and stay weekends quite often. Then other times I'd say, "I've got to get back tonight," and Tom would say, "No, no, no, don't go back yet. You don't want to go back to an empty house." Well, when I got back into my house, bear in mind it was probably a 40-minute drive, I would park in my little drive and get to the front door, and I would hear the telephone ringing. It was Tom, just sitting at the other end, "Just wanted to make sure you were back okay." He was such a lovely guy.'

When Janet was ready to visit a Grand Prix, in 1976, Bernie Ecclestone gave her a FOCA pass. 'I went as a guest of Tom and Nella and the Shadow team. Everyone was very kind to me.

'That year Tony won the John Cobb Trophy posthumously and I went to the RAC Club with my father to receive this. It was a beautiful trophy, shaped like a world, and had lots of very well-known names on

it. It sat very proudly in my little living room. At the end of the 12 months I had to return it, but Thomas suggested that he take some photos of it for me. Photography was one of his hobbies. I still have those photos.'

Tom's 1976 Formula One season began well enough, as the team fielded what amounted to a pair of DN5Bs at the Brazilian Grand Prix at Interlagos. He and Jean-Pierre Jarier had new monocoques, with subtly revised suspension, and Jarier qualified his car third behind Hunt and Lauda; Tom was 12th on the grid. In the race the Frenchman chased the Anglo-Austrian duo until Hunt crashed, and seemed set for second place, with fastest lap, until he crashed on oil from the McLaren. The beneficiary of this was Tom, who found himself running second on lap 34, but he was overtaken by Patrick Depailler's Tyrrell a lap later. The Shadow's rear tyres and rear brakes were finished, and he had also nearly become a victim of the unflagged oil in the Sargento corner. Nevertheless, third place and the second podium of his career was a satisfactory way to start.

Tom was faster than Jarier at Kyalami in South Africa, where he finished seventh just outside the points as Lauda led Hunt home. But for a puncture, and resultant oversteer from his replacement tyre, he would have been in the points again as he had been running fourth behind the Ferrari and the two McLarens. He was also strong at Long Beach, qualifying fifth and running fourth behind the two Ferraris and Jody Scheckter's Tyrrell until a driveshaft broke on the 32nd lap.

Neither of the traditional non-championship races at Brands Hatch and Silverstone allowed him to repeat the success from 1975; he was sixth at Brands, fourth at Silverstone.

The Spanish Grand Prix changed Shadow's season. That was when new rules came into effect, truncating the distinctive airboxes and bringing the rear wings further forward to reduce downforce. It was a complex race, in which Hunt beat Lauda (who had suffered damaged ribs the previous week after rolling a tractor at home), but was disqualified for a dimensional infraction on the McLaren M23's rear suspension, and would later be reinstated on appeal. None of this mattered much to Tom. Shadow had only tested briefly at Silverstone, where there seemed to be little difference between the old and new configurations. But in Spain there was and he qualified only 22nd in the short wheelbase spare car. He dropped to last place on the opening lap when his new airbox managed to inhale a cloud of dirt and the throttles jammed shut. After losing crucial time he managed to clear them and then spent his afternoon fighting his way back up to a frustrating eighth place finish. On the positive side, Jarier had enjoyed a strong race up to fifth place until his electrics failed, but on the negative side for Don Nichols' beleagured team, Spain marked designer Tony Southgate's last race before he left to join Team Lotus.

In Belgium they qualified 13th and 14th Tom a hundredth ahead of Jarier, and the order was reversed as they finished ninth and 10th.

There was more frustration at Monaco, where Tom placed seventh ahead of Jean-Pierre. Tom caught and passed Carlos Pace and then his team-mate by the 67th lap, following a brief rain shower that he didn't even notice. 'You certainly go very quickly in the wet,' Jarier observed in the debrief afterwards. Tom looked puzzled. 'Wet? Uh, did it rain today?'

Compounding Shadow's aerodynamic problems, changes to the tyres had been less favourable to an outfit that was in little position to do much to revise its cars to work better on the new rubber. It was a dispiriting time for all concerned, but while the mercurial Jarier let it get to him, Tom just kept pushing and emerged as the de facto team leader.

Shadow's Alan Rees and Jackie Oliver had interesting observations on their two drivers. 'When those two were with us there was more driver talent in our team than

Even in the wet, in practice in Austria, the DN5 was a busted flush, leaving Tom longing for the arrival of the Shadow DN8.

possibly in any other,' Rees thought. 'Tom would never give up, whereas Jarier would. There was nothing wrong with Jarier but, for whatever reason, things used to go wrong for him. He was quite hard on the car, but that was probably because he got the maximum out of it. It could have been that. He was a talented driver, he really was. That drive in Brazil in 1975 was staggering. But he had no application, that was the problem. If the car was good then he was more than very good. If it wasn't, he gave up.'

Oliver added, 'Jarier didn't know he was brilliant – so he couldn't control his brilliance.'

'It was easy to have a good relationship with Tom because he was so approachable, such an easy person to talk to,' Rees said. 'We didn't talk *much*, but his personality was such that is was pretty easy to have a good rapport with him.'

Oliver admitted that he didn't know Tom *well*. 'He wasn't very chatty, he wasn't like the other racers who were full of confidence. His confidence seemed to be from within and he didn't need to express it. It was like it came out when he drove.'

In the middle of the year, Tom made a brief return to Formula Two when he was invited to race at Rouen for Fred Opert's team as regular drivers Jacques Laffite and Jean-Pierre Jarier were on duty for Renault in the World Sportscar Championship race at Enna. Tom drove Laffite's BMW-powered B35 and absolutely loved it on the Frenchman's settings. He qualified third, only two-tenths of a second off Alex Ribeiro's works March. Unfortunately, the engine refused to pick up cleanly out of slow corners in the race and, after slipping to the tail of the leading group, he got into a slide while trying to use a lower gear to keep the revs up in a tight corner, lost hold of the steering wheel while simultaneously

The moment Tom tested the new Shadow DN8, at Snetterton, he knew it was a big step forward.

correcting it and trying to upshift, and parked the car in the catchfencing after only five laps.

He raced again in Formula Atlantic, too, for Chevron. Opert entered a car for him in the race at Trois Rivieres in Canada. Tom retired with brake problems as team-mate Jean-Pierre Jaussaud finished second in his B35.

Back in Formula One, Sweden brought only ninth place, France a gripless eighth. Not until Brands did Tom get a chance to shine again, and there he fought Gunnar Nilsson's superior Lotus in a mighty battle for fourth place that finally went his way when the Swede's engine broke. He actually finished fifth on the road, but this was the extraordinary British Grand Prix in which Regazzoni triggered a race-stopping first-lap shunt, and from which an apparently victorious Hunt – who, only the previous week, had got his Spanish victory back – had this one taken away from him by more of the pettifogging politics that were an additional, and crucial, factor in a gripping year.

In Germany, the Shadows' traditional sombre black – to which they had reverted after the flashes of orange the previous year – was complemented by the red and blue of the Villiger tobacco company's Tabatip cigarillos brand, bringing a much-needed financial boost. It didn't bring one to the performance, however, and Tom found his DN5 so unstable over the Nürburgring's numerous bumps that there were sections that had been flat the previous year on which he was now having to back off. Yet again he finished, eighth, two places out of the points. But of greater concern to all was the fiery accident suffered by championship leader Niki Lauda, whose Ferrari crashed heavily after suspension failure at the Bergwerk corner. For days his life would hang in the balance, before this quite remarkable man staged one of the greatest recoveries in sporting history.

The DN5 proved quite well suited to the Osterreichring. 'Oh, it feels really good, like it does at Silverstone. It seems to like smooth, fast circuits,' Tom told *Autocourse*'s Pete Lyons after qualifying sixth. Reversion to an older pattern rear wing had helped. Despite a banzai start he was still sixth at the end of the opening lap, but the Shadow quickly faded with failing brakes before retiring after 14 laps. The race provided John Watson with a brilliant maiden victory for Roger Penske's eponymous team.

Back at Snetterton, Tom was finally able to put some test mileage on the team's new Dave Wass-designed DN8, which was effectively a pukka upgrade of the DN5 to suit the new regulations. Tom loved the new car, and endorsed his feelings for it after briefly trying the older DN5 in practice for the following Dutch Grand Prix only to find it lurching into slides all by itself in the fast corners. The fact that he was given the new car, rather than Jarier as had been the case the previous year

with the then-new DN5, showed how far he had come within the team. Of the DN8 he said, 'It brakes far better than the old one and it doesn't scrub off speed when you put it sideways.' Yes, the old style was back, but Zandvoort was perhaps one of the circuits where that exacted little penalty on lap time, and he qualified third right behind poleman Ronnie Peterson, in a March, and Hunt, and just ahead of Watson's increasingly competitive Penske. The DN8 wasn't quite so strong in the race, and Tom's performance was overshadowed by the Titanic fight for the lead between Hunt, who eventually won, and Watson, who retired. After a great scrap with Scheckter, he dodged round the Tyrrell just as they came up behind a course car (after Larry Perkins spun his Boro), and though a fuel pick-up problem generated a high-speed misfire after half-distance, a fourth place finish was a great encouragement to everyone in the team.

Monza in Italy brought another bout of controversy as Hunt and Watson were moved to the back of the grid following checks on their cars' fuel. But it also saw the uplifting return of Lauda. Tom qualified only 15th after a minor off, and Alan Rees admitted that the DN8 needed more testing. The race brought another eighth place finish. Canada, at Mosport Park, was worse, 11th, as the handling deteriorated when the fuel load lightened. And America, at Watkins Glen, was equally disappointing, the DN8 running no higher than ninth before engine failure intervened.

Outside the Shadow camp, Hunt's series of victories and Lauda's courageous comeback had set up a dramatic climax to the season that overshadowed everything else at the final round at Fuji in Japan. And, to make matters worse, the race began in torrential rain.

He qualified the new car third in Zandvoort, and raced strongly against the likes of Clay Regazzoni and Jody Scheckter on his way to an uplifting fourth in the Dutch Grand Prix.

Lauda pulled out after one lap, bravely admitting that, with his scarred eyelids, it was impossible to see properly in the appalling conditions. Hunt, who eventually finished third after a late stop to replace a punctured tyre which had worn excessively on a slowly drying track, gained the one point he needed to snatch his World Championship crown.

As for Tom, the Japanese Grand Prix could have yielded him a much deserved victory. From 13th place at the end of the first lap he fought his way brilliantly up to fifth after 33 of the scheduled 73 laps, his wet weather skills transforming the DN8 into a genuine contender. After 39 laps he had climbed to second, having hounded Patrick Depailler until the Tyrrell driver needed to make a pit stop. Now only Hunt was ahead of Tom, and the McLaren driver would have to make his pit call on the 62nd lap. At this stage eventual winner Mario Andretti in his revamped Lotus was behind both Tom and the recovering Depailler. However, chunks of rubber from the Shadow's deteriorating tyres were beginning to block the exposed radiator ducts, and on the 47th lap heartbreak struck again when the engine failed as an indirect result. Tom abandoned his car stoically, and began the long, wet walk back. For once Nella was not there to console him, having stayed at home after breaking a hand in a horse riding accident.

So 1976, then, was another frustrating year for Tom,

one in which James Hunt scooped all the headlines. Tom, of course, was quite happy avoiding the limelight, but he would have preferred some decent results. Nevertheless, he remained his usual upbeat and philosophical self when Pete Lyons interviewed him in *Autosport* just after Monza. For a man of supposedly few words, he provided illuminating insights into the way his character was developing.

Lyons wanted to know how Shadow maintained its morale. 'Effort,' Tom said. 'Everybody has really been putting everything into it. Alan Rees, me out on the track, everybody. We've all been very keen to keep the thing going, except J-P perhaps.' At one stage the Frenchman seemed more interested in opportunities at Ligier-Matra, something that upset everyone in the team.

'When you've got problems, and you're not getting the results, you half expect the mechanics to lose heart, but the opposite has been the case. When we get a good race finish they're thrilled to bits. My main concern has been about their side of things, as it were, hoping that they wouldn't get fed up, so I'm very happy about it.'

Though Monza brought only an eighth place finish, Tom – seen here chasing Larry Perkins, Jarier and Mass and leading Stommelen, Hunt and Fittipaldi – drew great satisfaction from a relentless pursuit of Carlos Reutemann.

He said he didn't think his driving had suffered through lack of testing. 'I've gained a lot of experience this year, because, although we've been struggling a bit, it doesn't really affect my driving. I mean, if you start backing off accepting that you've got no chance of actually winning, maybe, then your driving will certainly change. So you can't afford to do that, and I've been trying as hard as ever, as if the car was fully competitive. I haven't been in Formula One long enough to get blasé about it, and I'll try hard in anything.

'When we first raced the DN8, people came up to me and congratulated me on "going better". Now that really annoyed me. Because the DN5 went downhill compared to the new cars coming out, they must have thought that I went downhill, too. That's just not the case. It's very rare that a driver loses his ability, it just doesn't happen often, and certainly my driving, in my opinion anyway, has stayed about the same. The car is better, and perhaps even my driving is a little better, too, because I've gained a lot of experience over the past year or so.

'Additionally, as the DN5 became less competitive I had to try all the more in order to get the maximum out of it, and my driving must have benefited from that. If you're up at the front – so I'm told! – it's often the case that you don't have to drive 100 per cent; in the midfield, of course, you do, to try and claw your way up there.'

By Canada the DN8's bubble of promise had burst. As the fuel load lightened the handling deteriorated, making it impossible to hold off Regazzoni. Tom finished 11th.

Lyons also touched on the thorny problem of Tom's flamboyant style. 'I don't throw it around as much as I used to. At Zandvoort I did, but that was because we were understeering a lot on the slow stuff, and I had to. In the old days I used to get it sideways, really enjoy myself, and scrub off speed until I almost came to a stop. Now I try to strike a sort of happy medium. It's something I have learned for myself and which Alan Rees has been telling me all along; it was difficult to make myself stop doing it, but it became easier as I got to get the feel of a Formula One car, as I got to know where it was losing time. Experience, if you like.

'When it's wet you can throw it about, and it's fantastic then, I really enjoy it. You can do almost anything you like with the car. Apart from the wet races, I must say that I don't enjoy racing as much as I used to. The way Formula One is at the moment, the car has to be just right and it doesn't matter how good the driver is.'

Bob King always thought that, certainly in his early days, Tom never really appreciated just *how* good he was. So his comments to Lyons were intriguing when the latter asked him where he felt he ranked overall, especially after what he had said previously to Nella in a private moment. 'Well! I don't know. I reckon I'm as good as anybody else, I suppose, otherwise I wouldn't be doing it. I'm in there to win, and I think I can beat anybody in the race. If I didn't think that, I'd be at a psychological disadvantage straight away, wouldn't I? I'm sure in my own mind that I'll be winning races as soon as we've got the Shadow done up properly and we start getting the breaks. If I don't win races next year I'll be very disappointed indeed.

'Whenever I'm racing, even in a dice, I feel completely at ease. I can't tell you why, but I always feel that there's plenty of time, and I never get irrational.'

The late Tony Lanfranchi recalled an eight-car Formula Ford shunt at Brands in which Tom was involved, which highlighted his calmness in the cockpit. 'I got them all to hold their hands out immediately afterwards,' Lanfranchi said. 'Tom's were steadier than mine, and I had only watched the accident!'

'Monza was very satisfying for me,' Tom continued, 'because, although I knew I had an understeer problem and was very far back, I was catching up slowly. James Hunt was behind me, but he had a problem getting past John Watson, and he wasn't catching me as quickly as I had thought he would. I could see them in my mirrors and I thought, "Well, there's going to be a bit of a dice

In the dry at Mount Fuji the DN8 remained a handful.

on here, we might be able to tow each other further up towards the front." But after he did get by John he was a bit faster than me on the straight, so he got past me. But after he came off, I caught up to Stuck and Ickx and Andretti. After Mario had passed Stuck, I was right up behind the March and he was looking in his mirrors all over the place, didn't know where he was. When he hit Mario, it was because of my presence just behind. He made a mistake because of the pressure I was able to put onto him. So then I had a clear road in front of me – great! Reutemann was way, way in front of me and I thought, "Hell, this is going to take forever." But I plugged away at it and eventually I got him. Just tenths and tenths. Very satisfying even though I knew that I could never catch the leaders.'

That was the thing about Tom, just as it had been with Roger and Tony, and just as it wasn't with James Hunt, who eventually would only give it his all if he felt he could win: they all loved racing for the sake of it. When the game was worth the candle James was a racer, no question, but they were racers *all* the time.

'That's why I do it,' Tom said. 'Because it's very exciting, it can be very satisfying. It's fantastic. I couldn't do anything else and get so much pleasure.'

There was another sign that season of how much he was maturing on the world stage, and it came from Brands commentator Brian Jones who would later tutor drivers in the art of public speaking.

'There was one occasion when Tom had to sing for his supper – well, his lunch, actually. Bear in mind that if you got a "Good morning" from him, it was a conversation. But this time when he got up and was required to speak he was articulate, urbane and looked incredibly handsome. He had lovely chiselled features and he spoke in a really very fine way. It was an amazing transformation and I was terribly impressed. He was very, very confident in himself now, he really was. To me, that just showed how much he had developed and matured.'

There was a nice little ego boost at the end of the year when former motorcycle and car racing legend John Surtees made it clear that he was interested in signing him to drive for his team in 1977. Tom had even considered it for a while, though it was a complex deal that involved more than just money.

Nigel Roebuck recalled a time when Tom and Nella were dining in the same restaurant as Chris Amon and his wife Tish. Amon had put in some stunning drives for Mo Nunn's little private Ensign team that year and, in his heyday at Ferrari, had been one of the few men capable of challenging Jim Clark on even terms.

'Eventually Tom came over, very shyly, shook hands with Chris and they sat down for a few minutes,' said Roebuck. 'He was so uncertain about his future, what should he do? He didn't really know Chris at all but wanted some advice. When Chris told me about it, I said to him, "Jesus, that's says everything about Tom Pryce that he came to *you* for advice..."'

Amon was legendary for making some unfortunate decisions about his own career, such as leaving Ferrari in 1969 just as its new flat-12 312B1 came right for 1970, or building his own car for 1974 and refusing to consider leaving that disaster behind, even when offered drives with Ferrari (again), McLaren and Brabham at a time when all three were winning races. He was the greatest driver never to win a grand prix.

'Chris thought it was very touching in a way that this young guy he didn't know very well was so sort of lost that he'd ask him. Chris was a friendly, approachable sort of man, and you could detect that very easily. But it was still very interesting that Tom barely knew him but so wanted to confide in him and seek his guidance.'

A complication in a possible Surtees deal was that Miles Warwick-Smith ran the team's sponsor, London Rubber Company. 'He didn't want to be seen to be saying, "I want my son-in-law to have the sponsorship," because that wouldn't have been fair and my father is very straight,' Nella explained. In the end, Tom's loyalty to Shadow, and in particular to the men he respected there – Alan Rees and Pete Kerr – won the day. New for 1977 was backing from Italian financier Franco Ambrosio. Tom agreed fresh terms with the team, in the expectation that it would now have sufficient money to develop the DN8 into the car that it needed to be.

'I know and like Don and Alan, and all the boys,' Tom said. 'We get along together and I am happy to stay with them. Now we have the new car I am sure we can get some better results than we achieved in 1976. I can drive as fast as the next man, it is simply a matter of setting up the car to achieve the potential I know it has.'

Completely jaundiced by Shadow, Jarier had quit to drive a 1976 Penske for mercurial German wheel manufacturer Gunther Schmid and his ATS team. As part of the deal with Ambrosio, Italian Renzo Zorzi – the man who had benefited from Tony's clash with Alex Ribeiro at Monaco two years earlier – stepped up to Formula One after only a couple of outings for Frank Williams, as Jarier's replacement.

Previewing the new year in *Grand Prix 77*, Andrew Marriott wrote, 'Tom Pryce's faith in the Shadow project could reap unexpected rewards in the 1977 season.' There was nobody in the pit lane who would begrudge the quiet but hugely popular Welshman his overdue – and deserved – success.

ABOVE: *In the dreadful conditions that were such a key feature of the Japanese Grand Prix, Tom chases after Regazzoni and John Watson.* BELOW: *His chances of a maiden victory, in conditions tailormade for his wet weather skills, evaporated as his worn wet tyres threw chunks of rubber into the Shadow's exposed radiators, overheating the engine.*

CHAPTER 19

A moment of desperate sadness

5 March 1977

'There was no time to think, I just reacted on pure instinct. I lifted off and made a big move to the right and, I tell you, I missed the guy by this much. Tom was running right in my slipstream, and he had no chance.'

Hans Stuck

Tom's last season began in Argentina. In the Parc Almirante Brown he qualified ninth, alongside Jody Scheckter, and liked the narrower rear track on the DN8. In a race notable for blistering heat, he hung on to the back of the leading group, setting the eighth fastest lap, only six-tenths of a second off James Hunt's fastest overall, until the gear linkage fell apart on the 45th of the 52 laps. After a long pit stop he was too far behind to be classified. By contrast Scheckter, who was having his first outing in the new Wolf WR1, went on to win.

Journalist Tony Watson saw Tom race in Formula One for the first time that year. 'I tell you, he was really giving that car the chopper. Really determined. He used to telegraph the car round the corner, blipping the throttle all the way round, really attacking the kerb. In those days that style wasn't so traditional. We have a saying here: he looked like a Spaniard driving a car. A Spaniard is very tough and determined and faces the

Hunt, Lauda, Pace and Scheckter have already gone out of shot, as Tom (16) appears to make a reasonable start further behind. For reasons never known, he would fall to the back of the field further round that opening lap of the South African Grand Prix.

bull, and Tom drove his car with the same heart. He was just like that, impressive.'

The Brazilian Grand Prix at Interlagos carried echoes of Fuji the previous year. Tom drove his usual intelligent and robust race in a less than fully competitive car that he had qualified 12th, two seconds off poleman Hunt. *Motoring News* described the way in which he had to drive the car to record his 1m 34.32s best as 'criminal', meaning that the vehicle squandered his talent. Tom regarded his lamentable situation with calm resignation, and told Alan Henry, 'I really shouldn't have to drive so hard to record those sort of times...'

When Jochen Mass crashed his McLaren on lap 13, errant catchfencing snared Clay Regazzoni's Ensign and obliged Ronnie Peterson to spin his already difficult Tyrrell six-wheeler. Tom thus found himself running in fifth place behind Hunt's McLaren, Carlos Reutemann's Ferrari, Mario Andretti's Lotus and Carlos Pace's Brabham-Alfa Romeo. Andretti retired after 19 laps with electrical problems, and Hunt then lost the lead to Reutemann on the 23rd of the 40 laps, immediately pitting for fresh front tyres, so Tom was suddenly

The DN8 went into 1977 unchanged but, despite this sort of handling behaviour, Tom was still able to set the eighth fastest lap in the Argentine Grand Prix.

running in second place, comfortably outpacing John Watson and Niki Lauda as they, too, struggled with excessive tyre wear. The Shadow squirmed and wriggled its way round the magnificent track upon which its predecessor had, for the previous two years, been the class of the field, Tom pushing for all he was worth as Hunt began to make inroads into his advantage after his tyre stop. At last he was genuinely satisfied with the way the car was handling once the fuel load had gone down, and just as hopes of a much-needed middle podium finish began to grow within the camp, the engine failed with fewer than six laps left to run.

'One day Pryce's irrepressible talent will triumph over mechanical malfunctions and he, hopefully with the Shadow team, will at last get a taste of real success,' Henry wrote.

The team went out to Kyalami early, ready to conduct intensive tests on a completely revamped DN8 prior to the South African Grand Prix. Components had been shifted around to improve the weight distribution, there was attractive new bodywork, and Tom's car sported a Shadow-modified six-speed Hewland gearbox. It was the first time the team had been able to do any serious development running in almost 18 months, and Tom relished the chance. The DN8 produced no meaningful times as the team

By Kyalami the car had been completely reworked by designer Dave Wass, with sleeker bodywork and a new livery to reflect the financial input of new sponsor Franco Ambrosio.

concentrated on going through every set-up combination so it could start to understand the car properly, and did not attempt qualifying laps. But times taken from the entry to Barbecue Bend and the exit of Juskei Kink, the fast back section that was generally regarded as the key to a quick lap besides performance on the long main straight, made interesting reading. Watson was fastest overall with 1m 15.23s from Scheckter (1m 15.54s), Lauda (1m 15.66s), Andretti (1m 15.83s), Vittorio Brambilla (1m 15.90s) and Hunt (1m 16.40s). Through this section Lauda and Scheckter were quickest with 9.20s from Hunt on 9.35s, but Tom, while not pushing as hard as he would have been on a genuinely quick qualifying lap, was next with 9.39s. He came away feeling that Shadow was at last making progress again.

Days before the South African Grand Prix, he dropped in on journalist Frank Keating on his way to Heathrow for an interview. He arrived during a domestic upset, as the family cat was stuck in a tree. Without a thought, Tom shinned up to rescue it. Over lunch, Keating, a thoughtful and perceptive interviewer, asked Tom for his thoughts on mortality, a question many writers fight shy of. 'I don't say I don't fear death,' Tom told him. 'But would I feel it?'

Two days before the race, an incident occurred that Nella never forgot. They visited friends at their farm just outside Johannesburg, swimming and eating with them.

When they returned from the pool, she and Tom discovered their clothes had been stolen. 'Our jeans had gone, and some photographs of Thomas and me from my purse. We didn't have many photographs of the two of us, and these were rather nice. And I thought, "Oh, damn!" And then I thought, "Don't be silly; it's only a possession, and you've got Thomas. The real thing. What do you want those silly old photographs for?"'

The atmosphere within Shadow was buoyant. It poured with rain during Wednesday's practice sessions, and there was a feeling of euphoria as Tom dominated the day. He simply destroyed everybody else, using his almost supernatural wet-weather skills, and his sheer enjoyment of such conditions, to the maximum. In comparison with his rivals he was on the power sooner and harder, gently holding the boxy white car in graceful power slides. His best lap was 1m 31.57s, almost a second clear of former champion Lauda in a Ferrari whose turbine smooth flat-12 engine's power delivery was significantly better suited to the conditions than the Shadow's peaky Cosworth V8.

A wet road can be a great leveller. During Wednesday practice at Kyalami Tom was uncatchable, outrunning second fastest Niki Lauda by almost a second.

'It was quite easy,' Tom remarked nonchalantly, omitting to mention a brake locking problem.

Lauda posted 1m 32.38s and was followed by Scheckter on 1m 33.23s, Pace on 1m 33.27s, Brambilla on 1m 33.91s and Reutemann on 1m 34.09s. It was a fabulous performance.

'I remember passing the butcher's shop in Ruthin later that day,' Jack Pryce recalled, 'and somebody popped their head out and gave me the thumbs up and said, "He's fastest, you know!" That was how we found out things in those days.'

Tom's showing was a timely reminder. 'I reckon Tom is as good as James,' Brabham's Herbie Blash remarked to journalist Peter Windsor, then the grand prix correspondent for *Autocar* magazine. 'I really do.'

It dried up for Thursday's session which was held in the afternoon, and I was incensed to read an ignorant piece of journalism in the *Daily Telegraph* in which the writer blithely reported that the rabbits had been put in their place as James Hunt set the pace. The wet was always a great leveller, and that Wednesday encapsulated all the great promise that Tom Pryce possessed. He

slipped back down the grid on a dry road, for the Shadow was happiest running a soft chassis set-up that favoured the wet and still required more development work. While Hunt was fastest on 1m 15.96s from Pace (1m 16.01s) and Lauda (1m 16.29s), Tom was 15th with 1m 17.11s.

There was a drivers' parade before the start of the race, and Alan Henry remembers waving to Tom from Crowthorne as he was driven round sitting on the boot of an MGA. It was a marque he always liked.

He made a poor start for reasons that will never be known. He was virtually last at the end of the opening lap, heading only Bob Evans in the lamentably tardy Stanley BRM. But, with a speed that would earn him the race's fifth fastest lap, he set about scything his way back through the field, the Shadow dancing on the limit of adhesion.

In Hunt's McLaren M23, Lauda's Ferrari or Scheckter's Wolf, such beautiful driving would likely have been rewarded with the lead of the race. Watching him, and judging his performance at the wheel against the quality of the car he was forced to use, veteran French journalist Jose Rosinksi turned to Windsor and simply said, 'Poor Tom.'

Brett Lunger in his March was the first to be picked off, then Tom's own team-mate Renzo Zorzi, both on lap two. Brazilian Alex Ribeiro and Dutchman Boy

Hayje, both driving Marches, followed next time around, and Austrian Hans Binder in his Surtees on lap five. From lap six Tom was hunting down Brambilla, before the Surtees team leader overtook Clay Regazzoni in Mo Nunn's Ensign. As Brambilla pulled ahead, Tom's progress brought him up to a strung-out group comprising Regazzoni, Gunnar Nilsson in the second Lotus 78 (the car that Tom might himself have been driving had the proposed swap with Ronnie Peterson happened at the beginning of 1975), Jacques Laffite in the Ligier, and Hans Stuck in the works Lexington-sponsored March. Tom closed on the Swiss driver for six laps before overtaking him on the 14th. Nilsson (a gritty, *hard* driver, remember, according to Nick Jordan) was passed on the 18th, Laffite on the 20th. Now Tom had risen from 22nd to 13th and had Stuck in his sights.

On the 21st lap, team-mate Zorzi hit trouble, his Shadow gliding to a halt on the side of the track opposite the pits, just over the distinctive brow and the bridge that spanned the main straight. There was a problem in the fuel metering unit and fuel was pumping into the engine's vee. Two factors prompted the tragedy that was to follow.

As Zorzi was climbing out of the cockpit smoke was rising from the hot engine. And he had trouble disconnecting his helmet's air-line.

'Renzo once told me that he always had trouble disconnecting the oxygen pipe on his helmet,' technical artist Giorgio Piola revealed. 'You needed to push it back to disengage a securing clip and then tug it downward to disengage it. He just used to keep trying to tug it downwards without activating the clip disengagement first. That was why he didn't get out of the car immediately at Kyalami.'

These two factors – the wisps of smoke around Zorzi's car and his initial failure to vacate the cockpit immediately – were sufficient for two marshals in the pits on the opposite side of the track to decide that this was an emergency situation that required action. They began to run across the track to deal with what was, by any standard, only a minor fire. One of them was a 25-year-old panel beater named William, or 'Bill' for short (despite copious efforts, nobody the author spoke to in South Africa could recall his surname); the other was a 19-year-old called Frikkie Jansen van Vuuren, who was normally employed as a ticket sales clerk at Jan Smuts Airport in Johannesburg. Like all other marshals the world over, they were working voluntarily.

Bill literally just made it to safety. Grainy film footage shot from the bridge, just behind the accident, reveals how close he came to death. Van Vuuren, carrying his 40lb fire extinguisher, did not make it. The same film confirms that he never had a chance. Even as the two men set off, four cars were approaching the brow, hidden in the dip that preceded it. Tom was now

ABOVE: *In the raceday parade, Tom was chuffed to be taken round the track in a red MGA. MG was one of his favourite marques.* BELOW: *The final photo: Tom was happy, relaxed and, as ever, optimistic on the last day of his young life.*

In a dramatic fight back, he soon caught Dutchman Boy Hayje...

right with Stuck, with Laffite and Nilsson following. Stuck and Tom approached the brow in line, the German only feet ahead of the Shadow which was jammed right in its slipstream as Tom prepared to overtake it before they reached Crowthorne Corner at the end of the straight. Laffite was close behind Tom, and Nilsson was a hundred yards further back. They were travelling flat out in sixth gear, at least at 170mph, moving at 250 feet per second.

The two marshals had 60 feet to traverse. Bill, with a marginally better start, just got to the other side. Van Vuuren, travelling at best at no more than 10mph or 15 feet per second, needed at least four seconds to cover the distance and was hampered by his hefty extinguisher. In that time, the quartet of speeding racing cars would have covered 1,000 feet, or just under a fifth of a mile.

Van Vuuren was 3.8s into his fateful sprint, three feet from his goal. In that time Stuck, Tom, Laffite and Nilsson had travelled more than 900 feet. It was at that point Stuck's March appeared, screaming atop the brow. Tom was mere inches behind it. Stuck sensed, rather than actually saw, van Vuuren and somehow jinked round him. Tom was on the left-hand side of the track, within three feet of Zorzi's car, and was so close behind Stuck's March that his view of van Vuuren would have been completely blocked until the moment of impact.

He missed Bill by millimetres, but had absolutely no chance to duplicate Stuck's avoidance of van Vuuren. There was simply no time, let alone room. Tom struck van Vuuren head on at 170mph, and as the South African's body was tossed into the air like a rag doll's, he and the fire extinguisher he had been carrying hit Tom full in the face. Van Vuuren was dead before his body hit the side of the track a few feet ahead of Zorzi's car.

The Italian had been walking away from his vehicle, but had turned and was walking back to investigate the smoke as the four cars approached the brow and the two marshals began their run. He was still bending over the engine, on the barrier side of the car, as the tragedy unravelled. As Bill made it across he knew how lucky he had been, for Tom had so nearly clipped one of his ankles. But neither he nor Zorzi were immediately aware of the tragedy unfolding only inches away.

In the cockpit of the Shadow poor Tom was already far beyond help, but his foot was still jammed down on the throttle. Chillingly, the now driverless car continued down the main straight at unabated speed.

'As he was coming through the field there was only one more car in that pack that he had to overtake, and that was Stuck's,' Rees said. 'Stuck was the one who avoided the guy who ran across the road, and he did it so quickly that Tom was left out there. He wouldn't have known anything about it, I'm sure of that. Stuck obviously saw the guy at the last moment and just swerved, and Tom was right in his slipstream.' Rees remains convinced that Tom would have scored points that day.

'I was a very lucky man that day,' Stuck recalled in 2005. 'We were a threesome, Tom, me and Jacques Laffite. One lap Tom got ahead of me and I was running behind him with Laffite behind me. But then I passed Tom again, so it was me, Tom and Jacques as we came up to that brow. Of course, when you were in the dip you could not see over it. As we got to the top I suddenly sensed this marshal running across the track from my right, carrying an extinguisher. I took a big chance and I don't know how I got away with it. There was no time to think, I just reacted on pure instinct. I lifted off and made a big move to the right and, I tell you, I missed the guy by this much.' He indicated a tiny gap between finger and thumb.

'Tom was running right in my slipstream, and he had no chance. He would just suddenly have been confronted with this guy, and he hit him head-on. I saw Tom overtake me and I could see the state of the cockpit... I knew he was already dead. That was one of the saddest moments of my life.'

In the pits, Rees was aware that one of the cars had hit a marshal, but not which one. In the Springbox Tower, commentator Roger McCleery saw something flutter into the air: 'I thought someone had left some old overalls lying by the side of the road.' Meanwhile, after striking Tom, van Vuuren's extinguisher was thrown over the grandstand and struck a parked car, jamming its door shut.

Chasing Stuck, Laffite and Nilsson avoided the debris by pure good fortune, and as the four cars continued to head towards the Crowthorne right-hander, 900 feet further down the road at the end of the straight, most spectators were completely oblivious to what had happened until the Shadow began to veer to the right. It left the track and bumped along the sandy edging strip, scraping down the metal barriers at still undiminished speed and flattening the braking marker boards. Stuck reached Crowthorne, and negotiated the right-hander safely. But, in his wake, the Shadow finally glanced off the right-hand barrier and veered to its left until it T-boned Laffite's Ligier, which had slipped by after the brow. The blue car and the remains of the white one were both then sent spinning by the impact into the catchfencing on the outside of the corner, the Shadow slamming very hard into the sleepers.

'Tom was in front of me and we came to the brow,' Laffite remembered. 'I was just far enough behind him not to see what happened. I just saw a car on the left, and I saw Tom's car slowing maybe a little bit, so I overtook him. Okay, he's very nice, he let me past. I came up to Crowthorne. Before going into a corner after a straight, especially one with big braking, I always

...before passing Brett Lunger and team-mate Renzo Zorzi, ironically at the very spot at which Fate would later intervene.

looked in my mirrors before turning. One of the reasons I had also looked that time was that I could hear this engine note, maybe not completely flat, but nearly. I watched my mirrors and suddenly I thought, "Ooh, he's arriving!" So I widened my line slightly. As we turned into Crowthorne, suddenly he clipped me, like that! (he smacked both hands together) I could not believe it. *Dang!* It was a really big hit. I saw him arriving, but I didn't know why, because he had let me past. I thought maybe he missed his braking...

'The worst thing for me was that, first he was killed. And Tom was as a character good, as a driver very good. A really nice guy who really loved racing. And the second thing, my wife was there this time and the speakers say, "Jacques Laffite is dead." Fortunately, somebody caught her and told her I was okay, out of the car, no problem.'

Had he not had that aural inkling of the Shadow's approach, and widened his line fractionally as a result, Laffite's Ligier would have been hit right in the side of the cockpit by the errant Shadow.

'Tom finished the trajectory on the left, and he was still in the car. I didn't know he was killed. I got out of my car. If he was on his own, I would have gone over to him. But I could see other people with him, so I thought, "All right," and I climbed up on to the bank. It was only later that I discovered what had happened. I could not believe it when I hear 10 minutes later that he had died.

'I'm sure Tom would have become a very, very big, big driver if he had the opportunity with a good team. He was clever, a natural talent.'

Several journalists had been watching from the bank on the outside at Crowthorne. Alan Henry was one of them. 'I saw it all,' he recalled, 'although it didn't register with me what was happening at the time. I just saw a car out of control.'

Henry also remembered journalist Denis Jenkinson's face as he breezed into the press room later. 'It was on the start-finish line and Jenks had been up at Leeukop, at the other end of the circuit, and hadn't the faintest idea this had happened. I haven't ever seen the wind taken out of his sails as it was then by sheer disbelief.'

Photojournalist Jeff Hutchinson was down at Crowthorne, covering the race for *Autosport*. 'I saw Tom's car coming down the straight and veer slowly to the right – our left – until it ran along the barrier about halfway down the hill, and then it veered left – our right – and headed for the outside of Crowthorne, where I was standing with AH (Henry).

'Laffite was in the braking area and just as he braked, Tom's car collided with his and was tossed up into the air and landed at our feet amongst the catchfencing. One of the poles actually flew between AH and myself, and injured someone up in the stands behind us.

Clay Regazzoni, in Mo Nunn's Ensign, succumbed on the entry to Crowthorne at the end of the main straight...

'Tom's car ended up on its wheels, and it was clear that there was no hope for him. Automatically I took photos, but ones that I never wanted to be used. The only paper that did use them was the *Johannesburg Star*, who had a runner who took off with my film before I actually saw what was on it.'

Henry took up the story again. 'What you've got to remember is that the two cars hit the bank so hard that there literally was a sandstorm of gravel. Momentarily we were almost completely enveloped in that so I wasn't really quite clear what had happened until Hutch pointed out to me afterwards the thing about the catchfence pole. I was aware of the car coming down towards us, out of control, but I had no idea what was going on. You know how your mind suddenly thinks, "There's a car coming down here and I just don't get this at all." That was it. When I looked up it was just kissing the barrier on my left; I hadn't seen anything of what happened at the top of the hill. It was only when it collided with Laffite, and they landed below us. I think Jeff said it was Tom, and then we looked down...

'Maurice Hamilton very kindly did my lap chart for the rest of the race, because I was a bit shocked. More than a bit.

'Once the race was over I crossed over the track and walked back on the left-hand side up to the pits in a fairly zonked frame of mind, because there was no doubt about Tom. And John Surtees popped out from one of those little caravans the teams had at Kyalami and took me in, sat me down and gave me a whisky, which I always thought was a nice gesture. I appreciated that a lot. He must have realised what I felt about

Tom. Of course, he'd been interested in running him that year, and I think they socialised a bit anyway because Tom and Nella were quite close to Edenbridge where John lived.'

Swedish journalist Frederik Af Petersens also saw the accident. 'I'd gone down to the first corner, and from the reaction in the grandstand I understood that something had happened. And then I saw this car coming down towards us, going along the guardrail all the way down on the driver's right-hand side. There was an opening where the ambulance could come through on to the circuit; it hit that opening and that turned it back in the direction of the outside of the track, and that's why it hit Laffite. I was standing there and some guys came with a stretcher, and I remember that I simply didn't recognise Tom. I haven't thought about that for a long time, but it comes to me every so often. They told me it was Tom, and that was a shock. I then went back up to the pits, and that's where I found out what had really happened.

'I remember that the doctor who opened up van Vuuren's overalls took one look and closed them again. That was horrible.'

The Shadow's designer Tony Southgate, by then working for Lotus, saw the whole incident from his position on the pit wall. 'It was so bizarre you just think his card must have been marked. The extinguisher ripped his helmet off and sheared the rollover bar clean off. Tom wouldn't have known a thing...'

'Kyalami was horrific,' former Shadow mechanic Trevor Foster remembered, 'because the race was still going on. The guy with the extinguisher was hit virtually straight in front of where we were; as it was then you went over the brow in front of where we were at Tyrrell. Obviously we were concentrating on the marshal and all we saw was him being run over. You think that there's plenty of time to lift off, but of course there isn't any at 170 miles an hour. The guy just went up in the air like a rag doll and came down at the side of the track. And because Tom's car carried on, I never thought anything else had happened. I couldn't see down the track to Crowthorne, so when he didn't come around again, and because they didn't stop the race, I thought he'd probably pulled off with a bit of damage to the car down the bottom of the hill. Nobody knew any different. I went down to parc fermé afterwards and remember talking to Jimmy Chisman, with whom I'd worked at Shadow and who'd gone to Brabham when I went to Tyrrell, and I said, "Are you all right, then?" never knowing any different. And he said, "No, I think Tom's dead. He's had a big shunt at the end of the straight." And then, of course, it all came out what had happened.'

Andrew Marriott was commentating that day. 'It was the first live televised motor race ever in South Africa. The country got television very late because it didn't want the natives to see what was going on in the outside world. Jackie Stewart was meant to be doing the commentary, but his mother had died. So I got the gig two days beforehand, and was on my own in this commentary box that they'd built about 60 feet in the

...and the gritty Swede Gunnar Nilsson did not last much longer before Tom overtook his Lotus.

Despite the brevity of his race, Tom's best lap would stand up as the fifth fastest overall, a fantastic achievement in an uncompetitive car.

air on some scaffolding, because they thought we'd want to see all round the circuit. It was the most frightening place.

'You couldn't really see what happened on telly, it was just a blur. I didn't *know* what had happened, and then about half an hour later some kid came in front of me in the commentary box. I'm commentating away, and he had a piece of paper in his hand. It was folded and he opened it, and it said four words written on it: "Tom Pryce is dead". And I was meant to carry on commentating after that.

'I'd actually had lunch with Tom and Nella two days beforehand at the Kyalami Ranch. It was *very* difficult to keep going...

'The worst thing was that Zorzi's car wasn't even burning, it was merely smoking. They could have left it. It was a disgrace, really, what happened there.'

Beulah Schoeman was working in the control tower for the organisers, right above the point of impact. 'This was one of the most horrific accidents I ever witnessed in motorsport, and one which is impossible to forget. Many of us believe that, in his eagerness to get to the other side of the circuit, van Vuuren forgot that there

was a blindspot along the straight, which would have made it impossible for him to see the oncoming cars. Sadly, this mistake cost him and Tom Pryce their lives.'

John Watson was racing one of Bernie Ecclestone's Brabham-Alfa Romeos, finishing sixth and setting the fastest lap. Three decades later he recalled bits of the race. 'All I remember coming on to the pit straight was that clearly there had been an incident, but there was *no* incident to see. You were getting flags and warnings, but it wasn't until half a mile down the road at Crowthorne that there was a car, in the catchfencing. Actually, there were two cars, but you didn't immediately see the other one. I didn't understand what had happened, and it wasn't until the race was over that the truth dawned. I'd just assumed there'd been an incident in the pit lane.'

Nella gradually became aware of an atmosphere. 'I was keeping my lap chart when Reesie came and said, "Nella, there's been an accident, Thomas has had an accident." And I just said, "Take me to him, where is he?" He replied, "Well, I can't – he's been killed." And I said, "Look, he's not dead, he'll want me there. Take me." But he wouldn't. I felt... If I'd seen Thomas, I might have been able to accept it more. I saw him get into the car, and I did my lap chart in the pits, and then he didn't come round. I began to suspect something, because people started sort of looking at me. And I thought, "Why are they looking at me?" And then Reesie came over. I think that the fact that I hadn't been able to see Thomas led to problems I had later. I'm not blaming Reesie because he obviously thought what he was doing was best. Of course he was trying to protect me, because Thomas had had a great blow to the head.'

Victory fell to Niki Lauda, the man who had been all but rejected by Ferrari after his courageous comeback the previous season from his near-fatal accident at the old Nürburgring. It was his first victory since receiving the facial burns that he would forever have to wear like an iconic mask, and the perfect riposte to both Ferrari and its new recruit Carlos Reutemann, whom Lauda detested. But it was a victory completely without joy, and there are photographs that capture the moment on the rostrum when the Austrian was told of Tom's death. Part of the Shadow's rollover hoop had become trapped beneath his Ferrari for much of the race, and he had been obliged to nurse the car home as it steadily lost oil and water as a result. He only just made it.

'I had absolutely no idea Tom had been killed,' Lauda remembered in 2004. 'When I drove past the brow there I didn't know what had happened. But I remember the scene and I remember that I hit something, but I didn't know what it was. It damaged my front wing and the car started to understeer a lot and to lose all the oil. That was the hardest race car I ever had to handle after that. Jody was right behind me, and I just said to myself, "If I can overcome the Nürburgring accident, this guy is not gonna pass me here." So long as I could get quickly on to the straight then I could live with the understeer in the other bits where he couldn't pass me.

'The red oil light was on most of the race from about lap 27, and I had to change my tactics again with 10 laps to go. The engine actually blew up as I went over the line.

'I was feeling really pleased with myself, with what I had done. It wasn't until I got on to the podium that they told me that Tom had been killed. I didn't know him well, but I knew he was an upcoming star and I respected him. There was no joy after that.'

Whatever had possessed the marshals to take such a seemingly incomprehensible risk?

George Witt was the chief pit marshal. In 2005, he spoke of the accident for the first time, and this is what he remembered: 'Zorzi stopped on the side of the track opposite the pits. His car caught alight, and our policy in such circumstances was that two marshals would attend every fire. Two more were ready to back them up if necessary, if their extinguishers were not sufficient to stop the fire.

'Bill and Jansen went over, and I had my foot over the Armco barrier, ready to join them if necessary.

'Nobody gave them instructions to go; there could not be any such instruction. What they did was automatic, they couldn't wait to be told what to do – that was the understanding of all of us. They acted spontaneously. It was their job to fight fire, so they attacked.

'I saw Bill run across the road, and one minute there was not a car in sight; the next, four were upon them. Bill was a marathon runner, so maybe he was that little bit fitter. I saw Jansen get hit, and his body fly into the air and land by the side of the track. I didn't realise that Tom Pryce had been hit by the extinguisher. It was all just too fast.'

In the immediate aftermath everyone had an opinion. 'Mine,' Witt continued, 'was that Zorzi should have come into the pits. He had been in trouble for two laps, and really he did not have to stop where he did, on the outside of the track opposite the pits.

'Everyone was in shock after the accident when the race finally finished. It was just tragic, because the marshals were doing their job for the love of the sport and they were acting from the best intentions. The accident just happened. You can always find fault later in these situations, but what did Jansen see? He saw a car on fire, opposite the point where he was standing, and he grabbed a fire extinguisher and ran to put the fire out. Zorzi was still in the car when Jansen grabbed the extinguisher, and who knew how big the fire might become? Look how quickly Niki Lauda's car had become a fireball at the Nürburgring the previous year. Zorzi's car could have done the same. You couldn't blame the marshals for acting how they did. It was impossible to place blame on anyone. It was just a tragic accident.'

Actually, Zorzi was finally out of the car and walking away from it before the marshals had even begun their trip. But Bill and van Vuuren believed they had a role to play nonetheless. Perhaps the saddest irony is that where Roger Williamson perished because of the appallingly low standard of preparation and training of the marshals in Holland, Tom died because one young marshal in South Africa simply tried too hard to do his job.

It was a shattered fraternity that left Kyalami and prepared to mourn the loss of one of its most loved members. Britain's third shooting star had fallen like a meteor reaching its apogee.

All over the motorsport world, the news of Tom's death hit people very hard.

'The way that Tom was killed was very tough, very upsetting,' said his old benefactor Bob King. 'The chances of that happening are so small. Certainly it cut short a fantastic career. One hell of shock, even more so as the facts surrounding it began to emerge.'

Ian Flux was racing in Formula Three at Silverstone. 'I was at Becketts watching the saloon cars, and it

With Tom dead at the wheel, the shattered Shadow heads out of control down to Crowthorne corner.

wasn't long before we were due to go out for our qualifying. Then I heard the news. I'd been through all that before, with the Graham Hill thing. It was just so sad, and I remember thinking, "How many more people I know are going to die before I reach 21?"

'When I talk to people, one of my favourite Formula One driver stories is about Tom sleeping outside Token for two nights, in my old caravanette, and then having to drive our Ford Cargo to the track because we were all so knackered. How many other guys do you suppose went through that before their first Formula One race?'

Brian Jones, like many, remembered exactly what he was doing when he heard the news. 'We were in the old clubhouse at Brands, in the bar. It was a very dark place with masses of atmosphere; there was racing memorabilia all round the place: a steering wheel from one of Jack Brabham's cars, half of Denis Jenkinson's beard which he had promised to shave off if Jochen Rindt ever won a grand prix, that sort of thing. It was Saturday lunchtime, we had finished running the racing school and a 'bike race was about to start. We were all sitting at the bar, and suddenly George Officer burst in and dragged me out. "Oh, Brian, there's dreadful news from Kyalami. Tom Pryce has been killed!"

'And we were all just devastated. There was me, John Webb, Geoff Clarke, Tony Lanfranchi, the usual mob. We had all known Tom and we all regarded him as the finest product of Motor Racing Stables, James Hunt notwithstanding. It hit us all hard, we really were shattered. He was a smashing lad, an absolutely terrific chap.'

'I can remember quite vividly where Karen and I were when Tom was killed,' David Richards said in 2006. 'We were in Kuwait and we were being hosted at a dinner party. We had not long arrived and were having a drink chatting to the other guests when somebody mentioned that they had heard on the radio about an incident at the South African Grand Prix. Karen and I were so upset we left the dinner party and went back to our hotel.'

David has kept in touch with Jack Pryce over the years, inviting him to test sessions when he was running the BAR Honda Formula One team. Like his son, Jack would sit quietly, assimilating everything that was going on around him without feeling any need to be at its centre.

'My lasting recollection of Tom is of someone of extraordinary talent who had been totally unaffected by the situation he found himself in,' David said, 'true to his roots in Wales and very appreciative of all the support he had from his many fans. What a contrast to today's Formula One driver!'

Over in Argentina, Tony Watson felt the aftershock.

His passion for the sport went a long way back. 'We didn't have television back in the old days, and I realised that motor racing was dangerous when my dad opened the paper one day and said, "Tony, Peter Collins has been killed."

'Well, back when I was a kid in 1958 there was a much better corner (at the Parc Almirante Brown circuit) than there is now after the Senna S; it was called the Toboggan and was a downhill, off-camber ess, one hell of a corner. I remember one Saturday afternoon there as if it was yesterday. They used to get me into the autodrome courtesy of the representative of Lodge plugs, and I was there with Peter Collins and his wife. Now that I am older I understand the real impact of a works Scuderia Ferrari driver watching the practice out there at that corner – with me, a 10-year-old kid! There I was with this chap beside me, and he was a god to me.

'When he was killed, nobody could console me. It was the end. Exactly the same thing happened when I heard of Tom's death. I was shattered.'

Jack and Gwyneth Pryce were at home, as usual, that Saturday.

'I wasn't going to work that day,' Gwyneth recalled, 'but then a colleague called me and asked if I would stand in for her as she was feeling unwell. So I went in to see our regular patients. One of them, I gave her the usual injection and helped her to get up. And every time I went to see her I always turned on her television so she could watch the one o'clock news. I have no idea why, but something told me not to do it that day. I even touched the switch, but for some reason I took my hand away and left the television set switched off.

'I was driving back home to make Jack his lunch when I saw my friend, who was supposed to be ill, following me in her car. I thought to myself, "What's going on with this one, then?"

'I pulled over, got out of the car, and went back to her and said, "Whatever's the matter with you?" And that was when I saw her face. And suddenly I just *knew*...'

Jack, meanwhile, had also learned of his son's death in the cruellest possible way. 'I turned on the television, to see if they had a bit of news from Kyalami...'

Niki Lauda felt he had driven one of the best races of his career, battling serious odds to enjoy his first success since the near fatal accident at Nürburgring the previous year. But, on the podium, his satisfaction was swept away as he was told the news of Tom's death.

CHAPTER 20

What might have been...

'The extraordinary thing is that they were three fantastic talents, not just very good but absolutely fantastic, and that all three could have been World Champions. I really believe that. And all better than James. No question.'
Andrew Marriott

With only two grand prix starts to his name it has always been easy for people to overlook Roger's Formula One career. After all, against James Hunt in ostensibly the same car, what had he done? But putting to one side the fact that there had been no time to test the March 731G prior to the British Grand Prix, or that the Hesketh version engineered by Harvey Postlethwaite was a very much more sanitary and competitive machine than the works car that Max Mosley hired out to Tom Wheatcroft, there was another indicator that provided a far more graphic illustration of Roger's true potential. This was the little-publicised test he did for BRM at Silverstone in February 1973. The circumstances were unusual, and Tom still suspects that he and Roger were set up by crafty team boss Louis Stanley.

Early one morning, Stanley called Wheatcroft, who was still in bed, and asked if Roger could test at Silverstone as regular driver Clay Regazzoni was fogbound in his native Switzerland. Since Roger was a rookie, team manager Tim Parnell first sent test driver Vern Schuppan out in the BRM P180 to set a base time.

In 1974 Emerson Fittipaldi (followed here at Watkins Glen by ill-fated rookie Helmuth Koinigg) played a percentage game on the way to his second World Championship. What might Roger have done in a similar car, fired with his usual determination and commitment?

Mario Andretti races in Argentina in 1977 in the Lotus 78. This would bring him within a whisker of the world crown before inspiring the 79 with which the American won the title in 1978. What might Tom or Tony have achieved in the same car?

This was the team's 1972 car, which had been designed by Tony Southgate before he left at the end of that year to join Shadow. The ladybird-shaped P180 had a significant rear weight bias, and though it had won the non-championship John Player Challenge Trophy race at Brands Hatch at the end of the previous season, in the hands of Monaco Grand Prix victor Jean-Pierre Beltoise, it was to be pensioned off for 1973 as BRM reverted to its trusty P160 which had been heavily revised by new designer Mike Pilbeam.

At that time the Silverstone lap record stood at 1m 18.8s or 133.72mph to former motorcycle champion Mike Hailwood in a Surtees TS9B, set during the 1972 *Daily Express* International Trophy race the previous April (the meeting in which Roger has so dominated first time out in the GRD). Since then, Regazzoni had recorded 1m 18.2s while testing for BRM. Within a handful of flying laps, Roger beat Hailwood's lap record and equalled Regazzoni's lap in a P160, even though everyone at BRM had deemed the P180 to be less competitive. Then a front upright broke.

Nick Jordan took up the story. 'Roger and I had driven down from Leicester, following Wheaty in his

BMW. That was mad, I can tell you... but good fun. After Roger took over the car from Vern he went quickly, but then the top right front wishbone broke at the inner joint, and the wheel just fell in and jammed on the monocoque. Roger was coming up through Abbey at the time. These were the days when you had that raised pit road at Silverstone, and after slowing it all down he crept into the pits and parked up, and just pointed at the front suspension...'

Wheatcroft then insisted that he was immediately strapped into a P160C – a car similar to that in which Beltoise had won in Monte Carlo the previous May, and with which Regazzoni had been so fast but by then less competitive than the Pilbeam-modified P160D which would be very quick on occasion in 1973.

Roger adjusted immediately to the P160C's different handling characteristics and soon lapped in 1m 18.0s, two-tenths faster than Regazzoni's previous best. To put that into complete perspective, the previous April World Champion-elect Emerson Fittipaldi had taken pole position for the International Trophy race there in 1m 18.1s, and BRM's 1971 Italian Grand Prix winner Peter Gethin had lapped a P160 in 1m 18.2s.

Roger was then given a new set of Firestone tyres and proceeded to lap consistently in the 1m 17s. Up until that time nobody had ever gone round Silverstone anywhere near as fast (though to be fair to Schuppan, the Australian has always maintained that he lapped faster than Roger that day). He tried several more sets of tyres and recorded similar times on each, indicating that the car had reached a plateau and that he'd got the absolute best out of it. The team was amazed by the metronomic consistency of his lap times.

Roger's performance made a big impression on Parnell, whose father Reg had been a grand prix driver, and who had himself raced in the top league. The big, no-nonsense manager from Derby was under no illusions as to what made a good Formula One racer. 'Roger was terrific. Without a doubt he was a future World Champion. That day he broke the lap record, and that was the fastest a BRM had ever been round there. He was very fast. He'd have been a top driver. There was real championship material there.'

On the way home, Jordan asked Roger what he'd thought of it all. 'He just smiled and said, "Fantastic!" He really enjoyed it. He really appreciated the fact that Tim Parnell and the boys had worked very professionally all through his test. That was typical of Roger; he would always come up to you afterwards and say, "Thanks, that's great."'

At the time BRM was still looking for a partner for Regazzoni and Beltoise. Parnell had called Stanley down in London to update him on progress as the day went on, and the BRM chief became very animated about signing Roger. He invited Wheatcroft to lunch at the Dorchester, on London's Park Lane, to discuss things further the following day. Tom went along, but was unimpressed with Stanley's traditional, and some felt pompous, way of trying to woo potential drivers or sponsors.

Wheatcroft ended up leaving his sweet course to Stanley and walking out. The latter had offered him £8,000 immediately, with a further £8,000 to come from the team's sponsor, Marlboro. When Wheatcroft first demurred, Stanley mistakenly believed he was trying to raise the ante and upped his offer, virtually proffering a blank cheque. Stanley even tried to bribe him with one of BRM's V16 Formula One cars dating back to the team's early years in the late-forties and early-fifties, for Wheatcroft's burgeoning collection. But when Tom remained adamant that Roger and he were not interested, lunch came to its premature conclusion.

Money was never the issue. 'BRM was on the way down, and if Roger were going Formula One he were going with the Cosworth V8,' Wheatcroft said trenchantly. 'It was a day I were conned, really, because they told me Clay were fogbound in Switzerland, and it were no such thing. It were just a try-on. Then Louis wants me in the Dorchester, brings a contract out, wants Roger to sign it, but no way.'

Derek Bell, with whom Wheatcroft had so nearly won the prestigious 1970 European Formula Two Championship, called Tom after seeing Roger that day at Silverstone: 'By God, Tom, you've got a fast lad there.'

'That were very nice of him,' Wheatcroft said. 'Drivers very rarely compliment another driver, and I appreciated that.'

Wheatcroft was also cheered to hear from Jordan what rival Formula Three team owner Mo Nunn thought. 'Mo was anti-Roger in 1972, I suppose, just because of the competition, really, nothing more than that,' Jordan said. 'It was nothing personal, though Tom used to wind him up. Mo was an ex-Formula Three driver and he would go out, lay on the road and watch cars out on the track. He said to me a few days later, "You know, Nick, I always thought that Roger just had good engines in Formula Three, but I watched him drive that BRM and, I'm telling you, that boy can drive."'

Nunn would go on to run his own Formula One team before switching to America's IndyCar series in the nineties and becoming one of the great race engineering forces with Jimmy Vasser, Alex Zanardi and Juan Pablo Montoya in Chip Ganassi's team. He was a very hard taskmaster, but knew his onions when it came to assessing drivers.

While he was chasing Roger, Stanley predicted that he would soon be the equal of Jackie Stewart. But when *Competition Car* interviewed him that April he made a fool of himself as being thwarted by Wheatcroft had provoked petulance.

'At the moment there's a slump in skills in English drivers,' he said. (Bear in mind that at this time Tony and Tom had also started to show their enormous potential, and James Hunt was obviously very quick, if still rather erratic and prone to crash.) 'You name me a British driver – apart from Stewart – who can win races! Who are they? There's only one bright star on the horizon, and that's Roger Williamson. I think he will be as good as Stewart in two years' time.'

Stanley went on to berate John Webb, the prime mover behind Brands Hatch, for the avant garde – and, as it turned out, far-sighted – assertion that Formula One teams should bring on young drivers far sooner than was the norm at that time.

'Williamson is a perfect example,' Stanley trumpeted. 'He's had two sessions of testing with BRM (sic), in one of which he broke a lap record on his first drive with a Formula One car. In spite of that, Williamson is not yet ready for Formula One racing for another year. If he is interested in reaching the top he must have a full season of Formula Two, spiced perhaps with one or two end-of-season Formula One outings. But to put him in a works team at the outset would be foolish, irresponsible and bad judgement.'

The fact that BRM had done precisely that with Stewart back in 1965 did not appear to occur to Stanley, any more than the recollection that he had offered Tom Wheatcroft a £16,000 contract for Roger to race a BRM only two months previously…

Stanley would, however, make amends for this bit of nonsense with the way he handled the terrible aftermath at Zandvoort, and the powerful prose with which he summarised that tragic day.

The BRM drive subsequently went to the young Austrian driver Niki Lauda, who was supposed to pay Stanley £35,000 for the privilege but never actually got round to it. Lauda was excused his financial liability as he comfortably upstaged Regazzoni and Beltoise to establish himself as de facto team leader long before the midpoint of the season, and he used some startling performances in the ageing P160D as a springboard to earn himself a Ferrari contract for 1974. By 1975, he had won the first of his three World Championships. Yet, at the time that he joined BRM, he was less highly rated than Roger...

Shortly after that BRM test, Tom and Roger went to South Africa to test a Formula Two March, and at one stage shared it with the great Ronnie Peterson. 'Ronnie jumped in Tom's March 722 and said he didn't like the way it was set up,' Jordan remembered. 'They softened the springs and messed about. Ronnie was a goer as well, one of my heroes, no question. He did a time that was very respectable. Roger went out in the car, came in again and said, "I can't drive it like this, can you put it how I like it?" So they did, and he went out and beat

Jody Scheckter, against whom Roger raced convincingly and competitively in his rookie Formula Three season in 1971, won the Monaco Grand Prix here in 1979, and went on that season to claim the championship crown with Ferrari.

Ronnie's time. Then Ronnie got in it again, and there was a bit of a needle match going on!

'Funnily enough, whereas Tony loved testing, Roger hated it. He just liked racing, and he liked his car stiff, like a kart. If it was twitchy, he'd say it was okay, so long as it was quicker.'

Wheatcroft remembered that trip as one of the best times of his life. 'We were there for six weeks. Then the Formula Ones come down to test for the Grand Prix. Alex Blignault still let us run after all the other teams had signed an agreement, and though the Formula Ones would flash past him on the straight, when the cars all went round the back section of the circuit Roger'd have passed them again! Niki Lauda were out for his first Formula One drive with March, and that's how I met him and Ronnie Peterson.'

In 1974, Emerson Fittipaldi won his second World Championship, in the Marlboro McLaren M23. It was identical to the car that Roger should have driven for Tom Wheatcroft's private enterprise, at a time when it was still possible for independent teams to leave their mark.

The day that Roger had hung around Tom's office, choosing his moment to voice his concerns about possibly leaving him to drive for Ken Tyrrell, they had made a pact. 'We rang Pat McLaren up and ordered two M23s,' Wheatcroft explained. 'Still in my workshop I've got all the stuff that we bought, never been unwrapped, to make a car for ourselves. We were going to make a Formula Two car and run it during the 1974 season in odd races, as well as do Formula One, and then we'd learn how to make a Formula One car off the Formula Two.

'The McLarens would have been private, for myself,

and Pat would have sold them to us; it was all laid on. Course, I knew her well 'cause I'd done quite a few deals when Bruce were alive, so we weren't like strangers, you know. I knew her like I knew Ken.

'Roger were very loyal. Never lied, never did anything like that. Never asked me for anything. I were ill for weeks after he were killed. Just the smell of burning... I were a bit ashamed of myself, sometimes, when I look back on how I was then. And after Roger, it weren't fair on any driver because he were so superior. Nobody could take his place in my heart.'

All Roger had wanted was the chance to drive racing cars, for Tom Wheatcroft.

'I never doubted that Roger was going to make it,' said Nigel Roebuck, 'but because I thought Pryce and Brise were all pure, flowing, natural ability, I always thought Roger was more of a Graham Hill than a Jimmy Clark, put it that way. The results would have been similar, but I always thought there would be more graft involved for Roger. He was a fighter, and very brave. I remember he won the Formula Three race at Clermont-Ferrand when I was there in 1972 – that was a helluva good race. I'd say he was in a similar mould to Alan Jones.'

'Roger could have gone all the way,' Jordan said. 'If you look at James and Alan, and then look at Roger, Tom and Tony, James and Alan were able to make their way through the programme and get on with it. Roger always used to say, "Jonesy's quick. He's not a slow driver, and he's tough, too." What you've got to remember is that all these guys were *on* it, regardless of the horse they had under them. Without a doubt, Roger could have made it, Tom and Tony too.'

'He was smashing bloke and I loathed the way he died,' Jeremy Walton said of Roger. 'It affected me and soured my view of Formula One. Add in Gerry Birrell's death in Formula Two the same year, and the fact that I had spent a lot of time with Gerry at Ford and knew the rest of the Birrell clan pretty well, I think I erected the same mental distance to driver friendship as Alan Henry had to adopt after Tom Pryce.'

For 1974, McLaren had found itself in a quandary. It had attracted the Yardley cosmetics company away from BRM for the 1972 season, but now McLaren had secured Marlboro funding and had persuaded '72 Champion Emerson Fittipaldi to join 1967 title winner Denny Hulme in its driver line-up. At the same time it was still contracted to Yardley, and therefore obliged to run three cars. Wheatcroft is adamant that he received a big money offer from Marlboro for Roger (presumably via Stanley at BRM earlier that season, as John Hogan said in 2006 that he didn't recall anything after that). But, logically, it might have suited everyone for Yardley to have transferred its sponsorship allegiance to a British driver – Roger – in a quasi-works McLaren M23 run by Wheatcroft Racing. The M23 would make Fittipaldi and Hunt World

Champions and, given everything he had done previously in racing cars, it is inconceivable that in the same car as those two Roger Williamson would not have vied for grand prix victories, perhaps even World Championships. All these years down the road, more than three decades on, the thought is still almost too poignant to bear.

'In one sense,' Alan Henry thought, 'Tom's accident was worse than Roger's. Whilst we roughly knew what had happened in the Williamson accident and there was the fire, it was the bizarre dimension of the Pryce accident. It haunted me for quite a while afterwards.

'Peter Windsor and I said at the time that we came from middle-class backgrounds where your parents might go to a funeral when they were 65 as their friends started dying. But suddenly, as motorsport reporters, we were presented with a situation where, at 25, 26, 27, we were the ones going to funerals. I don't think I'd been to one before Tom's, or at least his memorial which was held some weeks later. I didn't know what a funeral or a memorial was all about. But I think Tom's memorial in Ruthin was cathartic. As I recall, everyone was in tears. I went up with Nella and some other friends, and gave an address. I remember the place being absolutely crowded out, like some presidential campaign.'

Bill Harding was one of Tom's pallbearers. 'It was actually the worst thing anyone has ever asked me to do,' he recalled in 2006. 'But Nella was a friend for a long time, and afterwards. Tom just had this incredible talent that was never full realised.'

Team owner Fred Opert also went. 'I remember it being terribly moving, very poignant, lots of this haunting Welsh music... an unbelievable atmosphere.'

Brian Jones had previously attended Tom's funeral in St Bartholomew's Church in Otford. 'It was an extraordinary scene, and the church was just busting at the seams. The great and the good of Formula One were there, including Bernie Ecclestone. And it was a service in two parts. The first was conducted by the archetypal English vicar of the parish, smooth-talking and everything. The second was conducted by a Welsh firebrand who preached hellfire and damnation from the pulpit. At least, many of us could only assume that's what it was because it was all in Welsh. It was obviously not a harangue against poor Tom, but an outflowing of pure passion. It was an incredibly traumatic occasion, because everyone was very upset as they had been terribly fond of Tom.'

Henry made another point that places the seventies in their correct perspective. 'When you think of all the harooshe there is these days... Back then, there was one dimension in all this, a common factor: the race just went on. But why did the drivers do it? Looking back, it seems extraordinary. When I talked to Jackie Stewart in 2005 at a BRDC board meeting, he was this highly credible man, all suited and booted and a super-

In 1977 Alan Jones relished the wet road handling of a modified Shadow DN8 on his way to victory at the Osterreichring. If any race had conditions that Tom would have loved, this was it...

intelligent bloke. And I sometimes looked at him across the table and thought, "You must have been a complete fruitcake to drive those cars at that sort of speed on those circuits back then."

'If you actually take a snapshot from the seventies, knowing what you know today, the whole thing seems so thoroughly irrational that you can't understand why anybody did it at all. But those were the parameters back then. If you process forward what happened to Tom, or what happened to Roger, to this sort of environment today, and then consider the semi-hysteria that's attached to Kimi Räikkönen having a wobbly wheel and it falling off... They are just totally different eras, that's all you can say.'

Had Tom lived, the sodden Austrian Grand Prix in 1977 would have been Heaven-sent for his wet-weather skills and the further revamped Shadow DN8 in which his successor Alan Jones was victorious. What if he had followed the path eventually trodden by the Australian?

When Frank Williams cast around for a driver to lead his team in 1978, after setting up afresh in 1977 with a

talented engineer called Patrick Head, they settled for the no-nonsense Jones. He had actually signed a contract with Ferrari, on the strength of that Austrian victory for Shadow, but the Scuderia later decided not to take up its option. Williams signed him, not because he thought he was the star he would become, but because in restarting his team he wanted a solid professional in the cockpit. Jones went on to win many grands prix for Williams, and the World Championship in 1980. His successor Keke Rosberg was Champion in 1982. Tom might have raced for another seven or so years, which would have taken him right through Williams's initial years of success. Who knows how much of Jones's eventual success he might have emulated or improved upon?

'Unfortunately he didn't come to Williams in 1974,' Frank said, 'and he was right not to do so, but we rated him very highly as a likely Champion of the future.'

Only months after Tom's death, Gunnar Nilsson won a Belgian Grand Prix held in wet conditions, driving the Lotus 78 that Tom might perhaps have ended up racing had the proposed swap with Ronnie Peterson come off in 1975. Nilsson was later diagnosed with cancer and, by 1978, was too unwell to take up leadership of the Arrows team, a breakaway from Shadow; he succumbed to his illness that autumn. Had Tom gone to Lotus, either in 1975 or even later on when Colin Chapman was still interested, he could have been there in the ground-effect era that took Mario Andretti to his World Championship in 1978, working with his old compadre Tony Southgate.

'I think Tom would have made it,' Alan Rees said. 'I think he would have got to the right place because he was so quick, so good. Tony Brise would have got there too.'

It was equally conceivable that Tony, who after all had got his chance in the first place with Williams, could have won races with Frank right through to the end of the eighties. Don't forget that in their time as team-mates that year at Embassy Hill, he was considerably faster than Jones.

'Roger and Tony were more abrasive because they were more worldly,' Alan Henry thought. 'If anything, there was a tameness to Tom's personal character which might have affected him adversely in the end. But he was a very, very nice person. When you got to know him you could talk about anything for a long time, just sort of meander off on conversations about everything and anything.

'Equally, however, as Tom proved in his dealings over contracts with Geoff Clarke and Chris Meek, he was no pushover.'

'It's funny, looking back,' Nigel Roebuck suggested. 'I remembered going to Tony's house in Bexley to do that interview in 1975, and then I thought of grand prix drivers today. It was quite nice, but it was the original young couple's starter home, not some pad in Weybridge or Monte Carlo. And I don't remember him ever mentioning money. I don't know if, not knowing him that long, it would ever have got to that point, but it just seemed not to be a consideration at all. He just wanted to be a grand prix driver, that was all he wanted to do.

'In looks Jenson (Button) has always reminded me of Tony, but I think Tony had more steel. He was a hard old boy. I thought, of the three drivers of the 'Lost Generation', to me he was the one who would have gone the furthest.'

Andrew Marriott was adamant. 'The extraordinary thing is that they were three fantastic talents, not just very good but absolutely fantastic, and that all three could have been World Champions. I really believe that. And all better than James. No question.'

And so, the 'Lost Generation' leaves behind the sad memories that drift through the uplifting legacy of its inspiration, together with that most poignant and heart-rending thought of all: what might have been...

Jones, the man who had struggled against Tony at Embassy Hill, yet was rated a 'hard bastard' by Roger, won the 1980 British Grand Prix in this Williams FW07 on his way to that season's World Championship. What might Tony, or Tom, have done with the car?

Postscript

'Roger's accident changed my outlook on racing. It was the first time anybody had been killed in racing that I knew well and, yes, for a time I wondered, was it all really worth it?'

Ian Phillips

Life is no respecter of talent, character or potential. It is capricious, often stinting, in its favours. As Roger Williamson, Tony Brise and Tom Pryce were 'left behind', so others flourished.

Bernie Ecclestone went on to effect a revolution of the way in which the sport was organised, dragging it reluctantly into a modern commercial era. He made multiple millions of dollars as the csar, and along the way made many of the men who were once his rival team owners very rich, too.

Max Mosley, who co-founded March Engineering in 1969, went on to become the president of the Federation Internationale de l'Automobile, the sport's governing body, in October 1991. He remains one of the most controversial characters in its long history.

François Cevert, who finished second to Jackie Stewart at Zandvoort in 1973, and who, the Scot acknowledged, 'could have passed me at any moment' a week later at the famed Nürburgring, never knew he would have been Tyrrell's team leader in 1974. He was killed in practice for the 1973 United States Grand Prix at Watkins Glen, before he could be told that his legendary Scottish team-mate was retiring.

Stewart had become a World Champion for the third time when he quit at the end of 1973, never competing in what should have been his 100th and final grand prix following Cevert's death. After creating a new life as a businessman and motorsport ambassador he returned to Formula One in 1997 as joint-owner of Stewart Grand Prix with elder son Paul. Johnny Herbert won the Scot a '28th' victory in the Grand Prix of Europe at the new Nürburgring in 1999, just before the Stewarts sold the team to engine partner Ford. Stewart finally received a scandalously long-overdue knighthood and, today, continues to play a key role and to set an inimitable

In 1976 polesitter Eddie Cheever, Mike Wilds and David Purley sit in the pits at Brands Hatch at a celebratory meeting held in honour of recently crowned World Champion James Hunt.

example. He only stepped down as president of the British Racing Drivers' Club in 2006.

Niki Lauda moved from BRM to Ferrari for 1974, and after a near miss that year, won the first of his three World Championships for the Scuderia in 1975. A year later he went through the ordeal of fire himself at the Nürburgring before returning to the cockpit only weeks later. A second title followed in 1977. In 1979, he abruptly quit the sport to start LaudaAir, his own airline, before returning with McLaren in 1982 and winning his final title with the team in 1984. He retired for good in 1985 but remained a part of the scene as a television commentator and then as team principal at Jaguar (née Stewart) from 2001 to 2003. The battle-scarred Champion remains one of the most charismatic and plain-speaking people in racing, as a commentator for Austrian television.

After beating Lauda to win his first grand prix at Zandvoort in 1975, James Hunt won his title with McLaren in 1976 before moving on to Wolf and then retiring abruptly after the 1979 Monaco Grand Prix. He became a popular motorsport television commentator for the BBC, straightened out his boisterous life when he met artist Helen Dyson, and had finally shed his playboy image to settle down with her in a rambling house in Wimbledon where he liked to breed budgerigars. He died there on the weekend of the Canadian Grand Prix in 1993, following a massive heart attack. He was just 45.

Emerson Fittipaldi's career waned after that extraordinary decision to leave McLaren, until he re-invented himself in America's IndyCar series. He twice won the prestigious Indianapolis 500, in 1989 and 1993, together with the IndyCar crown. After retiring following a serious back injury sustained in an accident on one of the notorious ovals, he returned as the revelation, aged 58, of the Grand Prix Masters race at the new Kyalami in November 2005.

After a bruising season with Surtees in 1976, Alan Jones grabbed his chance with Shadow as Tom's replacement in 1977.

The loss of Tom shook Shadow to its roots, as had the loss of Peter Revson. Only days after the 1977 crash, Jackie Oliver and Alan Rees had to sit down and find another driver. They sat in Oliver's London flat, going through the FIA Year Book, but couldn't think of anyone.

'We got to Alan Jones,' Oliver said. 'We both said *Alan Jones*! We got him out of the book. I had his number in London and called him. It was nine in the evening. A guy with an Australian accent said Jonesy was back in Australia. We got him at two in the morning. Signed him on the spot.'

They also pitched for Zorzi. Oliver remembered kindly: 'He was the worst driver we ever had, but he brought Ambrosio along. Subsequently, after much negotiation with Ambrosio, we got Riccardo Patrese.'

Thus Formula One's wheel of fortune turns.

Later that season Jones scored the team's only grand prix victory in the rain-soaked Austrian Grand Prix. A year later his move to Frank Williams's revived team led to his World Championship title in 1980. He retired at the end of 1981, came back with Arrows in 1983, switched to Beatrice Lola two years later, and dropped out for good at the end of 1986, returning to Australia to race touring cars. Today he is a television commentator.

Jochen Mass, Patrick Depailler and Vittorio Brambilla all went on to win grands prix. The German was awarded the half-points Spanish race in 1975, where Tony had made his début. The Frenchman won the 1978 Monaco Grand Prix for Tyrrell, then hit a purple patch with Ligier in 1979 before smashing his legs in a hang-gliding accident. He was killed testing an Alfa Romeo for the German Grand Prix at Hockenheim in August 1980. Brambilla won the rainy half-points Austrian Grand Prix for March in 1975, but his career was effectively ended in the accident at Monza in 1978 that claimed the great Ronnie Peterson's life after he was struck on the head by an errant wheel. He died of natural causes in 1998.

John Watson also won races, frequently in fighting style, after his maiden success with Penske. In 1981 he won the British Grand Prix for McLaren and further triumphs followed in 1982 and '83 before he, too, carved a new career as a television commentator.

Hans Stuck's career eventually took him into sportscar racing where he blossomed, while Jacques Laffite won races with Ligier, returning after a spell with Williams to set a new unofficial record for grand prix starts. Sadly, his Formula One career ended in a first-corner collision at the start of the British Grand Prix at Brands Hatch in July 1986, but he remains as popular as ever today as a commentator for French television.

Gunnar Nilsson and Clay Regazzoni, the other men against whom Tom was racing that fateful day at Kyalami, had star-crossed lives. The Swede won the 1977 Belgian Grand Prix at Zolder for Lotus, and was to have headed the new Arrows team which grew out of Shadow for 1978, but was struck down by the cancer to which he succumbed later that season. Regazzoni raced with Ensign and Shadow after leaving Ferrari, before striking gold in 1979 with Williams. At Silverstone that year he scored the team's first triumph in an emotional British Grand Prix, but was sadly paralysed in a crash at Long Beach in 1980 after returning to the cockpit of Mo Nunn's Ensign. He remains a feisty figure when he returns to the Formula One paddock at Monaco and Monza each year.

Renzo Zorzi was replaced at Shadow after Kyalami

by upcoming Italian Riccardo Patrese, who himself would win races and set a new record for the number of grand prix starts before retiring at the end of 1993. Zorzi went back to tyre testing for Pirelli.

Token designer Ray Jessop died in 1976, while Ron Dennis, the man who had commissioned the car, finally got his toehold in Formula One when Marlboro arranged a shotgun marriage between his Project Four business and the ailing McLaren team. Subsequently, Dennis led McLaren to World Championship successes in 1984–86, 1988–91 and 1998–99, writing a massive slice of British motor racing history along the way. After starting afresh in 1977, Frank Williams, together with Patrick Head, steered Williams to multiple World Championships even though Frank – who was later knighted – was paralysed in a car accident in 1986.

Tony Vlassopulos lives in Weybridge and is working on a DVD of his life to give to his sons and their children.

Tom Wheatcroft won his battle to reopen Donington Park in 1977, and has since housed his wonderful Collection there. In 1993, he achieved another dream by staging a grand prix – the Grand Prix of Europe, won memorably by Ayrton Senna.

Ian Phillips had a spell working with Wheatcroft at Donington Park before picking up his pen again, then

Roger's Formula Three GRD 372, his Formula Two March 732, and his Formula Three March 713M remain on permanent display at Tom Wheatcroft's Donington Collection.

These are the trophies that Hilda Williamson so lovingly and so frequently cleaned for her son.

left journalism in 1987 to run the Leyton House March Formula One team for his friend Robin Herd. His rollercoaster life eventually took him, via a bout of meningitis, to a new role as commercial director when team owner Eddie Jordan graduated to Formula One in 1991. Phillips remained there after Jordan sold out to Russian entrepreneur Alex Shnaider in 2005, and when it was renamed Midland F1 Racing for 2006.

'Ironically, Roger had asked me if I would be prepared to go and work for them in setting up their Formula One plans for 1974,' he remembered. 'I had decided I was going to leave *Autosport*. Actually, the Monday after he was killed I was expecting to hear the news that he was going ahead with the plans with Tom. I got a different sort of call at nine o'clock that morning. I had been at the Formula Two race at Mantorp Park in Sweden when he was killed, and nobody heard anything while we were over there. When the phone rang I said to my girlfriend, "I don't want to talk to anybody." But it was Richard Feast, the editor of *Autosport*. He told me what had happened, and that while I'd been away I'd been made editor, so it was a bit of a mixed emotion day.

'Roger's accident changed my outlook on racing. It was the first time anybody had been killed in racing that I knew well and, yes, for a time I wondered was it all really worth it? I wasn't sure whether I wanted to be involved, but I think that's a natural reaction when you're young and you've never actually been touched by a tragedy. Unfortunately, it's a thing you have to become hardened to. I had to question if it was really all worth it, when a young life could be just wiped out like that. Being only 22, I couldn't comprehend it all, and I

suppose in a way you are always slightly reticent in relationships from then on. You can be close to people, but not that close. I mean, be good friends, talk or whatever, but keep your distance.'

Ben Huisman's two sons, Patrick and Duncan, children that terrible day at Zandvoort back in 1973, later raced in the Porsche Supercup. Huisman himself quietly visited the unveiling of Roger's statue at Donington in 2003, and, perhaps, continues to wrestle his own demons.

Chris Meek is still around the racing scene, while Bob King lives quietly in retirement in Watford. His son Stuart, after winning three BMX bicycle World Championships, raced cars for a while until the money ran out, and now works as a race engineer for Fortec Motorsport.

The indefatigable Nick Jordan is still in the business, working for Lola Cars on the sales side while keeping his hand in building Historic Formula Three engines.

Bit by bit, the families and loved ones of Roger Williamson, Tony Brise and Tom Pryce picked up the shattered pieces of their lives.

Dodge Williamson sadly never got over his son's death.

'I think what helped him afterwards was that Harry Downing, the rep for BP at the time, approached him,' John Upton revealed. 'He'd got to know Dodge and Roger well. Donington was reopening and BP was building a petrol station up there; would he be interested in running the petrol station? At first Dodge said, "No." But apparently he thought about it some time afterwards, saw Harry again and said, "Yes," he'd like to do it.

'Harry told me he was doing it to try and get Dodge to love his motor racing again, and that was one way of getting him back in without getting too involved. We used to go up there whenever there was a race on, and it got Dodge back in. He'd converted an old coach into a camper and we'd go up there on a Sunday with it, and a lot of the racing drivers would come in, have a cup of tea and talk.'

It is not difficult to detect the protective hand of Frederick Bernard Wheatcroft at work here...

Dodge died in 1987. His wife Hilda continued to cherish her son's trophies until she passed away in 1999, aged 85.

Barbara Upton lives quietly in Wigston with her husband John, alternating transatlantic visits with sister Nola who lives with her second husband Sonny on a dairy farm in Pennsylvania.

Jacqui Martin is now Jacqui Hamilton. 'After Roger, I got married on the rebound, in 1976, to actor Michael Hamilton. I love my ex-husband dearly, but I should never have married him. We were together for six years, and are great mates now.' She married again, 10 years later, to Derek Mottershead, who runs Bang & Olufsen in the UK. She puts on conferences all over the world, and they live in Hurley, near Henley.

'The thing that always gets to me is hearing that song by Roberta Flack, 'Killing Me Softly', she admits. 'It reminds me of the day Roger and I drove down to Goodwood, in a white E-Type Jaguar, with that song playing on the radio...'

In February 2002, a memorial tree was planted in Roger's honour in Abbey Park in Leicester. It was a wet, miserable day, but the faithful were there, including Tom Wheatcroft and his son Kevin, Barbara, Andy Morris, Roger's friend, and Dave Brodie. Touchingly, old Brode brought along a painting of Roger for display. In July the following year, a beautiful sculpture of Roger by David Annand was unveiled at Donington Park to mark the 30th anniversary of his death. It bears the poignant words: 'Nobody could take his place in my heart.'

In the aftermath of Zandvoort, the Roger Williamson Safety Fund was set up to help to ensure that such a tragedy could not be repeated.

In America, the Tony Brise Trophy recognises excellence at Long Beach.

And at Pembrey, the Tom Pryce Trophy is awarded annually to the most promising Welsh driver.

In December 2005, upcoming motorsport writer James A. Roberts's radio documentary on Tom's life was broadcast, to glowing reviews. Fittingly, Roberts now works for the crash.net website owned by Welshman Bryn Williams, who was a major fan of Tom's.

Bette Hill rebuilt her life after the trauma of her husband's death and the lawsuits from the bereaved families of his employees that left her in straitened circumstances. She remains an enthusiastic supporter of the sport, and the only person who can claim both a husband and a son as World Champion after Damon restored his family's financial well-being by winning his title with Williams-Renault at Suzuka in 1996. It was as much a victory for good sportsmanship as it was for talent and determination.

Tony's death shattered the tight-knit Brise family. 'John never spoke of Tony,' Janet Brise (now Janet Hunt) revealed. 'He really kept everything bottled up inside him. He was always a quiet man anyway, but he just couldn't talk about him. And even I found it strange. I almost felt I shouldn't talk about him in front of John, and yet I needed to. Pam was good and she would talk about him, and we would often talk together. John was just heartbroken. We all were, but he just bottled everything up. We both felt that his cancer had come about because of that; it can come as a result of that sort of stress and shock.'

John Brise never recovered from his eldest son's death. 'John never pushed Tony, but I'm sure that everything he ever wanted to do came out in Tony,' Pam said. 'When Tony died, I think John's cancer began to set in. He was such a fighter, such a stubborn man, but suddenly he just wasn't fighting any more...'

The accident at Arkley claimed not one World Champion but arguably three, for Tony would surely have made it and Johnny Brise had won three crowns in stock cars. Five years later he succumbed to his illness. It was 29 November 1980. 'Exactly five years later,' Janet mused. 'And it was a Saturday on which Tony had died. Those dates are so strange.

'The 29th is very spooky for me. Tony and I were married on 29 June. I never say it's a sad day, because I met my husband John on the 29th, and I got married to Tony on the 29th, but it is weird. For Pam it's terrible, because 29 November is when her eldest son died and her husband died. We always talk then. We don't always mention it, but I always say, "Are you okay?"'

'Last year (2005) was the 30th anniversary of Tony's

Thirty years after his death, this sculpture of Roger – flanked by two of his warmest supporters – inspires visitors to the Donington Garden of Remembrance.

Nella Pryce went to most grands prix with her husband, but admits that she never really trusted or understood the motor racing world.

death, and she and Tim went to the graveyard in Wilmington Church, near Dartford. He was cremated, but there is a little plaque.'

Thanks to her match-making cousin Richard, Janet married John Hunt in 1990. John recalled, 'I was being taken to the airport by a friend of mine, who said before I got on the plane, "When you come back, if you give Jan Brise a ring, and ask her out for dinner, you might not get refused…" Jan knew nothing about it at all and Richard was just playing Cupid. So when I got back I did give Jan a ring, and we went out for dinner – the 29th of November 1986…'

John competed in hillclimbs and circuit races, and Janet also tried her hand behind the wheel. 'Tony bought me a lesson, I think the Christmas before he died, at the Jim Russell School at Silverstone. I loved it!' she enthused. 'I thought it was wonderful. But Tony said, "One driver in the family is enough, I don't want you racing." And he wouldn't really let me have any more lessons.'

Reg Allen's daughter caught the bug early, thanks to his hydroplane racing. 'After powerboats, Dad went into sporting car trials. Tony did one once, because of us, after my father encouraged him. Tony got so interested that he drew up some plans for a new trials car with special suspension. I remember him discussing it with my father over the kitchen table. I had my own trials car after Tony died. Daddy was trying to get me back on the road, so to speak, and encouraged me to go racing. I was living in Bexley at that time, and he said, "Go down to Brands and I'll pay for you to have a course of lessons." He wanted to take my mind off things, give me something to do. I had one lesson, and John Webb called me up to his office and said, "I've been watching you and you showed promise. I'll be completely honest: you're a story and I can get a lot out of you, and you can get your racing out of me, I can get you sponsored. How serious are you?"'

Janet's first race was in a celebrity ladies Ford Escort clash on Bank Holiday Monday in 1977 when she finished second to Desiré Wilson, arguably one of the best female racers. She then raced Renault 5s whenever fellow hotshoe Juliette Slaughter wasn't driving the car, before graduating to Formula Ford in the Rolatruc series and then a Lola T490 sportscar under Kelly Girl sponsorship. 'Desiré was doing the same series, and we shared the same mechanic and the same truck. She became a good pal of mine because I kept asking her, "How do I go round this corner?"'

'John Webb was good for me too, I'd never have a bad word to say about him. He found me Kelly Girl and gave me the chance to race.'

The Hunts still go to the British Grand Prix every year, and watch most grands prix. 'It's so different now,' Janet says. 'You hear about people like Jenson Button living in a house on St George's Hill in their first year of Formula One, and we had our little town house in Bexley!'

Her comments were made with humour and no rancour. 'Because of the money it's got so very, very serious. It's not the same. The gym, and keeping fit? That didn't happen in Tony's day! You didn't think you had to have an early night. You didn't think you mustn't drink. Certainly in Formula Three there *were* drivers – not Tony – who I remember came up with hangovers at most races.'

Mention of Button's name prompted comment on how much he reminded several writers of Tony when he burst on to the Formula One scene. 'Oh, you sent a shudder through me!' Janet said. 'That's exactly what I felt, and then Pam said that to me as well. I said to her, "I can't believe you said that because I said exactly that, too, myself." I've never met Jenson, but watching him on television he seems so similar. It's quite nice, in a way.'

Pam Brise lives quietly in Hadlow, near Tonbridge, and sees her sons Tim and Simon and her grandchildren regularly. She also visits Janet and John Hunt in

Guernsey. 'She's like my mum,' Janet says. 'I lost my mother in 1986 and my father in 1989, and I suppose because I never went back to Birmingham when I lost Tony – my parents offered to buy me a flat up there, but somehow that would have seemed like going back a chapter in my life and I felt my home was now in Bexley – I wasn't far from the Brise family. So I had Tim, Simon and Pam. Pam was brilliant; she was always my second mum, and she's become like a best friend. We talk on the phone at least once a week. I always send her anything on Tony that I pick up. She says it's so nice when people remember him, and I guess that's how I feel.'

The moment she learned of Tom's death, Janet Brise called Nella's parents. 'I knew her mother and father, and I think I was straight down to see Nella as she had done with me. We were very close again then. We laughed and cried together. There had been so many parallels in our lives and we had so much in common. She couldn't go back to her house in Ightham, and she was staying with her parents because she couldn't bear going back. So I said, "Come and stay with me." By then I'd moved to Blackheath, and she came and stayed, and came out two or three times to my parents' holiday home in northern Spain. I just remember this one time, my father said, "Why don't you two do something together? Set up a little business or something, a shop." So we were talking about a shoe shop, but that never quite happened. She was working for Asprey's in the antique glass department, and I was working as a personal assistant somewhere in London. Then we came up with the idea of opening an antique shop.'

Thus was born Pryce & Brise.

'Nella had moved up to Blackheath by that time and had a flat round the corner from me, so we saw a lot of each other. We then found a property in Fulham that was going for auction. My father was a great one for egging us on, saying, "Go for it, it sounds good. Don't forget most other people will be businessmen bidding to make a profit. You'll be wanting it as a shop, so work out what you want to go up to."

'So we sat there in this auction amid all these businessmen with their briefcases, just two girls thinking, "We're never going to get this shop." It had been derelict for some years. Anyway, we did get it. I think it was £26,000, but we had to do quite a bit to it. This was 1982 and we opened in 1983.' They stayed in business for a decade, before going on to other things.

'There was one other thing about the day that Tony was killed,' Janet said. 'It was also Nella's 21st. So her birthday is always on the anniversary of Tony's death...'

Nella struggled for many years to come to terms with the loss of her beloved Thomas, and with not being able to bid him a final goodbye. 'Obviously I was terribly shocked by Thomas's death, and I think I couldn't grieve properly *because* I was so shocked. I became almost

The indefatigable Gwyn Pryce was very close to her son. Like Hilda Williamson, she was immensely proud and regularly cleaning his trophies.

hysterical. I'd just laugh all the time until I cried, because I couldn't let myself dwell on it. It was too painful, especially because of the fact that I hadn't seen him after the accident.

'My parents were fantastic, very supportive, and so were Jack and Gwyneth. But once I had got home, I started having very severe panic attacks. They went on for eight or 10 years afterwards. It took me a long, long time to get over them. I didn't react in the same way as Jan did, for example. Jan talked about Tony, and cried. I just dealt with it the only way I could. I couldn't express all my feelings.

'For the first year or so after Thomas died, I used to see these people who looked like him. Every time a door opened or closed – and I know it sounds silly to say it – but I'd look up, expecting it to be him. I think I was going round the bend, actually. Someone would pull into the drive, and I'd think it would be him. I'd just look round, expecting to see him. I'd be driving and would see a tall man with curly dark hair, and I'd have to go in front and look at this person, it was obsessive. It was

'They adored their kids. They were a lovely family,' Jenny Anderson said of Pam and Johnny Brise, seen here with 12-year-old Tony in the karting days. The resemblance between Tony and Jenson Button is uncanny.

really weird. I was really frightened by the panic palpitations, not being able to breathe properly. I'd moved to Blackheath by then, because I couldn't live in our house again, just could not spend another night there. To me it was Thomas and me, it was all too much. So I moved up to London and I saw this doctor; he listened to what I said about these attacks and then said to me, "Do you hear voices in your head?" And I said, "No, I don't!" And afterwards I thought, "He thinks I'm going round the bend. Like schizophrenia."

'If only they'd put two and two together and thought, "This girl's just lost her husband, in an horrific accident, and she's only 22..." What the hell are you meant to feel? It's not surprising I had panic attacks. But that was nearly 30 years ago. If it was now, I think somebody would have told me to go to a therapist and get all this out. It's different now, isn't it?'

Nella was also tormented for years by a dream in which she saw Tom sitting in his MGB in traffic in Sevenoaks, and would rap on his window. '"Thomas! It's

me!" And he would just look back at me without a flicker of recognition. "Thomas, look at me, I'm your wife!"'

Janet, too, had a recurrent dream. 'Pam had come to me and said that Tony hadn't been killed but had been very badly hurt – so much so that he would need lots of operations. I wanted to see him but she wouldn't tell me where he was because she didn't want me to see him. When I saw him I didn't recognise him. He wasn't the man I knew and loved. And he didn't seem to know me at all. I'm sure all this was because I never saw Tony after the accident and so a part of me couldn't believe he was dead.'

Nella drew heavily on the support of Janet. 'She was fantastic, especially as I had a different experience to her, with the panic attacks. I thought I was going mad – I was really frightened. I didn't realise at the time it was because of this grief, and that I couldn't cope with it. Jan was fantastic and became a very close friend, and we had lots of fun and adventures together, shared lots of things after motor racing, and as a result of motor racing, strangely.'

'We used to go to a wine bar in Greenwich called the Bar du Musee,' Jan recalled. 'One evening the local rugby team came in and began to chat us up. One of them noticed we were wearing wedding rings. "We're both widows," I explained. They thought this was a huge joke. After all, we were only aged 22 and 24. When they realised we were deadly serious they were so apologetic! After that they became best mates and were very protective of us.'

There had been further heartache in the immediate aftermath of the accident, when Tom's wedding ring went missing. 'My father told me it had gone,' Nella revealed. 'We had the same wedding rings, and I wanted Thomas buried with his. I don't know why, it was just important to me, it seemed the wrong thing to take it off his finger. I suppose you can think about it this way: people in South Africa don't have very much money, and perhaps someone stole it thinking it was riches to them. But eventually it was returned.'

Miles Warwick-Smith handled legal action against Kyalami which was eventually settled out of court. 'I was in no state to do it myself,' said Nella, 'but one of the reasons for doing it was to improve things for the future, because I'm a great believer in that. That should never have happened. It was a tragedy that it happened once, but if it had ever happened a second time...'

Somehow Nella avoided bitterness, as did Jacqui Martin and Janet Brise. And the view that Nella and her father took said much about their respective characters. 'My father said to me afterwards, "Nella, that poor man (Jansen van Vuuren) has lost his life and his family are grieving the same as we are grieving." He is a very sensible man and he said we should send the van Vuuren family some flowers, that you shouldn't hold it against them. "He has lost his life as well, and he did it because he was trying to do the right thing." He was just a young boy…'

Tom and Nella had planned to leave the oast house, and just before he was killed they had found a property in Ashdown Forest in Sussex. Instead, she sold up and moved to Blackheath.

Poignantly, Janet and Tony had also just made a successful offer on an oast house near Brands Hatch, which they were both very excited about. They had been due to exchange contracts the week after he was killed.

'Thomas was 27 when he died,' said Nella. 'When I reached 27, it felt really strange. And when I moved house to Blackheath from Ightham it was really weird, it was like, "How will he be able to find me if I'm not there any more?" I know it sounds really stupid, and I'm not a stupid person, but it is your sort of sub-conscience at work.'

When Pryce & Brise had run its course for the girls in the early nineties, and a relationship with property developer Andrew McCallum – whom she had met during the refurbishment of the shop – had run into problems, she moved to Toulouse to study French. Eventually Fate brought Nella and Andrew back together at a horse fair in Avignon in 2000, and now they breed horses just outside Nîmes.

She still detests Tom's sport, having once described it as 'one that kills people,' but has happy memories of old friendships with some wonderful people. 'Alan Henry was always my favourite, because he was such good fun. He used to make us laugh with his limericks. I can remember being out in Kyalami, the first time I went there in 1975, and they had this cabaret – people with these grass skirts and spears – and swirling round the dance floor with Alan as he was pointing out who was having an affair with whom. I couldn't believe it! I was just married and very idealistic. Thomas and I were going to be together forever, we weren't going to have affairs, and this was all very new to me…'

Jack and Gwyneth Pryce continued their roles of policeman and nursing home proprietor. On retirement, they built themselves a new house in the garden of their old one. They frequently receive visitors who pass through, and are happy to talk about the old days when their son was Britain's great hope and the best sportsman in Wales. Their hospitality is warm, and Jack draws pleasure in showing guests a beautiful photograph taken by Rainer Schlegelmilch, on a wall on the first-floor landing. It shows Tom in full flight at the old Nürburgring in the black, blue and red Tabatip Shadow DN8, in 1976. It was a present from Tom's friends at Shadow, as an engraved caption attests. The guest bedroom is beautifully decorated, with a selection of photographs of Tom and Nella, one of Jack as a younger man, and one of David John, the son the Pryces lost all those years before Fate took their beloved Maldwyn, too.

They have the dignity and the inner strength that cloaks the pain life brought them as they speak of their younger son, even when the subject turns to that day at Kyalami in March 1977. 'He still lives,' Jack says quietly. 'But sometimes we have low days, especially when we remember happy times from home life…'

Time has moved on, for all but the 'Lost Generation' who remain preserved in the amber of their harsh destiny. New heroes have come forward to bask in the spray of Champagne. But within their sport, those who loved or supported Roger Williamson, Tony Brise and Tom Pryce, or who just smiled with pleasure from the sidelines as they watched them race, have never forgotten their style, their personalities and their outstanding yet unfulfilled talent. Or the excitement of those distant days when their bountiful promise still blossomed like an awakening flower.

Nor has their conviction ever been shaken that, but for fortune and had Fate been more benign, all three could have reached their personal summits – and, instead, been remembered by history as British World Champions.

Tom is buried in St Bartholomew's Church in Otford, where he and Nella had been married two years earlier.

LIFE AS A LION

Four years after his heroic attempt to rescue Roger Williamson at Zandvoort, David Purley was back in the news headlines. But this time he had survived the severest deceleration ever known.

Purley had essentially walked away from Formula One at the end of 1973, making only sporadic appearances in the Token in 1974. Instead, he got his kicks in Formula Two that season before moving into the Shellsport Formula 5000 series in 1975 with a one-off Chevron B30 powered by Ford's GA V6 engine. The following year, he used a modified version of the car to clean up in the 1976 championship. That success prompted him to think about Formula One again, and he commissioned designer Mike Pilbeam to create his own car for 1977, which he ran under the aegis of his father Charlie's Lec refrigerator business.

His most memorable performance came in the rain-spoiled Belgian Grand Prix at Zolder. Conditions were very poor to begin with, but gradually the track began to dry. The hard-charging former paratrooper moved steadily up the field, from an excellent 13th on the grid to seventh place until the leaders began pitting. As this happened he actually found himself in the lead for one glorious lap. Inevitably he fell back, as he, too, stopped and the faster combinations got back into their stride, and there was an amusing post-race incident after he had upset World Champion Niki Lauda after holding off the Austrian's Ferrari for a while. Lauda remonstrated a little too much with him about 'rabbit' backmarkers, finally prompting an increasingly bored Purley to retort, 'I was leading at the time, and if you wag that finger at me again, I'm going to stick it up your arse!' After that the Lec bore

Token continued after Tom's move to Shadow. Here Neil Trundle, David Purley, Mike Earle and Ian Flux head back to the paddock at Brands Hatch for the 1974 British Grand Prix.

a white rabbit, and later Niki sported a rat on his Ferrari.

Purley was attempting to work his way through prequalifying for the British Grand Prix at Silverstone on 14 July when the Lec's throttle stuck open at Becketts corner. Earlier in the session he had made a pit stop and the engine had briefly caught fire. Marshals and team members quickly extinguished the flames, but the extinguishant then solidified and jammed the throttle mechanism. The Lec crashed head-first into the bank at Becketts, one of the fastest and trickiest sections of the track, and stopped instantly from 106mph. He suffered eight fractures in his left leg and two in his left foot, and seven fractures in his right leg, as well as seven broken ribs and five pelvic fractures. Only his remarkable physical condition saved him, but his racing days were surely over.

Purley then underwent months of painful rehabilitation. 'God, he could barely walk,' recalled Greg Field, who worked for Purley in Mike Earle's team. 'When he was on crutches he was grimacing. It was a real struggle to get anywhere.'

Leaving Earle's old Onyx workshop entailed driving 80 metres to a level crossing, getting out, phoning for clearance, opening the gates, getting back into the car, driving across the rail track, getting out of the car again, closing the gates, ringing up again to report that you were through, and then getting back in again! It could be tedious for a fit man, let alone one whose legs were still recovering their strength, yet Purley would never let anyone help him.

He did, however, seek assistance from time to time when he was cycling. He could not put his legs down when he came to a stop so he would take a run

In 1976 Purley was scheduled to be the driver of David Gossling's Project Blue Star land speed record contender, but the programme died when Gossling was killed in a car accident.

In 1977 Purley returned to Formula One, his moment of glory coming when he briefly led the wet Belgian Grand Prix at Zolder from Niki Lauda, after staying out as faster runners made pit stops to change their tyres.

past the workshop and call out for help – so that, by the time he came around again, somebody would be standing there ready to catch the bike so he could dismount.

Eventually he was able to walk again, but was frustrated that he limped because his left leg was now shorter. So he chose to undergo months of painful surgery in which the shorter leg was rebroken and then continually stretched just as it was beginning to heal. Each time the bone had to grow a little bit further as it knitted back together again, and that way his doctors 'found' an extra inch until the length of the leg matched the right.

During his prolonged recuperation he swam a lot and went to The Otters in Chichester, where disabled children could swim. He would be there with them, all the time, looking after them and motivating them because he loved helping them to cope with their lives.

In 1979, he returned to motor racing in the Aurora British Formula One series, first with the spare Lec and later with a Shadow DN9. At Snetterton, he took the Shadow to fourth place in a triumph of courage and bloody-mindedness.

Afterwards, he let the black car roll into the pit lane in front of Earle's garage. Earle explained, 'I was proud of him that day. I said to him, "Bloody well done, mate, I'm impressed! And if *I'm* impressed with you, that really *is* bloody well done!"' Purley then pulled off the silver and red helmet he had borrowed from his mate John Watson, smiled at Mike and then said very quietly, 'Do me a favour, Mike. I don't want to look a wally, but I can't move. Take the car round the back and I'll get out there.' And so they pushed him where nobody could

see, and lifted him bodily out. He had proved something to himself that day, and felt that he could quit the sport on his own terms. It had not beaten him.

When Donald Campbell was killed in January 1967, trying to break 300mph on Coniston Water, his engineer Leo Villa said he doubted whether British record-breaking would ever spawn a man of similar calibre. But in 1976 there was talk of Purley driving David Gossling's ambitious Project Blue Star land speed record contender, until Gossling was killed in a road accident. Purls would have been the perfect fellow to take up Campbell's mantle.

Purley's legacy was far greater than the sum of the results he left in the record book – and not just because of his heroic efforts to save Roger Williamson. Earle and Field both believed he was a much better driver than he was given credit for. 'He really was a very good driver,' Earle said. 'And he was also that rare thing: a man who really was larger than life.'

Field said, 'He was an absolutely brilliant bloke, and on the right day, in the right frame of mind, he was blindingly quick. He was probably fearless, mainly because he didn't understand what it was about. He felt he was invincible. He thought he'd go into a corner and sort it all out, and if he did spin he'd just stop in the gravel.'

On 2 July 1985, Purley was prodding the tiger yet again as he flew his bright red Pitts Special out over the sea off Bognor Regis. As a result of a technical fault it failed to pull out of a dive, and, this time, even 'Brave Dave' could not survive. He drowned while trapped in the wreckage.

'He was always going to go out the way he went, wasn't he?' Field said in 2004, as he looked back on his old friend. 'You know, hardly a week goes past when I don't think of Purls. I don't think I've ever known anyone else like him.'

Purley had an affinity with the Williamson family after Zandvoort, and visited the display of Roger's trophies at the Donington Collection with Dodge Williamson.

INDEX